1976

may be kept

The Spanish American Novel

The Texas Pan American Series

The Spanish American Novel

A Twentieth-Century Survey

JOHN S. BRUSHWOOD

UNIVERSITY OF TEXAS PRESS • AUSTIN AND LONDON

The Texas Pan American Series is published with the
assistance of a revolving publication fund established
by the Pan American Sulphur Company.

Library of Congress Cataloging in Publication Data

Brushwood, John Stubbs, 1920–
    The Spanish American novel.

    (The Texas pan-American series)
    Bibliography: p.
    Includes index.
    1. Spanish American fiction—20th century—
History and criticism. I. Title.
PQ7082.N7B7   863   74-32429
ISBN 0-292-77515-6

FOR DAVID AND PAUL,
with thanks for their interest

CONTENTS

PREFACE

The Spanish American novel burst into prominence in the 1960s for readers outside the Spanish-speaking world. Of course, there had long been a small but faithful public of specialists and *aficionados*. However, the new awareness was an entirely different matter: many people now found themselves interested in Spanish America as a result of reading its literature, rather than the other way round. This reader reaction is highly significant since many earlier novels were picturesque—exotic, the way travel books are. Undoubtedly, the basic explanation of the new interest in the 1960s is that Spanish American fiction shows more artistic originality than ever before. The books, therefore, are more likely to provide valid literary experiences, regardless of whether or not they have regionalistic aspects.

Often the word *boom* is used in connection with the phenomenon of the 1960s, in Spanish America itself and in other countries. The usage is entirely justified, because the amount of high-quality fiction has increased enormously. In terms of publicity, the increase in quantity and quality has been given a push by the international activity—the high profile—of writers like Carlos Fuentes, Gabriel García Márquez, and Mario Vargas Llosa. With this fact in mind, it is well to remember that two highlights in our enthusiasm for Spanish American fiction are writers who belong to an earlier generation: Miguel Angel Asturias and Jorge Luis Borges. Asturias won the Nobel Prize in 1967 in recognition of a body of work that fictionalizes the myths and problems of Guatemala. Borges, the great storyteller, has written only short fiction but has contributed as much as anyone to the Spanish American novel through his insistence on the novelist's right to invent. Both careers began in the 1920s. In an in-between generation, Juan Rulfo and Julio Cortázar constitute a similar pair, Rulfo mythologizing the reality of the rural Mexican, Cortázar annihilating logic in works where the regionalistic factor is of no practical importance.

The fact is that the tradition of the novel in Spanish America is long and substantial. Its recent excellence indicates an age of maturity that encourages the writers to invent and innovate. However, the boom should not be allowed to obscure all the good that has gone before; and, in fact, there are a number of studies that deal with the Spanish American novel (see Bibliography). Fernando Alegría's outline history is a handbook covering the subject from the Colonial Period to the early 1960s. Alberto Zum Felde's study is a history of the genre terminating at about the middle of the twentieth century. Both books are stronger on general trends than on critical analysis. More recently, Kessel Schwartz has published a history of Spanish American fiction from the Colonial Period to the late 1960s. Its organization is based on the traditionally recognized literary movements and phenomena. The study contains many plot synopses, frequent critical judgments, occasional analytical comment, and a copious bibliography. Another recent study, by Cedomil Goić, organizes the material by generations and concentrates on analyses of fewer novels. Arturo Torres Rioseco and J. R. Spell published collections of essays on authors, including most of the big names of the first forty years of the century. Spell's book contains detailed plot summaries and critical evaluations with a limited amount of specific analysis. Torres Rioseco's essays include the results of interviews with the writers as well as studies of their works. His critical observations place great emphasis on the psychological validity of characterization. Luis Harss's *Into the Mainstream* also uses a combination of interview and literary analysis in dealing with much more recent authors. The book is published in both English and Spanish versions and is the best way for a recently interested reader to begin learning about the novels and their authors. Harss makes some errors of fact as well as a few questionable judgments in his general statements about the novel's trajectory in Spanish America. However, his insight is often keen, and the best quality of his book is that it provides a sense of the work of each author.

There are, of course, many books that deal with the novel in different countries and with various aspects of prose fiction. My purpose in the present book is to study the development of the genre in Spanish America as a whole, during the twentieth century. Emphasis is on works rather than on authors, and I have resisted the temptation of putting all the works of a single author in one place. The study of fiction on an author-by-author basis is important and interesting. My purpose here, however, is to study the novel as a cultural organism; therefore, the structure of this book depends on the dynamic factors in the genre, rather than on biography. A novel belongs to a culture. It may transcend limitations of time and space, but even that fact is important to the understanding of the cultural milieu in which it is created. This consideration is not necessarily related to questions of ideological commitment. In many cases it is appropriate to show how a fictional experience of a given situation differs from a documentary recording of the same situation. The procedure, however, is not to dwell on contrasts, but to point out the factors that transform incident into art. Although I have used many sources of historical information, the basic reference used throughout preparation of the study is *A History of Latin America,* by Hubert Herring (New York: Knopf, 1968).

I believe it is reasonable to begin this study at the entrance to the twentieth century because Spanish American novels from 1900 to 1930 show all the major characteristics of fiction during the nineteenth century and, in addition, the earliest adventures in innovation. The termination of the study in 1970 is a matter of practical necessity. Its preparation demanded that cut-off point. There is, however, some reason to think the future may regard it as a good stopping place in any case. The new novel in Spanish America was well established by 1970. The writers now enjoy an unprecedented self-confidence. A spectacular decade has invited the attention of readers throughout the world. Although many excellent novels will surely be coming from Spanish America, it is not likely that they will create an effect as dramatic as the phenomenon of the 1960s.

There is always some question about the extent to which Spanish America can be studied as a whole. Even books that claim to do so very often turn out to have national or regional divisions. One of the secondary purposes of the present study is to test the possibility of dealing with the novel while avoiding such divisions. In order to enhance the effect of unity, I have not mentioned the nationality of novels gratuitously. When this kind of identification is necessary for clear explanation, it is included in the text. In other cases, nationalities of authors, and also their dates, may be found in the index after each author's name.

A list, at the end of the book, illustrates the basis of the book's organization. The list does not contain all Spanish American novels published during the years indicated; it is not supposed to be a bibliography. It serves as a graphic representation of the trends, coincidences, and contrasts that make up my concept of the Spanish American novel. In the text of the book, this material is presented in two different kinds of chapters. Some concentrate on particular years and depend primarily on a single novel, as in the chapter entitled "The Year of *Los de abajo*." The other chapters are panoramic and cover periods of intervening years between the appearance of key works. This organization has the advantage of adding a dimension to what we normally expect in a panorama of literature, because it permits us to see more clearly all the aspects of the genre at a specific point in time. Some of the novels included in the "Year of . . ." chapters would have to be left out if the book were entirely panoramic. Therefore, the two kinds of chapters tend to correct a distortion that might be created if either kind were used exclusively.

Naturally, problems of whether to include or exclude a novel become acute as the study progresses. The question of which ones to emphasize is just as difficult. It is the age-old problem faced by anthologists, and the solutions are never entirely satisfactory. From the beginning I have tried not to be unduly influenced either by traditional emphases or by fashionable canons of taste. As the study progressed, it is fair to say that I tended to emphasize overlooked novels that change our understanding of what prose fiction was like at a given time: *Op Oloop*, *La casa de cartón*, and *Novela como nube*, for example. I have also attempted to "rescue" some excellent novels—books whose merits are recognized by all their readers, but whose fame has been restricted by the general excellence of the last decade. Among them are *Job-Boj*, *La comparsa*, *El día señalado*, and *Los habitantes*.

Sometimes I have been aware of readers measuring the space allotted to particular works, in studies similar to this one. It should be clearly understood that in the present book there is absolutely no correlation between my estimate of a novel's aesthetic value and the number of words I have used in writing about it. In some cases, novels included in panoramic chapters receive much less detailed treatment than if they were in a "Year of . . . " chapter. In all cases, the amount of attention accorded a book is governed by what characteristics are most enlightening in a particular context. In speaking of the novels, I have avoided, as far as possible, words that have special meanings for particular groups of critics or teachers of literature. However, I have used two words that are important in my own vocabulary of criticism and that might create some confusion: *experience* and *dynamism*. I speak of the experience of a novel—by that I mean the process of its coming into being, whether from the standpoint of the author or the standpoint of the reader. This act refers to appreciation of a work of art, but as a dynamic phenomenon rather than as a *fait accompli*. To put it another way, a work of art is an experience, not a document; what we learn from it is not just the product of the experience, but the experience itself. My use of *dynamism*, or *dynamic*, is closely related. I use it in connection with the factors in a novel that vitalize the experience, transforming the anecdotal base of the work of fiction and sustaining the process of growth and change throughout the novel.

Several technical matters invite comment. First, the passages translated in this book are mine unless otherwise noted. Second, when referring to a novel several times, I have used a note citation only in the first instance. After that, page references appear parenthetically within the text. Third, and most important, it is desirable to clarify a term—*Spanish America* or *Spanish American*. I refer to the countries of the Western Hemisphere where Spanish is the principal language. The term is different from *Latin America*, which includes Brazil, where Portuguese is spoken, and Haiti, where the language is French. It may be convenient sometimes to speak of Latin America as a whole, in some political or sociological context. It is hardly ever suitable, however, in speaking of literature, because language is the primary ingredient, and this fact modifies all but the most general statements. Finally, readers interested in English translations of the novels studied here should consult *Latin American Fiction and Poetry in Translation*, by Suzanne Jill Levine (New York: Center for Inter-American Relations, 1970).

A matter that is decidedly nontechnical and of fundamental importance is the fact of my own foreignness. No one working in a foreign literature can possibly see his material with the sense of cultural identification that is natural in dealing with one's native literature. I hope that genuine interest in Spanish American culture, combined with visits to some of the countries, will serve as a reasonably adequate compensation. My efforts have been assisted by support from the General Research Fund of the University of Kansas and by a travel grant from the Joint Committee on Latin American Studies, awarded through the Social Science Research Council.

Prominent among my acknowledgments I am pleased to say that several libraries in Spanish America served me extremely well. These institutions have often been criticized harshly by scholars and even by the general public. In all cases, I was aware of the general shortage of funds; but I found a very high percentage of the material I needed, and much friendly assistance.

Many students have contributed to this study, particularly in seminars and in dissertations. Several are mentioned in the notes. I do wish to mention here the names of two former students who were also my research assistants: Stella T. Clark and Karen Hardy. Another group deserving special thanks is made up of four excellent critics, who unselfishly let me use manuscripts of their works prior to publication: Osvaldo Larrazábal Henríquez, Raymond D. Souza, Martin S. Stabb, and Jaime Valdivieso.

It would be impossible, of course, to name—or even remember—all the people who have contributed to this study. However, I recall with gratitude and admiration the names of some who made special efforts to help, in many different ways: suggesting books, resolving literary puzzles, reading manuscript, arranging interviews, and listening patiently. Prominent among them are Demetrio Aguilera Malta, Fernando Alegría, Pedro F. de Andrea, Jorge Barros T., Alfonso Calderón, Alberto Escobar, Sergio Galindo, Cristóbal Garcés Larrea, Juan Carlos Ghiano, Luisa Mercedes Levinson, Néstor Madrid Malo, Eduardo Mallea, Juan Mejía Baca, Pedro Orgambide, José Miguel Oviedo, Gustavo Sainz, Manuel Zapata Olivella, and Roberto Yahni. I certainly do not wish to hold them accountable for any shortcomings the book may have; rather, I hope they may find some satisfaction that suitably rewards their friendly cooperation.

JOHN S. BRUSHWOOD

The Spanish American Novel

CHAPTER 1

The Heritage (1900–1915)

A retrospective view of the turn of the century may create a false impression of serenity if we allow generalities to absorb and obscure illuminating nuances. In the political realm, for example, it is deceptively easy to focus on the peculiar stability of certain strong-arm governments while ignoring the general state of unrest. In literature, the period seems to find expression in two modes: a dreamily idealistic, art-for-art's-sake *modernismo*, and the earthy revelations of realism and naturalism. Actually, these three kinds of writing are more closely related than their definitions might suggest.

The meanings of realism and naturalism parallel each other and even join in Spanish American fiction. They are sometimes used indiscriminately to refer to novels that emphasize the seamy side of life to the exclusion of human goodness. There has been, and still is, a good deal of discussion as to whether one novel or another is deterministic enough to be considered naturalist. Realism sometimes refers to technique, sometimes to verisimilitude. Part of the problem is that, with rare exceptions, novels are not written to serve as examples of literary terms; rather, literary terms are a means of describing novels, always with reservations. The clinical view is the most interesting function of naturalism in Spanish America. It is more accurate to speak of naturalist tendencies in novels than of naturalist novels. Realism's most important function is to focus attention on the distinguishing characteristics of the New World. Narrative techniques overlap.

Modernismo is a more difficult problem. Often its importance in prose fiction is overlooked because poetry seems to be a more appropriate vehicle for the eternal search for beauty. *Modernismo*—the name of the movement itself—is highly significant because it indicated the intention of belonging to the mainstream of literature. Its writers reacted against many of the excesses of romanticism but retained the romantics' yearning for the unattainable. The search brought them into contact with the poetry of French symbolism and Parnassianism and strengthened their dedication to what may be called the grand poetic tradition—that is, all kinds of poetry of earlier times. Their interest in being modern also brought them face-to-face with the unimaginative society of the time and created an intense reaction that turned into hyperaestheticism. The notion was that everybody was against the artist. His subsequent rebellion— often taken for escapism—was an eloquent protest against the mediocrity of the world he lived in.

This idea related the *modernistas* to the French decadentists. It is also the most convenient point for the observation of *modernista* prose fiction. The year 1900, naturally, does not mark a specific point of change in the Spanish American novel. The tendencies apparent at century's end, and for some years thereafter, are characteristic of a period that may reasonably be dated from 1885. At the turn of the century, we have a showcase of what the twentieth-century Spanish American novel inherited from the past. Occupying prominent places in this display are several novels where the spiritual, vague idealism of *modernismo* is in obvious contrast to the practical outlook of realism-naturalism. The more practical way of looking at the world accepts objective awareness as the only knowledge and attempts to deal with humanity's problems on that level. The aesthete-idealists were not willing to settle for so little. Their search was based on the presumed possibility of cultivating an awareness that would separate individual men from the dull conformity exacted by a practical society. In spite of this diametrical opposition, both sides end in a sense of futility, although for different reasons in the two cases. Hernán Vidal discusses this phenomenon as it relates to Manuel Díaz Rodríguez's *Sangre patricia* (1902).[1] He deals with symbolism, one of the major components of *modernismo*, and with naturalism as we understand it in the works of Emile Zola. Relying principally on Ralph Freedman's *The Lyrical Novel*, he shows that symbolist perception of objects transforms them gradually into representations of the beholder's interior emotion. The object observed, therefore, transcends the reality it has as part of our objective awareness; but it ceases to be of worldly use to the symbolist, who, therefore, withdraws from the everyday, commonplace world. The creature of naturalism, of course, is defeated by physiological circumstances that repress his development. The two apparent opposites, therefore, come together as representations of futility, in terms of the everyday world. Hardly an optimistic start for the new century. There is more to the sense of futility, however, than this coincidence of literary philosophy with literary science. One of the reasons for the insistence on art was the feeling that the world—and life—was ugly. Resignation from this distasteful world was not just an escape; it was also a protest. The insensitivity of everybody else—the bourgeoisie because of materialistic greed, the masses because of ignorance—stood between the artist and the creation of a perfect society.

In *Sangre patricia*, Díaz Rodríguez brings this problem to life by using a shifting narrative point of view that Andrew Debicki has analyzed in his explanation of the novel.[2] The analysis shows that Díaz Rodríguez's reader sees the protagonist, Tulio Arcos, in two different ways: at times with intimate sympathy for his dreamy idealism, but often in a more detached, clinical fashion. Technically, there is no change in narrative point of view, since the entire novel is written in the third person. There is, however, a change in narrative attitude. The third-person voice alters the distance between narrator and character, sometimes standing apart from Tulio, then almost taking Tulio's position.

The anecdotal base of *Sangre patricia* is slight and commonplace except for one detail. Tulio Arcos is in Paris, awaiting the arrival of Belén, whom he has married by proxy. (This is the unusual detail.) The bride dies and is buried at sea. After that, nothing happens until Tulio commits suicide—in the sea, of course—at the end of the novel and after long and sometimes tiresome discussions with his friends about his lack of adjustment to the loss of Belén. What then makes this book come alive? Debicki has stated the basic experience very clearly in pointing out that "by making us shift, again and again, from one [narrative attitude] to the other, Díaz Rodríguez forces us to keep picking our way among two very opposite outlooks on life, one elevated and romantic, the other down-to-earth and pragmatic."[3] There is a second important factor in the reader's experience of this book. It is the translation of tangible reality into attitudes or feelings, by means of symbolist imagery.

First, it is convenient to observe that Tulio's problem of adjustment is more philosophical than psychological, though literary critics' love for psychological character development often produces a slightly oblique reading of the novel. Debicki suggests the philosophical nature of the problem when he speaks, in the lines quoted above, of "two very opposite outlooks on life." The contrast is personified later in two of the protagonist's helpful associates: Borja the idealist, and the pragmatic Ocampo. The author introduces a possible compromise in the person of Martí, a musician who has made his peace with social institutions. Within the experience of the novel, however, Martí never represents an acceptable choice, because his compromise always seems dull, mediocre. Tulio's ultimate decision is not the result of a neurosis, however neurotic he (and the other characters, for that matter) may be. It is his choice of a particular view of life.

The unusual detail of the marriage by proxy plays an important role in the communication of his attitude. Díaz Rodríguez constructs the narrative so we see Belén only in the first chapter, when she is on her way to France. The chapter ends with her death. In the second chapter, the narrative moves back with Tulio to a preceding time; and then the third chapter begins after Belén's death. This structure enhances Tulio's idealized vision of his bride. She is vanishing reality. Material reality also vanishes in the mist of symbolist imagery. The world of tangible reality becomes useless to Tulio Arcos, and suicide is the act that has most meaning. At this point, the reader has to be affected by the basic contrast in the novel, unless his own view of life corresponds to Tulio's. Within the novel, and within a nonobjective frame of reference, Tulio's decision is perfectly acceptable. But if we withdraw and take the clinical view, we face the problem of whether he was right. Certainly his solution does not promise a long future for humanity.

The idealist-pragmatist contrast in the philosophical problem of the novel corresponds to the symbolist-clinical contrast in the author's narrative technique. Thinking in terms of literary movements or modes, the same contrast corresponds to *modernismo*, on the one hand, and realism-naturalism, on the other. Then, moving outside the strictly literary world, the contrast lies between some kind of intuitional view of reality (Bergson, for example) and the practical world of positivism. The contrast also affects our understanding of Tulio Arcos as he is related to the world in which the novel was conceived and developed. Taking the idealist view, Tulio Arcos is a rebel against a materialistic, practical society; from the clinical position, he is an aristocrat who is out of step with social and political changes taking place in Venezuela, and with the more general predominance of an unimaginative bourgeoisie. Debicki speaks of Tulio's efforts "to rise above a pretty horrible world."

The world was, in truth, less than delightful. In addition to universal human failings, Spanish America suffered political problems that produced general unrest. Occasional references to a period of stability in the latter part of the nineteenth century are misleading. There are indeed some instances of strong-arm peace that fostered material progress. Railroads were built, for example, and also schools, but these were built with less enthusiasm than railroads. The presumably progressive programs, in any case, were carried out by leaders who desperately wished to transform backward countries into modern European states. In spite of this programmed activity, Spanish America was not relatively stable at century's end; it was chaotic.

Venezuela was still gasping from the Guzmán Blanco dictatorship when Cipriano Castro swooped down from the hills in 1899 and established a dictatorship that lasted until he turned it over to Juan Vicente Gómez in 1908. The Castro revolution was the first invasion of hill people (*andinos*) into the placid ambience of aristocratic Caracas. In Argentina, Leandro N. Alem led a middle-class revolution against ex-President Roca and the oligarchs, in 1890. Although the revolution was only a partial success, it forced Roca's puppet, Juárez Celman, out of office in favor of Carlos Pellegrini and solidified the Radical party, which rebelled again in 1905 and finally elected Hipólito Irigoyen in 1916. Colombia was embroiled in a vicious civil war from 1899 to 1902, after the death of Rafael Núñez left no strong leader. Jorge Montt, in Chile, became president after the civil war of 1891 and granted most of the executive power to the Congress. Eloy Alfaro returned to Ecuador from exile in Nicaragua, in 1895, and led a successful revolution against García Moreno. Uruguay was effectively divided into two parts in order to quiet the *blanco* rebellion under Aparicio Saravia in 1897; and war was necessary again in 1904 to reunite the country under President Batlle. Cuba was fighting for its independence from Spain and then was occupied by United States troops from 1891 to 1902. The Cuban experience, incidentally, was very important in Spanish America's identity problem. When Spain was overwhelmed by the United States in the war for Cuban independence, there was a resurgence of sympathy for the mother country, in spite of old wounds and libertarian inclinations. The United States occupation did nothing to comfort the wary Spanish Americans. They were right in regarding the occupation—and the Platt Amendment, which made Cuba a United States protectorate—as a statement of intent that was followed by a long period of interventions in Latin America.

Peace and stability, such as they were, existed in Mexico where the dictatorship of Porfirio Díaz, pestered by strikes and mumbled dissent, was building up to the biggest explosion of all—the Revolution of 1910; in Peru, where the nation was exhausted from the War of the Pacific; in Bolivia, also exhausted and caught now without a port; in Guatemala, where Estrada Cabrera, one of the worst of Spanish America's dictators, replaced an assassinated president in 1898; and in a few smaller countries, where economic adventurers from the United States were laying the foundations for exploitation.

There was certainly plenty of cause for rebellion against the course society was taking. The *modernista* influence in the novel naturally produces varied effects. The most satisfactory general description is "poetic," though even this word is open to varying interpretations. The novelists sometimes become humorously critical of the movement's hyperaestheticism, and they persist in their desire to shock the reader into thinking that change is possible.[4] At times, this anxiety turns into overt cynicism, as in *El desarraigado* (1907), by Pablo J. Guerrero. The protagonist finds life unworthy of his

concern. An interesting aspect of the novel is that its setting is Venezuela rather than Paris, the customary setting for intensely sensitive
protagonists of this period.

A different facet of *modernista* prose is apparent in *La gloria de
don Ramiro* (1908) by Enrique Larreta. Here the artist moves away
from worldly reality by retreating into the past. The novel is a kind
of love affair with the city of Avila; and Larreta's antiquarian aes-
theticism does as much to give life to the novel as do the contrasts
that form the basis of the action.[5]

The influence of realism-naturalism is apparent, frequently on a
philosophical plane, in the novels of *modernismo*. In *La gloria de
don Ramiro*, it is apparent in the accuracy of the historical background. Probably the realist-naturalist interest in the New World
experience prompted the setting of *El desarraigado* in Venezuela.
Yet all these novels are fundamentally *modernista*. Reversing this
priority and looking at novels that are basically realist-naturalist,
with *modernista* influences, we naturally find greater emphasis on
the clinical tone or narrative attitude, but not necessarily a more
effective social role for the fictional characters. They corroborate
Hernán Vidal's explanation concerning the futility of characters
created within both literary tendencies, even though the causes for
futility are entirely different. An approximation of the relationship
between *modernista* fiction and realism-naturalism may be suggested through an association of the work of Joris Karl Huysmans
with that of Paul Bourget and, in turn, with the work of Emile Zola.

Federico Gamboa's *Santa* (1903) is one of the most widely read
novels that can be considered basically naturalist. No doubt some of
its public has been attracted by its risqué theme—the rise and fall
of a Mexico City prostitute. However, the *modernista* influences in
Gamboa's novel give it a quality—"dimension" might even be a
suitable word—that attracts readers who would be repelled or bored
by *Nana*, for example. Suggestive associations transcend words.
Early in the novel, while Santa waits at the door of the bordello
where she intends to work, the sound of children's voices creates a
remarkable contrast. Later, the sound of rain turns into Santa's emotional state. This kind of transfiguration is "dangerous" for the
symbolist personage because the voices and the rain cease to be
practical realities for him, and the process gradually separates him

9

from the real world. Gamboa's novel does not go that far. The trans-figurational development is partial and serves to deepen the reader's experience. Other stylistic factors contribute to the same effect. Gamboa's prose style is visually unattractive. The reader's eye informs him that long sentences and paragraphs could be boring. The actual reading experience proves otherwise, and Seymour Menton's analysis of the style shows why.[6] Gamboa makes frequent use of verbs and derivatives of verbs to give motion to his lengthy utterances; repetitions or near repetitions of motifs, words, or families of words have a rhythmic effect; similes and metaphors contribute to the lyric sound of the prose as well as to the meaning.

Santa has a very controversial ending. The protagonist is rescued from the gutter by the long-suffering and devoted Hipo, dies of cancer, and is buried in a tranquil country cemetery. True love redeems the fallen woman. Some readers find all this insufficiently deterministic, some think it is overly dramatic, and some accept it as just right. As a matter of fact, the outcome has a structural importance and ought to be read that way. Any sensitive reader must know—or at least *sense*—from the beginning of the novel that it is not going to be a textbook example of naturalism. The symbolist devices are apparent enough. After the introductory scene, in which the children's voices emphasize the critical point between Santa's past and future, Gamboa shifts to the cause of Santa's plight. The flashback could be a short story and is more purely naturalist than the novel as a whole. It deals with her seduction, miscarriage, and dismissal from the home by her brothers. This episode modifies the contrast established by the children's voices, showing that Santa did not leave home of her own free will.

The second point in this fundamental development comes when Santa's grim-faced brothers appear in the middle of café gaiety to inform her of her mother's death. Here again the contrast, and also the information that the presumably idyllic side of the contrast is not real. The death of her mother removes the only comforting factor in Santa's memory. This event coincides roughly with the apex of Santa's career as a prostitute—there is a transition from the distinction of courtesan to the disgrace of whore.

The controversial ending is the third step. Santa's miserable condition certainly contrasts with the tranquillity of the cemetery. But the fact is that tranquillity was available to her only through death. Redeemed by true love or not, futility marks the life.

A clear reaction against this sense of futility is apparent in the novels of Carlos Reyles. They develop and illustrate his belief that the goal of living is the accumulation of power and money—a position that has not endeared him either to his contemporaries or to more recent generations. Gerardo Sáenz, author of the most extensive study of Reyles's work, considers the exposition of this ideology the fundamental goal of the novelist in *Raza de Caín* (1900) and in the rest of his work.[7] Through narrative techniques similar to many novels of realism-naturalism, *Raza de Caín* tells the story of the domination of a weak idealist by a strong, practical type. Artistic transformation appears to interest Reyles only slightly. The story is designed to inculcate the idea that progress is good, idealism is bad. The purpose apparently was to inspire activity rather than futility in the author's society.

Naturalist novels are not intentionally regionalistic. Their real purpose is to deal with human problems rather than political or social ones. However, the inclination to reflect the New World experience often produces interesting regionalistic detail in the realist-naturalist works. Hacienda life in Reyles's novels is an example; an equally rich example—this time of small-town life—is Manuel Gálvez's *La maestra normal* (1914). This novel probably owes its longevity to the integration of story line with setting, raising a question as to what actually underlies the fictional experience: the plot of seduction, or the slow movement of the provincial town. The life of the town is dull, crawling but inexorable. The novel could be described the same way, and so could the Solís-Raselda story line. Solís seduces the schoolteacher out of boredom. As a fictional personage, he could find a place in any novel influenced by end-of-the-century ennui and hypersensitivity. It would be possible to describe a line of development of the Solís-Raselda story and give an entirely erroneous impression of the novel. In fact, Solís is caught by the town as much as by the receptive Raselda, and it is only within the setting of the town that the seduction could have any interest.

Alegría calls this novel one of the masterpieces of Spanish American *costumbrismo*.[8] His reason is that Manuel Gálvez, instead of simply hanging types against a background of customs and local color, develops intricate relationships among the characters, making a world in which the reader can enter rather than simply observe. This differentiation is of some importance to an understanding of the function of the novel in Spanish America, because it is related to the writer's attitude toward reality. In general, the novels oriented toward human problems have more carefully made structures than those that emphasize regionalism. *La maestra normal* is a kind of bridge between two methods of novelization. To some degree, *Grandeza* (1910) by Tomás Carrasquilla also strikes a compromise. It has a more intricate structure than many *costumbrista* works, but interest in the novel depends largely on the quaint types chosen for portrayal. The use of identifiable types either enhances the verisimilitude of fiction or intensifies the illusion of reality. When types are caricatured, the increased sense of reality must be illusion.

A second effect of character typing in regionalist fiction is fragmentation of the narrative. Emphasis on types tends to make the narrative structure lineal and episodic. Two steps in this direction are the picaresque *El casamiento de Laucha* (1906) by Roberto J. Payró and the satirical stories of Argentine society by José S. Alvarez, published in a collection as *Cuentos de Fray Mocho* in 1906.

Local customs, recognizable types, and language peculiarities are the stock-in-trade of the *costumbrista* novelists. This kind of regionalism is not much concerned with the role of nature. The land may be superficially related to custom or type, but there are no more than faint suggestions of the man-nature conflict and combination that later characterized novels about the New World experience. The writing is influenced to some extent by Flaubertian realism, but Hispanic models like the traditional picaresque novel and the sketches of Mariano José de Larra give a better idea of what these works are like.

The reader's experience as he accompanies Laucha's narration is like that of any picaresque novel: the protagonist is a likeable acquaintance whose frame of morality probably differs from the reader's. Therefore, we either suspend our criticism and experience the story intimately, or we read it judicially and unhappily. Orgambide and Yahni, who obviously like this novel, point out two planes of morality and note also that the book is critical of certain social ills of the period, such as quick fortunes made by unscrupulous use of an unregulated stock market, and dishonest politicians.[9] The fact that the protagonist is a gaucho gives the book a certain regional interest. His *joie de vivre* is unusual. Life is a party at best, a practical joke at worst. This attitude is what makes the story move. The fact that his marriage is a fake is just part of the joke. Although Laucha is an interesting type, he is not well known in Spanish American literature. Much of the regional identification depends on the language.

The language of Carrasquilla, the Colombian regionalist, is probably his most useful instrument, but he is careful to keep it understandable. The same is true for *El casamiento de Laucha*, where the language becomes important as a unifying device, since the story line is episodic. Alvarez (Fray Mocho), however, swings more freely than either of them. He is not in the least concerned about the unifying factor since his stories ("vignettes" might be a better word) were not intended to be published together. They are intended to capture the reality of a time and place, as accurately as possible. The people in his sketches are those one sees every day, and his reports might seem to be dull if it were not for an unconscious transformation of reality, which Orgambide and Yahni have analyzed very cleverly.[10] They see the humor primarily in a situation which is announced in the title. The title itself is always in the form of a folk saying, or a pseudo folk saying made up by Fray Mocho. The dialogue tells the story, and the language is the soul of the dialogue. The personage, therefore, is actually revealed through the language, and Fray Mocho tries to make the language just exactly as the character would speak it. So, in the process of the story, the language itself actually becomes the source of humor and of reality. There is a similarity here to the role of language in the works of some novelists of the 1960s and 1970s.

Fray Mocho's satire may be the sharpest of all the *costumbrista* writers, but José Rafael Pocaterra's *Política feminista* (1913) will be a close second.[11] The political orientation of his novel makes it a special kind of *costumbrismo*. Everybody loses to political power, and there is not much hope for change. The author develops the idea through the use of familiar techniques that reveal his disgust. At the same time, he amuses the reader with his semidetached bitterness.

Characterization by Pocaterra is really caricature, because his technique is to emphasize a single detail. He is by no means objective, and his feeling of superiority produces a sarcastic tone. The effect almost amounts to a tradition in Spanish American literature. There is never any question that the novelist is the narrator. He creates his people, puts them on display, comments on their follies and peculiarities. The feeling he creates for the character is sympathetic, but patronizing; the reader has a choice of identifying with the character or of joining the author in his sarcasm. Pocaterra maintains the same attitude in his descriptions of situations, showing his impatience with the world he lives in. The setting of the novel is a provincial town, and "The Great Venezuelan Railroad station— because in Venezuela, among other great things, we have a railroad—was full of people" (p. 18).

Given the political situation in Venezuela early in the twentieth century, it is hardly surprising that fiction was used as a vehicle of protest. *El Cabito* (1909), by Pío Gil, is a denunciation of the government of Cipriano Castro. In an extensive essay on the novel, Guillermo Meneses points out that the Castro regime is not always considered as bad as Pío Gil makes it appear.[12] The same may be said for most denunciatory literature. However, that judgment refers to the work's value as a document, rather than to its merit as an experience. In the latter connection, Meneses points out that the narrative wavers between emphasis on individuals and emphasis on groups. Readers necessarily will appreciate the direction of his attack—the political opportunists who stand between the president and the people. However, the characteristics of individuals do not always contribute to this focus, and the end of the novel produces a dishonored heroine dying in a convent and a hero who misses his opportunity to kill the tyrant. This finale is a combination of the sense of futility observed in many novels of the period and the remains of romantic overstatement. It is an interesting corroboration— in a clearly nonartistic novel—of the protest found in several Venezuelan *modernista* novels.

A more searching appreciation of social disruption appears in *A la costa* (1904), by Luis A. Martínez. The organization of action and ideas in this novel has two essential aspects. One is the personal trajectory of Salvador Ramírez, a young man caught up in the conservative struggle against the Eloy Alfaro revolution; the other is the contrast between Salvador and his friend Luciano Pérez, a revolutionary and a liberal in the nineteenth-century sense—that is, a defender of the rights of the provinces against the encroachment of centralized power. Salvador's movement from the highlands to the coast gives the novel an underlying dynamism that contributes to the sense of loss of a traditional situation. The destruction caused by an earthquake foreshadows the changing circumstance which is personified in Salvador. In the aftermath of this natural disaster, the narrator's words associate decay with violence, in order to communicate the protagonist's state of mind.

Enrique Gil Gilbert, in an excellent study of the novel, notes that this feeling contrasts with Martínez's description of the overwhelming fecundity of the coastal region.[13] He also points out that Salvador, having traveled from one environment to the other, achieves happiness and dies almost immediately thereafter. There is something abortive about this development that may indeed leave the reader with a taste of pessimism. On the other hand, Salvador's movement from one zone to the other suggests the totality of Ecuador. The feeling of unity tends to make a contrast opposed to the division of the novel into two parts, and the reader's experience in this case is ambivalent—a paradoxical combination of wholeness and division. This ambivalence is an almost inescapable reaction to civil war, and it is Martínez's best communication. In addition, he allows Salvador to explain his ideas in expository discourses that bear a very faint resemblance to interior monologue. They do not work very well, because they do not sound like words a person might say, but rather like a contemplative essay. If there is any other message of importance in this novel, it is the suggestion, noted by Gil Gilbert, of man overwhelmed by nature, a theme of fundamental importance in communication of the New World experience.

Awareness of this experience deepened gradually. Basically, literary expression of the New World phenomenon takes into account the most obvious factors that distinguish it from the familiar European environment—for example, the strange flora and fauna, or coexistence with a non-European people. Toward the middle of the century, writers also show an appreciation of more subtle differences —for example, the amazing range of civilization, from savagery to cosmopolitanism, within a small area. The development of the novel in Spanish America is based on the accommodation of technique to material and vice versa. It is very likely that a sense of the uniqueness of the material tended to modify the literary influences from Eu-

15

rope. On the other hand, Spanish American writers were bound to tradition closely enough to make them respect the general lines. The heritage on which they have based the novel during the twentieth century amounts to a combination of *modernismo*, realism, naturalism, and an ever persistent romanticism—all these terms understood as referring to tendencies, rather than as restrictive schools.

The question of whether there were any notable changes in the novel during these first fifteen years of the century is rather like asking when the century begins. Superficially, the question may sound frivolous; actually it is of great importance, because our customary use of centuries as units of history is simply a convenient approximation, like the names of literary movements or schools. Beyond the reference to the century as a unit, most people look for a point in time when some general direction or attitude changes. A Chilean critic has said that for his country the twentieth century began in 1925 when church and state were finally separated. He notes that the orientation of the society and of the novel changed around that time.[14] There is little doubt that for Mexico the crucial date is 1910, the year that marks the beginning of the revolution and the end of the Díaz regime. In Argentina, a possible choice might be 1916, when the Radical party succeeded in electing Hipólito Irigoyen president. Cuba's independence almost coincides with the century, but some might pick 1934 (the abrogation of the Platt Amendment) as the crucial year. In Uruguay, a new era might date from the beginning of Batlle's second term, after his trip to Switzerland where he studied the social structure; or it might date from 1917 when the country adopted a new constitution that provided for a commission-type government.

Although it would be impossible to pick a single date for all of Spanish America and propose that our century begins then, it does seem safe to say that the early part of the century saw a number of attempts to improve on various nineteenth-century circumstances. Changes in the novel are similarly elusive, and the most striking change coincides with the most basic social movement, the Mexican Revolution.

Outside Mexico—specifically and somewhat surprisingly in Chile, where traditionalism in prose fiction has been a persistent characteristic—two writers produced novels that subtly suggest change in the function of the genre. One of them, Pedro Prado's *La reina de Rapa*

Nut (1914), uses a theme that provokes an examination of generally held values. The other, Eduardo Barrios's *El niño que enloqueció de amor* (1915), is interesting because of the consistency of its narrative point of view, which is the diary of a ten-year-old boy.

The title of Prado's novel means "The Queen of Easter Island." The narrative is in the form of a journalist's diary and consists of episodes about people who belong to an ancient civilization. The totally fictional situation allows the author to invert commonly held beliefs or change the perspective in which we see social reality. A natural problem, the shortage of water, destroys the civilization, and Prado's invention remains inviolate. The author's respect for his right to invent is as important as any of his unusual ways of seeing reality. The diary form is also interesting, but is not as important as in *El niño que enloqueció de amor*. Barrios turns the story over to the diarist except for the frame, which is the work of the novelist who finds the diary. This technique is of considerable importance because earlier novelists found it very difficult to surrender the narrative voice, even when the third-person omniscient was obviously inadequate. There may be some room for debate about the psychological validity of what Barrios's ten-year-old protagonist does and says, but the book is consistently written within the limits of the presumed characterization.

The sharpest turn from traditional ways of making fiction is *Andrés Pérez, maderista* (1911), by Mariano Azuela.[15] Several earlier novels by the same author are safely within the realist-naturalist tradition. Some of the themes show dissatisfaction with the state of society, but there is nothing unusual about the means Azuela uses to communicate. *Andrés Pérez, maderista* is an entirely different matter.

The anecdotal base concerns a man who becomes involved accidentally in the Madero phase of the Revolution, and who with growing cynicism exploits the opportunity. Azuela makes the point by creating an idealist, Toño Reyes, who emphasizes the opportunism of Pérez. The author turns the narration over to Pérez and lets his antihero tell his own disgrace. The fact that he tells the story himself adds insensitivity to opportunism. The author does not leave Andrés standing alone, however. The negative message comes through in a different way. The novel introduces a considerable variety of people who are willing to come to the feast even though

17

they had nothing to do with its preparation. The emphasis, therefore, in the contrast between Andrés and Toño, has to be on Toño, whose idealism is unique and destined for defeat.

Putting aside the old custom of long descriptions, Azuela emphasizes dialogue as a means of moving the plot and making characterizations. The story moves fast and is, in fact, short. Speaking of Azuela's persistent war against the opportunists, Luis Leal quotes the author regarding *Andrés Pérez, maderista*: "I wanted to condemn, in less than a hundred pages, an aspect of the Madero movement whose rapid triumph was the major cause of its downfall, because it did not have the time to mature in the consciousness of the people."[16] The statement is interesting for the opinion expressed; it is even more interesting because it suggests that there was in the mind of the author a relationship between the length of the work and the time factor in the anecdotal matter. This concept of fiction and the techniques used in *Andrés Pérez, maderista* appear again, and under more complete control, in his masterpiece, *Los de abajo*.

CHAPTER 2

The Year of *Los de abajo* (1916)

Mariano Azuela conceived and wrote *Los de abajo* during, and immediately following, one of the decisive stages of the Mexican Revolution. He was a medical officer attached to the forces of General Francisco (Pancho) Villa. From about the middle of 1914, what had started as a revolution turned into a civil war, with Villa and Venustiano Carranza as the principal leaders. Although Villa seemed more powerful for a while, Carranza gained the upper hand by the end of the year; 1915 was a long period of withdrawal to the northern part of Mexico by the *villista* forces. By October, Azuela was in El Paso with two-thirds of the novel written. He wrote the rest of it in the office of *El Paso del Norte*, the newspaper that first published the book.[1] It appeared serially from October to December, then as a book in 1916.

One of the outstanding characteristics of *Los de abajo* is the author's ability to transform experience and observation into fiction in an on-the-spot situation. Other novels of the Revolution, although written years later, are less successful in transforming anecdotal base into artistic narrative. In fact, Azuela's rapid assimilation of the circumstances placed him so far ahead of his time that *Los de abajo*

19

came into its own after a decade had passed. The novel was "discovered" in 1925, and rapidly gained international recognition. The year of *Los de abajo* could be 1915 or 1916 or 1925. The choice of 1916 shows some interesting comparisons and contrasts with other Spanish American novels published the same year.

Los de abajo is one of the most-written-about books in the history of Spanish American letters. If a devoted investigator cared to search long enough, he could find practically anything said about the novel. Analyses conflict with each other, and changing principles of literary criticism shift the focus of interest as time passes. Torres Rioseco says the book is an epic poem in prose, but does not pursue the point. Alegría says it is an antiepic. Leal says the structure is original, not influenced by any foreign novel. Menton says the structure is epic and explains this description in an analysis of the novel.[2] Prominent in discussions of the book is the question of what the author thought about the Revolution. The result is often more biographical than literary, but it does underline the fact that, whatever else *Los de abajo* may be, it is involved with the human condition in a particular situation. These opinions regarding structure and epic character indicate that something about the book goes beyond the local scene, that there is a heroic element, and that the structure communicates some kind of knowledge that cannot be stated in a summary of the novelist's ideas extracted from the work.

Demetrio Macías, the protagonist, dies in a losing battle at the precise scene of his first triumph as a revolutionary leader. To that extent, at least, *Los de abajo* is circular. Hardly anyone would care to argue the point. This awareness, however, becomes a part of the reader's experience gradually, and it is not complete until the end of the novel. Meanwhile, other factors also follow a circular course and combine with the sense of movement necessary to the creation of a circle, which is indeed important in the understanding of revolutionary activity.

The opening episode of *Los de abajo* deals with Macías's flight from home and organization of a band of revolutionaries. Federal soldiers invade his house and then burn it. Azuela reveals his basic narrative techniques from the beginning. The novel opens with a person speaking, in the middle of an episode that becomes clear gradually. The clauses tend to be short and create an effect of sim-

20

plicity and tenseness. As Macías goes up the mountain, Azuela allows himself a typically brief descriptive passage—imagery that says more than objective awareness, but used with severe restraint. He accomplishes character portrayal with just a few observations. The procedure is much like caricature, but with the important exception that Azuela does not exploit a characteristic to the point of making it absurd. Just as a few words make a personage emerge clearly, so later on a few more words can add to the characterization.

Demetrio Macías is ingenuous, strong, patient, independent. Azuela invites the reader's outrage over the invasion of the man's home. There is no sense here of the semislave living in subhuman circumstances. He is a humble man, certainly. His reaction, however, is not that of a wretch who finally reacts against a lifetime of misery, but rather of a man whose rights have been disregarded in a particular situation. This point of departure, for those interested in the author's ideology, speaks eloquently with regard to his view of society. For the reader who is interested only in the experience of the Revolution through the novel itself, it means that his original sympathy is for a man who commands respect as an individual, not for an anonymous mass. However tempting it may be at times to say that the Revolution itself is the real protagonist of *Los de abajo*, the fact is that the reader's sympathy toward Macías is basic from the start of the novel, and concern for him is active throughout the book.

From this point—that is, beginning with the picture of Demetrio Macías climbing up the side of the mountain—the novel is in motion, the protagonist's power grows, and the circle begins to form. Motion is physical movement from one place to another, and it has a corollary spiritual effect of liberation. Together, these phenomena are the very essence of revolution, in the sense that revolution is the opposite of a static condition created by a repressive society. The sense of movement comes via Azuela's quick, clear statements, by his leaving pieces of action unresolved as the narrative jumps to some other situation, through objective observation of the pleasure the soldiers take in simply roaming about the country, and, of course, by gradual appreciation of the circular movement of the book's structure.

Still early in the novel, Azuela introduces Luis Cervantes, a city slicker who teaches Demetrio that the Revolution is more than a local protest. Cervantes turns out to be an opportunist, a characterization similar to Andrés Pérez in an earlier novel. Another character introduced later, Solís, is to a considerable extent the opposite of Cervantes. The Cervantes-Solís contrast is similar to the Andrés Pérez–Toño Reyes contrast in *Andrés Pérez, maderista*, but in *Los de abajo* the pairing is not as important to the structure. The importance of Solís is more contemplative than functional. The presence of Cervantes is needed to bring about the change in Macías and stimulate the circular movement. The first effect is to indicate that Macías and his men don't have the slightest idea what they are fighting for. Then, in a kind of double-take reaction, we realize that revolutionary ideology is of the least importance. Revolution is movement; ideas are secondary. Indeed, the men of ideas have little or no revolutionary effect in Azuela's novel.

Encouraged by Cervantes, Demetrio acquires more power and more followers, but loses the human touch. The subtitle of this novel is "Scenes of the Revolution," and it indicates what the author was probably thinking when he wrote the episodes. Effects like the sense of movement caused by absence of detailed transitions arise from the set of circumstances in which the artist works, rather than from his plan. Azuela might well have said "Scenes and Portraits of the Revolution," because he introduces a wide variety of people. Like the scenes, the people are based on experience and observation. Apparently, he took a few of the minor characters completely from real life, even keeping their nicknames. Others are composites of two or more people.[3] The variety serves to give a broad personality base to the revolutionaries. The gamut of human emotions parallels a long series of reasons for participating in the Revolution. The procedure communicates a sense of general unrest, but it does not create the feeling of a faceless mass of people united in a common cause.

As the Revolution expands, Demetrio Macías loses his keen awareness of relationship to all his men. Then as *villista* fortunes decline, his forces become fewer and fewer. Once when a subordinate reported to him that his men were killing each other in a brawl, his unemotional retort was to order them buried. But back in the ravine where it all began, now with fortunes reversed, Demetrio sees his men falling one by one, and he thinks of them separately and by name. The circle—if it really is a circle—is complete in more than the geographical sense. The reborn feeling of proximity to his men is a psychological or spiritual return. He has been a general and now is once again undistinguished by rank. This, also, is a return.

If all these factors that contribute to the feeling of the circle did in fact close, then the movement of making a circle would not be revolutionary at all. But that is not really the experience of the novel. There is a point in the story when Demetrio goes home to visit his wife and child. He could elect to stay; but, in this much commented on scene, he tosses a stone and lets it roll down the side of the mountain. And he explains that he has become like the stone, caught up in the movement of the Revolution. Maybe this inexorable, primordial movement comes to a standstill when the circle closes there at the end of the second battle of the ravine. In the last sentence of the novel, Azuela says, ". . . Demetrio Macías, his eyes fixed forever, keeps aiming his rifle . . ." (The second suspension points are the novelist's.) Our first reaction is that Azuela has found a poetic way of saying that Demetrio is dead. Then we wonder, without denying the positive reality of that statement, whether there is another level of understanding, which informs us that the circle doesn't close, but makes a spiral. No matter how often we return to what seems to be a past condition, it turns out never to be exactly the same.

Reference to more than one way of understanding *Los de abajo* does not mean that Azuela's disenchantment with the Revolution was unreal or unreasonable. His involvement dates back to the last years of the Díaz regime when he became a supporter of Francisco I. Madero. The novelist's political ideas, like Madero's, were not very startling. They called for political reform—democratic institutions, civil justice, a fair economic opportunity—rather than profound social reform. The Madero revolt triumphed in the middle of 1911, and Azuela was given a political appointment in Lagos de Moreno. Madero's government was riddled with hangers-on from the old order, and it soon fell. Reactionaries and foreign interests brought about the assassination of Madero early in 1913 and Victoriano Huerta was made president. Villa, Carranza, and Emiliano Zapata continued the Revolution. With a change in United States recognition policy, the Huerta government fell in July 1914. At that point, the Revolution turned into civil war between Villa and Carranza. A Villa-Zapata alliance gained strength very briefly, but the alliance did not hold. Azuela served the *villista* cause in both civil and military-medical positions.

The revolutionary movement culminated in the new constitution of 1917. Throughout its course, the Revolution had placed increasing emphasis on social reform. In other words, it had both bourgeois and proletarian aspects, with corresponding emphasis on political and social change. Although Azuela spent much of his time in the service of the poor, he never favored proletarianism in politics. He was disillusioned by the general course of political developments, and even more by the behavior of men. His bitterness is apparent in *Los de abajo*. However, it does transcend documentary-type exposition because Azuela discovered, probably without knowing it, the proper medium for the material. The matching of movement in the novel's structure with the primordial movement of revolution is the basic cause of the novel's surpassing its initial and most accessible meaning. However, behind this cause is the author himself, who was willing to depart from traditional procedures in order to accomplish something new.

An Uruguayan novel of the same year, *El terruño* by Carlos Reyles, also has much to say about internal upheaval. There is even a hint of the inexorable movement of revolution. However, Reyles's narrative techniques—unlike Azuela's—are all within the naturalist manner that is now referred to as "traditional." Its structural base is the characterization of Doña Angela, known also as Mamagela, the owner of a *pulpería*. She represents Reyles's ideal of the realistic, hardworking opposite of the dreamy intellectual. We appreciate her character through third-person omniscient narration—a point of view entirely in accord with the narrator's eagerness to coordinate several facets of the novel. In addition to the practical-idealistic contrast exemplified in Mamagela and several other characters, *El terruño* also contains a story of adultery and the author's arguments in favor of sheep raising for the good of the agricultural economy. This campaign, of course, underscores the plea for common sense as seen through characterization.

A feud between brothers, in the first part of the novel, foreshadows the fratricidal war that dominates the second part. We assume, because of the novel's stereotyped idealist, that intellectuals

24

will not solve the nation's problems. However, revolutionary activity is also of questionable value. Many people join the rebellion for reasons that have nothing to do with ideas—it promises a degree of freedom, irresponsibility, and food. This motivation recalls *Los de abajo* and the Mexican revolutionaries' appreciation of wandering about the countryside. The sense of movement never develops beyond a hint. Therefore, it remains in the background of our experience, particularly because Reyles uses lyric repetition to emphasize moments of important emotional response.[4] This stylistic device is not used with reference to the movement of revolutionary action.

The dynamism of *El terruño* is produced by the build-up of tension in the first part, followed by its release in the second. Mamagela's practical good sense, which Reyles probably would have liked to be the dynamic factor, often finds expression in static exposition. This common sense provides an optimistic ending for the novel, but experience within the work informs us that words are very fragile.

Shifting the scene to Argentina, Benito Lynch's *Los caranchos de La Florida* touches on problems of the rural economy because one of the protagonists has studied agronomy in Germany. However, Lynch decided to base his story on a tragedy caused by the violent tempers of Don Francisco (Pancho) Suárez Orono and his son, Panchito. The complications resulting from their personalities constitute a spinal column rather than a base for the novel. Nothing very complicated happens between the time the conflict is established, early in the novel, and the tragedy right at the end. Along the way, Lynch supplies a number of good pictures of gaucho life and a considerable comprehension of social attitudes. These factors take their place along the line of continuity maintained by the very slight plot.

Lynch first establishes the character of Don Pancho, the father, by commenting on how men have trembled in his presence. Then he provides a kind of prologue, a condensed history, of Don Pancho and the *estancia* named "La Florida." This part of the novel is not a flashback in the usual sense, because the author's purpose is to give as much information as possible in very little space. Artistic creativity is not a consideration. Real novelization begins when Don Panchito returns from Germany. Given the setting of the novel, we might reasonably expect a conflict between rural common sense and

25

book learning, or between traditional ideas and urban enlightenment. But there is no such contrast. The elder Pancho is a man of some sophistication, though he freely discards any of its aspects that stand in the way of his enormous ego. As for the effect Europe has had on young Panchito, the father wavers between wondering how six years abroad could have changed the boy so little and, on the other hand, berating him for shaving off his moustache in order to be fashionable. The tragedy of the novel is caused by the greatest similarity between the two men: their foul temperaments.

Lynch narrates in the omniscient third person. Since the characters of the two men are so important to his story, some deviation from this point of view could have been very helpful. And as a matter of fact, there is one part of the novel—Panchito is taking account of his relationship with his father—when the narrative comes close to being interior monologue.[5] The change is probably instinctive rather than intentional, because Lynch did not use it in other places where it would have served well.

His prose style, although it does not make use of brilliant effects, is useful to the communication of the narrative. Occasionally, he makes the reader focus on a person or an object by repeating the object of emphasis in a following phrase. Apparently he does this when he wishes to communicate a feeling of warmth for what he is talking about. He uses dialogue extensively, and his use of gaucho speech is a major technique of characterization. In general, it has a natural, authentic ring, and he uses it consistently and unobtrusively. That is, he does not call attention to what he is doing. Torres Rioseco points out that the speech of the gaucho in Lynch's novel reveals either low intelligence or limited opportunity to cultivate his natural advantages.[6] His very limited expression is entirely consistent with a servile attitude that comes as no surprise in view of the fact that, if he says the wrong thing, either of the two masters of La Florida is likely to belt him in the mouth with a riding crop.

The amazing thing is that the gauchos do not hit back. They only predict that such violence will lead to no good. Father and son are named *caranchos* about one-quarter of the way through the novel, by the half-crazy gaucho who foresees disaster (p. 47). A *carancho* combines the characteristics of eagle and vulture.[7] While the description is accurate enough for this father-son combination, Lynch does not emphasize the theme. The conflict between the two men develops over their interest in the same girl, who is by age better suited to Panchito. In the violent end, son murders father and is murdered in turn by the overseer of the *estancia*. Two very important conditions define the nature of Panchito's crime. First, on the night of his arrival from Germany, Panchito's father forbids him, under any circumstances, to go to a certain part of the *estancia*. The young man reacts understandably to what amounts to a dare, but he does not disobey. When he does go there, it is because he is lost in a storm. There he finds Marcelina, the woman in the case. Second, Panchito is quite a hand with his pistol. Repeated reference to it makes the reader expect him to commit murder. However, when he kills Don Pancho, he does so with a wrench he happens to have with him at the moment. The initial step toward disaster is pure chance; the murder itself is clearly not premeditated, but is caused by the passion of a moment.

Lynch does not suggest that the violence of his protagonists has any relationship to the environment. It appears to be hereditary and susceptible to aggravation by practically anyone or any circumstance. Between the establishment of the plot line and the final disaster, *Los caranchos de La Florida* levels off into a series of episodes of about equal intensity. The only development in the story line is Panchito's progress in finding out the exact nature of his father's relationship with Marcelina. Throughout these episodes, Lynch makes word portraits of a variety of gaucho types, of the country schoolteacher, and particularly of Panchito's cousin, Eduardo. He is particularly important because of the role he plays in the revelation of class consciousness.

As Don Pancho sees them, the gauchos are subhuman: half-savage, dirty, immoral, and stupid. He insists that they recognize his superiority. Panchito may be slightly more enlightened, but only to the extent that he is less consistently cruel. Like his father, he maintains a general policy of aloofness. Eduardo, on the other hand, fraternizes with the gauchos and enjoys a more relaxed though less respectable life. His relatives do see him, but they deplore his disgrace.

An appreciation of this class system develops naturally as Panchito goes from place to place. It is the most interesting aspect of the book. The basic plot is so slight we hardly notice its movement in a large part of the novel. The reader tends to look for plot development and, in the process, becomes involved in the apparently incidental communication of social attitudes.

The problem of the unappreciated artist seems far removed from the ways of life novelized in these three works. The publication of Manuel Gálvez's *El mal metafísico* in the same year calls attention to the great disparity between society in rural Spanish America and in the great urban centers. It is the story of a poet, Carlos Riga, in Buenos Aires during the early years of the twentieth century. Gálvez's sympathetic treatment of the dreamer by means of realist narrative techniques produces a contrast very similar to the contrast one recognizes in the confused literary scene at the turn of the century and for a decade or more beyond. Orgambide and Yahni say circumstances and personages are taken from real life and are identifiable.[8] They regard the book as an important document for Argentine letters. Indeed, it has a similar importance for Spanish American literature in general. And, by even further extension, the novel is important as a portrayal of gradual alienation. The artist's particular attitudes separate him more and more from the ordinary social process. Because Gálvez intended to make his work as a whole a portrayal of Argentine reality, there is every reason to believe that he did place real people in the novel. The discovery of equivalences is fascinating. However, if we put aside the game of identity and deal with the book as pure fiction, we find the author has used a changing narrative tone to give the novel vitality.

The story of *El mal metafísico* is divided into three parts. The function of the division is simple—it provides for a lapse of four years between the first two parts and a lapse of three years between parts two and three. Involvement of the reader in the life of the novel depends not on an obvious structural pattern, but on the establishment of a particular tone right at the beginning. Gálvez is gently ironic. Carlos Riga, a law student aged twenty, is waiting for friends to arrive at a café where he is to read them one of his poems. "Every night he used to meet some of his colleagues in literature and illusions at a coffeehouse, and there, carefully nursing the inspirational coffee, they would spend long hours defining Life, organizing Society, cursing the hateful Philistines who ignored them, and deceiving poverty and the thirst for glory with vague, easy dreams."[9] The narrator's tone is partly critical, partly nostalgic. And even if the past might have been a bit pretentious, it was important and understandable.

In an immediate flashback, Gálvez deals with Riga's family, then he goes to the *pensión* where the poet lives, and from there into his literary life. The tone of gentle irony pervades all this introduction. Then on page forty-five, one of the young men defines the "metaphysical illness," saying it is the sickness of creating, of dreaming, of thinking. The tone has shifted. This is a serious matter. Gálvez's reader discovers a sense of frustration increasing at the expense of pleasant nostalgia. The tone of gentle irony still appears from time to time, but unhappiness becomes dominant. This change gives the book vitality. It also gives it meaning for any age, because Gálvez deals with the dark tragedy that is another facet of when-we-were-young-and-foolish.

The first part of the novel has to do with Riga's first literary steps. One of the most perceptive episodes shows that his trouble with his father is of two kinds. First, the elder Riga thinks Carlos's literary pursuits are a waste of time. Later, having been persuaded by an old-fashioned writer that literature may even help an attorney's career, the father objects to Carlos's *modernista* efforts. Gálvez builds on the latter conflict to make a point of society's reluctance to accept innovation in the arts. Each characterization, major or minor, relates one way or another to the acceptance or rejection of the artist. The triumph of the first part is publication of the first number of a new cultural magazine, which is supposed to revitalize the country.

Part two carries Riga into greater difficulties. He has trouble scratching out a living. And his literary work is appreciated only by a few. Part three is about alcoholism, loneliness, sickness, and death. The novel has some of the romantic qualities often associated with bohemianism, but there is no melodrama unless it is created by the discomfort of particular readers. The calmness of Gálvez's prose lends dignity to situations that might have been ruined by overstatement.

Modernismo's exquisite sensitivity, while a subject for Gálvez's irony, was still cultivated when he was writing his novel. *El hombre que parecía un caballo*, by Rafael Arévalo Martínez, is an excellent example of symbolist transformation. This short novel, or long story, is the expression of a human relationship. The narrator is pleased, and later disillusioned, by his friend. The positive aspect of the relationship is expressed in terms of jewels; but even these become more brilliant than substantive. The negative aspect is expressed by association of the friend's movements and mannerisms with those of a horse. While this imagery contains an element of bestiality, there is also an element of graceful beauty. Therefore, the presumed positive and negative factors are not absolute. Each contains elements of the other.

It has long been taken for granted by most people that the friend in the story, Señor Aretal, is a fictionalization of the Colombian poet Porfirio Barba Jacob—otherwise known as Ricardo Arenales and Miguel Angel Osorio. The accuracy of this assumption makes no difference to the story. Recently, Daniel R. Reedy has explained that the author is talking about two aspects of himself.[10] The argument relies heavily on the ideas of Carl Gustav Jung. Without going into the pros and cons of the new interpretation, it is worth noting that it retains the essential communication of the traditional reading: an appreciation of the contrast between the fine and the gross. Apparently, the reader's experience depends on the author's shift of balance within the two systems of imagery. In spite of this tour de force, what one remembers of *El hombre que parecía un caballo* is more likely to be the clever descriptions of the man-horse. The associations are amusing and invite the reader to look for person-animal similarities in his own world. These effects—both the serious and the frivolous—make the story seem more innovative than it really is. Its freshness is the product of Arévalo Martínez's personal way of seeing things. Technically, it was old-fashioned in 1916.

CHAPTER 3

From *Los de abajo* to *Don Segundo Sombra* (1917–1925)

The novelists became more and more aware of their immediate surroundings, and this growing regionalism found its place in conjunction with themes inherited from the turn of the century, rather than in opposition to them. The hypersensitive, dreamy protagonist was still a major interest, but by this time he often found himself in circumstances far different from the Parisian settings of earlier years. In fact, regional awareness discovered a possible cure for his condition in the milk-and-honey beneficence of the simple life. In turn, this idealization of rural life indicates that the protagonist's troubles come from city life in general, rather than from Paris specifically.

The characteristics of the hero himself become less restrictive. He is not necessarily the bored aesthete whose symbolist transformations alienate him from real life. He may be alienated because he is an intellectual—as is Tocles, in *El terruño*. He may be simply the ingenuous, pampered son of a wealthy family; and, of course, this condition makes a very credible combination with the idea of the bored aesthete.

The transfer to the country doesn't always work the cure. It may be only temporary—Mariano Latorre's *Zurzulita* (1920) is an example. There are also times when the curative agent is not the country itself, but a rural woman overflowing with good health. Eduardo Barrios's *Un perdido* (1917) is such a case; and Joaquín Edwards Bello persistently reveals his fondness for the "woman of the people." To avoid any possible misunderstanding, it should be clear that these novelists were not members of the proletariat, nor were they proposing to let down class barriers. Their view of the robust and cheerful woman of the people is similar to their view of prize livestock. This view is hardly an enlightened one, but it is a step ahead of not seeing the common people at all. The so-called popular classes were also apparent in the cities where a novel of protest started developing.

Dissatisfaction with the state of society is apparent in a large percentage of novels. It is implicit, of course, in the novels where the protagonist tries to grasp reality more firmly by seeking a different milieu. However, it is far more apparent in novels that deal with urban society, by Azuela, Gálvez, Edwards Bello, and Carlos Loveira, and in stories by Elías Castelnuovo. Again in a rural setting, the feeling of discomfort focuses on the plight of the Bolivian Indian in Alcides Arguedas's *Raza de bronce* (1919). None of these books amounts to a crusade. Rather, they acknowledge the existence and problems of people who are not members of the oligarchy. Their cautious investigation—examining, but not daring to make any fundamental changes—is entirely in accord with the political mood of the time.

It is hardly necessary to say that political circumstances were not the same in all the countries of Spanish America. At any given time, the spectrum provided by nearly a score of political entities is likely to show widely divergent extremes. It is often possible, however, to find similarities in several countries—enough to justify some general assumptions provided we expect them to be suggestive rather than definitive. There were, in fact, several political moves that indicate awareness of the need for social improvement, but they tended to fall short of radical change. The Mexican Revolution was the most apparent and the most effective. A new constitution was promulgated in 1917, and through it a considerably larger portion of the population was given a chance at economic improvement. Much of its potential went unrealized because a great deal of the nation's political energy was spent in power struggles. By 1925, a political revolt by Adolfo de la Huerta and a vicious religious controversy emphasized the need for stability rather than programs of social improvement. In Chile, antioligarch sentiment produced the organization of the Communist party in 1920 and the election of Arturo Alessandri in the same year. He was able to bring about the enactment of a progressive labor code, but was unable to secure consistent legislative cooperation. In 1925 he was replaced by a military coup. The Radical party of Argentina succeeded in electing Hipólito Irigoyen in 1916. Unfortunately, he was a personalistic and indecisive administrator. During 1919, he tolerated strikebreaking tactics. Marcelo T. Alvear, an aristocrat who was an Irigoyen partisan, became president in 1922. Within three years, however, the two politicians had broken their alliance, and the influence of the Radical party was practically over. The new Uruguayan constitution of 1917 set up a commission-type government and made provisions for labor and social welfare that were similar to those in the Mexican constitution. There were no provisions for land reform. President Batlle had said in 1910 that this problem would be solved effortlessly by the general progress of the country. Ex-President Augusto B. Leguía of Peru seized the presidency in 1919. A new constitution with electoral reforms went into effect in 1920. However, Raúl Haya de la Torre, then a rising young politician, was exiled. He was in Mexico by 1924 when he organized APRA (American Party of Revolutionary Alliance).

In several other countries, there were major changes or tragedies important to the social situation, even though they were not related to planned social reform. Petroleum was discovered in the Maracaibo area of Venezuela in 1918. Guatemalans overthrew dictator Manuel Estrada Cabrera in 1920. Costa Rica endured Federico A. Tinoco for only two years, 1917–1919. Ecuador suffered a massacre of strikers in 1922 and a frustrated revolt in 1925. Gerardo Machado was elected president of Cuba in 1925. His administration turned into a repressive dictatorship that eventually produced Fulgencio Batista.

The picture of social change runs from armed revolution to nothing at all. It portrays an inadequate awareness of a complicated society, but it also indicates some recognition of a new era. Indications of a new era in the novel appear in the form of changing thematic interests and also in experimentation with narrative technique. These two lines of innovation cross each other rather than coincide. That is, thematic change may be apparent in a novel that uses well-established techniques. Rómulo Gallegos's protagonist in his first novel, *El último Solar* (1920), is basically a turn-of-the-century sensibility type, and his presentation is in the realistic manner. The author expands the thematic material to show, through his hero, a good deal about Venezuela during that time. Torres Rioseco points out that it is a country where dishonesty and opportunism are rampant.[1] He also says artistic talent is a liability—a condition apparent in the novels of Manuel Díaz Rodríguez. It is tempting to blame all the troubles on dictatorships, but in all fairness we must note that the problem of the unappreciated artist is as fundamental in Gálvez's *El mal metafísico* as anywhere else. Indeed, thematic change is apparent in *El último Solar* precisely because Gallegos uses a traditional theme as his base, then goes beyond that point in response to his specific surroundings. This expansion is the prime characteristic of his novels.

It is not so easy to point out cases of static themes developed by experimental techniques. A case might be made for Eduardo Barrios's *Un perdido* because psychological character analysis acts as an important narrative technique. The difficulty—not just in the case of Barrios's novel, but in a general sense—is that experimental technique actually changes the theme. However traditional the story may be, a new way of telling it makes it a different experience. Ricardo Güiraldes's first novel, *Raucho* (1917), is an exemplary case. Its autobiographical aspect tends to distract critics from its importance as fiction. There is no reason to doubt its reflection of the author's life. Juan Carlos Ghiano points out that the subtitle, "Moments from the Life of a Contemporary Youth," strongly suggests the relationship of the author to a particular social situation.[2] The anecdotal base is the experience of a boy with a natural affinity for *estancia* life who lives an alienating odyssey through city life and a trip to France, then returns to the *estancia* and rediscovers his identity.

The disoriented protagonist is saved by wholesome rural living, just as in many other novels. *Raucho*, however, is different from the rest. The principal difference is the structure of the narrative. "Mo-

34

ments," in the subtitle, is the key. There are nine of them, each one intended to communicate the feeling as well as the fact of a given moment. Even the first one, "Prólogo," is an integral part of the story—a word game that the customary realist-naturalist attitude would not likely permit. Concentration on the nine moments separates Raucho's life from humdrum reality. It is by no means a repetition of what the reader has experienced, and does not intend to be; therefore, it transcends documentary value. In other words, nine moments cannot possibly be a re-creation of real life. They are a distillation of it, as is the case of Güiraldes's novel, or they fail to be anything.

This structure is surprisingly similar to that of *Los de abajo*—a comparison likely to pass unnoticed, since the subjects are so different. Azuela even announces the structure in his subtitle, "Scenes of the Revolution," just as Güiraldes does. The effect is the same, if we take into account the difference between the odyssey of a single life and the movement of social upheaval. That is, Azuela's scenes amount to a distillation of his knowledge of the Revolution, just as Güiraldes's moments are a distillation of Raucho's youth. It is also interesting that the protagonists of both novels make a geographical circle, but each return is sufficiently different from the beginning to suggest a spiral rather than a closed ring. This last coincidence, while interesting to contemplate, is probably unimportant in a consideration of experimental techniques. There is no question of influence in the case of these two books. Their similarity amounts to two authors searching for adequate expression. Azuela found it, probably unconsciously, because his material suggested it. Güiraldes was aware of the search. His work prior to *Raucho* shows his desire to find some way to transform his feeling toward rural Argentina.

In his story of Raucho, Güiraldes reinforces the effect of the structure by using a narrative point of view, which Ghiano describes as grammatically third person, but with the psychological presence of the first person.[3] Actually, this narrative position acts as a liaison between the author and the protagonist, with the result that Güiraldes's reader tends to accept this multiple identity. The effect is created by having the presumed third person say things about Raucho which we may take to be Raucho's sentiment. It is this projection of one person into the other which makes the narrative almost first person. What the author accomplishes by all this is a communication of what a certain kind of life (a set of circumstances) means to him. It is a significance discovered via a profound emotional response rather than by observation. Recognition of this attitude on the part of the author will also illuminate his intent in *Don Segundo Sombra* and should silence discussion about whether the author painted a true picture of gaucho life as compared with, for example, Benito Lynch's *El inglés de los güesos* (1924). Nothing could be more real than *Raucho* or *Don Segundo Sombra*, though neither approaches a one-to-one correspondence with objective awareness. One of the extraordinary characteristics of readers of Spanish American fiction was for many years the willingness to accept as real the highly improbable scientist of Lynch's novel (a combination of caricature and misconception) while considering Güiraldes's creations as somehow separated from reality.

They are separated, of course, in the sense that they are transformations rather than documentations. And Güiraldes was not alone. Azuela, after continuing to deal with the Revolution in several works using most of the techniques of *Los de abajo*, became even more experimental in *La Malhora* (1923) and *El desquite* (1925). He intensifies the use of selected moments, adds to the effect by using a style that often seems to select words just as the structure selects incidents. This procedure minimizes the importance of a cause-effect sequence, and Azuela goes even farther, using an antichronological development of the story. He also experiments with interior monologue. The product is not always successful, but these works leave no doubt about the author's vanguardist tendencies.

If Azuela had been an influential author at that time, we might consider his work the inspiration of other novels, or even types of novels, that transcend documentary recording by experimenting with techniques. Actually, vanguardist trends in Mexico and the rest of Spanish America come from European influences and from a pervasive sense of a new era. A Mexican phenomenon called the "colonialist novel" is particularly interesting because its theme is really determined by the attitude of the author and because communication of the theme depends to such a great extent on the prose style of the narration. It is a highly specialized historical novel cultivated by Artemio de Valle Arizpe and several other young writers who were trying their wings in the postrevolutionary years. The novelists are more antiquarians than historians—they treat the past with possessive regard. Herein lies the theme. It is not simply the historical event or personage that inspires the novel, but the attitude of the author with reference to the historical fact. The theme comes to life through language that becomes precious in its attempt to create the ambience of a past time. To a considerable extent, these works recall Larreta's *La gloria de don Ramiro*. However, a difference of fundamental importance is that the Mexican writers were reviving the past of their own country, and their works serve as a means of identifying their particular reality. They contain an element of New Worldism that is not present in Larreta's novel.[4]

By transferring the experience of the novel to the past, the author places the present in a different perspective—for the reader and for himself. Historical fiction, therefore, can be a means of appreciating the present. The effect is different, of course, from the distillation of present reality as in *Raucho* or *Los de abajo*, for example, but the motivation of the authors seems rather similar. Still another way of changing perspective is the use of an imaginary situation like Pedro Prado's *La reina de Rapa Nui*. Like good science fiction, it affords the author opportunity to comment on his particular circumstance. Prado used a different approach, with much the same motivation, in *Alsino* (1920). Reduced to its minimum, this novel has the fantasy and charm of a story for children. A crippled boy grows wings and flies around the Chilean countryside becoming involved in situations that are quite ordinary until they are changed by his aeronautic capability. Allegorical implications deepen the experience of reading the novel. Association with the Icarus myth is inevitable; and given the boy's condition of being chained by his physical disability, Prado's reader is flooded with multiple implications relating to freedom—the restraints of social order, the problem of individual commitment, and concern for others. To make matters more complicated, Alsino is by no means a poet, or even a standard hypersensitive type; he is a country boy of very humble circumstances. One of the interesting aspects of the novel is Prado's insistence on a deterministic view of his protagonist in preflight stage and of the country people in general. The view is in marked contrast to the sense of freedom and also to certain passages that may be considered slightly excessive in their poetic rapture. The contrast provokes considerations of psychological validity that detract from the more imaginative implications of the novel.

Something—or perhaps several different phenomena—called "psychology" takes on increasing importance during these years. As applied to some of the novels built around the turn-of-the-century aesthete, the term could well be discarded in favor of "philosophical." At times it seems to mean any kind of searching character delineation. And it also refers to the psychological validity of the novelist's creation. For Eduardo Barrios it was the basis of fiction. Psychological analysis is actually the dynamic factor in some of his novels. On this foundation, he built his studies without great concern for their relationship to society. Rather, he thought in terms of universal human problems and, as is very often the case, produced incidentally some fascinating comments on his own cultural system. The best known of his novels is *El Hermano Asno* (1922), whose title refers to St. Francis of Assisi's "Brother Brute," the inner force for evil. Barrios narrates through the diary of Fray Lázaro. The story concerns Fray Rufino's saintliness and concern for his loss of humility. The final tragedy is an expiatory act—or some prefer to think it is the triumph of the brutish side of Fray Rufino. Fray Lázaro's narrative shows his own involvement, and astonishment. The reader joins him, but with no feeling of incredulity. The basic concept of this novel is the spiritual problem of a single individual. It arises from a Christian paradox—saintliness invites the reverence of others, which produces sinful pride in the saintly person. In addition to its meaning for the individual, this paradox is significant in various national cultures and in a whole civilization. It is a part of the identity of Spanish America.

It is possible to discuss psychological validity or psychological penetration in practically any of the novels written during this period. The heart of the matter is that novelists were responding to the popularization of the science of psychology. However, the use of psychology as a critical criterion is not very productive unless psychological analysis is the dynamic factor in the novel, as in *El Hermano Asno*. If the movement of the book comes from some other source—the combination of symbolist imagery and nostalgic recall in Reyles's *El embrujo de Sevilla* (1922), or the selection of moments in the composition of *Raucho*—the discussion of psychological factors has little to do with appreciation of the work. Undoubtedly, the writers' awareness of the new science encouraged, in many cases, a deeper understanding of visible reality, and prolonged the influence of realism-naturalism.

In spite of an occasional variant like Pedro Prado, the Chilean novel was for years the stronghold of realism-naturalism, the bulwark against vanguardism. Four of the stalwart defenders are prominent in this period: Eduardo Barrios, Joaquín Edwards Bello, Mariano Latorre, and Marta Brunet. The novels of Edwards Bello are a good example of a growing awareness of social problems, and one of them, *El roto* (1920), has enjoyed a large public because its treatment of a type is almost documentary.

The novel actually defines its title as part of its message. However, this definition is more illuminating if it functions as an addition to a prior understanding of what *roto* means. It is, in fact, a variable or relative term used to refer to an individual representative of the dregs of society. Depending on the attitude of the speaker, the word may refer to a person who has reached this sorry state through his own doing, or one who has been forced into it by social circumstances. The *roto* may be simply down-and-out, or he may be vicious. Generally, his inner resources are meager. In a review of the novel, Omer Emeth, a French critic who lived in Chile, wrote almost entirely of the meaning of the term as it is revealed by Edwards Bello's work. By request of the novelist, this review appears at the end of the definitive edition of *El roto*, published in 1968.[5] The critic enlarges its meaning to include anyone who is morally reprehensible. His comments probably coincided with the author's intention of chastising society. The role of environment is important in the book and in Omer Emeth's review, particularly as it applies to the boy Esmeraldo.

The childhood of Esmeraldo was very likely the embryo of Edwards Bello's story. He grows up in the slums, as close to a bordello as is possible without actually living there. In addition to the characterization of Esmeraldo, the novelist develops others to fill out his picture of the slums. Some of them become almost as important as Esmeraldo; and the bordello itself, La Gloria, becomes the center of the story. The chapters mainly portray aspects of life in and around La Gloria, and frequently have the tone of a newspaper feature story. This quality encourages the reader to think of the novel as documentary. Undergirding this effect, moreover, was Ed-

39

wards Bello's commitment to visible reality. Complicated and copious files of political events and human behavior were the source
of his information. Torres Rioseco, who certainly expresses many
doubts about Edwards Bello's success as a novelist, points out that
he does avoid the sociological tract in favor of novelization.[6] Indeed,
El roto may be a good example of minimal transformation. That is,
it may answer the question of how much novelization an author has
to effect in order to differentiate his work from a documentary
report. The line is an important one in many Spanish American
novels because social protest is frequent and because awareness of
the New World is, in its initial manifestation, a documentary impulse.

El roto opens with the description of a slum area—not the de-
cayed center of a city, but a new settlement on the periphery. Its
miserable condition is an appropriate setting for the misery of the
people in the story. Alfonso Calderón, in his preface to the 1968
edition, says that the time of the novel is prior to the period of *alessandrismo*, and refers to it as a time of "abominable bossism, of
corrupt paternalism, hiding below the surface of constitutional
order."[7] It is interesting that the opening scene, although very detailed, does not set the time precisely. The author includes a number
of side remarks more characteristic of a human-interest story than
of a novel—about foreign influence, building of the railroad, the
provincialism of Santiago, the physical appearance of mestizo types.
They provide atmosphere and tend to generalize the situation. In
contrast, the sixth chapter concludes with statistics and references
to dated sources—in other words, unmitigated documentation. The
time references are specifically to the years 1908–1915, and the
annotated edition carries a footnote explaining that publication of
the novel was delayed by World War I (pp. 26–27). The statistics
are a reminder of what documentary information is really like. By
comparison, the author's comments in the introductory passage seem
imaginative. In reality, they are based on facts and filled out with
opinion. Edwards Bello extends another invitation to the reader's
imaginative response, still in the first chapter, by introducing an episode involving people from both social spheres. A lady of quality has
her purse snatched by a boy from the slums, assisted by his two ac-
complices. No one can catch the boy who has the purse. He runs to
La Gloria. Esmeraldo is the smallest of the three involved in this

operation. The theft could well have been witnessed by Edwards Bello, and it is as appropriate to a feature story as are the observations made earlier in the chapter. Its significance is increased by two important phenomena of novelization in the latter part of this chapter. First, when Esmeraldo runs into the house next to La Gloria, one of the prostitutes comments on what his mother would say—a piece of information not likely available through observation. The second is much more important in the structure of the novel: the flight of the child from the world of respectable people into the world where he feels he belongs. At the end of the novel, Esmeraldo flees from his supposed benefactor back into the slums. This social dichotomy is reinforced throughout the novel by a contrast which Calderón describes as parallel miseries. One is a physical misery; the other is a moral misery. Respectively, they apply to the underprivileged and to the people of quality. Calderón says only the latter wish to preserve their miserable condition.[8] It is clear, however, that the protection of Esmeraldo by the newspaperman, Lux, separates the boy from his sense of belonging. This feeling of alienation is augmented by the physical destruction of his world.

Near the end of the novel, Esmeraldo leaves his benefactor's room, late at night. In the space of one page, Edwards Bello develops the boy's feeling of alienation by three expanding references to sadness. First, ". . . the street was lonely and sad"; shortly after this, "Winter was coming on, sad and monotonous"; and then, "He remembered Lux and the days spent with him as something sad and foreign to his temperament" (p. 148). He enters his old neighborhood and finds it changed. Several references give it a spectral quality (p. 152). In a kind of epilogue, Esmeraldo finds out what has happened to his friends, his relatives, and the house he once lived in. His world has been destroyed; effectively his roots have disappeared while he was in prison. When he leaves his benefactor, Lux, he actually has nothing to return to. Later the police approach him in his old barrio and he flees from them. He turns and stabs the closest of his pursuers and then eludes the others by dashing in front of a moving train, leaving them separated from him. We see no more of him, but learn that the man he stabbed was Lux, the reporter who struggled to save him. In his flight from the police and from Lux, the boy repeats the flight from the world of respectable people that had taken place as part of the purse-snatching episode.

41

In this early flight, Esmeraldo runs from a threat and toward the security of his barrio; in the second flight, he runs from the possibility of a new security, but there is no haven for him in his world. The implications of this contrast constitute the suggestive aspects of the novel.

The tone of protest is not nearly as strong in novels that take place outside the city. Spanish America's two related rural problems, ownership of the land and social justice for the Indian, are suggested in several novels, and the Indian problem is the basis of Arguedas's *Raza de bronce* (1919). The principal function of the rural novel, however, is to clarify the relationship between the human European transplant and the world into which destiny has cast him. This process has two important aspects, one of them basically bucolic and the other heroic. The bucolic aspect includes the country-against-city contrast, the idea of abundant good health and moral improvement through hard work, and awareness of the picturesque quality of rural customs. The heroic aspect includes the notion that man has to fight and conquer nature; his awestruck condition when he confronts the vastness of plain, jungle, mountain, or river in the New World; his sense of foreignness in a nature for whose objects he does not even have names; and the nagging fear that he will be beaten by the enemy he is supposed to conquer.

José Eustasio Rivera's *La vorágine* (1924) includes both the bucolic and the heroic aspects, though it is usually remembered for the heroic—adventurous man swallowed up by the jungle. In spite of much adverse criticism, principally related to its hyperdramatic protagonist, Rivera's novel hangs on to its place on most lists of landmark novels in Spanish America. The anecdotal base of the novel is multiple, a series of events in the jungle and on the plains of Rivera's Colombia. He brings them together around his invention, Arturo Cova, adventurer, poet, and lover. At the beginning of the novel, Arturo has captivated Alicia, another in his long line of amatory triumphs, and is being pressured by her family to express his good intentions in a marriage ceremony. Since he prefers not to give up his freedom, and Alicia does not wish to make him unhappy, Cova decides they should flee from Bogotá into the hinterland. This decision is our initiation into the characterization of Arturo; and, although he does change in some ways in the course of

42

the novel, he never becomes more reasonable. Separation from Alicia follows the escape to the plains. Arturo goes into the jungle, seeks and rejoins Alicia, and disappears. Action is slight. The addition of subplots increases the activity, and some of it enhances the ambience of the novel. However, it is really the characterization of Arturo Cova that makes the novel what it is. He is its greatest asset and its most objectionable fault.

Insofar as Arturo is melodramatic because he is a poet awestruck by nature, he provides the heroic factor that saves the novel. What nearly destroys it is the extension of his exaggeration into an unconscionable egocentricity. The trouble comes from the author's mishandling of first-person narration. The saga of Arturo Cova is supposedly in diary form. Therefore, he tells his own story. Unfortunately, his creator could not shift completely from the third-person view of the narrative. So it is that Arturo says things about himself that should be revealed by what other people say and do. That way we would be spared Arturo's overwrought explanations of his own sensitivity, his pseudoastonishment when various women throw themselves at him, his eternal rhetorical questions designed to reveal how deep the currents run beneath his debonair surface.

Reaching for an understanding of the protagonist, we feel a certain sorrow for the novel. The story develops in three major stages: (1) the experience on the plains, (2) the experience in the jungle after separation from Alicia, and (3) reunion with Alicia followed by disappearance into the jungle. Events are foreshadowed by Arturo's dream early in the story. The novel's vitality depends less on actions that constitute the plot line than on what Arturo observes on the periphery. The first stage of the novel is mostly bucolic. The plains are vast, the beauty of nature astonishing. Rural customs and characteristics of rural people are the most important factors. They are not idealized except to the extent that any city dweller thinks life in the country is desirable. Griselda, the coarse country girl, makes a contrast with Alicia. In truth, they have one thing in common: they both fall in love with Arturo against his will. One noteworthy narrative technique is the introduction of Griselda into the story line and the incidental description of her, rather than a preliminary character sketch in the realist manner. The unspectacular effect of this technique makes the characterization of Arturo all the more flamboyant.

There is a considerable feeling of discovery in the first part of the novel; it becomes more intense when Arturo goes into the jungle. The things of nature are strange; the Indians are strange; Arturo finds himself face to face with life in a circumstance where the trappings of civilization are minimal. He suffers hallucinations, thinks the trees are talking to him. His person shrinks; and, at the end of the novel, a third-person narrator informs us that he and his companions were swallowed up by the forest. They find no way to defeat nature, nor do they see a way of meeting it on equal terms. The role of the jungle is important in Spanish American fiction, and *La vorágine* is a forerunner of many novels insofar as the recognition of the environment is concerned. As for the relationship of man and nature, novelists have discovered that man is not inevitably swallowed up by surrounding nature. They discover the meaning of the relationship through a process that is either mythologizing or something closely akin. The same process applies also to the plains, and it began there earlier. This characteristic is the underlying importance of *Don Segundo Sombra*.

CHAPTER 4

The Year of
Don Segundo Sombra (1926)

Ricardo Güiraldes's major novel, *Don Segundo Sombra,* is a narrative representation of the author's attitude toward rural life. It is important, however, to notice that the author's attitude, in this book, is not the basis of the novel's tone. The tone is controlled by the expectant attitude of the novice who tells the story in the first person. The author's more general, and more fundamental, attitude is a combination of the concept of beneficent rural life as seen in *Raucho* and the technique of narrative-embellished-into-poetry as seen in *Xaimaca* (1923). It is an attitude effective on a plane more basic than the apparent narrative tone of the novel. There is more than one myth in Güiraldes's creation. Don Segundo is a myth, but so is the boy, the almost nameless Fabio Cáceres. His near anonymity is perpetuated by Güiraldes's critics, who prefer using almost any appellation for Fabio, so long as it is not his name.

The protagonist of *Raucho,* Güiraldes's first novel, has a natural affinity for *estancia* life. Sophisticated city life nearly destroys him. He rediscovers his authentic self by returning to the country. The benefits are physical and moral. They are also spiritual. Güiraldes sees rural life as noble and inspirational. It fulfills a need not just for physical activity, but also for self-expression—the kind of expression that makes him internally certain that he is doing something he ought to do. In order to put this feeling into a novel, he needs a living, breathing representation. Don Segundo serves, but he is a vanishing breed. Therefore, he becomes something more than real—the myth of the ideal gaucho. A vanishing ideal, however, cannot correspond satisfactorily to the complex feeling suggested by *Raucho*. There must be a transmission of some part of the myth of Don Segundo to a type that promises to endure. And so, Fabio. So also one of the novel's problems. Fabio is not a real-life boy; he is the generalization of the city boy with romanticized ideas about the manliness and solid camaraderie of life in the country. The type suffers from a tendency to wilt rapidly when placed in an authentic working situation. However, Fabio endures; then, in addition, he reconciles himself to becoming a cultured gentleman. The combination stretches probability to the breaking point, or beyond. In other words, the narrator created by Güiraldes is an idealization. He has it both ways and, therefore, is a representation of what the author thinks ought to happen, rather than a re-creation of probability. Güiraldes has, in a way, mythologized himself.

Taking the casual view of *Don Segundo Sombra*—that is, the view of an ordinary reader whose appreciation of factors like myth, style, and structure is subconscious—it is the story of a boy who leaves a dull home and enjoys a more adventurous life before settling down to take his place in respectable society. Fernando Alegría, commenting on the novel in the same way, says it is a perfect "novel for young people" that can be enjoyed by readers of any age.[1] He may be right, but it seems more probable that *Don Segundo Sombra* is a book parents would like to be a favorite of their offspring, but which young people find inauthentic because its rich imagery and mythologizing become fairly cloying. Reading Güiraldes's novels is a more satisfying experience if one is willing to suspend his adverse reactions in order to appreciate fully the positive qualities of the book.

The action of the novel divides naturally into three different stages. Juan Carlos Ghiano notes that each stage consists of nine chapters. The first part deals with Fabio's leaving home and his commitment to the nomadic life with Don Segundo; the second part is about Fabio's difficult apprenticeship; the last nine chapters include the culmination of the adventure and the readjustment to a sedentary life.[2] There is nothing extraordinary about this narrative organization. There are some time lapses. (It is of some importance to an appreciation of Fabio as a myth that, within this tripartite structure, the first and last chapters identify the novel as a book of reminiscence. Therein we become aware of Güiraldes, the maker of Fabio.) Imagery based on the movement of water indicates the intensity of action in each part: the first is an arroyo, the second is a river, the third is a lake. Ghiano finds a reaffirmation of this division in a contemplative passage near the end of the novel, where the three stages are referred to in terms of morning, midday, and evening.[3] One might think this would be enough reaffirmation, but not for Güiraldes. Two pages later, just to be sure we don't miss the point, he says: "It is apparent that in my life water is like a mirror that reflects images of the past. On the banks of an arroyo, long ago I recalled my childhood. Watering my horse in a river ford, I reviewed five years of gaucho wandering. Finally, seated above the small inlet of a lake, on my own land, I mentally went over my calendar of obligations as owner" (p. 127).

Güiraldes is not subtle. His overclarification works disadvantageously in almost all aspects of the novel. Alegría objects to the loss of epic quality following the first third.[4] He points out, with considerable justification, that the author simply drops the line of development that would have served him best—that is, the nomadic commitment that culminates, at the end of the ninth chapter, in the words "Riding, riding, riding" (p. 39). The second part of the novel consists of episodes or scenes from gaucho life, and they alter the mood of the book. However important the poetic aspects of Güiraldes's writing, the truth he communicates through his two protagonists is related to the absolute reality of daily tasks. His devotion to clarity forces him to write the second part of the novel as it is, even though it may disappoint a reader who prefers to maintain the established mood.

Güiraldes's style, fundamentally, is as unobtrusive as his organization of the narrative. There are no problems. When gauchos speak, he reproduces their peculiarities phonetically. This practice was a century old in Argentina when Güiraldes wrote the book. His first-person narrator uses normal speech with vocabulary that is natural for an *estanciero*.[5] His imagery constitutes the extraordinary aspect of his style. A keen visual sense produces pictorial descriptions that are more natural in the framework of reminiscences by an adult than as products of Fabio as a young boy. Near the beginning of the novel: "The narrow road stretched out darkly in front of me. The sky, still blue with sunset, was reflected in the irregularly formed puddles or in the water held in the deep tracks made by a cart, in whose furrow it took on the appearance of carefully cut steel" (p. 7). Often the imagery seems extraneous to the story, more decorative than functional. And its presence is emphasized by Güiraldes's vanguardist tendency to look for the unusual metaphor. "The spurs resounded in chorus, tracing their suspension points on the ground" (p. 25) is quite a description of some gauchos walking toward their horses. The novelist invents imagery in both of his two basic styles— the normal and the homespun. In the latter, he uses commonplace objects, and the images tend to be more functional.

Many images add to our appreciation of Fabio as he projects his own feelings onto nature. Fabio, the first-person narrator, is our informant, of course, and we know everything the way he knows it. The characterization of Fabio is really the only one in the novel. No interiorization is possible in anyone but Fabio, since the narrative point of view is consistent except for the slight variation observed in the first and last chapters. The people other than Fabio and Don Segundo have peripheral roles and often seem appended to the narration, just the way some of the imagery does.

The Don Segundo we see is the Don Segundo seen by Fabio Cáceres. From early in the novel we know he has a special quality, thanks to Fabio's much-quoted and not very subtle "It seemed to me I had seen a phantom, a shadow, something that fades away and is more an idea than a being" (pp. 7–8). The noble myth embodied in Don Segundo, however, does not have very much importance unless it is joined to the qualities Güiraldes imagined in Fabio. Ghiano says Güiraldes was interested in "the relationship between the pampa and the man who lives it."[6] This essence has its importance in Fabio as well as in Don Segundo. Also referring to the relationship of man and the earth, Iván Droguett Cz. considers Don Segundo Sombra an American projection of the myth of Antaeus who gains strength from contact with the earth.[7] One could argue that this contact is more important to Fabio than it is to his mentor and guide. The latter's *modus vivendi* is disappearing. It is Fabio who is influenced by its importance. Fabio is a myth created by Güiraldes; and Fabio, in turn, makes a myth of Don Segundo. It is important to clarify that Don Segundo Sombra is a very different creation from the psychologically valid gauchos of other novels, and his characterization is also very different from the aesthetic overtures toward life on the pampa made by Enrique Larreta in *Zogoibi*, a work generally considered a failure and remembered mainly because its author wrote better things. It is in the peculiar chronological position of having been published the same year as *Don Segundo Sombra*. The difference is remarkable, mainly because Larreta's novel is absolutely static—an attempt to paint a picture from imperfect memory. The comparison emphasizes the dynamic quality of Güiraldes's novel, even though it is reminiscence. The relationship between the pampa and the man who lives on it is actually discovered in the course of the narration.

Roberto Arlt's *El juguete rabioso* is as interesting an account of city life as *Don Segundo Sombra* is of life on the pampa. Arlt, though almost antiliterary in some respects, uses some techniques not generally cultivated by Spanish American novelists before his time (dreams and long interior monologues). His protagonist moves through a series of changing circumstances which relate to his understanding himself and which suggest several philosophical concepts often associated with literature—existentialism, a kind of pleasure principle, awareness of the creative moment. Influences may have a particular significance in the case of Arlt, because it seems he read extensively and well, though rather haphazardly. Silvio Astier is narrator and protagonist of *El juguete rabioso*, and he is to a very considerable extent a novelization of the author's youth. At one point, when Silvio explains his unusual intellectual interests, he says he owns works of Baudelaire, Dostoyevsky, and Baroja.[8]. A collage made of the reader's memory of these three authors is likely to furnish a good idea of what Arlt's work is like.

For many years appreciation of his work was negligible, in spite of the fact that he has always had a small number of dedicated supporters. Not surprisingly, his first novel has never been a favorite even among his most avid readers. However, in recent years his work has attracted attention because of its innovative characteristics, and in this context the nearly forgotten *El juguete rabioso* becomes more important. One of the general criticisms of Arlt's works is that his style is uncultivated and disagreeable. Orgambide discusses this matter, pointing out the novelist's interest in improving his writing, and also specifying positive aspects that contribute notably to the narration.[9] Since *El juguete rabioso* is a first novel, the problem of style is present; and, in order to deal with the more interesting aspects of the book, the style problem should be taken into account and then suspended. The disturbing stylistic faults are ambiguities arising from unclear association of relatives with antecedents, and unfortunate word choices that place two words of the same family in juxtaposition or that make accidental rhyme or alliteration. Their effect is to dislodge the reader from his close association with the narrator and place him temporarily in an objective situation. The shock is undesirable but not disastrous. These errors have absolutely nothing to do with the author's right to use language more natural than the customary usage of belles-lettres. There are, in fact, times when he follows a very commonplace statement with a rather poetic descriptive passage. This contrast also shocks, but the results are positive because they are creative and draw the reader even closer to the narrator. Arlt's use of dialogue is still another matter, and in this connection critics find no fault. He came from the humbler segment of the population of Buenos Aires; his ear for oral speech was sensitive; and he reproduces common urban language authentically.

Arlt proclaimed that he was unable to follow a plan in writing his novels.[10] However, *El juguete rabioso* reveals the youth of Silvio Astier in four stages that correspond to four chapters. The time span is approximately four years, beginning when Silvio is fourteen. The narration is in the first person. This point of view is consistent and entirely credible. It affords unobtrusive use of interior monologue and dreams, and it is virtually indispensable as an undergirding for Silvio's lonely search for self-understanding.

The novel opens with reference to a specific place in Buenos Aires and to a specific stage in the narrator's development. The description gives the feeling of exact detail, of a circumstance within the author's experience (or the narrator's experience), and this feeling of reality strengthens the presumed single identity of author and narrator. The narrator introduces the shoemaker from whom he used to borrow books, and he reproduces phonetically the shoemaker's speech peculiarities. In this way, Arlt advises his reader of the novel's basic characteristics, within the first two pages. The first chapter then develops on the basis of Silvio's reaction to reading books about Robin Hood–type bandits. He and two friends form the "Club of the Midnight Cavaliers" and actually do steal. Their plans are considerably more ambitious than their escapades—a fact that adds to the sense of boyish invention communicated by this chapter. Silvio, always the inventor, makes a cannon. One of his friends wins an air rifle by falsifying a picture needed to win a contest. The narrative tone in this chapter is gently ironic, similar to the tone at the beginning of *El mal metafísico*. It is mildly derogatory, yet indulgent. However, the thefts are real, and this fact makes the basic game seem distorted. The boys' last act as a club is to burglarize a library. (Books are a constant concern throughout the novel.) Orgambide points out that all of Arlt's works are a search for some way to be happy, in the sense of enjoying some luxury.[11] The books are important in this regard. However, the importance of imagining and of inventing (really the same thing) is just as apparent.

In the second chapter, the narration acquires a very picaresque tone. Silvio's mother tells him he must earn his way, and he finds work in a bookstore. Selected episodes show the frustration of working for the penurious owner, who is constantly at odds with his wife. Silvio's attempts to better his condition are futile. The heroic possibilities of the first chapter disappear as Silvio is reduced to the function of a servant. Life takes on an aspect of suffering. His friends from the first chapter have disappeared, and a sense of Silvio's loneliness grows.

Chapter three is the episode of the golden opportunity. Silvio has a chance to become an airplane mechanic, but is dismissed because the army officers decide he is too imaginative for their purposes and really should be in school. The mood by this time is complete loneliness. Silvio has practically nothing to do with anyone else. He discovers that his ambition is not to possess things, but to be admired by others. This feeling is in perfect accord with the development of the story, which has left him isolated. A dream sequence (pp. 97–98) is one of the better examples of Arlt's use of this technique, which effects an interiorization of Silvio that goes beyond self-study by the first-person narrator. He attempts suicide at the end of this third part.

In the last chapter, Silvio is working as a stationery salesman. He meets one of his old friends from chapter one and learns the other one is in jail. So much for his friends. The significant action in this part is an invitation for Silvio to take part in a burglary. Instead, he betrays the instigator. Preparation for this act comes in an interior monologue (pp. 141–142) that reflects Silvio's confusion by degenerating into fragmented language that finds masochistic beauty in his treachery. He is absolutely alone. After refusing a reward for his act, he attempts to explain his feeling of relief for having done what he knew inside was inevitable. By this time he is trying to explain his act to someone else (the intended victim of the burglary). He speaks of his sense of change, of having recently come into being, and of feeling consequently the real beauty of life. The loneliness surfaces: "And I say to myself, 'What am I to do with this life that is within me?' And I would like to offer it . . . to make a gift of it . . . to go up to people and say to them: 'You have to be happy! Do you understand? You have to play pirates . . . build marble cities . . . laugh . . . set off fireworks'" (p. 152). At the end of the book, the intended victim offers to help Silvio find a job, and Silvio asks for one in the south (where there are few people). As he turns to go, he stumbles over a chair.

Although Arlt reveals a good deal about the less blessed aspects of life in Buenos Aires, *El juguete rabioso* is clearly not a social novel. It is primarily concerned not with the organization of society, but with the organization of an individual. Moreover, it is not really concerned about the peculiarities of an American city, but with a more universal set of problems. It is generally characteristic of vanguardist fiction to be universal in its concerns. Sometimes this attitude makes it appear separated from the real world. Arlt's concentration on Silvio tends to separate his novel from the real world, because the focus on an individual, in this case, prohibits the fictional creation of a cross section of society. Some vanguardist novels purposely blur the line between objective awareness and some other way of knowing. Arqueles Vela's *El Café de Nadie* erases it by making objects and ideas equal to each other.

Two fictionalizing procedures are basic to this short novel. One is a contrast between a presumed reality and the dreamlike condition of the café. The second is a contrast between two shadowy characters (obviously members of the literary movement, *estridentismo*, to which Arqueles Vela belonged) and the comparatively realistic presence of Mabelina, a representation of eternal woman. The two contrasts come to life thanks to the novelist's unusual imagery, which is attractive because its strange associations communicate ideas or feelings rather than because they produce beautiful mental pictures. Since imagery is the dynamic factor in the novel, the experience of reading it is rather like reading poetry. A single word or phrase may produce a drastic readjustment in our reaction; the work as a whole produces suggestions rather than proposals or expositions.

Vela first sets the scene by removing the café from the concrete world. Its threshold is like the "last step in reality."[12] His descriptive vocabulary suggests half-seeing, silence, timelessness: "Everything, in its alchemist atmosphere, hides itself, taking on the patina of retrospective irreality" (p. 11). All is covered by silence. The light suggests dawn or sunset. The two vaguely seen customers enter and the narrator (third person) develops the association of things and ideas. From the beginning, entering the café is like entering the "subway of dreams, of ideations" (p. 11). Once the two customers seat themselves, they "inspect the various psychological planes of the café" (p. 12). Their waiter is hypothetical, and the customers do not order anything. "Intermittently, from the other ideological floor, comes a muffled feminine laugh which, like the JAZZ BAND, smashes within the customers the cups and glasses of their sentimental restaurant" (p. 13).

About one-fourth of the way through the novel, Mabelina enters the café for the first time, and Vela makes use of his inventive language, referring to "her lively, her perversatile eyes" (p. 17). She looks over the numbers of the dining alcoves, selecting the one that corresponds to her "sentimental equations" (p. 17). The mathematical suggestion of this figure of speech invites attention to a number of images based on technical devices. Like the reference to jazz, they show how the vanguardist writers thought of their epoch as a new era.[13] The specific interest in technical innovations probably comes from Italian futurism. Successful use of this kind of imagery is far from certain. Sometimes its shock effect turns out to be more amusing than meaningful. During an episode when Mabelina feels more amorous than her partner, she has to restrain herself before his indifference and feels as if she were in "the electric chair of love" (p. 22). This image evokes surprise and then a smile, but it doesn't really communicate much about Mabelina's feeling. Vela, fortunately, does not leave matters there. Like most weavers of imagery, he frequently follows one attempt with another, hoping to come closer to the mark. In this particular case, he succeeds admirably. The extension of the image has Mabelina feeling as if she were in a clinic where an experiment with some kind of ultraviolet rays disintegrated her spirit and separated her from her body (pp. 22–23). The ideas of electricity, of light contrasting with shadow, and of shadow images joining, all carry out the action of the episode (p. 23).

The freshness of Vela's imagery was the factor that attracted attention in the twenties, and it is still what his reader notices first. Since it is tempting to quote example after example simply because they give a new view of recognizable reality,[14] we lose sight of the fact that these images actually do move the story because they communicate the difference between one moment and the next. Vela writes very short paragraphs, which contribute to the epigrammatic quality of his images. They also tend to fragment his prose, thereby encouraging the reader to think of isolated pieces of the novel.

The sense of fragmentation, however, is important to the experience of the work. Vela communicates it through imagery, through paragraph organization, through the shreds of conversation at a dance (p. 24), through reference to constant change in the human condition (p. 28), through the variety of Mabelina's lovers, and finally through her awareness that she is really a jumble of parts created by her response to different men (pp. 38–39). (There is also a suggested second plane, on which she is the creation of the two shadowed customers who always occupy the same place.) The narrative line finally moves to a time of introspection by Mabelina. She arrives at a relatively objective awareness of herself through a process that Vela identifies by having her write her name until it seems not to be hers. There is one notable deviation from the normal practice of this universally recognized act—each time she writes her name, the letters are farther apart. This effect appears graphically within the story (p. 40) because vanguardist novelists favored visual effects. Mabelina's self-awareness translates this stretching out of herself into a feeling of identity with everyone else. She classifies her memories, pushes the call button to summon reality, and each time the bell seems more distant. She closes her thoughts within her purse and starts to leave the café. Looking back before leaving, she notices that the two faithful customers are in their usual place; for a moment she appears indecisive, then walks out into the dawn-illuminated city.

An obscure line between objective reality and dream reality—similar to the corresponding line in *El Café de Nadie*—is the dominant characteristic of Pablo Neruda's *El habitante y su esperanza*. This short novel consists of fifteen sketches in which a first-person narrator tells a story of love and loneliness, of a crime of passion, and of a sense of vengeance. Typical Neruda imagery (particularly reminiscent of his *Residencia en la tierra*) produces a transition from anecdote to dream. The relationship of these two sides of reality is apparent from the beginning of the story; however, there is a climax in the structure about halfway through, and dream reality predominates from that point until the end. The last deed in the story belongs only to dream reality; it is unable to cross the line into objective reality.

In the 1920s, vanguardist fiction in Spanish America tended to be short. The authors may not have been able to sustain themselves so "far out" for a long time. They may have felt a certain urgency about showing their latest productions to their friends. Certainly they were inhibited by an overwhelming tendency to deal with social problems. Whatever the reasons, there were no full-length innovative novels, though vanguardist influence appears in some—Arlt, for example. Short vanguardist fiction was common, at least in the major cultural centers.

In many cases, volumes of stories acquired a special unity or progression within the collection—a characteristic which, along with many other aspects of early vanguardism, is very apparent in some of the most recent Spanish American fiction. *El Café de Nadie* appeared with two shorter pieces, one of them first published in a newspaper in 1922. They share Vela's interest in topographic effects, his shocking imagery, a sense of the universal feminine, and a question about the plane of reality to be accepted as truth. Eduardo Mallea's *Cuentos para una inglesa desesperada* are six stories that move progressively toward a feeling of worldliness; they alternate a first-person narrator with third-person omniscient, creating a rhythmic variation within the overall progression; and the sixth unit, "Six Poems for Georgia," has its own half-dozen pieces.

Mallea's collection is a kind of bridge between certain aspects of *modernismo* and the new sense of the mid-twenties, though there is no reason to think the author intended it to be so. They are somewhat reminiscent of the suggestive writing of Darío in "La muerte de la emperatriz de la China," for example. However, they are not all alike. The three stories narrated in the first person tend to be decadentist in tone; those written in third person are more like the bucolic works of the *modernistas*. Still, within these characteristics, there are modern associations that identify the stories with their time: automobiles, jazz, and Yale banners. These new-age features become increasingly important throughout the volume. The first-person narrator of "Cynthia" is more worldly, more aggressive than her counterpart in "Arabella y yo." Georgia, in the last story, is a flapper, very art nouveau.

Mallea's prose tends to sound staccato, an effect that enhances the feeling of the jazz age. He frequently omits finite verbs, particularly in sentences used to set the mood at the beginning of a story. Sometimes the sentence consists of only one word—a technique most frequently used in "Seis poemas para Georgia." (For the sake of accuracy: these six poems are not poetry in the traditional sense; they are prose poems or poetic sketches.) The author's keen sensitivity to the value of words is apparent in two superficially similar cases which in reality are fundamentally different. In "Arabella y yo," he develops a sense of boredom by beginning four consecutive sentences with "Días . . . ," the last three with "Días en que . . ."[15] However, in "Sonata de soledad," the effect he wishes to create is slightly different from boredom or ennui—it is a sense of restless yearning for many kinds of human contact. The novelist suggests both the basic mood of bored dissatisfaction and the desire for variety by beginning four consecutive sentences with synonyms rather than four repetitions: "Ansias," "Voluntad," "Deseos," and "Ganas" (pp. 43–44). He also uses unmodified substantives to create a mood or ambience. To emphasize the absence of the feminine ingredient, for example, he lists objects associated with masculinity in his story (p. 63).

The dynamism of each of the individual stories in *Cuentos para una inglesa desesperada* comes from a change in mood within each story. However, the reader's overall experience is a feeling of progression into worldliness, with a persistent, nagging sense of being alone. It is important, for an understanding of the epoch and for an understanding of Mallea, that in this first book his technical virtuosity demonstrates his awareness of the author's fundamental right to novelize.

Within the general inventive euphoria of 1926, Genaro Estrada's *Pero Galín* sounded a note of good-natured self-criticism that could be extremely helpful to Spanish American literature if it were more generally cultivated. This one novel by itself cannot be considered a work of fundamental importance, but it has characteristics that identify it as a book likely to be "discovered" repeatedly throughout the years.

Fundamentally, Estrada's novel is a satire on the colonialist novel in Mexico and on the taste for fake colonial in general—"Even if the Americanism of jaguars and the virgin forest turned into a fiasco, we must agree that local color, so cultivated in the nineteenth century, is saved by the works of colonialist art, which, little by little, in Mexico as in Argentina and in Chile—and in the United States through imitative architecture—attracted interest and inspired vocations that might have failed in the English essay or the Russian novel."[16] However, as may be seen at the beginning of the quotation, he comments on Spanish American literature in general. His outlook is cosmopolitan. Regionalism is suspect and is justified as "a vigorous movement toward autochthonous art" (p. 9). The quotation marks are Estrada's and they illustrate one of his ways of detaching himself from ideas he does not approve. His satire is penetrating, challenging, but not vicious.

The novel is set around a young man, Pedro Galindo, who is so taken with everything colonial he changes his name so it will sound colonial—Pero Galín. Estrada uses him as a pawn and frequently wanders away from him almost to the point of forgetting he is writing a novel. In fact, the novel itself is a bit of a joke. The author brings about a solution by having a woman save the protagonist. After their wedding, she provides a shock treatment by taking her husband to Los Angeles and Hollywood. He finds the country he travels through devoid of the things that have made up his world. And, in addition, he becomes accustomed to modern conveniences. At the end of the novel, we find him cured of his colonialist dream and active in the modern world.

The dynamic factor in the novel is the satire. However, it is successful because of Estrada's control of the language and of the joke itself. He writes a colonialist version of a commonplace dialogue (pp. 30–31); he furnishes explanatory footnotes for a line of regionalist poetry (p. 10); he composes a jargonish, noncommittal evaluation of a piece of colonial art by an expert (pp. 65–66); he becomes very vanguardist in his use of highway and hotel signs as part of his narrative (pp. 99, 104); and the end of the novel is a satire on his own solution to Pero Galín's situation. Persistently he is sharp enough to make many people think, but without really damaging anyone. More novelists could have read him profitably.

CHAPTER 5

From *Don Segundo Sombra* to *Doña Bárbara* (1927–1928)

During the 1920s, literary experimentation sometimes became so much more sophisticated than the general culture that it provoked an adverse reaction. Since vanguardism tended to be cosmopolitan, the countertendency was regionalistic. Experimental writers often addressed themselves to an "in" group, and as a reaction, many other writers bent over backward trying to reach a large audience. Sometimes the search for a mass audience was related to Marxist ideology. At the root of all these attitudes was the persistent need to identify and name the objects and circumstances of the New World and the experience of living with them. Experimentation in literature does not necessarily run counter to that need. Indeed, in general it did not do so, but its New Worldism is often subtle and was frequently overlooked under the pressure of anxiety that existed during the 1920s.

The course of vanguardism in this period is most readily apparent in literary magazines.[1] The obvious genre is, of course, poetry. Avant garde magazines were founded by young writers, and the very large majority of authors produced poetry before anything else. The magazine *Martín Fierro,* one of the most famous in Argentina, was founded in 1924. By 1925, it was flooded with free verse. Among its contributors was Jorge Luis Borges, who also helped found *Proa* at about the same time. Even earlier, Borges and friends had edited *Prisma,* a review that lasted for two issues and was circulated by pasting it to walls. This extraordinary means of distribution certainly indicates that the editors hoped to reach a large public, even though their techniques were vanguardist.

The cosmopolitan writers in Argentina became known as the "Florida" group—a name that implies social distinction, good taste, wealth, and sophistication. Some other writers, Roberto Arlt among them, formed a group known as "Boedo"—a name which suggests their interest in the common people. The existence of these two schools has led to misunderstanding from time to time. They were not violently opposed to each other. Friendships existed between members of the two groups. Their designations indicate two general ways of looking at literature's function. The reputation for snobbishness suffered by the Florida group was shared by the writers associated with the Mexican review *Contemporáneos.* The slightly earlier *Horizontes* and *Irradiador,* principal organs of *estridentismo,* were less prominent and also less maligned. The problem of cosmopolitanism versus regionalism was apparent also in the *Revista de Avance* in Havana, and the same general polemic is apparent in the reaction to the work of the Peruvian writers of the group that included Martín Adán and Emilio Adolfo Westphalen.

Of course, vanguardism was not felt with equal intensity throughout Spanish America. Experimental activity was greater in the major cultural centers. It was nourished by contact with Europe and discouraged or fostered by a large variety of local conditions. As for the effect on fiction, it is probably fair to say that the most frequently mentioned names were Proust, Joyce, and Benjamín Jarnés. Observable experimentation includes excruciating interiorization in characterization, use of interior monologue, sometimes variation of narrative point of view, interest in the new things of a technical age, startling imagery, some playful use of the language, interest in typographical effects, and the conviction that the novelist is under no obligation to reproduce visible reality.

The novels published during the two years between *Don Segundo*

Sombra and *Doña Bárbara* cover the spectrum from very vanguard-ist to very traditionalist. The extremes are best represented by Owen's *Novela como nube* (1928) and Carrasquilla's *La marquesa de Yolombó* (1928). Most of the novels line up on one side or the other, but at least two really belong somewhere between the poles— *Royal Circo* (1927), by Leónidas Barletta, and *El pueblo sin Dios* (1928), by César Falcón.

Gilberto Owen's novel might well be interesting to a Jungian critic, since it is based on the myth of Ixion. On the simpler basis of reader-meets-novel, it is the story of Ernesto's quest for the eternal feminine, identified first as Eve and later as Helen. The movement of the book is effected by the author's changing use of images to communicate the attitudes of Ernesto. There are times when Owen appears to have reversed the normal process of observation followed by multiple associations—he seems to give the associations first, allowing his reader to find the observation somewhere in the maze of reactions. Sometimes it is simply playful— what a pity it is that a beardless young man is unable to write a poem comparing the delights of shaving with a sojourn in Naples.[2] Others are more direct suggestions of the protagonist's mood, or even of his actions. Sometimes Owen puts aside his surrealist imagery and becomes almost matter of fact.

The novel has to be read with very close attention. Narration is third person, but it is only what Ernesto perceives. The images lead into a structure that progresses away from his boredom with conventionality, which is his condition in the initial scene. The novel then raises a question about the reality of its beings, via association with the cinema; it erases the line between life and death; time in sequence then ceases to have meaning; and ultimately the whole matter of identity becomes absurd because Ernesto doesn't know whether several women are all the same or all different, and he ends up committed to one he does not know at all. He finds himself with a woman who is like a cloud; and we find ourselves with a novel that is like a cloud, which is exactly what Owen told us in the title.

There is a certain amount of frustration involved in reading a book of this kind, but it is also fun. For example, with reference to one of the Eves, the one Ernesto meets at the shore: "Mounted on wave number seven hundred, Eve approaches Ernesto, stepping newly born from the liquid shell like a very conventional, immense

Venus, and hands him an identification card with her home address and telephone number, which is a procession of swans: 2222222" (p. 174). There is some of the same kind of joy in Salvador Novo's *El joven* (1928), especially because of its rapid, almost subliminal, references to lights, advertisements, and movement of the city. Jaime Torres Bodet's *Margarita de Niebla* (1927) is more reminiscent of Proust in its very detailed description of attitudes and the very slow movement of the story.

It is probably safe to say that most vanguardist prose of the 1920s deals with wealthier people or with creative artists. Martín Adán's *La casa de cartón* (1928) is a novel of youthful experience in Barranco, a seaside suburb of Lima. More accurately, Barranco was an entirely separate city when the book was written. The ambience, however, is urbane, and the people in it are worthy precursors of Vargas Llosa's Miraflores creations.

La casa de cartón's most readily apparent characteristic is an almost overwhelming wealth of unusual metaphor. Its richness (frequency and uniqueness) comes close to repelling the reader. However, the author controls it to the satisfaction of most people's taste, and the positive influence of the imagery becomes a dynamic factor, inviting the reader to continue. Fortunately, the function of Martín Adán's metaphor making is apparent from the beginning of the novel—it uses a physical condition to communicate a psychic state. Often there is gentle humor within a perfectly serious image of this kind: "Breakfast is a hot ball in your stomach, and a hardness of the dining-room chair on your backsides, and the solemn wish that you didn't have to go to school, throughout your whole body."[3]

The narrator uses the second-person singular (*tú*), but its significance is not clearly consistent. At first the narrator appears to be addressing himself; then in an episode referring to the setting sun and the Plaza of San Francisco, the "you" seems to indicate a person other than the narrator (p. 19). The end of this passage suggests a union of persons that makes identities indistinct: "And there is no one who is not you or I" (p. 20). Immediately following, the narrative voice mentions Ramón, using the third person. At times, Ramón seems to be a more realistic side of the poetic narrator; at times he is a different person.

The story also achieves a fusion of the aspects of time: "Now we are going by the Plaza of San Francisco, . . . It is not today when we go by the Plaza of San Francisco; it was yesterday when we did it" (p. 19). The effect of timelessness created by these telescoping realities is in tension with certain topical references. Speaking of Nietzsche, the narrator says Ramón knew that "Superman was an alias of Firpo."[4] Other references, like those to Blaise Cendrars and to Rolls Royce automobiles, tend to emphasize specific time. However, Martín Adán's style suggests timelessness by using repetitions whose rhythm and repeated sense cause the passage to take on special significance that transcends ordinary narration. "Beatas que huelen . . ." begins three sentences (p. 18); "tuve que . . ." begins three consecutive sentences (p. 63).

The author produces more than a single effect by repetition. When he repeats a sentence in toto several times, it communicates boredom (p. 80). He stabilizes the scene on a streetcar by making observations without finite verbs, introducing a wide variety of people. The ever present metaphor comes so close to being epigrammatic, in many cases, it begs to be lifted from the novel. Therefore, it works against the unity of the book. However, Martín Adán seeks the exact word within the writing itself, or imprisons the meaning within a series of approximations. At times these methods of transforming objective awareness spill over into fun for its own sake, producing episodes in which pure joy becomes more important than the anecdote from which it grew.

The novel contains some clever satire on the culture it represents. There is a delightful passage concerning what a Latin American expects from his visit to Paris (p. 32). Showing his cosmopolitan orientation, Martín disparages the old-fashioned, traditional Hispanic literary tastes of Lima's literati. They of course have a "taste for Pérez Galdós, practical and dangerous, with consumptives and madwomen and criminals and the pestridden, but viewed by the reader from a safe distance" (p. 51). Martín Adán, in expressing this opinion, indicates the dynamic component of his own novel, the factor that makes *La casa de cartón* more than a simple account of youthful experience. His comment about reading Galdós apparently refers to the possibility of seeking a deeper involvement of the reader. In his own narrative, he works for this effect through the telescoping of identities. He uses observations of people and things as a real basis. The transformation of them serves chiefly to identify the narrator; but the joining of identities keeps him from being clearly individualized. Therefore, the activation of the reader's role.

It is important to an understanding of experimentation and cosmopolitanism that all these works are specifically and obviously tied to a locale identifiable as the author's country, regardless of what the critics might have said. Owen writes with poetic suggestivity, in a seriocomic vein, of the Mexican city of Pachuca; Novo's city of modern miracles is the capital of Mexico; Torres Bodet's Paloma suggests provincial Mexican culture; parts of Barranco still correspond to the ambience of *La casa de cartón*. True enough, none of the novelists sets the reproduction of local color and customs as his goal, but it is equally true that not one is alienated from his culture. The factor that caused some critics to consider them too Europeanized must have been technique rather than subject matter. One might argue that *La marquesa de Yolombó* is removed by time from its own epoch, since it begins in the middle of the eighteenth century and covers the period through the War for Independence. That argument, however, would also be specious, because the history of Colombia is very much a part of its present. No one attacked the novel, of course, on the grounds of foreignness, because Carrasquilla's stock in trade was a feeling of familiarity communicated to his readers with no great subtlety and certainly with no technical innovation.

From the very beginning, Carrasquilla cultivates a narrative tone appropriate to the novelization of a legend. Specifically, he creates the impression of oral storytelling by suggesting the narrator's presence without his actually entering to participate in the action. The effect is enhanced by a looseness of style which sounds casual, conversational, but which obtains a favorable response that comes from careful planning rather than from improvisation. When he says, for example, that "Mass was said there, if there was a priest, for he *llegó a faltar* on occasion,"[5] the italicized words resemble the sort of paradox suggested in English when we say "he turned up missing." This narrative tone affects the point of view, which is third person but not objective. In *La marquesa de Yolombó*, the author owns the story and is regaling his listeners. This characteristic is similar to some of the Mexican *colonialista* novels. There are also

64

times when the novel's colloquial dialogue and, to an even greater extent, the affectation of old-time speech become dangerously cute. In some passages, Carrasquilla puts aside the raconteur tone and relates facts of the plot in a less committed way. The change is very effective in the epilogue because it needs to be differentiated from the rest of the novel.

The book is about an extraordinary woman, an early feminist, who is in the mining business. She is also a faithful royalist and is rewarded with a title of nobility. Her experience with a confidence man leads to a dramatic ending that need not be revealed in a commentary on the novel. Carrasquilla prefaces the story with a brief account of Yolombó's history. He then presents the lineage of his protagonist and follows with a detailed characterization of her as a young woman. We come to know her through her actions and words, and through the novelist's specific comment. Having accomplished this much, Carrasquilla holds up the progress of the novel to give us more information about colonial Yolombó. About one-third of the way through the book, the narrator begins the consistent development of the story. Cause and effect operate uninterruptedly to the end. The epilogue jumps fifteen years to tie it all up.

It is probably Carrasquilla's fond lingering over costumbristic tidbits that has made this novel beloved among Colombians and relatively unknown outside his own country. It is doubtful that this novel differs very much in technique from those written during the same years by Carlos Loveira, Manuel Gálvez, and Joaquín Edwards Bello. The most apparent difference is Carrasquilla's familiar tone.

Leónidas Barletta, probably better known as a political writer than as a novelist, deals with some of the less fortunate members of society in *Royal Circo*. Like those of his friends Roberto Arlt and Elías Castenuovo, however, his people are unusual, not the commonplace, proletarian mass. There is more Dostoyevsky than Marx in novels by these writers. The principal experience of *Royal Circo* is the awareness that long-suffering ordinary people show compassion toward each other. The narrative is rather awkward. Although Barletta seems to have been somewhat aware of new techniques of narration, he did not really appreciate their potential for carrying the message. Therefore, the novel is basically within the limits of traditional realism, even with the addition of a small

amount of warmed-over romantic sentimentality. The same characteristics make a satisfactory general description of Falcón's *El
pueblo sin Dios*. Here the novelist squanders a promising beginning
by introducing too many themes. Basically, the novel deals with a
love affair colored by a contrast between urban sophistication and
provincial conservatism. However, the author's tendency toward
denunciation produces lines of action related to exploitation of the
Indian population, dishonesty in politics, and freedom of the press.
The narrative moves toward making the town itself the protagonist.
This effect might have been achieved by more use of unidentified
dialogue, and the various sins of the town might have appeared
more closely related to each other. As it is, Falcón relies very heavily
on the realist manner, and his lines of action produce a poorly unified novel.

Surely many writers must have felt a great uneasiness about their
right to depart from the most obvious description of what they
saw. Moreover, it should be clear that near-documentary narration
does not prohibit good writing. Probably the best narrative prose
of the time is in Martín Luis Guzmán's *El águila y la serpiente*
(1928). In it the author narrates his experiences with some of the
leaders of the Mexican Revolution. They are memoirs, rather than a
diary; and the episodes mainly portray certain personalities revealed
to the author by his own ability to appreciate details of human behavior. Guzmán's gift for writing suspenseful narrative is apparent
in many episodes of *El águila y la serpiente*. The nature of the book
requires episodic development rather than a single, unified story.
He deals with well-known leaders and some lesser ones. Each has a
public image, and the purpose of the book is to reveal the personality behind the image. The process is interesting in a consideration of
the art of novelization because Guzmán obviously does not reproduce the image that is generally known. He deals with what his
own experience has revealed, and communicates it through description of the personage and reference to the narrator's reaction in
the presence of the well-known figure. One year later, Guzmán
published *La sombra del caudillo*, a political novel dealing with
Mexico after the Revolution. Many of the characters can be identified. However, their development must be different from those in
El águila y la serpiente because Guzmán cannot be present in the
novel. Since it deals with politics, identification of characters is an

interesting game. Though possibly less stimulating, the same problem of re-creation and invention is important in any novel dealing with the observable circumstances in which the author lives. *La sombra del caudillo* was published the same year as Rómulo Gallegos's *Doña Bárbara*, a novel that has always presented a problem with respect to the reality-versus-fantasy of the protagonist. Since the book has regularly been taken as a true picture of Venezuelan reality,[6] the ambivalent condition of Doña Bárbara herself takes on special meaning.

CHAPTER 6

The Year of *Doña Bárbara* (1929)

Doña Bárbara is the novel of the *llano*—the plains of Venezuela. Much of its material is the picture of the region: its appearance, the mood it inspires, the types of people who inhabit it, their customs, and their legends. All these factors become functional in a story that interweaves personal emotions with the contrast between undisciplined power and the law. Gallegos's novel, like Azuela's *Los de abajo*, is one of the standard reference points of Spanish American literature, and, in the years since 1929, practically everything has been said about it. There has always been general agreement regarding the author's success in portrayal of the milieu. Differences have arisen among Gallegos's critics with reference to the validity of characterization, particularly of Doña Bárbara herself.

The discussion probably has its origin in Gallegos's use of symbolically suggestive names. His story line develops around the efforts of Santos Luzardo (a name that suggests honesty and progress) to save his family estate from the depredations of Doña Bárbara (suggestion of primitivism). The corresponding estates are named "Altamira" (connotation of highmindedness) and "El Miedo" (the word means fear). Given this basis, the focus of the novel easily becomes an exposition of civilization versus barbarism, a traditional Spanish American theme. It is a very important one because the tendency has always been to develop culture—even overdevelop it sometimes—in certain centers without providing for the necessary diffusion throughout the provinces. The resulting contrast is apparent not only in the fine arts, but also in political awareness and in economic integration. The problem was a valid concern when Gallegos wrote his novel, and it is still important even though its outward appearance may be somewhat modernized.

No one quibbles about the theme itself. However, readers insisting on psychological validity find fault with some aspects of characterization. Doña Bárbara is particularly bothersome because, for some readers, an act of abnegation on her part, at the end of the novel, is not consistent with her general ruthlessness. Actually, the narrator lays the foundation for her ambivalence early in the novel by pointing out the memory of a frustrated young love as a functional parallel to her lust for vengeance created when she was raped.[1] His care is not enough for everyone, and some find fault with her and also with other characters—the stiff, toy-soldier quality of Santos, for example. Discussion about characterization in *Doña Bárbara* contributed little or nothing to appreciation of the novel until the recent suggestion that Doña Bárbara doesn't have to be psychologically valid for the novel to say what Gallegos was writing. In addition to the obvious symbolism, recent criticism points out the use of animals as a means of communicating the novel's reality. This procedure is more fundamental than foreshadowing the development of the story by suggested comparison of animals with personages. It is a novelization—not fully developed in Gallegos's work—of native American myth, which assumes the ability of a person to convert himself into an animal. This transformation is of fundamental importance in the work of many Latin American novelists—Miguel Angel Asturias and Demetrio Aguilera Malta, for example.

Sturgis E. Leavitt points out that Gallegos, in making his protagonist a symbol, also made realistic probability unimportant.[2] More recently, Andrés S. Michalski has taken Leavitt's opinion as a starting point and further revealed the extraordinary characterization of Doña Bárbara.[3] In all fairness, we must approach his analysis with caution, because his enthusiasm has led him into some poorly founded statements. It is not true, for example, that the development of Doña Bárbara as a symbol destroys the realism of the book. Moreover, the description of the novel as a fairy story (prince, sleeping beauty, and witch) really says only that Gallegos uses a standard plot line. The important aspect of Michalski's study is the exposition of several means by which the author makes his protagonist a special kind of person, one whose presence in the novel has a meaning more transcendent than the participation of a simple flesh-and-blood person. Through a combination of fantastic elements with ordinary ones, Gallegos makes her a reconciliation of the two; and, by extension, the novel itself transcends its own realistic base. The process is an example of the search for an appropriate way to translate the New World experience.

The narration is third-person omniscient. It never leads us inside a character, though it sometimes informs us about such an interior stage—one that would not be apparent to other characters in the novel. There are times when the narrator manipulates the story unduly and makes the reader feel closer to the author than to the novelized reality. We experience the total work (that is, the combination of plot line and ambience) in three stages that correspond to the changing attitudes of Doña Bárbara and Santos.

The first of the three parts is really an extended introduction. We meet city-oriented Santos on his way to Altamira to sell the estate. Doña Bárbara has taken the law in her own hands and is gradually taking over the Luzardo holdings. Flashbacks reveal the backgrounds of both protagonists. In general, style and structure are traditionally realist. However, the narrator does suggest a special quality in Doña Bárbara by means of a sort of incantatory repetition (p. 26); there are also passages of lyric description. In general, Gallegos's prose style works to his disadvantage now in the last third of the century. It sounds old-fashioned—stiff, strange because it belongs to another time, but still without the aura of classic status. A similar sense of the *passé* comes when the faithful peons gather around Santos upon his arrival at Altamira—rather like a movie about the Old South.

A subconflict develops in this first part—the struggle within Santos between his inclination simply to sell his property, on the one hand, and his growing sense of belonging, on the other. We are again in the presence of the man-land complex, as in *Don Segundo*

Sombra and other examples of New Worldism. The effect of Doña Bárbara in this part is fear—the threat of lawlessness, even bodily harm. This malevolent factor becomes part of the countryside itself. In the second part, Santos becomes the militant representation of civilization, resolved to defend his property rights by legal means. Doña Bárbara is more human and less legend in this part. The "devourer of men" wavers, not because of a new respect for the law, but because of a new interest in Santos. This part contains a great deal of information about life and work on the two *hatos* (ranches). Gallegos succeeds in making most of this information functional in the development of the story. Moreover, his short chapters—effective throughout the novel—are especially productive here because they take advantage of the reader's interest without abusing his patience. With regard to the protagonists' attitudes and their implementation, there is little that promises the reign of justice.

In the third part, Santos decides law is not enough; force must be met with force. Doña Bárbara loses and fades away. On the least imaginative level, a reader may take this fact as the flight of the losing lover. For most readers, however, Doña Bárbara will have been sufficiently identified with the sense of fear (rather than primitivism), and her disappearance removes that factor from Santos's relationship with the land. Her departure is the happy ending in the development of this relationship as we understand it through the characterization of Santos. The development of climax and denouement is somewhat inhibited by the narrative tone, which may have seemed natural in 1929 but now sounds out of date. In one tense moment, for example, Gallegos narrates (the translation is an approximation of the style, not a literal interpretation): "Meanwhile, 'The Tiger' had managed to edge over in the direction of a rifle and was reaching for it when Luzardo brought him down— a curse on his lips—with a neatly placed shot in the thigh" (p. 240). Exigent readers have to suspend their reaction to this kind of writing. It is asking no more than in the case of Roberto Arlt, for example. Some readers, we must confess, probably find it entirely acceptable.

Doña Bárbara is a novel rich in possibilities for discussion: the role of the Yankee intruder, Mr. Danger; the rescue and rehabilitation of Santos's teen-age cousin, Marisela—referred to by the author as "The Sleeping Beauty" (p. 90), but also interesting as Galatea;

the parallel degeneration of the property and the relatives of Santos Luzardo. The essential communication, however, is the reconciliation between the urbane Santos and the reoriented Santos at the end of the novel. The acceptance accorded the novel at the time of its publication indicates that it was meaningful for the time, or appeared so. It is hardly surprising that this should be the case, in view of the generally presumed interest in the New World experience, in those years. An examination of the other novels published in 1929, however, provokes some second thoughts. Although several of them emphasize the re-creation of objective awareness, their concern with the New World is anything but standardized.

Martín Luis Guzmán, continuing his scrutiny of Mexican reality, turned to post-Revolution politics in *La sombra del caudillo*. The anecdotal base of this novel is a presidential campaign in the late 1920s. The theme that controls the course of action is the constant presence of the *caudillo*'s will—a theme of more general significance in Latin America than the details of political maneuvering. In Guzmán's novel, the leader's limited appearance on the fictional scene does not correspond to his importance in the book. His functional role is the exercise of personalistic will, behind the scenes.

Although *La sombra del caudillo* appears, at first glance, to be entirely different from *Doña Bárbara*, the novels share two important characteristics. One is thematic—both illuminate the problem of personalism against the collective will. It is significant that this conflict is evident in a postrevolutionary context and also in a situation where there had been no revolution. The second similarity is in the art of novelization. Both novels take identifiable circumstances as their base, and the authors face the problem of balancing creation with re-creation. Once this problem is established, the two novels differ fundamentally. Gallegos's fantasy element adds a considerable amount of intuitive communication to the basic facts. The intuitive communication of *La sombra del caudillo*, however, derives principally from the theme itself—that is, the pervasive shadow. The implementation of the theme becomes almost single-mindedly political. There are factors not related to the campaign itself that do function in the development of the plot—the several households maintained by one of the candidates, Aguirre, for instance. However, the narrator reveals very few details of this private life. The intricacies of the plot are mainly political details, and the effect is likely to remind readers of a recent best seller in the United States, *Advise and Consent*.

Guzmán very wisely makes the opposition candidate (the reader's choice) less than perfect, though certainly more attractive than the *caudillo's* man. However, in a second clever move, he gives the opposition candidate an ally and friend who is a model of rectitude. This way the novel does not depend on a simplistic opposition. Instead, the fundamental contrast is an appropriately complex basis for the development of the story. The novel is in six parts. The first sets the political scene and reveals some aspects of the private lives of some of the principals. After part one, the private aspects are not developed, although the information provided has a function later on. The second through the sixth parts may be identified by reference to some particular personage. In fact, the author names the parts for the people who trigger the novel's progress, except for the fourth part, and it would be quite appropriate to do so there if it were not even more desirable to emphasize an incident. The arrangement of emphasis places much importance on individual people; but Guzmán does it without making vignettes, because the protagonists maintain their position of importance while the key people in their plans differ from one section to the other. The development of the novel produces a feeling of frustration. People are maneuvered, used to the advantage of others, worked into traps before they realize what is happening. The frustration builds gradually as humane relationships deteriorate. Reconciliation becomes impossible; double-crossing follows; then violence begins and finally reaches the ultimate stage—murder.

Guzmán's prose is simple, perfectly clear. The action itself, though complicated politically, gives the impression of being trimmed to the bone, because of the scarcity of extrapolitical factors. The narration is consistently third person. In view of these facts, we wonder what is the source of the book's life. The political plot itself could be news from the daily paper; and that is indeed interesting, but *La sombra del caudillo* obviously has some additional dynamic factor. It is probably the narrator's use of the third-person point of view to achieve by description effects that generally come from more complicated techniques. On the first two pages of the novel, we see the difference between two people in an analytical passage

73

that leaves no doubt about its third-person condition, but achieves an exceptional communication through its organization.[4] First, it describes the conversational manner of Aguirre; second, the very different manner of his friend Axkaná; third, it states flatly that one is a military politician, the other a civilian politician; fourth, it states briefly how each thinks of his role. We know not only what they are like, but also how each one feels about a certain aspect of himself.

This early passage is indicative of a narrative technique which is not flamboyant, but is very effective. Guzmán describes, in another place, the fusing of two concerns in the thought of Aguirre during a contemplative moment (p. 12). The effect, although it is narrated in third person, is hardly different from interior monologue. The same technique communicates Axkaná's awareness when he is "taken for a ride," blindfolded, by political enemies (pp. 128–130). At the point when Aguirre begins to realize that a break with the *caudillo* is inevitable, the two men are talking at Chapultepec Castle, and the panorama of the trees and the city takes on an entirely new appearance (pp. 53–54). Sometimes a very accurate and economical description communicates as well as many pages. Describing Aguirre's conversation with one of his mistresses, the narrator says, "But he spoke on the periphery of what he was thinking, just as he thought on the periphery of what he was feeling" (p. 15). Interior imagery can be equally effective when it is exteriorized to communicate visual experience—"He fell as if the pistol that killed him had fired not the bullet intended to kill, but the corpse itself" (p. 194).

Narration of this kind adds an interior, intimate, individualistic factor to an otherwise exterior novel. The effect is to produce a closer person-to-person relationship between reader and personage than is likely in the typical New World novel where the exterior theme or a mythologized protagonist is likely to predominate. The more intimate basis functions also in Roberto Arlt's second and best-known novel, *Los siete locos*. However, the nightmarish, edge-of-insanity circumstance of this novel tends to reverse the effect of intimism, making it centrifugal and productive of irrational anguish.

Just as each of Arlt's madmen functions on the edge of sanity (the normal condition), so they function collectively on the edge of society. Their goals are destructive with respect to society and also with regard to themselves. They are participants in what they want to destroy. The novel's tone is set by the fact that everybody is obsessed by some interest, idea, or goal that seems completely reasonable to him but madness to someone outside his personal orbit. The *locos* organize a secret society—it is really the *astrólogo's* obsession—which will change society (there are fascist overtones) and which will be financed by a chain of brothels. Another expects to find gold where it cannot be found. Another has a formula for making a killing at roulette—a system learned from Christ himself. Incidentally, this one is recognized as mad within the novel. Still another finds satisfaction in exploiting prostitutes although he is rich and has no need for the money.

The tone established by these strange fixations becomes a basis for understanding the characterization of Erdosain, the protagonist and presumably a novelization of Arlt himself. He is an anguished man, full of doubts about the meaning of his existence and in search of some way of affirming it. The role of Barsut in the novel is to torture Erdosain for no apparent reason. He is, therefore, an externalization of an aspect of his victim's personality. His function is metaphorical, and the effect is similar to the one achieved through the imagery used by Arlt to create a feeling of alienation by changing abstract elements into concrete things: ". . . each hurt was an owl that jumped from one side to the other side of his misery."[5] Erdosain is a kind of personification of disquiet. In a way, he incorporates within himself the absurd aspects of all the obsessions of his fellows.

This novel presents a problem of style similar to that of *El juguete rabioso*. The quotation above exemplifies a stylistic paradox often found in Arlt's novels. Some of his most awkward-sounding lines contain some of his most perceptive observations. Similarly awkward but less successful is his experimentation with stream of consciousness. It is possible to guess his intent, but the passage itself is likely to sound more like a telegram—or perhaps a list of errands on today's calendar—than like a fluent stream of associations. The novel is interior, however. The technique that relates Arlt most closely to the vanguardists is his use of interior monologue—and, we might add, his habit of shifting point of view without warning. Actually, the occasional confusion created by these switches enhances the sense of chaos, the atmosphere of near lunacy. Interior monologue is the basic narrative manner. Since that is the case, *Los siete locos* becomes a caricature of society, because each character thinks of his own obsession as perfectly normal, and the totality of these presumed normal situations is a monstrous absurdity. The effect it produces is disquieting, not humorous. The great difference between Arlt and the vanguardists of his time is the economic-social class he deals with. In general, his characters belong to the least privileged ranks of the middle class; and, although social reform is not likely to take place in the ways indicated in *Los siete locos*, his people exhibit a profound dissatisfaction with society as well as with themselves.

This dual dissatisfaction is another of Arlt's distinguishing qualities. On balance, Arlt probably has more in common with his vanguardist contemporaries than with the more realistic novelists of his time. However, the literary vanguard rarely concerned itself with the problems of society as a whole, regardless of how perceptive the novelists might be with regard to the complex interior reality of an individual. Jaime Torres Bodet's *La educación sentimental* is such an extreme case of interiorization the novel almost destroys itself. The narrator-protagonist tells of his friendship with another boy, Alejandro. A family vacation takes the narrator away from Alejandro's company for a while; then he returns and looks for his friend. That is practically all the exterior change there is. Some recent novelists who produce fiction in which nothing happens might find solid inspiration in Torres Bodet's novel. Its point, of course, is to recount interior change, with specific reference to a moment in the protagonist's emotional growth. The word *moment*, in this case, is particularly significant because there is a conflict between exterior time and interior time in *La educación sentimental*. Communication of emotional growth does not always coincide logically with the procession of outside events.

Torres Bodet sets up the novel by having an anonymous "editor" introduce the protagonist. The story is his diary. Interiorization takes place with such intensity there is hardly any dialogue; and when there is, it serves only to illustrate an observation already made. There is also a slight inconsistency in the narrative attitude that affects the communication of the novel. In the first part of the story—before the protagonist goes away with his family—the narra-

76

tion is not credible as the diary of a young boy. Rather, it is the memoir of an older man looking back on his youth, and the resulting tone is partly, and indulgently, humorous. When the boy goes away, the narrative attitude comes much closer to coinciding with what we may presume to be the attitude of the protagonist. It makes a significant difference, in the experience of the novel, that this change takes place when the context of the narrator's problem changes. His response to Alejandro's friendship continues to be the focus of the narrative, but it is more independent in the new circumstance. The reader's sense of this growing independence is greatly strengthened by the fact that the adjusted narrative attitude lends a feeling of greater authenticity to this part of the book.

Even so, the overall reaction produced by narrative ambivalence is an appreciation of contrast between a youthful view and a mature view of the same situation. It intensifies the complexity indicated when the protagonist, about to leave one quandary, walks squarely into another, at the end of the novel. Such problems of human relationship formed the basis of most vanguardist fiction, and the novelists considered them more fundamental than the problems of society or of institutions. The best narratives of this kind elicit close reader participation. The techniques intended to involve the reader in *La educación sentimental* are the editor-narrator-protagonist arrangement—which allows the reader to choose his position, even suggests that he make the choice—and the open-ended conclusion. This latter technique may be a somewhat tardy way of involving the reader, but it unquestionably extends the life of the reader-novel association.

The writings (and the word is used advisedly) of Macedonio Fernández constantly invite the reader to participate. The structure —if it can be called that—of any collection, work, fragment, or piece is so chaotic it remains open to the reader's entrance on various levels. The most basic is a challenge to join in the fun; the next step is to wonder what in the world the man is writing about. Then a more manageable frame for wondering makes its presence felt. This stage tends to be philosophical, and it probably causes some readers to ponder a question about the author's understanding of reality, or the difference between materiality and nothingness. Even if his reader is not philosophically inclined, he participates on this level in an intuitive way, sensing that this man's work is somehow saying that real things are not real after all.

Fernández's writings defy classification. They even fight against collection. *Papeles de Recienvenido* is about fifty pages long. It has a narrative constituent, but it is more like a rambling essay than anything else. Its anecdotal base is a street accident soon after Recienvenido (New Arrival) reaches Buenos Aires. A chapter functioning as prologue refers to the accident. Then the first-person narrator, Recienvenido, wanders through a series of wild associations, discussing anything that suggestion indicates. It is funny because the author's oblique view of the world he lives in puts everything in an unusual perspective. Even the most external aspect of this series is humorous because of the unexpected combinations of stimulus and result that underlie the associations. The reference to the accident turns miraculously into a brief dissertation on the wisdom of dividing time into forty-year intervals. From here we slide into a proposal that a statue be erected in honor of the man who invented the difference between left and right. This possibility brings up the narrator's dislike of statues: he loathes those folds of cloth that should be rippling in the wind, but really never move. Somehow these thoughts lead him to comment on an account in the newspaper *La Prensa*, concerning a disaster that really wasn't a disaster at all. From this point, the essay-narrative wanders to hunger in Germany, to the dangers of travel, back to the street accident, and on to boring literature.

A chapter directly concerned with the street accident follows this preface. Policemen and newsmen concerned about the accident are the objects of the New Arrival's sardonic humor. The following chapter is an introduction by the "editor" to the rest of the book. Macedonio Fernández loves this confusion of narrative identities. The natural effect of the trick is either to alienate the reader and cause him to lose interest, or to entice him into the identity trap. The effect is intensified in both possible directions when the narrative voice speaks directly to the reader.

Following this introduction of the "editor," the book enters into the literary life of the time and becomes basically essayistic. The "in" joke is an important factor in the humor, but it is not pervasive enough to discourage a reader unacquainted with Fernández's specific time and place. Humor is, of course, the book's outstanding characteristic. Nélida Salvador says the basic humorous technique is the insertion of a variant into a known mold.[6] There are, however, other ways of describing Macedonio Fernández's writing. He calls attention to the irrational by highlighting paradox. Very detailed description where we normally do not expect or need detail produces the same kind of humor Julio Cortázar achieves in his how-to-do-it manual. The mad associations used in the prefatory chapter of *Papeles de Recienvenido* are a standard technique. Syntactical marvels challenge the reader's ingenuity as well as his language.[7] Exaggeration produces a sense of incongruity that borders on the grotesque, but never crosses the line.

This kind of book has to fight its way through life the way a nonconformist person must. Frequently it is pushed aside by a serious book which appears to be more meaningful, or even better because it is serious. Readers are reluctant to accept humor as having unquestioned importance. Macedonio Fernández would be more appreciated (and many other writers along with him) if readers would at least change the humorous-versus-serious dichotomy to humorous-versus-somber. In this book, he uses paradox as a means of unifying (or reducing) time and space to the point of capturing a sense of origin (p. 39). This tour de force does more than supply grist for the nothingness-reality philosophizers; it is one of the reasons Macedonio Fernández is a writers' writer since it cleans the slate for creating. To put it another way, it makes possible the appreciation of the point before creation.

Since *Papeles de Recienvenido* is obviously not a novel according to any generally accepted definition, notion, or custom, there is a legitimate question relative to its usefulness in a book about the novel. The explanation is that it has to be taken into account not for what it is as an accomplished literary work, but for its function as a dynamic experience for its readers, particularly those who are themselves writers. Fernández is more than willing, he is eager, to go beyond the limits of objective awareness. He is irreverent toward anything except the authentic human condition. He does not hesitate to make sacred cows look absurd. There is about him a certain *joie de vivre*, a condition of being a free spirit, that provides an unusual kind of witness to life. What he knows makes him reject the inhibiting aspects of structure, of formalization, of organization. There is an astonishing parallel between him and Roberto Arlt. *Parallel* is the important word—not *coincidence*. It is as if they traveled, slightly separated, from similar but not identical origins to similar but not identical destinations.

The contrast between this work and *Doña Bárbara* is very apparent. There would be little point in observing that the two books belong to two different national cultures, because there were novels generally similar to *Doña Bárbara* nestled closely to *Papeles de Recienvenido*. Fernández's work is a kind of superexpression of the vanguardism of the 1920s. It asserts an essential aspect of literary art—the author's right to create his fictional reality. Its importance becomes even clearer when we look at the books of 1929 with an eye on developments in fiction during the last half of the century. It is unquestionable that a special set of circumstances (not all of them literary) focused attention on Gallegos's novel; it is equally apparent that the development of the genre in Spanish America owes as much—and probably a great deal more—to Macedonio Fernández.

CHAPTER 7

From *Doña Bárbara* to *Don Goyo* (1930–1932)

In a book published in 1939, Arturo Torres Rioseco says, "The purely psychological novel with no external movement, and the metapsychic novel oriented toward the realm of dreams, have had their cultivators in our countries (C. A. Leumann, Torres Bodet, etc.), but they are inappropriate forms of expression for peoples of such an intense objective life and of such limited literary culture."[1] The accuracy of the critic's terminology might supply fuel for a debate, but there really is not much doubt about what he means. Certainly he is not against the use of psychology in the narrative process. In fact, his foremost criterion for judging the quality of fiction is its psychological validity. However, Torres Rioseco's evaluation of this factor corresponds roughly to a layman's test of reasonableness. The kind of novel he considers inappropriate for Spanish America is the interior study cultivated by the vanguardists; and, though he does not say so, his judgment probably included other narrative techniques as well as narrative point of view. His opinion is interesting in a study of the novel's history because it says, a decade after the year of *Doña Bárbara*, that the most original works of that year were not appropriate to the culture.

Gallegos's novel itself is safe, of course. One of its major factors is the faithful reproduction of the typical, the picturesque. During the years immediately following the publication of *Doña Bárbara*, we find ourselves facing one of the great conflicts of Spanish American literature—regionalism versus cosmopolitanism. These years, 1930–1932, are crucial ones with regard to the effect of this conflict on artistic creativity. Or, to shift the perspective, they are crucial years with regard to what the novel reveals about Spanish American culture. If we look only at the year 1929, it appears that, in addition to Gallegos's novel, the offerings are fairly standard works by established writers, plus some vanguardist writing on cosmopolitan themes. These innovative works look much more modern than *Doña Bárbara*. However, during the next three years, purely cosmopolitan fiction disappeared. Many novelists use vanguardist techniques to reveal social deficiencies in a particularized context. The intensity of protest varies among the novelists, and the relationship of artistic novelization to social message becomes a matter of fundamental importance.

Undoubtedly, Torres Rioseco's observation about the appropriate kind of fiction is worth consideration. It apparently recognizes part of a very complex situation. His emphasis on the exterior novel appears to reflect the New World impulse, the need to see and to name the things of this miraculous hemisphere. However, the orientation of prose fiction from 1930 to 1932 clearly shows an additional concern—the problem of social justice. In this connection, support for an antivanguardist position comes from an interesting source, Roberto Arlt. In a preface to *Los lanzallamas* (1931), apparently defending himself against attacks on his stylistic shortcomings, he refers to James Joyce as a kind of darling of the literary snobs and defends the urgency of his own writing: "But today, midst the noise of a social edifice that is inexorably crumbling, it is impossible to think of decoration."[2] Obviously, his concern is different from New Worldism.

The specific world of Arlt clearly justified his anguish as a writer concerned for the welfare of the lower middle class. Hipólito Irigoyen was reelected president of Argentina in 1928. This man, once the hope of antioligarchic liberalism, had proved largely ineffectual even during his first administration, 1916–1922. His political resurrection turned out to be a sad mistake. His personalism had grown and was now allied with an unreasonable nationalism—a very unproductive combination. Disenchantment with his regime supported a coup led by Gen. José F. Uriburu in 1930. The Radical party was through. Middle-class apathy had prohibited any fundamental change in the Argentine situation. The generals and the oligarchy were supreme. The Uriburu regime was characterized by insistence on order with some Mussolini-like qualities that were especially favored by Uriburu's principal intellectual supporter, the poet Leopoldo Lugones. The political position of Lugones was probably inspired by a complex of anxieties somewhat akin to the anguish of Roberto Arlt, in spite of the very different outlets discovered in the two cases.

Los lanzallamas is a sequel to *Los siete locos.* If there is any difference worth pointing out between the two novels, it is that the feeling of near lunacy is even more intense in the later book. There is only one outlet for Erdosain's anguish—it is the road to murder and suicide. Arlt is probably the only Latin American writer of his time whose work discovers such an individualized resolution to a general problem. The combination reveals an extraordinary grasp of the relationship of the individual to society. It is ironic that for many years the readers who most appreciated Arlt's qualities included many of those against whom he felt he had to defend himself.

In part, the messy world of Arlt was caused—or, at the very least, nourished—by the international economic depression. In general, the problems growing from this crisis caused conservative retrenchment in Spanish American politics while encouraging literature of social protest often based on radical ideologies. The most notable exception to this generalization was Mexico where the Revolution found itself in a major political crisis. As the crisis cleared, one of the most revolutionary administrations became a reality, with Lázaro Cárdenas as president. A contrary example was Peru where Raúl Haya de la Torre probably won election in 1931. The declared president, however, was Luis Sánchez Cerro who outlawed Haya's party.

Economic problems make up one of the many ingredients in the Spanish American novel of protest. It is not a proletarian novel in the usual sense of the term, because the proletariat was not of the usual kind. An industrial workers' class was acquiring considerable strength in a few places. However, a greater problem was land distribution, and a related problem was the status of the Indian, particularly in the areas where advanced Indian cultures left dense indigenous populations. It is not hard to understand, given these facts, that folkloric elements become mixed with protest, and the line between New Worldism and social protest is not always clear.

In novels where the circumstances suggest the possibility of proletarianism, writers tend to focus on the individual misfit rather than on the masses. This preference, clear enough in Arlt, is even more apparent in *Larvas* (1931), a volume of stories by Elías Castelnuovo, who also belonged to the Boedo group. The stories are related to each other by a narrator who teaches in a correctional institution for delinquent boys. Each story concerns a particular boy; each boy is in some way a social misfit. There is no exploited working class visible as a segment of society. In a similar way, José A. Osorio Lizarazo, in *La casa de vecindad* (1930), veers away from proletarianism. The narrator-protagonist is a victim of burgeoning technology, and this situation could well lead to a novel about the laboring class. Instead of developing in that direction, the book turns into the story of human concern on an individual basis. Thomas E. Kooreman, in a study of urban problems in the Colombian novel, shows that the narrator's character partly explains this orientation— his apparent unreliability is actually a revelation of his inability to comprehend a society that is too sophisticated for him.[3]

César Vallejo comes closer to what we usually think of as a proletarian novel, in *El tungsteno* (1931); but even here, the special circumstances of the New World create a special emphasis. The novel offers an interesting combination of factors to readers who know something of Spanish American literature: first, the industrial connotation of the title; second, the leftist ideology of the author; third, Vallejo's basic identification as a poet deeply affected by the realization or frustration of human brotherhood. Once inside his novel, we find Vallejo has provided a setting around the establishment of a mining operation (United States ownership, naturally) in Peru, but concerns himself with the dehumanization of people caused by the advent of this capitalistic ogre, rather than with its actual operation. The condition of the worker is not an important part of the book. In the last forty pages, something less than the

last third of the novel, the book becomes more proletarian; there is
a mass rebellion against police brutality (not directly against the
industrialists). This popular movement creates a leader, the black-
smith Servando Huanca. Vallejo makes him the very unnatural
mouthpiece for Leninist ideology in the final thirteen pages of the
novel. The effect is as deadly as it sounds. Fortunately, the author's
instinctive human concern makes the novel in general more convincing than its last pages. The major part of the book is not devoted to the economic class struggle, but to the brutal self-interest
of individual men.

The narration is consistently third-person omniscient. Even hallucinations are described in the third person. In spite of this awkward-
ness, however, the novel shows a good deal of narrative cleverness.
Vallejo's use of an individual, rather than the mining company, for
ideological propaganda is one example. Another is the way he slants
the novel toward the Indian problem. *El tungsteno* is, in fact, an important *novela indigenista* (one that deals with the Indian's problem
in terms of his own heritage). The blending of European and Indian
in the name of Servando Huanca is an important factor in shading
the novel. Another is the sympathy elicited for the two military
recruits. Vallejo points out that the men had never been a part of
the Peruvian civic-economic organization. This revelation is the
culmination of many examples that show the conflict between two
cultures, with no attempt on the part of the intruding whites to find
out why the Indians act as they do. Vallejo does not actually write
from the standpoint of the Indian, but he is able to appreciate, from
where he stands, what the Indian attitudes are.

It is apparent that Castelnuovo, Osorio Lizarazo, and Vallejo
were concerned more with the point they were making than with
the effectiveness of narrative technique. This attitude is one characteristic of the reorientation of the novel during the period 1930–
1932 and continues to be important for quite a long time afterward.
Techniques introduced by the more innovative writers of the 1920s
tend to get lost—not because they are absent, but because they are
obscured by the regionalist-cosmopolitan conflict. A fuller appreciation of the experience of the Spanish American novel comes from
recognizing the need to deal with some specific, localized circumstances and responding to the varying creative intensity of the
writer—that is, the extent to which he employs nonsimplistic nar-

rative techniques in order to make his statement more than a dialogued document.

The most spectacular case of localized theme was the novel of the Revolution in Mexico. Its heyday was the early 1930s. It is surprising, at first glance, that the Revolution was not an important theme during the first decade after its violent phase. A second thought suggests that it was quite logical for the Revolution, which was a series of interrelated rebellions as well as a civil war, to acquire very gradually the degree of unity and heroic status needed for it to be assimilated into literature. The years between actual participation and recall were marked by more abstract products of the movement: a sense of newness, cultivation of the arts, an awareness of the common effort, for example. Then, in the late 1920s, the Revolution started growing as a theme, and a few years later, it was almost alone in the Mexican novel. Scores of writers needed to tell their experiences, or those of some acquaintance or friend. Often these semifictional tales follow a straight line of narrative development, very appropriate as an expression of revolutionary movement, and have the urgent tone of an author's desire to tell it all. Some novels, however, use interesting techniques that deepen the experience of the narration without losing the sense of movement. Gregorio López y Fuentes, in *Campamento* (1931), uses a composite of shifting scenes to illuminate the reality of an overnight encampment of revolutionary soldiers. Not exactly movement; rather, the other face of movement—the halt, the respite, the moment that corroborates movement itself. In another novel, *Tierra* (1932), the same author tells the story of the segment of the Revolution led by Emiliano Zapata. His purpose is to glorify Zapata, protesting the political villainy that worked against the agrarian leader. To this end, he sets out to turn Zapata into a legend and brings it off by developing a double paradox, or a paradox-contrast. He gives the novel a documentary appearance by using years as chapter titles: 1912, 1913, 1914, and so on. Then he enhances this effect by quoting some of Zapata's utterances on the Revolution and land reform, and by novelizing one version of the murder of Zapata. The leader's charisma makes people remember his words as if they had some magic quality; and after his murder they will not believe he is dead. The novelist turns reality into unreality. Parallel to this development, he deals with a completely fictional character, Antonio Hernández, in a completely realistic way, thereby turning unreality into reality. As the two lines of development flow together, there is as much reason to believe one as the other.

Novels of the Revolution followed the course of the struggle itself—that is, from portrayal of the fighting to novelization of the aftermath. Postrevolutionary governments and the corresponding fiction had to deal with some very complicated social problems created by agrarian reform, rapid urban growth, and industrialization. *La luciérnaga* (1932), by Mariano Azuela, deals with the uprooted provincial who cannot find a place in urban society. The theme is recurrent in Azuela's novels and is an important aspect of the social change taking place in much of Spanish America at the time. In this novel, Azuela achieves a particularly accurate communication of the situation by distorting his protagonist's view of reality so that it corresponds to the awry appearance of a culture that is changing so rapidly its individual constituents cannot adapt themselves to it.

The novelist uses a number of techniques that easily qualify as vanguardist. Basically, he creates the effect by beginning the narration in the middle of the action and also in the middle of the protagonist's drug-affected perception of the situation. Both factors are necessary. Dionisio, whose thoughts we experience, is the driver of a bus involved in an accident. His uncertain grasp of reality joins the reader's sudden entry on the scene to create a simultaneous feeling of alienation and involvement.

Azuela's principal tool is interiorization via interior monologue. A variation of this technique resembles what the person might say aloud, but to himself. In addition, he uses stream of consciousness that is apparently chaotic association. The interiorization of Dionisio is set against a very real view of the city that is presented most effectively in a style that suggests movie-camera panning—lists of substantives that make the mind's eye sweep across the urban panorama. The contrast points up Dionisio's failure. A second contrast sets him against his brother who stayed back home and whose view of reality is as distorted by miserliness as Dionisio's is by drugs. Interiorization reveals the latter's failure even before coming to the city. Azuela correlates the importance of individuality with the creation of social problems as a consequence of rapid urban growth.

87

There is a relationship between his view and the bucolic themes of some novels of a few years earlier—*Raucho*, for example. The healthy rural values are similar, but Azuela has provided the flamboyant exception of Dionisio's brother. And the emphasis is also on the negative aspect of city life, rather than on the curative effect of country living. What is more, the destructive effect of the city is no longer the decadent bourgeois problem, but the poor man's difficulty in making a living.

The similarity and the difference are both important. One stresses the continuity of emphasis on New World phenomena—the social problems of this hemisphere are still another reality to be recognized, identified; the other points to the fact of social change—Latin American cities traditionally had not been causes of the distortion apparent in *La luciérnaga*. Although in later years Azuela himself questioned the validity of his vanguardist techniques, the fact is that he successfully used new ways of communicating new circumstances.

Imaginative use of history is an important factor in two Venezuelan novels that deal with the national reality: *Cubagua* (1931) by Enrique Bernardo Núñez and *Las lanzas coloradas* (1931) by Arturo Uslar Pietri. The role of history in these two books is probably more than coincidence. Venezuela was under the rule of Juan Vicente Gómez and had been since the early years of the century. The country was as rich in oil as it was poor in liberty. Its economy was bringing about profound social changes—a process that often fosters national self-analysis. In a repressive political situation, invocation of history may permit comments on the national circumstance that otherwise could not be said.

The basis of *Cubagua* is a mixture of history and legend surrounding a "lost" city on an island off the Venezuelan coast. Its charm is similar to that of science fiction, and Núñez creates the effect mainly by intercalating present and past. The primary time, the book's present, is around 1925. The novel begins with a presentation of some people in La Asunción, a town on Isla Margarita, who will participate in the story. We soon realize, however, that the narrator has transposed us to the time of the Conquest and the tyrant-explorer, Lope de Aguirre. Larrazábal Henríquez regards this unobtrusive transition and others like it as the principal means by which Núñez creates the novel's atmosphere.[4] He shows that the mention of a place or an object may trigger a return to the past. These evocations are not like ordinary flashbacks, because they do not necessarily explain the background of a particular person. They belong rather to the situation as a whole. Instead of setting them apart as flashbacks, Núñez makes them arise naturally from the interests of the characters, who are functioning in the present time. When this suggestion occurs, he simply follows it without breaking the narrative flow, allowing it to be the main story line for as long as development requires.

Cubagua is more oriented toward its social environment than might be expected in a novel based on the quasi-magic evocation of a legend. Class distinctions are apparent, and exploitation of the Indians is one of the factors contributing to the notion that civilization corrupts, that simple joy has escaped us in a poor trade for anguish.

Las lanzas coloradas takes its title from a statement by José Antonio Páez, a patriot general in the war for Venezuelan independence from Spain. It refers to a sergeant's admonition to his men that for their own good they had better come back with their lances red with enemy blood. Uslar Pietri portrays a stage of the war as it affected a particular set of people, using the larger historical reality as background and also as instigator. The novel tells its readers a fact of history that memory tends to write off: the war for independence was more complicated than a neatly drawn battle line with Spaniards on one side and patriots on the other. It enlarges on the symbolic memory that Bolívar won the independence of Venezuela. The experience of the novel is the translation of this awareness of history into an intimate study of two participants, Fernando and Presentación (landowner and slave), whose paradoxical allegiances during the war reflect the confusion of the struggle. This lack of clarity in the fight for independence is undoubtedly an important part of Venezuelan reality, and, with slight variations, it may be understood as generally true for Spanish America.

The chronological setting of the novel is the period between the defeat of the first great patriot leader, Francisco de Miranda, and the assumption of leadership by Simón Bolívar. The *llaneros*, the plainsmen, led by a Spaniard, José Tomás Boves, were royalists.

Las lanzas coloradas reveals some of their personal reasons for taking this side—not always a logical step in terms of the larger picture, but quite reasonable from their limited point of view. Eventually, José Antonio Páez convinced Boves that the battle was not between the plainsmen and the city people, but between the new republic and Spain. This accomplishment was an important contributing factor to Bolívar's ultimate success. It did not, however, resolve the conflict between capital and province, a persistent problem throughout Spanish America.

Uslar Pietri begins his novelization of this historical moment by introducing, in his first chapter, three basic elements of the story. First we read the novelist's version of a legend told by a black slave. It is not actually the slave's narration, but the author's interpretation of it. Repetitions of motif words, phonetic rhythms, and open-ended verbless phrases produce an awareness of the slave's superstition, feeling of repression, and potential violence. The second part of the chapter introduces Presentación Campos, a slave who functions as overseer. He is a natural leader and, by that fact, a step higher on the social scale than the average slave. Uslar Pietri changes his narrative manner, describing the qualities of Presentación through what others say and think about him. Then he cuts in a third scene to introduce Fernando, the young owner of the estate, his sister Inés, and Captain David, a young Englishman dedicated to the patriotic cause. This scene is typically romantic drawing room. Its refined, almost dilettantish atmosphere contrasts in one dimension with the forcefulness of the overseer, and in another dimension with the primitivism of the slaves.

After establishing the novel's present time in the first chapter, the narrator goes back into the past and presents the history of the estate, of the family, and of Fernando himself up to the time of the first chapter. This section of the novel is partly a kind of capsulized history of the country, with a spicing of legend. It also takes us to colonial Caracas, where Fernando goes to complete his education and where he meets a group of young patriots. Here the narrator again increases the amount of detail, putting aside the capsule of history and creating an active picture of the young revolutionaries.

When the narrator brings the story back to the initial point in time, in the sixth chapter, he has created a historical perspective that gives a feeling of present time to what really took place in the second decade of the nineteenth century. This condition, combined with the persistently intimist interpretation, creates the illusion, noted by Alegría, that it is possible to determine the course already taken by history.[5] From this point, the contrast between Fernando and Presentación Campos develops. The latter's circumstance and character are reemphasized in a passage where a remembered voice seems to remind him of his inferior position. It has some of the effect of interior monologue, but leaves the clear impression that this other voice represents something imposed upon Campos, not caused by his own actions. He joins Boves—the slave becomes a royalist soldier. Fernando, the vacillating aristocrat, half-heartedly joins the patriots.

The narrator builds tension around the fearful expectation of attack by Boves and his troops. The account is interspersed with variations on a statement to the effect that Boves is coming. They are not quite the same, but are similar enough to function as a leitmotif. This tension refers to an anonymous group and also intensifies Fernando's questions about how important the venture is to him personally. Presentación's self-concern is just as strong as Fernando's, but it leads him in a different direction. His hallucinations after being wounded include a recapitulation of the novel, and the story fades into the coming of Bolívar, anticipated with a relevant leitmotif substituted for the earlier repetitions referring to Boves.

By the end of the novel, Uslar Pietri has identified the historical moment unmistakably; at the same time he has created the possibility of a reader response that is not limited in time and space, one that is based on the appreciation of personal conflict related to social conflict. In other words, the dynamic factor in the novel is dual. Conflict exists both inside and outside the characters and is a more fundamental reality than the war itself. The anecdotal base of *Las lanzas coloradas* is certainly an important part of the New World experience, but the novel itself probes beneath the picturesque.

The effort to reach some firm base for understanding the meaning of America—the New World, that is—emphasized a wide variety of thematic material and employed very different forms. Thematically, both *Cubagua* and *Las lanzas coloradas* move away from the present in which they are written in order to capture the reality of society at a particular moment in the past. An appreciation of the New World experience, however, requires identification of another aspect of reality—myth. European man tends to identify myth with history because he is trapped in the pattern of chronological progression. Myth, however, is functionally timeless, and so is the indigenous New World concept of reality. The novels of Miguel Angel Asturias persistently make this point. His first book, *Leyendas de Guatemala* (1930), is an early effort to re-create material that was an almost hidden factor in his self-awareness. Away from his homeland, Asturias became objectively aware of native Guatemalan culture and felt the vibrations of kinship.

It is important to recognize that however intense the function of Indian myth in Asturias's psychic condition, the stories must possess an exotic quality when presented to western-oriented readers in a western form. Otherwise, they would be inauthentic. It is equally important to remember that the stories have cosmogonic significance and, therefore, need to be differentiated by stylistic elegance from everyday, prosaic living. Basically, Asturias accomplishes this separation by repeating words, phrases, and syntactical constructions. In the legend of the volcano, he tells of the six men who peopled the Land of Trees. Three of them came by wind and three by water, and the narrator counterpoints these two sets of men.

The three who came in the wind, like birds, nourished themselves on fruits.
The three who came in the water, like fish, nourished themselves on stars.[6]

The repetition of words or phrases, particularly as the repeated beginning of a series of statements, produces an incantatory effect. The obvious association with oral repetition is enhanced by the exact syntactical equivalence of the two sentences. This technique is very similar to the duophrasing (*bifrasismo*) used in pre-Hispanic literature. It is a slightly altered rendition of a previous statement, possibly to make sure that the communication is really effected. A slightly different approximation of the same effect is apparent in "Tree that walks . . . Tree that counts the years, each of four hundred days, according to the moons it has seen; tree that has seen many moons, like all trees; tree that came, already mature, from the Place of Abundance" (p. 41).

Each of the passages quoted contains an element particularly stimulating to the imagination: the allusion to stars in the earlier quotation, and the notion of trees that came, already mature, in the second. This kind of suggestion, supported by Asturias's highly original images, enables the storyteller to move his reader into a very exotic world where he will accept animism as normal, and even the transformation of a braid of hair into a snake. Here is the most important aspect of Asturias's use of myth. He feels no need to explain such strange happenings, not even to say they are magic. He simply assumes they are part of reality. This progression is the dynamic process of the book. Obviously, it depends to a great extent on the use of language, and Asturias has never hesitated to deal with language in any way that will contribute to his artistic goal. A play (or a legend in dramatic form) called *Cuculcán* is frequently published with the *leyendas*. Richard Callan suggests the appropriateness of the combination, pointing out that Asturias does not list it among his plays.[7] The title refers to the feathered-serpent god common to several indigenous cultures of Mesoamerica. Its structure and theme have their own fascination—it is a single piece in nine scenes divided into three sets of three scenes each, each set of three having scenes identified by the colors yellow, red, and black, and made to correspond to morning, afternoon, and evening. However, the factor that makes it the perfect companion to the legends is its language. By the end of the play, rational language disappears and only sound remains.

Another volume of stories, *Los que se van* (1930), deals with the ethos of humble people, emphasizing cultural and economic conflicts. The collaboration of three young writers makes this book a kind of generational view of a particular situation. The book contains eight stories by each of three authors: Demetrio Aguilera Malta, Joaquín Gallegos Lara, and Enrique Gil Gilbert. In a brief preliminary statement, they say the book is a unit, not three parts. They hope that the work will be cohesive just as the dream that created it was cohesive.[8] The title suggests the authors' basic awareness: that a changing society necessarily marks the end of the relatively unsophisticated life style of the *cholo* and *montuvio*.[9] Thematically, the stories depend on details of this life style, particularly their contrastive effect against the reader's background of western culture and progress. They are strong, violent people.

Tragedy is a natural factor in their lives. Certain violent acts are cathartic and accepted as inevitable. Codes of honor justify death in situations where the white community might not accept it. Superstition and psychological motivation often lead to violence. When the individual cannot cope with the problem, he reacts physically and may even destroy himself.

Technically, the three authors also have some common denominators. The plots stress physical movement more than emotion, but the stories tend to be elliptical, highlighting key moments. Characterization tends to be stylized in a similar way. The people in the stories reveal their feelings in what they say, and the authors frequently reinforce these emotions by lyrical reference to nature. The effect is greatly enhanced when the author personifies nature and depersonifies man. In the process of depersonification—or deindividualization—the stories use some anonymous dialogue that carries the action forward and builds tension. These techniques isolate the *cholos* and *montuvios*, emphasize the qualities that are out of the ordinary. Repetitions in the form of refrains or introductory phrases also enhance the atmosphere of otherworldliness.

There are individual differences among the three writers, of course. Aguilera Malta's stories are theatrical in their dependence on dialogue for the intensification of emotions. He also makes the greatest use of repetitions, of short sentences sometimes verbless, of the repeated use of whole names of characters. These techniques move the Ecuadorean themes in the direction of *Leyendas de Guatemala*. They also foreshadow some of the author's work of the sixties and seventies. Speaking of his own novel, *Siete lunas y siete serpientes* (1970), and of some others with similar characteristics, Aguilera Malta has remarked that he and other writers of his generation would have written novels of this kind when they were young, if there had been anyone willing to publish them.

Gil Gilbert probably makes the greatest use of anonymous dialogue. He is also more explicit than the others about the conflict between *cholo* and white man. Plot is more apparent in Gallegos Lara than in the others because he is fond of ending with an ironic twist. Returning to the original proposition of the book, however, the important point is not the differences among the three authors, but their similarities. Theirs is a sense of change, of something disappearing. Their literary creation of this sense amounts to another act of naming the aspects of New World reality. Like many novelists in these years, 1930–1932, they were taking account of the New World, experiencing the *criollo* circumstance. Often the mention of *criollo* fiction suggests immediately the novel of customs in the realist manner. Clearly, this view is much too limited to satisfy what was happening in Spanish America. True enough, these years saw a turn toward noncosmopolitan themes. However, the novelists' attempt to communicate their particular reality led them not to traditional realism, but to many kinds of technical experimentation.

CHAPTER 8

The Year of *Don Goyo* (1933)

To a considerable extent, the novels of 1933 offer a concentrated view of the crisis of cosmopolitanism apparent during the years immediately preceding. Demetrio Aguilera Malta's *Don Goyo* meets this problem with a combination of narrative art and regional theme. The effect achieved—rare during the first half of the century —approximates the transcendent regionalism of more recent fiction. In this book and in some others of the same year the authors contribute to the New World identity by focusing on some social group that is less sophisticated, less cultivated (in the European sense) than the city-dwelling members of the ruling class.

Definition of this phenomenon brings up a number of problems because the various groups under the spotlight are not identical to each other. In some respects they are widely disparate. Aguilera Malta deals with the humble people on the Ecuadorean coast. Alejo Carpentier, in *Ecue-Yamba-O*, develops his story on the basis of Afro-Cuban culture and the sugar industry. *Toá*, by César Uribe Piedrahita, uses a contrast between rubber gatherers in the Amazon region and an outsider, sent in by the government. In *El muelle*, Alfredo Pareja Díez-Canseco reverses the contrast by placing simple people in a very complicated, urban setting. A tendency to speak of these groups as primitive or native risks both oversimplification and inaccuracy. Their common quality is that they reveal characteristics and problems that are fundamental in the regional cultures to which they belong. When Carpentier and Aguilera Malta deal with the two groups highlighted in their two novels, they tend to set the groups apart and to emphasize their basically human traits. In this way, the selected groups seem more authentic—more closely identified with man's basic nature—than their sophisticated counterparts. This process associates man very closely with nature, and the naming process is apparent and satisfying. In many ways it is like a botanist discovering and naming a plant—an act that is still fairly common in the New World.

Don Goyo and *Ecue-Yamba-O* have an exotic quality not found in other novels of this year. Its source is the authors' interest in identifying the two fundamental social structures on which the novels focus. These structures are different from the ordinary experience of the writers and readers of novels, so Aguilera Malta and Carpentier use particular techniques to set their created realities apart from the commonplace. However, they always make their readers aware of the role of the apparently exotic within the ordinary experience. The function, or experience, of *Toá* and *El muelle* is an entirely different matter. The use of contrast between cultivated society and the unsophisticated group does contribute to the identity of each, but not quite in the sense of discovering and naming. Rather, the discovery is made in terms of conflict, and the medium for revelation is protest regarding a social problem. In a sense, this, too, is a way of coming to grips with the nature of the New World experience; but its contribution to self-understanding is less fundamental.

This second kind of novel demands less in the way of experimental narrative technique than books that must transport the reader into an entirely unknown situation. Of course, the good ones are always the product of good narrative procedures; but they rarely invite attention to technique, and are likely to be called traditional. Taking these four novels into account along with others published in 1933, the turn toward regionalism is very apparent. Nevertheless, it is wrong to assume that regionalism and traditional realist narrative techniques are the only characteristics of the novel at this point.

97

In fact, there is a strong element of interiorization that emphasizes individuals rather than groups. This characteristic is as important, in the development of the genre, as the presence of vanguardist techniques in some fiction oriented toward social protest.

Don Goyo deals with the fishermen who inhabit the islands close to the port city of Guayaquil. Aguilera Malta establishes his novel on the basis of two complementary personalities. One of them, Don Goyo himself, is both legend and man. The other, Cusumbo, a *montuvio* (inhabitant of the river shore) whose troubles drove him from the mountains to the coast, is entirely a man of flesh and blood. This condition, however, does not mean that he is Mr. Average Ecuadorean. The whole reality created by the novelist is different and apart from the world of white culture. Given this primary step away from the experience that one anticipates within the white culture, Cusumbo then incarnates the circumstances created by the novelist. Don Goyo is its essence. Implicit within the novel are all the abuses found where a subservient group comes into contact with the ruling class, but there is no voice of protest complaining about the problems. The feeling produced by the intrusion of the white man into the life of the islands is a sense of losing something that is irreplaceable.

Traditionally, the islanders are fishermen. The effect of progress is to turn them to cutting the mangrove trees among which they live. The novel transcends the economic implications of the problem by balancing emphasis on Cusumbo and Don Goyo, and by using several stylistic devices that establish the reality of this unusual world. The narrative structure is a perfectly balanced organization in three parts. The first part is about Cusumbo—his situation within the novel's present, plus a flashback concerning his origin. Don Goyo does appear in this first part, but in a shadowy way. He passes in his canoe saying "Buenas noches de Dios," more presence than personality. A flashback to Cusumbo's past shows the degraded state of the worker in the highlands. Then the contrast between the strong, natural life on the islands and the corruption of Guayaquil clearly implies a sorry future for the fishermen.

In the second part of the novel, Cusumbo and Don Goyo are equally balanced. In this part, Don Goyo is very human and exerts his influence as the leader of the people. The difference between

Cusumbo and Don Goyo still holds, however, because the old man, no matter how human he may be, is cast in a hero role, while we see Cusumbo mainly in his passionate relationship with la Gertru. Even in this part, the extraordinary qualities of Don Goyo are very apparent. He is 150 years old—a condition that has not bothered readers of Spanish American fiction since the advent of Gabriel García Márquez, but was uncommon in 1933. The novel's central incident arises from a mystical experience in which a mangrove tree tells the patriarch that the trees are like people and must not be destroyed.

In the third part of the novel, Don Goyo is completely dominant. This part also effects the definitive transition to his legendary state, which was foreshadowed in part one. In a flashback that strikes a balance with the Cusumbo flashback in the first section of the novel, the narrator reveals how Don Goyo came to be the patriarch of the islands. At the end of the novel, he remains in the islands as a spirit. The feeling, however, is that the inhabitants will give way to the white man. The spirit of Don Goyo is a reflection of the defeated leader in part two.

The dynamism of *Don Goyo* is produced by the human-legend ambivalence in the characterization of the protagonist. It is a dangerous game for an author to play, because it involves moving back and forth between reality and suprareality. Aguilera Malta employs several techniques that make this situation plausible. It is very important that photographic accuracy is never one of his goals. Rather, he captures the emotional quality of a situation. None of his characters is supposed to know himself completely. He grants Cusumbo's power of memory, for example, a credible degree of fallibility that does not limit appreciation of his personality. In the passage where Cusumbo remembers killing the unfaithful Nica and her lover:

All this, even after so many years, he remembered perfectly. What happened after that was blurred in a series of superimposed images—macabre, absurd, disjointed. Sometimes it was like a whirlwind in his hand. A whirlwind of steel that kept on cutting dark flesh and white flesh. Then a sea of blood covering faces, whole bodies. Cries of anguish; insults, curses, moans. Two bodies that stop quivering. A long hesitation. The forebears who jump over their blood. A whole race protesting. The mad flight, crossing the jungle-mountain, crossing the rivers. Stung by mosquitos. Watched by snakes, by jaguars, by wild hogs. Hunger. Hunger.

99

Maddening hunger. Delirium. Fury. Thirst. Fever. Hunger. Does the sun exist? Is there a God? Am I still alive? Which way to go? Hunger. Octopus jungle. Vampire jungle. Jungle and hunger.[1]

This passage contains an enormous quantity of characterization, accomplished by intensifying emotion. In fact, the variation in this intensity is really what communicates the action that takes place. In a somewhat similar way, Aguilera Malta conceives his entire narrative as a series of key scenes that communicate action through emotion. This procedure leaves an impression of a highly stylized reality, a kind of distillation of the course of events. He adds to the unusual effect through the use of repetition, and by never hesitating to personify nature. When he deals with nature in conjunction with dialogue, it deepens the emotive quality of the characterizations without destroying the simplicity of the characters. In a scene between Cusumbo and la Gertru, the narrator first establishes the setting: "They were sitting on the trunk of a mangrove tree, right on the edge of the bank, sensing the water almost lapping their feet. Indifferently they watched the canoes skipping over the water, illuminated by the profile of a first-quarter moon. They pressed closely together, as if engraved on each other" (p. 71). We know the attitudes of the two people. What they actually say to each other reveals hardly anything, but reinforces their image as simple souls:

"Do you remember, Gertru?"
"Remember what?"
"When I told you . . ."
"Oh . . . No! I don't remember."
"Yes you do. You just don't want to tell me." (p. 71)

It is simple, and not improbable, certainly, but hardly informative. In order to fill out the meaning of the incident, the novelist turns again to nature: "The mangroves seemed to bend over, smiling, to hear them. The wind from the north blew stubbornly, insistently, slapping their clothing against their bodies, then blowing it out, as if it were trying to undress them" (p. 72).

By associating human emotions with the scenery, Aguilera Malta embellishes the love affair, maintains the character's simplicity, and avoids a possibly trite scene. The personification of nature is particularly meaningful with regard to the mangrove trees because it is

100

consistent with Don Goyo's mystic experience, makes it credible that the *cholos* accept Don Goyo's saying that cutting them down is like killing their own kind, and reinforces the symbol when the patriarch's death coincides with the fall of the oldest mangrove. It is this persistent intercalation of the nonliteral, in various guises, that sustain's Don Goyo's movement between man and legend.

Carpentier's *Ecue-Yamba-O* shares with *Don Goyo* the search for basic cultural characteristics—a similar inquiry through attention to people who are separated from the currents of change that we think of as civilization. Exact words are hard to find, even more in the case of *Ecue-Yamba-O* than in the case of *Don Goyo*. In Aguilera Malta's novel, the roots of custom, found in the ultimate appreciation of the society, are indigenous to the land. The corresponding roots in the Afro-Cuban culture are transplanted. However, this very fact gives the novel a particular value, because it shows that man's basic qualities (the characteristics that cause us to consider him natural man) comprehend a good deal more than his relationship to place. This revelation becomes especially effective in *Ecue-Yamba-O* through repetition of "Initiation" and "Therapy," essential steps in the life of the protagonist, Menegildo Cué.

The novel's theme assumes the existence of four identifiable circumstances: the natural world, the natural black, the citified black, and the white society. The values assigned to these circumstances are basic to the novel. The first two are positive factors, the last two are negative. This contrast of values interrelates, in an interesting way, with the characterization of Menegildo's cousin, Antonio Cué. The cousin lives in the city and is known as "el negro Antonio"— an epithet used regularly in spite of the fact that the descriptive adjective appears gratuitous. It is appropriate, however, in connection with the real world of Antonio. Within the white society, he shines shoes and makes music for the entertainment of the whites. His role reveals his blackness as cultural, in addition to the matter of pigmentation. However, the role into which the white men cast him is only part of his black experience; when he is with other blacks, especially as a participant in a fraternal organization, his personality changes from subservient to self-assured, even aggressive. The ambivalence in Antonio's personality illustrates the contrast in values

101

present in the four basic thematic circumstances, and, of course, the reader's awareness of the contrast is the key to appreciation of Antonio's characterization.

Generally speaking, characterization is minimal in *Ecue-Yamba-O*. The characters other than Menegildo serve mainly to reveal the protagonist more fully. This procedure has the desirable effect of maintaining the simplicity of people whose authentic human qualities are supposed to be in contrast to white civilization. An occasional use of nature has a similar effect, enriching the emotive quality of a situation without complicating it. This technique is similar to one that is of inestimable value in *Don Goyo*. In Carpentier's novel it is less prominent.

In addition to the contrast of cultural values, the theme of *Ecue-Yamba-O* must be understood in terms of a circular series of events. Menegildo's son is born and is given his father's name in circumstances like those that surrounded the early years of the first Menegildo. This circular action suggests the durability of the black culture and the individual's inevitable adherence to its pattern. On the other hand, it suggests that total adherence is impossible, that pressure from white society will always force the Menegildos out, and that white society will destroy them, only to have the cycle repeated infinitely.

The visible narrative organization of the novel is in three parts: "Childhood," "Adolescence," and "The City." At first glance, these titles look like one of those puzzles that challenge youngsters to pick out the element that doesn't belong with the rest. In reality, "The City" is one of the ages of Menegildo. It is when he meets white society and also his death. Within this tripartite division, Carpentier makes very short chapters and in some cases uses the same chapter title several times. This technique is the most unusual characteristic of *Ecue-Yamba-O*, and it turns out to be the most effective. The repeated chapter titles are used in two ways: repeated one right after the other—"Storm (a)," "Storm (b)," "Storm (c)," "Storm (d)"— or recurring once in each of the three parts. The two arrangements have different functions.

When Carpentier uses the conjoined series, it serves to fragment an experience, so many facets of it may be seen. On the other hand, the recurring chapter titles (one in each of the novel's three parts) are more related to the movement of the story than to the ambience.

They are diverse in time, but equal in thematic reference. Three chapters entitled "Initiation" deal with three stages in the life of Menegildo: his infancy, his sexual illumination, and his entrance into the black urban society. Each case produces trauma. In the first two instances, there are related chapters entitled "Therapy," in which Berúa, the natural black, cures Menegildo. In the third case, this ethnic authenticity is not present, so there is nothing to save the protagonist as an individual; however, the ethnic circumstance continues in the birth of his son.

César Uribe Piedrahita's *Toá* is considerably closer to the standard idea of what a *criollista* novel is like. It is also much less satisfactory as a literary experience, and much of its value lies in its possible documentary use as an exposé of the plight of Colombian rubber gatherers. The story divides into two parts and two emphases. In one, Antonio de Orrantia, a representative of the government, goes into the Amazon region to investigate the problems of the workers; in the other, Orrantia falls in love with Toá, a primitive siren of apparently overwhelming charm. She certainly overwhelms the novel's protagonist to the point of making him utterly useless so far as his assignment is concerned.

Although the author does not divide his novel into sections, its effect is clearly divided into two parts, with the division marked by the center chapter (the ninth of seventeen), entitled "Toá." The first section is by far the more successful of the two. Uribe Piedrahita establishes the necessary contrast by inserting his sophisticated protagonist into a world completely unfamiliar to him. The reasonable assumption is that this world is also unfamiliar to the reader; and, indeed, the narrative tends to join the identities of protagonist and narrator, and even the reader. At times the narrator moves away from Orrantia, but the distance is never great, and emphasis is always on him. Characterization of the protagonist employs description through the view other characters have of him, and also some brief, omniscient observations by the narrator. After revealing Orrantia's thoughts and dreams, the narrator may intervene to comment on them. This commentary, however, is not very different from omniscient description; and, since it is never extensive, it does not become a bothersome intrusion.

Indeed, the whole complex of narrative techniques used in the first part of *Toá* operates in a very subtle way. Basically, Uribe Piedrahita's procedures are those of the realist novel. Descriptions of setting, introduction of characters, movement into action are particularized by Orrantia's encounter with a less sophisticated culture. The meeting produces regional types, folk philosophy, and a special kind of identity search on the part of Orrantia. There is, however, a further difference from the typical realist novel in which the various steps of narration (setting, characterization, action) are always apparent. Uribe Piedrahita moves rapidly back and forth from one narrative factor to another, melding the various aspects rather than isolating them.

Toá is not a repetition of *La vorágine*. Orrantia's comprehension of the jungle is far more objective than that of Arturo Cova, whose life is joined to the life of the jungle. (That is, at least, the suggestion of *La vorágine*. It is doubtful that this joining becomes an actual part of the experience of the novel except for readers who are sympathetically disposed from the start.) The destruction of Orrantia comes not from the jungle, but from the pressure of the culture to which he belongs. The novel itself disintegrates just as the protagonist does. In the second part, there is no effective protagonist. He does appear, but he no longer has any relationship with the problems of the laborers. The narrator's emphasis, consistently on Orrantia throughout the first part of the book, shifts to the struggles of the rubber gatherers in the second. Retrospectively, this parallel disintegration of novel and protagonist seems to reinforce the element of social protest; but that is not what actually happens during the reading, because the loss of the protagonist is disconcerting, not stimulating.

The quest for cultural identity is of primary importance in the first part of *Toá*. However, the protest against exploitation of humans and also against official apathy becomes stronger as the narration progresses, and it ends with an effect very similar to that of a clearly proletarian novel. A further step in this direction is apparent in *El muelle*, by Alfredo Pareja Díez-Canseco. The whole point of the novel is to register a strong protest against social injustice. The author develops his message in terms of class discrimination in a social context and also in an economic context.

Since the basic setting of *El muelle* is Guayaquil, it combines with *Don Goyo* to make an interesting pair. Although the conflict in

104

Don Goyo arises from the intrusion of urban-oriented white culture, the novel's basic circumstance is on the margin of the city. The conflict in *El muelle* develops within the city itself. The exploited class is entirely removed from contact with the natural surroundings that provide the people's basic security. They are the victims of the defeat suggested by the narrative development of *Don Goyo*, and indeed their condition is very similar to that of the citified black in *Ecue-Yamba-O*. To put it another way, we can appreciate, in *El muelle*, a stage in the development of Spanish American fiction made almost mandatory by the circumstances of the society.

Guayaquil is a commercial center rather than an industrial center, and does not have the big-city ambience usually associated with the proletarian novel. Pareja Díez-Canseco compensates for this lack by using New York as a secondary setting. That is, New York is thematically secondary, but he balances the weight given the two aspects of his narrative locale by opening the novel in New York. The protagonist, Juan Hidrovo, is an unemployed merchant seaman involved in a laborers' demonstration. His young wife, in Guayaquil, accepts economic adversity as a matter of course, and suffers social discrimination abjectly but less stoically than she accepts poverty. The men of the ruling class consider her body their rightful possession, and her only defense is a kind of fundamental virtue that remains intact in spite of their abuse. Juan's experience in New York shows that, even in a much more highly developed society, human respect is in short supply. The two sides of the novel's plot join when Juan returns to Guayaquil and secures a job as a construction worker on a new pier. Then he loses it because of his employer's spite.

The message of the book is vigorous protest. The author invites his reader's sympathetic reaction toward the underdog, and he is convincing in his defense of human decency. However, his repeated cases used to illustrate the point would be static if a kind of dynamism were not provided by the split scenario and its ultimate joining. This narrative organization points out a common denominator in the fact of social discrimination and, at the same time, shows the difference between two stages of economic development. Aside from this structural device, *El muelle* does nothing that is not characteristic of the typical proletarian novel. The plain, straightforward prose makes a presumably accurate word picture. The narrator sometimes reveals the inner reality of characters, but he is always completely in control of their destinies. As for values, there is nothing that approaches the basic considerations of Aguilera Malta or of Carpentier; but there are many judgments: poor people are fraternal, rich people are inhuman, politicians are opportunistic and insensitive, policemen are brutal, and so on through a fairly standard list.

It seems natural that a novel so dedicated to the exposition of social problems should put aside interest in narrative innovation. This is not to say that innovation would be inappropriate—quite the contrary—but that the crusading intensity of the novel causes the author to believe that the most direct statement is the most effective. That is why the vanguardism of María Luisa Carnelli's flamboyant protest—*¡Quiero trabajo!*—is so notable. The best effects are achieved by interior monologue, exterior sound with cut-in glimpses of the protagonist, and some very surprising visual effects. Among them is a collage of newspaper stories about unemployment, with the names of companies and of wealthy men superimposed. Another collage features brand names. These representations suggest a capitalist conspiracy against the defenseless worker. By far the most effective graphic device is a kind of mandala. In the form of an asterisk half the size of a page, the author uses as each arm the words "¿Quién me dará trabajo?" ("Who will give me a job?"). The figure produces an astigmatic effect that accords well with the protagonist's confusion. This troubled state is also heightened in effect by repetitions, hiatuses, and series of verbless phrases.

Aside from the social protest, the novel is attractive because of its feminist orientation. The cultural sophistication of Buenos Aires not only fostered artistic innovation, but also encouraged women to step forward, daringly and hesitatingly, from their traditional roles. In an entirely different social context, Norah Lange's *45 días y 30 marineros* makes a similar feminist point. The author was a member of Buenos Aires's most cultivated literary circle. This novel is a product of rich-girl effervescence and should not be taken as typical of Norah Lange's work. It is, however, indicative of an epoch. Its very simple story is the experience of a girl traveling to Norway on a freighter. She is the only woman on board. The author uses no particularly interesting techniques, but within the story she shows her independence and her hypersophistication via language aptly described by Nélida Salvador as "ironic and casual [*desenfadu-do*]."[2] Since the feminism of Norah Lange's book is in no way related to social problems, it highlights the intimate experience of the protagonist.

Laberinto de sí mismo, by Enrique Labrador Ruiz, is an extremely introspective novel, far removed from the social protest found in some other novels of 1933. It is a kind of self-critical autobiography based on the author's standing apart from himself. On the one hand, he sees himself in ordinary perspective, just as any person is self-aware; on the other hand, he is able to withdraw, to stand apart and put his self-awareness in an entirely different perspective. The novelist sets up this duality by having his protagonist-narrator, who is a writer, described by the tools of his trade (his pencils). Their comments about him are similar to a conscience, if considered as belonging to the writer-narrator-protagonist. However, the effect is somewhat different because the physical separation of this voice gives the illusion of objectivity. The pencils refer to the writer's work without the commitment an artist feels to what he has created.

The effect of this dichotomy is enhanced by use of the narrative second person, you (*tú*), which is presumably one aspect of the writer addressing another aspect of the writer. Still a third narrative technique contributes the feeling of divided self—a conflict between the ordinary and the grotesque. Within the framework of everyday living, the narrator focuses on incidents that seem distorted. These episodes trigger a shift from the expected to the unusual.

The dynamic factor in the novel—the force that creates change within the novel and within the reader—is the contrast between union and disintegration. The narrator-protagonist is a writer by profession—a fact that equates him with Enrique Labrador Ruiz. But this unification immediately encounters the disintegrating effect of the creator watching himself create. Some of the novelist's best moments are passages of lyrical contemplation that are born of the book's fundamental contrast. Labrador Ruiz occasionally gets lost in his lyric enthusiasm. At times his style becomes aphoristic; and although some of these sayings are very quotable, they tend to give the novel a didactic tone.

The most interesting aspect of the novel is its introspective quality, and it fills out the many-colored picture of the novel in 1933: New Worldism and cosmopolitanism, traditional techniques and innovation, exterior reality and inner searching. All these factors existed together, sometimes in conflict, but also sometimes in direct association. The most apparent characteristic of these novels taken as a whole is the universalization of particularity, whether it be of a regional or a personal nature.

CHAPTER 9

From *Don Goyo* to *Todo verdor perecerá* (1934–1940)

Novels during the 1930s fall into two very broad classifications: those committed to dealing with some social problem and those that deal with the human condition in a more universal context. Still relying on the broad generality, it is reasonable to say that books in the first group often deal with masses rather than individuals and are more concerned with theme than with technique. Books belonging to the second group usually deal with individuals and are written with greater artistic awareness.

The novels of the year of *Don Goyo* and *Ecue-Yamba-O*, however, show clearly that these dichotomies cannot be trusted too far. The categories are not mutually exclusive, and they can be very deceptive with regard to the development of the novel. Although socially committed novels do not emphasize technique, they are not all written the same way. It is also important to clarify that, although this period is generally recognized by specialists as a time of social fiction, books of a more introspective nature appear in considerable quantity.

From *Don Goyo* to *Todo verdor perecerá* (1934–1940)

There is no break in the line of fiction established by the van-guardist writers of the 1920s. It is true that socially committed fiction became predominant for several years, but the other kind did not disappear. The possible error comes from assuming there was a period of social novels during which no other kind was written. It comes as a surprise to some people, for example, that María Luisa Bombal's *La última niebla* (1935) was published the same year as *El indio*, by Gregorio López y Fuentes. One is a technically complicated study of a woman's love; the other is a plea for social justice. Similar contrasts could be made with other pairs.

In order to create a useful perspective for the novels of this period, it is necessary to see several kinds of socially committed novels, divided by general thematic concerns. The main classifications are the *novelas indigenistas*, the books dealing with the problem of land distribution, and novels about the urban working class. Once this part of the picture is finished, a consideration of the more artistically aware novels will reveal, through analysis of narrative techniques, the common denominators in the novels of both general classifications.

Among the *novelas indigenistas*, Jorge Icaza's *Huasipungo* (1934) is probably the most violent denunciation of injustice. One of its characteristics is the use of repugnant scenes that shock readers into a state of indignation. While these scenes are the most memorable aspect of the novel, Icaza also uses other, less flamboyant, techniques that contribute to the overall experience of strong protest.

Irony is extremely important. Don Alfonso, the *patrón*, orders some Indians to work in a swamp, knowing that some will die; and he remarks that great accomplishments require great sacrifices. Don Alfonso, of course, is willing to sacrifice the Indians. This kind of irony increases as the repugnant scenes increase, the scenes persistently making the irony more pungent. By the end of the novel, a reader—unless he resists the process totally—finds himself caught in the working of these reciprocating aspects of a single technique, designed to produce an indignant reaction.

Behind this technical factor, however, Icaza deals with his characters in a way that most readers forget. Speaking in general terms, he humanizes them much more than is usually the case in novels written on this theme. In the first place, he opens the book with the spotlight on the *patrón*, rather than on the Indians. Interior monologue reveals the motivating forces in the lives of Don Alfonso and his family. The revelation is oversimplified, and we see them mainly in terms of their defects, but they at least have their own problems as individuals. They are not typecast, nor are they an amorphous group of oppressors. Even more important is the protagonist-hero, Andrés. Icaza characterizes him as having a rather complicated reaction to his wife and capable of fantasizing on the basis of his emotions. Obviously, these human qualities prepare the reader for the progression toward indignation. Added to them is the author's careful persistence with regard to Andrés's deep feeling for his home. The title of the novel, in fact, means his home, and the theme carries throughout the story.

Through all this, the narrator maintains a safe distance. He does not editorialize or moralize about what happens. His effect is most apparent in the episodic nature of the book. True, it is planned. The carefully worked out introductions early in the novel prove Icaza was aware of its structure. Later, the concentration on repugnant incidents indicates deliberate choice. This process intensifies our indignation, assuming we do not resist it, and the emotion is a generalized protest against injustice, although the catalyst is Andrés.

Narrative techniques vary considerably among the *indigenista* novels; and the reading experience differs accordingly, even though the novels tend to come together in one's memory because of their basic thematic similarity. In *El indio* (1935), López y Fuentes studiously avoids the individualization that Icaza uses as the basis of *Huasipungo*. He uses no names at all, referring to his characters by physical condition or by role: The Cripple, The Hunter, for example. This technique sets the Indians apart as a group, tends to make their reality different from ours. The substitutes for proper names suggest archetypal treatment, and this unusual condition combines with a system of correspondences that turns the novel into an allegory. All the events in *El indio* refer to life in postrevolutionary Mexico, but they suggest the history of the Indian since the time of the Conquest. At the beginning of the novel, some white men come to an Indian village and demand they be shown where to find gold. From that point, the author develops parallel lines of native Indian customs and the influence of white civilization. Lack of understanding is general; progress, in the terms of those who promote it, seems impossible. The effect of *El indio* is to create

111

a feeling of frustration, rather than indignation. However, the anonymity of its characters grants dignity to the Indian because he is Indian, rather than because an individual's personality is persuasive.

Both Icaza and López y Fuentes use an approximation of Indian speech mainly for atmosphere. Icaza uses starkly simple dialogue passages that make his Indian characters seem nearly inarticulate. Unlike the simple dialogue used by Aguilera Malta, Icaza's is not enriched by the natural surroundings. It does, however, achieve a rhythmic effect through the use of repetitions which make it different from ordinary speech. López y Fuentes also uses repetitions, but with a somewhat different effect. His style of repetition, like the paraphrases that employ the same construction (this is the death of brave men, the parting of stalwart brothers), creates a feeling of primitive nobility; Icaza's communicates stoic endurance of hardship. The difference is entirely appropriate to the two novels, one working better with López y Fuentes's generality, the other more suitable to the greater individualization in *Huasipungo*.

All *novelas indigenistas* necessarily find some means of making the Indian's state of separation a part of the reader's experience. Since the root of the problem is the peripheral existence of the Indian with respect to the social organization, a sense of this condition is basic to the novel. In *El resplandor* (1937), Mauricio Magdaleno uses a comparison of the Indians with the arid land they inhabit. He makes the point with descriptive adjectives and through characterizations, somewhat generalized, that emphasize the dogged persistence of the will to live. Magdaleno is more interested in prose style than most authors of this kind of novel, and his experiments with stream of consciousness and with neologisms suggest that these techniques will be an important factor in setting forth the reality of the Indian. Actually, they contribute much less than the organization of the narrative contributes. Magdaleno sets the misery of the Indian settlement against the fertility of a neighboring hacienda. By narrating the history of the hacienda's masters, retrospectively, he develops a countertheme of endurance, which also refers to belonging to the land. The strength of the hacienda tradition intensifies the feeling of separateness and hopelessness that we feel for the Indians. Then Magdaleno develops another contrast—this one in present time rather than in historical perspective. This novel is postrevolutionary, like *El indio*, and there is a possibility that political commitment may lessen the agony of the miserable people. They do in fact become tools of a politician who uses them mercilessly. Although Magdaleno's novel is not completely devoid of hope, such glimmers as remain hardly indicate a real solution.

Two other *novelas indigenistas* of this period take a rather different approach by entering the Indian world: *La serpiente de oro* (1935) by Ciro Alegría and *Yawar fiesta* (1940) by José María Arguedas. Both novels indicate a trend that this particular theme has followed in more recent years—to enter into the Indian world rather than look at it from outside. The Peruvian critic Alberto Escobar enhances the experience of Alegría's novel by emphasizing awareness of men who have an uncommon relationship with nature.[1] The fact that they are Indians is less important. By trade, they are *balseros*, raftsmen, on the Río Marañón. This river is more than just a part of the life of the people who live near it and by it; it is a character in the novel—and rightly so because it is, in effect, a member of the community. Life here is full of hazards and hardships, as seen from the standpoint of the outside world. However, readers who persist in seeing Alegría's novel this way do so because they insist on maintaining a predetermined expectation. It is far better to surrender to the novelist's basic narrative technique.

This fundamental device is the invention of a narrator who comes to the village as a stranger, then gradually comes to belong to the culture. The reader shares with the narrator this condition of outsider. If we continue the process of identification with the narrator, we appreciate the native culture as one in which the man-nature relationship emerges from complementary roles, rather than from polarities. This reaction to the novel depends more on characterization of the narrator than on the characterization of others in the novel. There are moments in the story when the narrator may not seem authentic, and fullest appreciation depends on the reader's ability to suspend such negative reactions. A similar problem exists in *Yawar fiesta* because Arguedas seems to feel himself a part of the Indian world. He invites us to participate as outsiders. The next step, almost immediate, is very difficult because the omniscient narrator is obviously not really an outsider. His use of Indian words, the special quality of his narrative style, and his description of what the town really is, as contrasted with what a stranger sees—all these factors tend to identify the narrator with the Indian community.

113

His prose style has two fundamental characteristics: rhythmic repetition and an ingenuous simplicity that may reflect the indigenous culture but is more suggestive of a sensitive child than of exoticism. Therefore, it is the reader who feels foreign to the narrator and the circumstance. However, there is a third step that reveals a disconcerting ambivalence on the part of the narrator. After a considerable introductory chapter that pictures the town and identifies the narrator as belonging to the Indian world, he suddenly withdraws from it: "When the Indians look and speak that way, a different hope shines in their eyes, their true souls reveal themselves. They laugh aloud, perhaps they also rage inside."[2] The narrator certainly feels apart from the Indian reality at this moment.

The problem of landownership turns into an octopuslike theme in Spanish American fiction. In the first place, it is one aspect of the *indigenista* novel. The injustice is more than a matter of economics; it involves the human sense of belonging. However, the complications do not stop there, because the sense of belonging evokes folkloric references and even the traditional theme of rural life against the corruption of urban living. The range of novels touching these aspects of the basic theme runs from the *indigenista* type to works by novelists of the Mexican Revolution and also to intensely regionalist works in which *costumbrismo* is the dominant factor.

Enrique Amorim's *El paisano Aguilar* (1934) expresses doubt with regard to the feasibility of ranching as a way of life in Uruguay. The narration is entirely third-person omniscient and this technique enhances the case-history tone of the book. The basic communication depends on a condition suggested by the name of the ranch, El Palenque (hitching post). Amorim's protagonist returns from the city to take over the family ranch. He readjusts his way of thinking to conform, more or less, to his new situation. However, the only reward is a certain amount of prestige. Economically, Aguilar goes from bad to worse. Every avenue of escape is closed; even in his attempt to save himself by rustling cattle, a flood thwarts him and keeps him on El Palenque. Decay, loss of ambition, spiritual drifting are the only possible results.

Two factors are operative in the reader's experience of *El paisano Aguilar*. The presentation of the central character as a rancher returned from the city suggests the theme of corrupt city versus

114

salutary country, especially when it becomes apparent that Aguilar has to relearn his rural frame of reference. This theme is an old reliable one in Spanish American fiction. In part, it represents nostalgia for a disappearing world. However, the second important factor in Amorim's novel is Aguilar's inability to extricate himself. This second factor underscores a problem to be solved by society; the first refers to a kind of myth that is part of the process of cultural identification.

The problem of landownership in the context of economic change is naturally most apparent in works by novelists of the Mexican Revolution. The familiar term "novel of the Revolution" must be used very cautiously with respect to the novels of protest published in Mexico between 1934 and 1940. They refer not to the battles, but to the aftermath. Mariano Azuela deals with the agrarian reform in two novels: *San Gabriel de Valdivias* (1938) and *Avanzada* (1940). Both novels are designed to show the program's failure— not for the lack of well-meaning theory, but through an abundance of individual human failings. The novelist forsakes the vanguardist techniques of some of his earlier work and is intent on the clear revelation of his disgust.

The Revolution, in the 1930s, had acquired a historical personality and could be perceived as a whole rather than as a fragmented series of rebellions. It was also the epoch of Lázaro Cárdenas, the most radical of the postrevolutionary presidents. This situation invited evaluation of what the Revolution had accomplished. Gregorio López y Fuentes's *Mi general* (1934) offers a commentary on the new society that recalls the career of Demetrio Macías in *Los de abajo*. The protagonist of *Mi general* is a rural man who becomes important during the Revolution, but lacks the sophistication to maintain the same level of relative power after the fighting is over. The novel uses a first-person, autobiographical frame; however, in this novel as in Azuela's, the communication is direct and obvious, with few overtones that might add to the experience of the work. The economic problem and the sense of belonging to the land become intimately related.

Somewhere on the periphery of this complex made up of the economic and psychological implications of the land problem, we find some regionalistic fiction that tends toward the folkloric. Rómulo Gallegos's *Cantaclaro* (1934) is almost an anthology of

From *Don Goyo* to *Todo verdor perecerá* (1934–1940)

Venezuelan legends, popular sayings, and history. Bernardo Arias Trujillo's *Risaralda* (1935) is interesting because of its emphasis on black culture. The author's prose style is rather declamatory, in spite of an original promise of a cinematographic technique.[3] At a time when the cinema could be expected to exert an influence on Spanish American fiction, Arias Trujillo seems to have glimpsed the possibility without discovering how to develop it. The most interesting novel of this kind—probably because it is more introspective—is Eduardo Zalamea Borda's *Cuatro años a bordo de mi mismo* (1934). This book is the journey, recounted in first person, of a youth from Bogotá who comes to know the coastal Guajira area and gradually becomes involved with the people of that area. It is his transition into manhood. The novel involves a combination of learning with contemplation; or to put it another way, there is an outside experience of perceiving folkloric elements that belong to the narrator's world and the inside experience of his contemplation of himself. These introspective passages can be fairly tiresome, especially early in the book before the narrator really establishes a relationship with the people. Fortunately, he controls enough narrative techniques to keep the book moving. One particular device, used in mood or atmosphere passages, is a kind of repetition that picks up the last word, or one of the last words, from one sentence and uses it as the first word of the next sentence. Often used in the description of a scene, this line of repetition gives the passage a special phonetic structure, and the effect is something like a darkened line in a drawing. Regional exoticism is more intense on account of it, naturally. In addition, Zalamea Borda enhances this sense of the unusual by a technique that communicates the narrator's enthusiasm—a list of the characteristics of people in an almost breathless sequence.

One damaging technique relates to the contemplative passages. The narrator indulges in self-questioning that tends to remove him from the scene of the novel and place him by the side of the reader. The compensating factor is the growing relationship with the people. What he says about Indians and blacks is one man's discovery. Clearly his experience helps him identify himself, and it is similar in one particular way to all successful adventures in the folkloric-rural, including some of the *novelas indigenistas*—he sees the contrast between simple men and technological civilization.

116

Novels dealing with urban problems may be described better by reference to a tone of general dissatisfaction than by calling them novels of protest or proletarian novels. The expression of proletarianism is mitigated by the circumstances of developing economies where the level of industrialization varies from place to place. Among the several types of novels that belong in this general category, one requires special attention because of its theme rather than because of its technique: *Puros hombres* (1938) by Antonio Arráiz. The author was imprisoned during the last years of Juan Vicente Gómez, dictator of Venezuela for more than a quarter of a century before his death in 1935. The book is an account of life in prison, and it makes no attempt to hide the author's indignation. Protest as such is more strongly present in this novel than in works dealing with the social organization, and *Puros hombres* is far from alone in Spanish American letters as a protest against political imprisonment. The theme almost constitutes a subgenre. There is—or was—a note of minor-key optimism about *Puros hombres* because the dictatorship was over and the novel was published in Venezuela. Unhappily, the retrospective view informs us that only a few years passed before another dictatorship was in control.

In the realm of economic protest—rather than political protest— José A. Osorio Lizarazo is one of the most committed. In *La cosecha* (1935), the scene is rural—the world of the coffee growers. However, *Hombres sin presente* (1938) is entirely urban. It is a defense of the laborer, an explanation of the power to strike, and an attack on white-collar pride. The narration is as obvious as any novelist could be expected to make it. Using traditional realist techniques, the narrator describes people and then sets them in motion. The same didactic tone and technique are found also in *El criminal* (1935), a semidocumentary account of the characteristic course of syphilis. The case history is novelized to a limited extent by parallel degeneration of the protagonist's health and relationships with others. At times the third-person narrator gives way to his protagonist's musings and imagination.

Osorio Lizarazo's novels are clear examples of work produced by the proletarian impulse to write for the good of the people. However, the standard idea of a proletarian novel requires a more complicated plot and more specific ideology. *Los hombres oscuros*

(1938), by Nicomedes Guzmán, conforms more closely to this standard. The novel develops along three story lines: scenes among the humble people of the barrio (including remnants of a rural heritage although the setting is urban), the theory and practice of labor unionization, and the love affair of Pedro and Inés. Pedro, the protagonist, is the unifying factor. He brings the three lines together principally in his contemplative passages. Guzmán is capable of using first-person narration very convincingly. He does so in these contemplative passages and also at the beginning of the novel where the narrator, a shoeshine boy, describes his situation and even uses an immediate present like the narrative voice of some much more innovative novels: "I am striding along on my way to work."[4]

Although this stylistic technique begins to incorporate the reader into the novel, it really is not exploited, and *Los hombres oscuros* becomes strongly expository. In the preliminary pages (dedication, quotations, introductory note, etc.) much is made of the author's being a man of the people, tough, realistic, and willing to deal with matters as they really are. The scenes of the barrio are sketches of customs and are, in fact, fairly strong as to theme and tone. There is a fiesta, but there are also a death, a murder, and a typhus epidemic. An episode of children watching copulating dogs adds a touch of innocent vulgarity. The labor-unionization line of the story produces most of the ideology. The crusade acquires some historical perspective when a Marxist labor organizer recalls meetings held in 1920. It takes on a broad social meaning because the novel emphasizes two principles of public morality—the need for temperance in the use of alcohol and the idea of the faithful woman, seen mainly in Inés.

The European immigrant in urban society appears in Max Dickman's *Madre América* (1935). The novel deals satirically with the spectrum of Argentine society, using types rather than well-developed characterization. However, Dickman also knows the value of interior monologue, and he experiments with other techniques that enhance the novel's scepticism.

The discovery of petroleum in Spanish America produced a special kind of protest novel in works like *Huasteca* (1939) by Gregorio López y Fuentes, *Mancha de aceite* (1935) by César Uribe Piedrahita, and *Mene* (1936) by Ramón Díaz Sánchez. Presentation of the problem has several general characteristics. It contains a protest against economic imperialism on the part of the United States. This protest is intensified by a sense of having been sold out by a compatriot. There is also, deep within the protest, a kind of culture shock caused by the invasion of exploiters from the United States. The novel by Díaz Sánchez strives mightily to turn these concerns into a viable fiction, and succeeds to some extent.

The title of the novel is a Venezuelan word for petroleum, *Mene.* Its effect is like giving a novel in English the title *Oil.* The novel itself is not as starkly dramatic as the title might indicate. Díaz Sánchez begins with a passage of unidentified dialogue, made up of voices in the crowd. The purpose is to communicate a feeling of camaraderie, regional folksiness, a time of fiesta. The general passage fades into the specific reality of opening a new street in the town, Cabimas. The author continues to use the device of unidentified dialogue as a means of maintaining awareness of the town as a whole. This is the trap—an image of the town as friendly and unspoiled. He sets the trap right at the beginning and keeps it operative. The exploiters of petroleum intrude upon this placid scene, and the narrator compares the invasion to the coming of the Spaniards at the time of the Conquest. There is no plot line that carries all the way through the novel. Several different episodes illustrate the exploitation and cultural conflicts provoked by the presence of the oil company. The episodes are not woven together, but the narrator ties up the ends by referring to some of the people at the beginning and also at the end of the novel.

A theoretical line between the socially committed novel and the artistic novel is handy for purposes of generalization, but in specific cases the line twists so vigorously we cannot hold on to it. There are actually four factors operating along this line: the social problem, identification of the New World experience, cosmopolitanism (concern with universal human values), and technical innovation. No two of these factors are dependent on each other, nor are any two mutually exclusive. Common to all types of novel during this period is a feeling of dissatisfaction with social values, whether in terms of problems of justice or in terms of individual identity and personal relationships. In this connection, it is impossible to overlook José Rubén Romero's *La vida inútil de Pito Pérez* (1938), even though the novel's idiosyncrasies set it apart from general classification.

Romero uses the picaresque mode to produce an extreme, sometimes amusing, example of disenchantment with the system. Some of Pito's acts are morally wrong from the standpoint of society, but justifiable in the context of his nonconformism. He cannot conform, because he finds no fundamental honesty. Some of the scenes are boldly satirical and clearly humorous; others follow the narrow line of tragicomedy. Since what we know of Pito reaches us through an invented narrator, we tend to observe his disquisitions rather than experience their cause. The thought-provoking aspects of this novel coincide with a number of essays of this period that take account of the position of man in America, by writers like Eduardo Mallea, Ezequiel Martínez Estrada, and Samuel Ramos.

This kind of introspective writing, since it is clearly related to the New World experience, provides a link between the two large groups of novels during this period; that is to say, between the books that deal primarily with social problems and those that deal with the general human condition. One unusual satirical novel— unusual in its attack on Lima's country-club set in the 1920s—also contributes to this link: José Díez Canseco's *Duque* (1934).

Duque satirizes Anglophiles specifically, but its more general target is the group that thinks everything good must come from Europe. The satire does not create the impression of an outraged writer, but of a disgusted one. The tone is teasing, rather than moralistic. The beautiful people are morally degenerate. The narrator is omniscient, uses a great deal of dialogue and a telegraphic style that moves the story rapidly. The story itself has the quality of a cartoon. It is the very superficiality of the novel that makes it move. Ultrasophistication satirizes itself.

Thinking in terms of novels that are the best examples of introspective concern for the human condition, it is helpful to think of a line created, during this period, by the works of María Luisa Bombal, Jaime Torres Bodet, Eduardo Mallea, and Juan Carlos Onetti. Closely related, but slightly apart for one reason or another, are works by Enrique Labrador Ruiz, Juan Filloy, and Vicente Huidobro. Bombal's *La última niebla* (1935) is fairly typical of this line of development.

The novel tells the story of the protagonist and her fantasized lover. Amado Alonso, in a prologue to the 1941 edition, explains that we see the reality that surrounds the protagonist only as she sees it,

120

that there are no settings as in the realist or naturalist novel.[5] He takes this characteristic to be the factor that involves the reader. Indeed it is extremely effective, especially when the first-person narrative operates in the absolutely immediate present, effecting the combination of novel time with reader time. However, there are several other techniques of equal importance in the experience of the novel. Nothing seems normal. The movement of the characters in the reality passages is stiff, unnatural; and this condition dulls the contrast with the dream passages. The mist (*niebla*) is a leitmotif that activates the fantasy. The development of the story is marked by it, and the end is entirely dependent on an alteration in the function of the mist. Rather than a signal of change, it has become a sign of a static condition. The protagonist, resigned to old age and a broken dream, refers to herself and her husband: "Around us the mist gives everything an appearance of absolute immobility" (p. 85). Her fantasized reality develops in counterpoint with an externally observed reality: her husband's sister-in-law, Reina, and Reina's lover. There are three corresponding stages in the fictional development of the two realities. The protagonist's night of love corresponds to a scene with Reina and her lover in the parlor of the protagonist's country home. Later, the protagonist thinks she sees her lover, but is really not sure. This episode corresponds to an interim event in the objective world when Reina does not come to the tenth wedding anniversary celebration of the protagonist and her husband. Finally, the protagonist's suicidal thoughts and subsequent resignation correspond to Reina's suicide attempt. The factor that cannot be well described in analysis is the overlapping of reality and fantasy—or to put it another way, the planes of reality. For example, when the protagonist is uncertain about whether she has seen her fantasized lover a second time, the uncertainty places this fantasy episode on a different level from the primary fantasy.

The cast is small and the focus very fine. That is the case generally in novels of this kind. Torres Bodet's *Primero de enero* (1934) confines the development of the novel to a single character and a single day. The novel deals solely with Gonzalo Castillo's desire to renew his life, to be something different from what he is. The author makes good use of a third-person narrative voice that speaks from the point of view of the protagonist. Gonzalo Castillo discovers that he cannot change his identity, because he is already identified definitively by

121

others. He does see the possibility of renewal by increasing his awareness of other people.

Juan Carlos Onetti's first published novel, *El pozo* (1939), focuses down as closely on a character as is possible.[6] Readers generally agree that the protagonist, who is a writer, is an extension of Onetti rather than an invention by him. The extension is, of course, an invention in itself. Hardly anything happens in the novel beyond the protagonist's anguished doubts about why he should do anything at all. The dull, pointless pessimism of the novel—more than pessimism, the lack of decision—raises the possibility that *El pozo* actually goes beyond the revelation of an individual human circumstance and relates itself to Uruguay's atrophying society. The dictatorship of Gabriel Terra ended in 1938 and the commission form of government was reinstituted. Both Onetti and a very different kind of novelist, Enrique Amorim, suggest a society that is anything but dynamic. We may speculate, in a similar way, about the possible relationship of Torres Bodet's *Primero de enero* to the institutionalization of the Mexican Revolution.

One of the most interesting novels of the period, especially with regard to technique, is Juan Filloy's *Op Oloop* (1934). It is one of those works whose impact cannot possibly be estimated, because, in spite of not being well known, it has always had a small and very dedicated audience.[7] The story shows the disintegration of a personality within a period of twenty hours. The chapters, if they may be called that, are indicated by clock time, in boldface type, at appropriate intervals in the narrative. The opening time reference is 10:00 A.M.; the last episode takes place at 5:49 A.M. the next morning. These references to time do not actually separate segments of the narrative from each other. They are simply indented along the left margin. Their effect is immediate and important because they are the first indication of the orderliness of Op Oloop's mind.

He is a Finnish resident of Buenos Aires. The first of four major steps in the novel's development reveals the regularity of his habits, his exquisite taste, his belief that everything fits a pattern that is equal to a harmonious whole. He accepts the principle of man's rationality. Filloy narrates basically in the third person but also uses interior monologue, which establishes very effectively an ambivalent quality in the protagonist. Beneath the perfect façade lurks an in-

122

voluntary rebelliousness. This interior problem becomes intense, in the reader's reaction, because Filloy uses typographical distortion to make the point. An expression of impatience ("I don't have a night available.") grows in type size in a sequence of three repetitions (p. 33). They communicate the developing tension of Op Oloop's impatience. The omniscient narrator makes clear that this typographical change represents what is happening inside the protagonist, not what he is saying. Then the same sentence is printed backward, as if seen in a mirror, and in capital letters. Still in capitals, it then appears divided into syllables and with the order of the syllables changed. Still another appearance follows, maintaining the illogical order of syllables, but now as the mirror image of the next-to-last version. Tension has changed to confusion.

The second narrative step involves the protagonist's love for Franziska. It should be a perfect love, but it persists in overstepping the bounds of reasonable idealization. In this part, Op Oloop has conversations of a fantasized or transcendent nature with his beloved. They communicate "telesthesically" (p. 109). Few writers compare with Filloy in language facility. He is in the Joycean tradition and clearly a precursor of Cortázar, Cabrera Infante, and other more recent novelists.

The third narrative step is a banquet given by Op Oloop for his friends. It is filled with philosophical and artistic allusions, erotic humor, language play and corresponding number play. Much of it is humorous, but intercalated is the growing confusion of the host. Here emerges a kind of philosophical basis for what is happening to Op Oloop. In a rational world, it seems absurd that love, an irrational state, should be the only means of making life a fulfilling experience (p. 174). This attitude is a partial statement of the ambivalence communicated through the novel, and it leads into the fourth narrative step, which culminates in the protagonist's suicide.

There is some justification for saying that Argentina naturally produced more sophisticated literature during this period than any other Spanish American country. Its ties with Europe were close. The literary tradition was robust, and Argentine activity during the vanguardist years of the 1920s was outstanding. Nevertheless, it is difficult to reconcile some apparent contradictions. For instance, María Luisa Bombal published *La última niebla* in Buenos Aires. Amado Alonso, in his introduction to the first Chilean edition, almost a decade later, chastises the Chilean literary world for being too backward to accept Bombal's novel. This view makes Buenos Aires look like a mecca for the innovative writer. On the other hand, Filloy was in Paris when he wrote *Op Oloop,* and published the novel privately in Argentina. There are, of course, many possible explanations involving personalities and literary feuds or prejudices, as well as authentic cultural trends. Certainly narrative experimentation was widespread throughout Spanish America, though its intensity varied greatly from place to place, and it also took many forms. Enrique Labrador Ruiz continued writing the fiction he referred to as *novela gaseiforme.* His *Cresival* (1936) is less innovative than the earlier *Laberinto de si mismo,* but it is of the same general kind.

Vicente Huidobro's *Cagliostro* (1934) is important because he recognizes the possibilities of cinematographic techniques in fiction.[8] It would be silent film in this case. In fact, the dialogue is synthesized and abrupt, just like the dialogue at the bottom of a screen. His scene changes achieve a degree of simultaneity. The theme, however, is far from psychological. It concerns a magician of sorts, more than three thousand years old, with remarkable powers for making gold and enlarging jewels. The story denies ordinary concepts of time and space and is closer to science fiction than to psychological study. The narrator makes a case for the reality of imagination.

The most prominent literary figure during the period 1934–1940 was Eduardo Mallea. His first works of fiction appeared during the vanguardist years of the 1920s; then a number of years passed before he published two relatively minor works in 1935. One was a novel, the other an essay—a suitable combination because he has continued to write in both genres, and with an intermingling of the characteristics of both. Mallea is interested in the novelization of the human spirit, and he has carried out this project within an Argentine context, searching for what is authentically human. In 1936, he published a volume of related stories, *La ciudad junto al río inmóvil,* which are penetrations into the human life of the city. *Historia de una pasión argentina* appeared in 1937. It is a spiritual-intellectual autobiography which asks many of the questions raised generally throughout the western world during the years between the two world wars. It was widely read by young intellectuals throughout

Spanish America. In 1938, Mallea published *Fiesta en noviembre*, a novel well known for its intercalation of two separate stories. *La bahía del silencio* (1940) is one of his most widely read books. Some consider it a novelistic treatment of the themes in *Historia de una pasión argentina*. It is a massive book and is a search for some constant in the human experience and for a way to put that constant into words.

Much of the commentary on Mallea's novels tends to interpret the ideas contained in them, rather than deal with their artistic qualities. There is plenty of reason for this emphasis since the characteristics of essay and fiction intermingle in his work. The basis of much interpretation is Mallea's distinction between a "visible Argentine" and an "invisible Argentine." Stated with flagrant oversimplification, this difference refers to superficial human relationships as contrasted with deep human concern—the kind that makes an individual feel ultimately inadequate with regard to his role in life. The visible Argentine is the veneer of the society—the false but accepted values, the forms, the prejudices; the invisible Argentine seeks the most basic human values, knows the meaning of struggle and of anguish. The pessimism of Mallea's novels is generally recognized. As a matter of fact, some novels are much more pessimistic than others. However, in any of his novels, the meaning of pessimism comes through completely only if the reader understands that authentic life is a search rather than a discovery. The fact that Mallea raises questions without answering them has little to do with the value of his work. The experience of his novels is the experience of the question itself.

Novelization, in the case of Mallea, includes commentary by a narrative voice that is committed to the anecdotal circumstance, but is not a participant in it. This aspect of his narration reveals the influence of the essay form. Some readers react to it as a kind of editorializing that interrupts the flow of the narrative. At times the narrator's style becomes aphoristic, and that is when his commentary is most distracting, because we take time to ponder the meaning of the saying. It is important to recognize, however, that the author considers this kind of narrative voice a valuable and legitimate technique in the creation of fiction. He believes it is possible to *narrar definiendo* (narrate defining), making a unity of action and

125

knowledge.[9] *La bahía del silencio* is one of the better examples of the technique.

The narrative structure is based on three stages in the life of a writer, Martín Tregua: youthful commitment, experience in Europe, and return to Buenos Aires. The details of the story are as typical as the outline. The young writer and his friends publish an ephemeral magazine; the period in Europe reveals the alienated condition of many of Tregua's acquaintances; the return to Buenos Aires brings on a period of disillusionment because the protagonist cannot discover the Argentina he expected to find. Mallea uses a first-person narrator, the protagonist himself, who addresses a "you"— an elegant, sophisticated woman whom he knows only by sight and by reputation. He reacts to her physical appearance and to what he considers indications of deep sensitivity. She is a symbol of the solid values Mallea finds in the more desirable aspect of Argentina.

The feeling of silence (lack of communication) that is an important part of the experience of the novel derives from the protagonist's addressing himself to the woman, and also from the many conversations in which Tregua himself is always the central character. The conversations often deal with art, literature, and politics. Tregua's friends talk with him, but hardly ever with each other. The effect, therefore, is often expository; that is, the dialogue has an essayistic quality. The success of this technique ("narrate defining") depends on the reader's taking one of two attitudes: either to surrender to the author's concept of the technique, or to read the novel primarily as literature of ideas. The latter attitude seems to be quite common, and it has produced many ardent admirers of Mallea. Its drawback is that it obscures the novelist's aesthetic process. Where his art is allowed to function, much of the message comes to the reader through carefully worked out associations, a phenomenon that is entirely in accord with the experience of questions rather than of answers. Communication by association is the effect of the unusual structure of *Fiesta en noviembre*, one of Mallea's better novels, judging it artistically, and one of the more interesting reflections of the world of its time.

The novel is easily recalled by the common description of its alternation of two entirely unrelated stories. This observation evokes an almost ritual association with William Faulkner's *The Wild Palms*, an intercalation of two novelettes by techniques entirely

126

different from those of *Fiesta en noviembre*, and with equally different effects. Faulkner put together two works of presumably the same importance, alternating the five chapters of each. The psychological experience of one story is an inversion of the experience of the other. In *Fiesta en noviembre*, one story is clearly more fundamental than the other, the intercalation is not as symmetrical, and the secondary story becomes dominant right at the end.

The opening scene of *Fiesta en noviembre*, which takes place in Europe, is printed in italics. In approximately one page of narration we learn that some soldiers have come to a poet's house to take him away. Two details of the scene stand out: the soldiers' appearance is dirty, not carefully disciplined, and the poet clutches a piece of homemade white bread. His aura of essential humanity contrasts with the soldiers' condition of playing a role. Changing to ordinary typeface, the narration also changes scene. It is the Rague home in Buenos Aires, on the evening of a dinner party. Eugenia Rague, grande dame, descends the stairs. She fits her surroundings as surely as Mauricio Magdaleno's parched Otomí Indians fit the calcium-dry earth they live on. "On the last step she paused, one clawlike hand clutching her lorgnette, the other rigid on the dark rail of the stairs . . . Her eyes, cold, uncompromising, swept the twenty square yards of the Renaissance hall, seeking some dissonant detail, some alien note in the perfection of its order . . . Standing in the half-darkness, her lips moved soundlessly, enumerating her treasures . . . a huge tapestry depicting a hunt, the dark splendor of a candelabrum, statuettes of ivory and bronze, paintings, vases, glass coffers, bric-a-brac of every conceivable description."[10]

The scene set around Eugenia Rague establishes the tone of the basic story. The guests reveal their concept of sophistication. The conversation is arty, pseudointellectual, with an underpinning of prejudices and opportunistic anxieties. Two expressions of authenticity develop within this framework of pretentiousness. One of them, Marta Rague, the daughter of Eugenia, is synonymous with responsibility; the other is a painter, Lintas, who refuses to negotiate his stand on artistic validity. The communication between Lintas and Marta is typical of Mallea-created relationships in that it comes to no resolution, but is a profound experience for both people, and for the reader. The development of this basic story is broken four times by italicized insertions that continue the story of the poet.

127

There is no overt connection between the two stories. However, at one point Lintas tells Marta of an incident in Buenos Aires when a band of Argentine fascists severely beat a Jewish bookseller. *Fiesta en noviembre* achieves two levels of simultaneity. One is the suggested simultaneity of the two unrelated stories; the other is produced by the juxtaposition of episodes that occur during the time span of the dinner party.

When the party is over and Marta is alone again, the novel switches definitively to the story of the poet. The narrator repeats all the segments interspersed throughout the main story, then continues the account for several pages. He keeps on emphasizing the contrast between the soldiers and the poet, seen in the first passage of the novel. We learn that the locale is Europe. It ends with the execution of the poet. In this way, the secondary story really controls the mood of the novel at the end. The associations develop in the following order: authenticity versus role playing in the poet's story, role playing in Buenos Aires society, the longing for authenticity subordinated in Buenos Aires society, violence and injustice in Buenos Aires, and violence and injustice in the poet's story.

Fiesta en noviembre emerges from a time when civilization descended into the nether regions. The Spanish Civil War was a training ground for militarists who were to rip the world apart. It had a profound effect on Spanish American artists and intellectuals, and ultimately on Spanish American culture. Fascism grew and precipitated the Second World War. It was a time of mounting crisis for all Spanish America. There were Axis spies in several countries. In Colombia, their presence led to the reformation of the airline and the creation of AVIANCA in 1940. Of more serious political consequence, Presidente Eduardo Santos declared, in 1939, that Colombia would protect the Panama Canal, in spite of Jorge Eliécer Gaitán's advocacy of neutrality. This difference was an early instance of a political trend that ultimately led to *la violencia*. Mexico turned to the right economically, toward industrialization, when Manuel Avila Camacho followed Cárdenas as president in 1940. Mexican cooperation with the Allies was not seriously in question, but fascist influences did have to be controlled. In Argentina, fascist elements had been active even in the late 1920s. The crucial date in hemispheric politics was January 1942, when the United States asked for Latin American support against the Axis. Argentina preferred a neutral position, which actually favored the Axis, and held out at Río for a recommendation rather than a resolution. Chile supported Argentina at that meeting.

These political facts do not appear as such in the novel, of course. Nor does the period described in this chapter reach the year 1942. The fact is, however, that the problems of international politics were making the Spanish American novel look outward. Artistic awareness and narrative experimentation were sufficient, even during a period noted for social protest, to assure continuation of the novelist's transformation of reality.

CHAPTER 10

The Year of *Todo verdor perecerá* (1941)

Todo verdor perecerá is the quintessence of Mallea's portrayal of the unresponsive human; or, if we look at it from a slightly different angle, it is his clearest communication of the anguished search with no end. While the human condition created in this novel may be taken as an entirely personal phenomenon, it is much easier to believe that in some way it belongs to, or to some extent reflects, a more general cultural state. This possibility is certainly supported by the nihilism of Juan Carlos Onetti's *Tierra de nadie*, a novel whose title suggests the indifferent attitude of the Buenos Aires people it portrays. Because these novels have characteristics frequently associated with post–World War II developments, it is informative to examine the other novels published during the same year, as a kind of cross section of the novel at that time—the year that pinpoints this hemisphere's involvement in the war.

No novel of 1941 can be taken as a standard. *Todo verdor perecerá* may be the best known book of the year; however, we could argue that Ciro Alegría's *El mundo es ancho y ajeno* has enjoyed just as much fame. Its strong nativism, as a *novela indigenista*, is a far cry from the sophisticated view of America in the novels of Mallea and

Onetti. There is an equally great difference between the kind of human concern expressed in Mallea's novel and the specific concern for material welfare (social justice) in Carlos Luis Fallas's *Mamita Yunai* or in Enrique Gil Gilbert's *Nuestro pan*, another novel that deals with a specific group of workers—in this case, those in the rice paddies of Ecuador. Attitudes toward the social function vary from the nihilism of Onetti's characters to the dynamics of a changing society in Azuela's *Nueva burguesía* and Amorim's *El caballo y su sombra*. As for technique, the narrative voice varies from first-person autobiographical in *Mamita Yunai* to the virtual absence of a narrator in *Tierra de nadie*. Other technical devices show a steadily decreasing need for traditional plot development, with Mariano Azuela among the more innovative—a spot frequently occupied by this famous novelist of the Mexican Revolution, somewhat against his will. Although several of the novels are direct narratives of personal experience, the degree of fictionalization in many of them is considerable; and in this connection, it is important to note the appearance of Jorge Luis Borges's *El jardín de senderos que se bifurcan*. The title story in this collection is a combination of spy adventure and science fiction. It is by no means a novel, and the author never has written a novel, but his stories have been of inestimable influence on longer fiction because they assert the novelist's right to invent his world.

The text of *Todo verdor perecerá* is preceded by two epigraphs that are more functional than usual for such quotations. One is from Isaiah, the prophet, and it warns of a time when the land will be desert and "there is no green thing."[1] So much for the title of the novel, and probably the physical setting. Then the second epigraph immediately humanizes the prophecy by reference to man and suggests man's helplessness within his circumstance. The novel begins with a completely impersonal setting—a landscape scorched by drought and fire. Mallea makes the scene overwhelming by communicating a sense of endless distance and at the same time intensifying the sensation by reference to all the different objects before the eye. A repeated adjective, *blanco*, refers to each of these objects; and its simplicity tends to counterpoint Mallea's metaphors, which, given this modification, can function without jeopardizing the leanness of the passage.

With the first introduction of a person, Nicanor Cruz, the unsympathetic quality of nature turns into personality and corresponds to the irascible spirit of man. "On very rare occasions, after many weeks of waiting, the storm clouds would conspire in the atmosphere and ignite an angry hope in the heart of Nicanor Cruz."[2] The key words here are *conspire* (*confabular*), *ignite*, and *angry* (*colérica*). The clouds do not simply gather; they act with malice. The effect here is not to personify nature in the romantic fashion, but to reflect the way Nicanor Cruz feels about the clouds. To ignite is, of course, a natural association with a storm. However, it applies immediately, in this case, to the extraordinary condition of the man's hope, which is not pure hope, but the grudging hope of a man pushed to the limit. In this sentence, Mallea defines rather clearly the character of the man and his relationship with nature. The scene shifts to Agata, his wife, in the house preparing a meal. A half-witted farm hand, Estaurófilo, lurks on the periphery of the scene— a constant presence of possible violence that never materializes. Nicanor arrives. The relationship of husband and wife is characterized by their speaking in impersonal constructions, avoiding personal pronouns and so eliminating the possibility of intimate address. This fact is basic to the description of their relationship. It is as sterile as everything else. The only difference between the two is represented in Agata's afternoon walks—an act of searching, without definition but also without rancor.

With Agata observing Cruz, this strange man to whom she is linked, the narration enters a long flashback. It is initiated by Agata's memory, but the narrator is omniscient. He describes the past as it affected Agata, but knows things she could not have known. The flashback recalls her growing up in Ingeniero White, a suburb of Bahía Blanca. Her father was an immigrant physician, widowed and alcoholic. Certainly he was not a vicious man, but ineffective as a father and as a doctor. The characterization of this human failure is the principal method of showing Agata's youth. The flashback introduces Cruz, considered a good catch in those days; the wedding; and the fifteen years of married life prior to the novel's present time. The narrative manner, during the flashback, is rather more succinct than in other places. This compactness tends to remove it from the realm of actual experience, but Mallea's imagery creates interest in the people and elicits concern for what happens to them. In some of the most persuasive instances, he attributes the image to his character, though he remains as narrator. Soon after Agata first becomes aware of Cruz's interest in her: "Agata went indoors laughing, willing to forget it or jokingly talk it over with Delia. But as she went to her room, she sensed the physical presence of a door leading out of that closed house."[3]

Part one of *Todo verdor perecerá* could stand alone. The novel returns to the time of the opening scene, a period of discouragement after forty-four days of drought. When the rain finally comes, Nicanor Cruz gets wet and catches pneumonia. Agata permits him to die and she herself plans to die—both from exposure. Agata survives—the Agata who sensed the door and took the afternoon walks. Here ends part one.

The second part of the novel begins with a description of Bahía Blanca, where we find Agata. In a brief flashback—again initiated by Agata's memory but controlled by the narrator—we learn what happened between the night of crisis and Agata's coming to Bahía Blanca. It is significant in her characterization that she feels no desire to go to Ingeniero White. In Bahía Blanca, she finds a friend —a party-loving woman with just moderate scruples. Agata finds herself in an unfamiliar social whirl, and briefly she glimpses the possibility of establishing a genuine relationship, but that also turns false. During this period of hope, there is more dialogue than in any other part of the novel. It communicates the possibility of Agata's coming out from her shell. With this exception, the style is like the style of part one. The narrator tells us about Agata and comments occasionally from a position that some readers consider too removed. Actually, Mallea-the-narrator uses three degrees of distance with respect to his character. On one occasion, for example, Agata considers her situation soon after coming to Bahía Blanca. First, the narrator is very close to Agata, even approaches interior monologue. She observes herself in a mirror, bites her lip to bring some life to the image. "Everything that could be taken as her adversary seemed to materialize in her very own face. Was she going to say something to herself sometime?" The narrator, asking the question, is almost the same as the protagonist. She herself could well be asking the question. Then, immediately, the narrator moves away to a position where he is obviously talking about Agata. "She was disgusted with herself and what she wanted was to give herself as soon as possible to someone else so she might be free from her own self."

133

Obviously, the narrator has moved far from interior monologue. It is inconceivable that Agata would say this. In the third position, the narrator moves from the individual situation of Agata to a general reference: "We end up resembling what we hate."[4] The shift seems more natural in this case, which involves three steps, than in a situation where the narrator moves directly from the first position to the third. This last narrative position is the one that often evokes an unfavorable reader reaction.

When the illusion of a relationship is shattered, Agata finally makes it to Ingeniero White, and her visits there become regular. They are like the afternoon walks on the *estancia*. At the end of the novel, the poor woman, apparently demented, invites the cruel attentions of some street urchins who pester her as if they were furies unleashed against her. Totally disoriented, she finds herself at her old house. Nothing opens a path, not even the ironic presence, on a nearby church, of the legend "I am the Way, the Truth, and the Light." After a period of silence, Agata "got up suddenly, as if summoned by a scream and, without knowing or caring where she was going, started running against the darkness" (p. 175). Again it is the Agata of the imaginary door and of the afternoon walks.

The characterization of Agata develops steadily on the basis of that first knowledge of her on the *estancia*. That is where the novel begins. The fact that she returns to the scene of her childhood suggests a circling narrative structure that is not the case. The childhood of Agata appears in a flashback and adds to the characterization that has already been established. The development of *Todo verdor perecerá* is a matter of intensification.

If the inhabitants of Onetti's *Tierra de nadie* ("No man's land") are less anguished than Nicanor and Agata Cruz, it is because they care less. Indeed, this no man's land deserves the name not because nobody can hold it, but because nobody wants it. Harss and Dohmann quote Onetti as saying: "I paint a group of people who may seem exotic in Buenos Aires, but are nevertheless representative of a generation . . . The fact is that the most important country in the young South American continent has started to produce a type of morally indifferent individual who has lost his faith and all interest in his own fate . . . Let no one reproach the novelist for having undertaken the portrait of this human type in the same spirit of indifference."[5] It would be appropriate to add a further plea, asking

134

that the novelist not reproach us for reading his novel with the same spirit of indifference, and probably without finishing it.

There are indications in *Tierra de nadie* of the novelist to come (in *El astillero*, for example), but Onetti was still groping uncertainly when he wrote this book. He deals with a dozen or so characters (reminiscent of the characters in the novels of Roberto Arlt) in a multiplicity of relationships. They meet in bars, in hallways, in apartments where they appear looking for someone else. They become friends, enemies, lovers, or any combination of the three. A relationship may end as abruptly and as fortuitously as it began. The narration is made up of segments that skip from one set of characters to another. Unlike some segmented novels, *Tierra de nadie* does not employ the segments to create a multifaceted awareness of a particular situation. The novel has no particular situation; therefore, the result of the segmentation is a sense of chaos, which is very likely what the author wished to create. The trouble is that his reader is not likely to care whether it is chaotic or not; and that is where Onetti's game backfires. Or maybe that is part of his game.

In the early episodes of the novel, it appears that a man named Aránzuru will be a unifying factor. He appears frequently, but the segments do not add up to a whole. Another character, Casal, gives the novel a kind of philosophical base by suggesting that he and his companions have nothing to hold on to. He admits that one or another may hold on briefly to something that has happened, but for no more than a few days.[6] This feeling is a fair description of the reader's experience with *Tierra de nadie*.

In terms of developing narrative technique, *Tierra de nadie* is of considerable importance—not because we can claim much success for Onetti, but because his interest in experimentation suggests possibilities that could enhance the communication of fiction. It was true in 1941, as it has always been true, that novels not centered on social justice were expected to be more innovative technically than their fellows. While there are obvious modifications to this proposition, it contains a substantial grain of truth. In large part, that truth depends on the assumption that experimentation in technique goes with the invention of the novelist's reality. Onetti does, in fact, invent, even though he points out that he is dealing with a very real generation. The influence of Jorge Luis Borges in the area of fictional invention acquires importance in 1941; and it would be also

very unjust to omit the name of another writer whose role was similar—Macedonio Fernández, whose *Una novela que comienza* was
first published in 1941. Its style is very similar to the one we have
already seen in *Papeles de Recienvenido*. The structure of this short
piece is that of an essay addressed to the reader about the narrator's
writing, with observations about two women he sees by chance. The
point that really matters here is that he needs to have one of the
women contact him so he can finish the novel. This trick of com-
posing about the composition becomes extremely important in more
recent novels, particularly because it refers to the whole matter
of inventing, the crux of creative art.

It would be absurd to say that *Todo verdor perecerá* and *Tierra
de nadie* are not committed novels. Clearly they show their concern
for a social problem; and though this problem may be significant beyond national boundaries, the two novelists obviously develop their
stories within a particular cultural context. The great difference between their novels and Ciro Alegría's *El mundo es ancho y ajeno* is
that the problems Mallea and Onetti deal with do not involve questions of social justice, and they do not specify identifiable social
groups who are victims of the problem. Alegría's novel—his most
widely known work—is basically the story of an Indian settlement,
Rumi. Problems of social injustice involve the settlement as such,
and also a number of its people who go out into the larger world.
In some passages, the novel communicates a sense of the Indians'
native dignity. Its general effect is to make readers feel that something should be done. This message very likely helped it win a prize,
awarded by Farrar and Rinehart, for the best Latin American novel.
The narrative structure of *El mundo es ancho y ajeno* is extremely
disjointed. Its major unifying element is an expanding protest
against injustice. This function is implicit in the title, which informs
us that the world is wide and belongs to somebody else. That is indeed a fair statement of the book's theme. Even the narrow world
of Rumi belongs to somebody else. However, if a reader does not
take titles very seriously, he may well be deceived by the first chapters of the novel where it seems that the narrative focus will be on
the village. As the novel develops, Rumi becomes the place from
which the structure emanates. The switch actually takes place when
the people of Rumi are despoiled of their land. At that point, the

outside world increases in importance. In a study of the effect of various narrative techniques in this novel, Alfonso González notes that the prose style changes at this point in the story.[7] He shows that the lyric passages belong for the most part to the early chapters of the novel, when the Indians can still live in peace and according to their own traditions. The picture of this life is idealized, rather Arcadian. Then the spell is broken when the white world intrudes, and the language becomes coarse, corresponding to the change in fortune.

The novel opens on a scene in which Rosendo Maqui, aged and wise headman of the community, is hunting down a snake of evil omen. The tone suggests the possibility of too much noble-savage decoration, but some reassurance comes when the narrator tells us that, if some of Rosendo Maqui's people had seen him, they would not have known what he was doing. This reassurance is doubly comforting because it indicates that we may possibly see things as the Indians see them. While the narrator doesn't exactly speak from within the Indian culture, he seems at least aware of the details. However, the narrative point of view turns out to be disturbingly inconsistent. It is basically third-person omniscient; but the narrator changes roles at will, shifting to "we" in order to comment editorially on what he is saying. In the first chapter, this editorial voice intervenes to express the opinion that Solomon is the world's most famous sage—this in justification of Rosendo Maqui's knowing who Solomon is. The author also uses the same voice to take issue with a characterization he has created, and even hides behind it to excuse himself for not penetrating more deeply into the inner reality of one of the characters. The effect of this apparent anxiety on the part of the narrator is that he practically pushes his own characters out of the way so he can enjoy the spotlight.

The opening chapters of the novel define the roles and relationships in the village. Then a chapter entitled "Juicio de linderos" (a legal determination of property lines) forecasts the dispersion of the people of Rumi. This chapter is interesting from a technical standpoint. It is highly fragmented and some of the narrative segments are chronologically simultaneous. The effect is to portray an alliance of the large landowner with the civil power, against the Indian. In fact, what happens to Rumi has all the characteristics of conquest, and, given the Arcadian setting of the first chapters, the association of this crisis with the Spanish Conquest of the New World is almost inevitable. The suggestion is not carried out, however, as it is in *El indio*.

The chapter called "El despojo" marks the dispossession of the lands of Rumi. The people seek a new place. Some go out into the world and suffer injustices in various contexts. From this point, it is apparent there is no structure within the work itself. What holds it together is the expanding role of injustice. One chapter deals with those who become outlaws; another deals with laborers in the mines; another with workers in the cultivation of *coca*; and still another with injustices suffered in the city. These paths do not cross; they radiate outward from what once was Rumi.

The novel reaches a point where there is a reconcentration of attention on the people of Rumi, now in Yanañahui. A native son returns and has some ability as a leader. He inspires the people to rebel, and they are virtually wiped out. The author's apparent anxiety is probably a reflection of his struggle for social justice. He had been an APRA partisan, suffered imprisonment, and was allowed to leave the country in 1933. It is reasonable to think, for example, that the vignettes of the prisoners, in the chapter that shows Rosendo Maqui in jail, are drawn from real life. On a different level of suggestion, the multiplicity of the areas of injustice probably reflects the concern among APRA partisans. Its effect on the novel is to change its emphasis radically. González very aptly points out that, after the Indians are deprived of Rumi, *El mundo es ancho y ajeno* ceases to be a *novela indigenista* and becomes a general novel of protest (pp. 64–65). It is consistently a didactic work, and that, too, intensifies its proletarianism.

Among the novels of 1941 that deal with possible social reform, Alegría's may well be the most proletarian, thanks to breadth of its emphasis. Azuela's *Nueva burguesía* deals with an appropriate locale and with suitable people, but his tone is satirical rather than fully sympathetic. It certainly does not tend to idealize the working man, as does the work of Nicomedes Guzmán, for example. *Nueva burguesía* is a series of sketches of the inhabitants of a *casa de vecindad* (a compound housing arrangement used by the urban poor in Mexico). The district is Nonoalco and the predominant occupation is railroading. The narration skips from one character to another with no apparent design. The only unifying element is the place where the people live. The incidents are not related to each other to form a plot. Characterization is never deep and tends toward caricature. To a considerable extent, this exaggeration of types reflects the author's displeasure with people for letting the modern world corrupt their values. In a larger sense, the novel reflects Azuela's disillusionment with the Revolution. He wanted people to have a better life, but in *Nueva burguesía* he shows new opportunities wasted on things that do not really improve the condition of the people—at least not according to Azuela's criteria. He is criticizing what has more recently come to be known as a consumer society.

Azuela's novel, in spite of its lack of a structural unifier, has coherence—a coherence of tone provided by the narrator's concerned disapproval. This effect maintains the reader consistently in the same position with respect to the novel's message. This position may be antagonistic; satire always runs that risk. However, there is enough solidly based humor (some picaresque types, for example) to win the confidence of many readers. It should be clear, in any case, that Azuela does not make fun of misfortune. He is merciless with all that appears to him to be stupid or dishonest.

Mauricio Magdaleno presents a very different view of Mexican society in *Sonata*. The protagonist is a writer, primarily a poet, who finds his integrity threatened by all segments of society. As a commentary on human behavior, Magdaleno's novel fits somewhere between the satirical tone of *Nueva burguesía* and the nihilism of *Tierra de nadie*. It never really comes alive, because he insists on an unremitting third-person narrative voice in a novel that desperately needs interiorization in the form of stream of consciousness or interior monologue. The absence of some technique of this kind is puzzling in view of Magdaleno's having experimented with stream of consciousness in an earlier work, *El resplandor*. We might suspect that *Sonata* was really written earlier though published later, as sometimes happens, but the date of composition is indicated as 1937–1938 at the end of the text. In any case, the closest approach to interiorization is some association of memories in one passage.[8] One other device is used extensively, but with limited success—references to music designed to create an atmosphere or correspond to an emotional state. The technique works reasonably well for readers who have a fairly sophisticated knowledge of music. One needs to know, for example, *La création du monde* by Darius Milhaud, should have an idea of what Erik Satie's music is like, and must recall the development of Beethoven's Ninth Symphony in some detail. A reader who has not listened to music to this extent, will gain nothing from the intended association. It will only seem pretentious.

Sonata's protagonist, Juan Ignacio Ugarte, lives through a series of disillusionments: with the relationships that exist in his own middle-class family, with his education, with his first love, with the business world and civil service, and with men of letters. He becomes involved with a Marxist group, takes part in an uprising, spends time in jail, and finally discovers that the movement's fearless leader has made a private compromise with the established party. Compromise is the ordinary act. Juan Ignacio's unwillingness to compromise robs him of success, but not of a sense of freedom. The narrator tells us about this conflict, but it never becomes an intimate experience.

The protest that is closest in spirit to *El mundo es ancho y ajeno* rings loud and clear in *Mamita Yunai*, by Carlos Luis Fallas. The novel contains two stories and two objects of protest: meaningless elections and economic exploitation. The title refers to the United Fruit Company ("Yunai" is a phonetic rendition in Spanish of "United"). The novel is narrated in the first person by the protagonist. The tone is, therefore, autobiographical, and there is good reason to think that the facts are as autobiographical as the tone.[9] The two stories are connected only by the presence of the narrator-protagonist.

The first story involves a trip by the narrator to a remote village to observe election procedures, as a member of the opposition party. It is possible that what he sees should not be called corrupt. The people of the village are Indians, and considerably less than well informed about the politics of their country. The representatives of the party in power maneuver them, get their votes, and sponsor a victory celebration that seems a lot more important to the electorate than the business of voting. There are several incidents that fatten this basic story. Mainly they deal with the opposition's attempt to keep the narrator from getting to the village in the first place, and

140

then with some of the village types. *Mamita Yunai* is, in part, a *novela indigenista*.

At the end of this experience, the narrator goes home. And that would be all if fate had not caused him to run into his old friend, Higinio, who used to work with him on a coastal banana plantation. This is where *la Yunai* comes in. The encounter provokes a flashback that starts with the narrator's youth and recounts his adventures as a *bananero*. Principally, the protest concerns an occasion when a paymaster refuses to pay due wages to Higinio, the protagonist, and a third friend. They have to accept a more dangerous job, the third friend is killed by a falling tree, and Higinio attacks the boss with a machete. That is why the narrator has not seen Higinio for so long. In a kind of epilogue, the narrator tells what has happened to him while Higinio was in prison.

There is not much to be said in favor of the joining of two stories. Mariano Azuela did something similar to *Avanzada*, and it didn't work any better for him than it did for Fallas. The fact is that we feel we have read not a single novel, but two separate ones. The combination should not be confused with the coherence achieved in *Nueva burguesía*, an effect which anticipates more recent writing in which apparent fragmentation turns out to have produced an unexpected sense of unity. Agustín Yáñez also does something like this in *Flor de juegos antiguos*. These are evocations of childhood— separate episodes that together communicate an ambience, almost reveal an identifiable personality. Here we are dealing with straws in the wind, however, anticipating a development in prose fiction that is to come later. Even though it is easy to describe a difference between *Avanzada* and *Nueva burguesía*, for instance, with respect to the effect of unity or disunity, it is far less simple to include a book like José Revueltas's *Los muros de agua* in the same description.

This first novel of Revueltas is another prison story. *Los muros de agua* is based on personal experience, but, unlike Fallas, Revueltas uses a third-person narrator. The author allied himself with leftist movements from his early teens, and at the age of twenty he was convicted of subversion and sentenced to a term in the prison of Islas Marías. These are islands off the coast of Mexico, and their use as a prison gives the novel its title, which means "walls of water." The book is, for the most part, a series of episodes about

141

the various prisoners. The stories begin on the train to the coast, and the first deals with the natural leader of the group. Of course, a flashback is needed to complete the presentation. Other flashbacks follow; but all the while, the basic story is moving forward in time, to the ship, to the island itself, and then to life in prison.

One of the more interesting aspects of *Los muros de agua* is that the problems and personalities of nonpolitical prisoners tend to obscure the fact that others are there for purely political reasons. A possible explanation of this emphasis is the familiar leftist desire to humanize the repugnant—that is, to emphasize the basic human qualities in people whose actions disgust those who condemn them. In spite of this, it seems that the author might have made more of the political issue. It is also interesting that Alfredo Pareja Díez-Canseco, in *Hombres sin tiempo* studiously avoided writing a political work. Although the author was imprisoned for political reasons, he makes clear in a preface to the novel that the fiction has no political intent.[10] He does not hide his political affiliation in the preface, but he invents a narrator who is imprisoned for a crime that has nothing whatsoever to do with politics. It is on this basis that the account of prison life grows.

The argument for change is far more generalized in such a presentation than it is in a novel like *El mundo es ancho y ajeno*. There probably is good reason for both types. Indeed, there is still another type, or aspect, of the novel of protest: a kind of novel in which change is inevitable. That is one of the aspects of the experience of *Nueva burguesía*. Whatever the narrator's attitude, changes are taking place in the society. The possibility of change in Alegría's novel seems all in the wrong direction. Undesirable change is forced on the people, and their struggle against it is frustrated. The problem is complicated by the fact that a native Indian tradition exists. Where that tradition is less important, change takes on a different aspect. It is often portrayed in an urban situation, but that is not necessarily the case. Enrique Amorim, for example, in *El caballo y su sombra*, deals with the restructuring of rural society.

The basic theme of the novel is the beneficial effect of European immigration. Its narrative structure depends on two important contrasts. One is the conflict between a traditional *estancia* and a farm run by a group of immigrants; the other is a class line between the landed aristocracy and the common people—a division which,

142

in the experience of this novel, encourages sterility. Relating these factors to each other is still another conflict seen through characterization: two brothers, Nico and Marcelo, represent traditionalism and change. They are not allegorical figures, but all their actions indicate diametrically opposed social views.

The narrator sets the character opposition at the beginning of the novel when Marcelo visits the *estancia* after having been in the city for many years. His expectations provide all the necessary background. Although the narrative point of view continues in the third person during the description of what Marcelo anticipates, it is closely related to Marcelo's position. There is a kind of rapport between him and the narrator, even though the narrator rarely comments.

The reason for the return of Marcelo is that he is in trouble in the city for aiding the illegal entry of refugees from Europe. Nico, on the other hand, finds his way of life threatened by the immigrant farmers close by. He considers himself king of the range; small farmers are inferior to him. He is the *macho* in every respect. The basic difference coincides with the traditional Latin American theme of urban progress against rural backwardness. The modern touches— automobiles, radios, refugees from Europe—do not change the basic theme.

Marcelo not only favors the immigrants, he is permissive with regard to class lines and sires a son by a peasant woman. This union has a parallel in a trick played on Nico by some of his ranch hands. They mate his prize stud (Don Juan, no less) with a pitiful nag. It is significant that both unions are illicit, and equally important that both are productive. The aristocratic unions made by Nico and by his horse are sterile. The system of contrast indicated by this parallelism is apparent throughout the novel and is reinforced by a characteristic of style that uses contrasting expressions in the same sentence, or close to each other.[11]

Marcelo returns to the city halfway through the novel, and the narrative then concentrates on the immigrant's farm and its troubles with Nico. Gradually they reach the point of crisis: Nico is indirectly responsible for the death of a baby of an immigrant couple, and the father kills Nico. Trimming the action to the essentials this way, Amorim's message probably seems about as subtle as a sledge hammer. Actually, the development of the novel shows a good deal

143

of finesse. The action of Nico that brought about the child's death, for example, is not the direct result of his conflict with the immigrants, but of a combination of many factors, some of them totally unrelated to the foreigners.

El caballo y su sombra is the closest to the standard idea of a nineteenth-century novel of all those published in 1941. Its author is an old-fashioned writer; even his social theories are the progressive ideas of an earlier generation, in spite of his updating them by reference to more modern situations. An appreciation of this year as a cross section must not overlook the fact that Juan Carlos Onetti, another Uruguayan, published *Tierra de nadie* the same year. Although contrasting themes among the various novels of 1941 are apparent enough, they are not very different from what we might expect on the basis of what has gone before. It is probably fair to say that eagerness to describe the New World experience is giving way to emphasis on social problems, in those novels that describe objective reality. However, the more interior novels seem to be giving a rather different view of the New World experience (*Todo verdor perecerá, Tierra de nadie,* and even *Sonata*). Obviously, narrative techniques have moved a long way from nineteenth-century realism. The newer techniques are still not very successful. In fact, it is sometimes impossible to tell whether a structural characteristic is a technique that did not work well, or the result of poor planning. In general, however, the indications are that the novel is in a transitional state in Spanish America by 1941, though its future would hardly have been predictable from that point.

CHAPTER 11

From *Todo verdor perecerá* to *El Señor Presidente* (1942–1945)

The landmark novels mentioned in the title given this chapter can be significant indicators only if they are viewed in a double perspective that includes characteristics of both past and future. We have seen, in the 1941 cross section, that there is no novel that can be considered a standard work that year. *Todo verdor perecerá* and *El mundo es ancho y ajeno*, two spectacularly different works, are also the two best known. *Todo verdor perecerá*, however, is the more significant in the eventual development of Spanish American fiction. Then, looking just past the period 1942–1945, we discover that *El Señor Presidente* is the first of several novels that mark the beginning of the "new novel" in Spanish America. The choice of Asturias's novel does not necessarily mean that it is the most important of the several highly significant works that appeared in successive years. It is simply the earliest of a very important group. The line of development that connects *Todo verdor perecerá* with *El Señor Presidente* involves five factors: (1) awareness of cultural identity, (2) freedom from nationalistic exclusivism, (3) interiorization in character portrayal, (4) exercise of the novelist's right to invent reality, and (5) technical experimentation designed to carry the experience of the novel beyond the limits of objective perception.

This line of development and the characteristics that identify it can be said to bridge the years 1942–1945; but the line is not exclusive, nor does it become so even during the remarkable development of the late 1940s. The line we describe is one way of identifying the mainline of Spanish American fiction in view of the characteristics it has acquired in the last quarter-century. The brief period 1942–1945 is by no means determinative. Indeed, it offers very little that is new. Reading the books of this period, we have the feeling of a holding action—the moment of pause before a happening. Four writers published first novels of interest: *El balcón hacia la muerte* (1943) by Ulyses Petit de Murat, *Babel* (1943) by Jaime Ardila Casamitjana, *Cada voz lleva angustia* (1944) by Jorge Ibáñez, and *Juyungo* (1943) by Adalberto Ortiz. Two writers published second novels that are notably different from their first works: *El luto humano* (1943) by José Revueltas and *Dámaso Velásquez* (1944) by Antonio Arráiz. A considerable number of novelists continued writing novels that are important among their complete works, but that do not indicate significant changes in the course of the novel as a genre. Their variety indicates a continuation of the broad spectrum seen during 1941. They include the *indigenismo* of López y Fuentes, the transcendent New Worldism of Aguilera Malta, the anguish of Onetti, the proletarianism of Nicomedes Guzmán, the psychological realism of Barrios, the contemplative search of Mallea. Narrative techniques tend strongly away from the traditional, in general. A few novels stay close to the traditional concept, but most of them experiment in some way. Agustín Yáñez published another volume of related stories; the presence of Borges was still felt in the realm of invention.

Juyungo is probably the most interesting of the first novels, because it combines the characteristics of a novel of protest with the protagonist's search for individual identity. It deals with the position of a black man in several social contexts, and the episodic structure is typical of many social protest novels. In this case, the novel is saved by the growing importance of the protagonist's search for an explanation of what he is supposed to do in the world, what he represents, how he fits in with others. The racial issue tends to become less important. Ascensión Lastre relates to blacks, to Indians, and to whites. "Juyungo" is a derogatory term used by Indians to refer to blacks. (Ascensión has both friends and enemies among Indians.)

Ortiz precedes the action of each chapter with a section of poetic prose called "Eyes and ears of the jungle." The effect of these pieces is not consistent. They tend to communicate a sense of determinism—that there is something behind the actions of men that is more persistent than they. However, the mood changes somewhat from one to another, enough to make the reader notice but probably not understand the difference. The story of Ascensión begins when he is ten or twelve, so his search for meaning is related to his growing into manhood. Oversimplifying somewhat, we may say that social protest in the novel comes through most forcefully in the protagonist's search for work, episodes dealing with sexuality are the best revelation of his personal quest. There is, of course, no clear dichotomy in the novel. Racial awareness is a strong factor in the sexual interests of Ascensión and his friends. The white woman is desirable because she is forbidden; the black woman because her feminine qualities are considered superior.

The importance of race awareness diminishes in Ascensión's definition of himself when he understands that his allegiances depend on other factors as well as on race. This concern for his own identity makes *Juyungo* a much more subtle novel than most novels dealing with racial groups, and it also relates *Juyungo* to the trend toward interior novels. There is, however, a social generalization related to Ascensión's introspection. The result is a protest that youth's talents are wasted because of class lines, formed not entirely on the basis of race; and this waste is related to the defeat of Ecuador by Peru in a boundary dispute. The war becomes a means of ending the novel.[1]

José Revueltas, in *El luto humano*, uses a different means of making a protest novel profound. The means is mainly structural. The basic story is that a group of rural people are trapped by a flood. Through the eyes of several people, we come to know a leader, one who is already dead. This technique—a very good one—is not original with Revueltas, but was something of a novelty in Spanish American fiction. Unfortunately for Revueltas's novel, the characters in it become symbols rather than real people. We find

147

representations of the future of the country, of violence, of the past, of the Christian-pagan mixture. Since the characters speaking in the novel's present time reveal the character of the dead man, a large part of the novel is made up of flashbacks. The end of the story, however, brings about a melding of these two levels of time. All the struggles the people have gone through have been unproductive. At the end, facing death on the level of present time, they find that the meaninglessness of the past joins the present.

Comparison of these two novels, *Juyungo* and *El luto humano*, with some other novels of the period 1942–1945 clarifies some of the crossing lines of similarity and difference. *Juyungo* has aspects of the *novela indigenista*, and it certainly is a story that deals with groups outside the power structure. Gregorio López y Fuentes's *Los peregrinos inmóviles* (1944) deals with a tribe's journey to find a home. Some of the implications of this novel are like those in *El mundo es ancho y ajeno*. It is important for the people to retain their identity as a group, and that is a very different thing from the identity problem in *Juyungo*. The novel by Ortiz makes a social protest, but in some respects it is like Onetti's *Para esta noche* (1943). Granted there are fundamental differences in social class and sophistication. A personal identity problem, nevertheless, is a personal identity problem, whatever the related circumstances. The protagonist in *Para esta noche* discovers that he is really a different person from the one he has assumed himself to be. His life becomes a flight toward death. Such an end is not as different from *Juyungo* as one might think.

It is also interesting to place *Para esta noche* by the side of *El luto humano*. There is a remarkable similarity in their sense of futility. Revueltas's novel, however, also has much in common with proletarian novels. The proletarian tendency, never very important in Spanish American fiction, generally tends to fade during this period. In *La sangre y la esperanza* (1943), Nicomedes Guzmán uses portrayal of the working class as the basis of the novel, but it really serves mainly as background. Guzmán's narrative techniques are very attractive and are much more sophisticated than those in *Los hombres oscuros*.

He establishes the tone of chapters by beginning with some animating image: autumn has a beggar's drawn face, the barrio is like an abandoned dog, the bells are like the laughter of hysterical women. The principal narration is in the first person, from the point of view of a boy who is the son of a worker on the streetcar line. Through this narrator we see the strikes, the family problems, the personal honor of a laboring man. The lineal structure of the narrative, as well as the emphasis on the worker's life, is modified by a romance between the narrator's sister and a revolutionary poet. The account of this romance is in epistolary form, so preserving the authenticity of the narrative point of view, since the boy presumably would not have this information.

It is possible that Spanish American emphasis on the importance of the individual has always had a diversionary effect on the expression of proletarianism. Obviously, respect for individuals has its limitations in Spanish America just as it has anywhere else; but there are also extraordinary—and sometimes eccentric—manifestations of its strength, for example, as in political personalism and in *machismo* (he-manism). Even so, it is surprising to see the turn taken by a novel like Osorio Lizarazo's *El hombre bajo la tierra* (1944). Given the title and the author's well-known concern for the common man, we naturally expect a novel of protest about working conditions in the mines. Actually, it is a novel of transition into manhood. The story is straightforward, with a third-person omniscient narrator and a lineal narrative structure. The narrator introduces the eighteen-year-old protagonist, Ambrosio Múnera, right at the beginning, with the suggestion that he is uncertain about what direction his life will take. The antagonist, Pedro Torres, appears in the first chapter and scorns the "tenderfoot." In the last chapter, Múnera kills Torres and realizes that he has proved his own *machismo* and has also committed himself to the life of a miner. The story is really not a protest though it is obvious that life is hard. It is basically a novel in praise of hard work and strong men.

There is something of an identity problem in *El hombre bajo la tierra*, but it is more exterior than the anguished questions about the meaning of life. Ambrosio Múnera is primarily concerned about how to make a living. Of course, the two types of concern are not entirely independent of each other. *Juyungo* shows their relationship. However, factors other than the search for identity make *Juyungo* look quite different. Although it too is strong on the experience of growing into manhood, the process is influenced by racial considerations; and the author's use of preliminary prose poems in

149

each chapter suggests a quality of reality created by the relationship of man to his environment. In this respect, Ortiz's novel belongs to the same tradition as Aguilera Malta's *Don Goyo* and *La isla virgen* (1942). This association brings up again the matter of the New World experience, which refers to cultural identity more directly than to individual understanding of self.

Many of the characteristics that persist as particularly Spanish American qualities form a coalition that tests credibility in *Dámaso Velázquez* (1944), by Antonio Arráiz. It is a novel of the sea, of adultery, of contrabandists, of murder, and of myth. The variety of themes is the novel's worst enemy. At the beginning, it appears to be a story of the sea. The narrator creates an appropriate ambience by having one brother in a seafaring family question his own adaptability to the sea. This circumstance, in view of what happens in other novels of the same period, suggests the identity search, but it should be clearly understood that it is not a major theme of this novel. The protagonist, Dámaso Velázquez, is introduced indirectly. Early in the novel, some contrabandists escape arrest because their boat belongs to Dámaso Velázquez, and we discover he is a man of power in official circles. References to him increase, in the midst of action. Then, by meeting Fernando Robles, the protagonist's bookkeeper, we learn more about his employer's activities; and there is a flashback into the protagonist's past, through the medium of the memories of others. He is a real swashbuckler, personalistic, close to his buddies. He pampers his wife with luxuries while keeping a more folkloric way of life for himself. It is, of course, a very solid life—nothing but the best, so long as it is not fancy.

The novelist weaves into this character development a good deal about the sea, a fine description of the island of Margarita, and a lot about the appearance and customs of the people. Arráiz invents attractive metaphors, but tends toward excessive detail. The plot of the novel struggles to avoid disappearing under a torrent of ambience. As for the story itself, by the middle of the book it becomes more a novel of adultery than a novel of the sea. In a moment of closeness, after witnessing a murder, Fernando the bookkeeper and Rosario, the pampered wife, make love. Given the extraordinary qualities of Dámaso Velázquez, only disaster can come of this infidelity. Several aspects of the work contribute to an appreciation of this period. It is clearly an idealization of the strong man. In this connection, it is important to point out that his active role in the novel is slight. We see him mainly through other people. It is his shadow, his influence, that we are aware of. The leader type often appears this way. It may be the powerful shadow of the dictator, or the inspiration of a folk leader, or the righteous force of an upstanding man. This archetype incorporates the value (or status) of the individual with the desire for leadership, which is the other side of the coin. The significance of his shadow role appears to be that he exists in principle as well as in person—an apparent paradox that makes an abstraction of individuality.

A second notable factor is awareness of the unexploited place with supernatural connotations. It is the experience of the New World—first geographically, then historically. This awareness is an important part of cultural identity. It has tended to turn inward from objective, visible reality and to relate men's deeper, inward reality with the outward circumstance. Going beyond this point, the experience of the New World becomes individualized and relates to the strong-man archetype. In addition, there is a third factor with a possible relationship to the other two. It is a very intense emotional response that appears disquietingly exaggerated to Anglo-oriented readers, and to many Spanish Americans. It may well be that this kind of expression is related to respect for individuality; it is certainly a folkloric reality. There are conventional responses that sometimes seem close to hysteria, used in fiction and in reality, and generally recognized as legitimate conventionalisms, though many people who recognize them would not say or do them. There seems to be a generational difference operating with regard to this characteristic, with younger people tending to discard it. This change may be the result of cultural internationalization.

In many ways, *Dámaso Velázquez* is the most typical Spanish American novel of the years 1942–1945, in terms of its predecessors; even novels as strongly localized as *Juyungo* and *El luto humano* show signs of moving from an old standard to a new one. Three of the works by new novelists during this period are more introspective. One of them, *Cada voz lleva angustia* by Jorge Ibáñez, has an externally based problem as its theme—erosion of the land and the effect on those who work it. *Babel*, by Jaime Ardila Casamitjana, has an introspective base and refers to the exterior. The first-person narrator offers a kind of testament to the role of subconscious and

151

apparently fortuitous factors operative in his awareness of being. There are many fragmented memories, often evoked by his reactions to present-time circumstances, dreams, and disordered ruminations. This tormented, Proustian soul seeks some kind of commitment that is deeper than that offered by exterior reality. He thinks about doing, but passes his time in contemplation.

Ulyses Petit de Murat's *El balcón hacia la muerte* (1943) is closer to what we normally think of as a psychological novel. Its anecdotal base is the experience of a tuberculosis patient in a sanatorium. Within this setting, the novel develops a microcosm with one unusual characteristic: life goes on accompanied by the persistent awareness of death's presence. The scenes move around among several situations, but are related to each other. The unifying factor, which also provides the novel's movement, is the relationship of the protagonist's psychological disposition to his physical health. Its principal stages are despondency, anger, hope, and cure.

The importance of psychological penetration in the works of Eduardo Barrios always worked as a path away from regional limitations. Surprisingly, *Tamarugal* (1944) contains many of the conventionalisms of Spanish American fiction at a time when we might expect the author to emphasize more universal characteristics. The novel is actually accompanied by two stories; the subtitle of the book is "A distant tale between two related stories," and this structure does, in fact, provide some unusual interest. The first story is narrated by a visitor to the site of the Tamarugal Nitrate Co. Ltd. The narrator describes, with repulsive detail, an accident to one of the workmen. The feeling communicated is that man is endangered by a technological world. The story also introduces "El Hombre," a type who could be the twin brother of Dámaso Velázquez.

Tamarugal itself deals with several different notions that make it a novel of protest: the threat of the machine (as in the story that precedes), economic imperialism, and official corruption. There is a suggestion of proletarianism in the circulation of the ideas of the Party among the workers. The most penetrating aspect of the novel is a love triangle involving El Hombre, Javier, and Jenny. The girl is really the protagonist, and the story, though it is narrated in third person, sees things as Jenny would see them. The two men have very different personalities: straightforward, down-to-earth sincerity versus Javier's intellect and sensitivity. The lady has her choice. In a last chapter that serves as an epilogue, we find out how things developed forty years later.

The love story furnishes the movement and most of the thought in *Tamarugal*. The novel gets fairly heavy during the discussions between the two men. The story that follows the main event is more typical of Barrios. The protagonist is an employee at Tamarugal. He travels through a night fog, thinking of enemies he has made. He sees two blotches that appear to be men waiting for him to pass, and little by little his fear increases. A surprise ending detracts from the very credible development of tension. However, this characterization is in no way the same as the anguished introspection of some other novels of this period. Barrios embarks on a type of meditative characterization in the basic novel of *Tamarugal*, but it remains cerebral, and didactic in tone. What is lacking is a combination of this intellectual exercise with the emotional interiorization of the closing story.

It is amply apparent that during the period 1942–1945 the Spanish American novel shows a balance between approaches that are cosmopolitan in nature, on the one hand, and allegiance to traditional nativism or regionalism, on the other. The balance is apparent in the comparison of selected novels, and it is also apparent in the comparison of selected factors from a single novel. If we could find ourselves in the position of a literary critic in 1945—without the benefit of hindsight—we probably could not guess the direction the novel might take in the future. The perseverance of a less traditional attitude might seem likely, especially since it is in accord with European literature, but there is always the possibility of a reaction that will renew certain aspects of a traditional approach.

The general cultural state of Spanish America, during this same period, bears a marked resemblance to the balancing of factors in the novel. In the long run, the effect of World War II was internationalizing. However, there were a number of conditions, during the war years, that promoted nationalism and, sometimes, a high degree of cultural defensiveness. The one certain condition is that change was taking place at a pace faster than average. Quite a few political events promised to liberalize the social organization, weakening the traditional power structure. The outcome of this widespread dynamism varied from place to place, and, although definitive reversals of traditional patterns are not apparent, the activity had some degree of permanent effect.

A major event in hemispheric politics was the Río conference in January 1942, during which the United States asked for support against the Axis powers. The principal opposition came from Argentina, with agreement on the part of Chile. However, some governments who were affirmatively disposed found that substantial numbers of their citizens felt otherwise. Their motives were to some extent genuinely nationalistic, but they also contained a good deal of anti–United States sentiment. The most confused situation was in Argentina. Because of the illness of President Roberto M. Ortiz, the vice-president, Ramón S. Castillo, took over the executive power in 1940. The orientation of his administration was pro-Axis, and this inclination was intensified by cultivating awareness of the Spanish heritage, at the expense of other European influences (English, French) that had been important in Argentina for many years. The pro-Axis orientation survived the military coup, in 1943, that ousted Castillo in favor of a junta that included Juan Perón. The future strong man functioned as minister of labor. Students of literature particularly are interested in the fact that a well-known, third-rate novelist, Hugo Wast, was minister of education.[2] By 1945, Perón was the real power, though Edelmiro Farrell was president. Perón had still not quite consolidated his power, but he was close to that point. It must be remembered, of course, that the Perón dictatorship was always somewhat disorderly.

In Ecuador, the support given by Carlos Arroyo del Río to the United States was deeply resented by the nationalists, and their sentiments were fanned by the boundary war with Peru, which was settled to Ecuador's continued dissatisfaction at the Río conference. In Colombia, President Santos supported the Allies, in spite of the strong opposition of Jorge Eliézer Gaitán and nationalist leaders. Santos showed his liberal inclinations by making a pact with the Vatican that limited the influence of the church in education. However, in 1942, the split among the liberals that ultimately led to *la violencia* was apparent. In 1946, the liberal split led to the election of the conservative Mariano Ospina Pérez, and chaos followed. Although nationalism can be very counterproductive in many ways, it can also promote an evaluation of a nation's position in the world—this too has its merits as part of the identification process.

The liberalizing movements have many different aspects. Whatever the overall opinion we may hold of the Perón regime in Argentina, there is no doubt that it gave the little man more attention than he had ever enjoyed before. In Bolivia, the president was forced out by liberal opposition in 1943, but the move was not really productive. In the same year, Manuel Prado, president of Peru, allowed Raúl Haya de la Torre to return to his country. By 1946, the APRA, headed by Haya de la Torre (now strongly pro–United States), was the real power in Peruvian politics. The vested interests, however, allowed this situation to last for only about two years. Fulgencio Batista, in Cuba, retired in favor of President Grau San Martín in 1944—another shortlived liberal move. Venezuela's Acción Democrática was formed in 1941; Rómulo Betancourt took power after an uprising in 1945. The much heralded election of novelist Rómulo Gallegos to the presidency in 1947 amounted to very little. His administration lasted ten months. President Alfredo Baldomir, in Uruguay, liberal in orientation, had to steer a careful course, taking into account the pro-Axis leanings of his conservative countrymen, being wary of Argentina's ambitious Perón, and courting United States aid to shore up the country's shaky economy. Guatemala rid itself of Jorge Ubico, in 1944, after thirteen years under his rule. Even Paraguay, rarely blessed with enlightened leadership, enjoyed the relatively commendable administration of Higinio Morínigo from 1940 to 1948.

The change in Mexico was different. Lázaro Cárdenas, the most radical of the post-Revolution presidents, finished his term, and President Avila Camacho took office in 1940. With his administration, the country entered a period of industrialization and again encouraged foreign investment. Industrial development was also the basic policy of the administration of President Juan Antonio Ríos, in Chile.

The period 1942–1946 was, then, a time of change but certainly not of revolution. The kinds and degrees of change varied. The two new tendencies were cultural internationalism and political liberalism. They did not necessarily accompany each other in a given situation, however. Nor can it be said that their opposites, nationalism and conservatism, went hand in hand. The tendencies of change crossed each other, just as happened in the changes taking place in the novel.

These years bring us to the edge of the literary phenomenon that deserves to be called the "new Latin American novel." Not everything about it will be new by any means. In fact, one of its most interesting facets reveals new ways of dealing with themes that are very old. It is also apparent that the post–World War II novel releases a cultural impulse that has been partially held in abeyance for half a generation.

CHAPTER 12

The Years of the Reaffirmation of Fiction: *El Señor Presidente* (1946), *Al filo del agua* (1947), *Adán Buenosayres* (1948), *El reino de este mundo* (1949)

The repeated brilliance in this series of novels, published over a four-year period, clearly indicates a direction for Spanish American fiction. They all deal with the Spanish American world, but they are excellent examples of the difference between personification and novelization. In other words, they are all based on objective reality, but they accomplish more than the addition of life to the facts of history. They transform objective reality, create worlds within the novels. The youngest author in the group was forty-three years old in the year of publication; the oldest was fifty. These ages hardly indicate a group of neophytes. In fact, they were all accomplished men of letters. Nevertheless, these works exhibit freshness of attitude and interest in technique because the writers belong to a generation that was late in coming to fruition in the novel.

Miguel Angel Asturias, Agustín Yáñez, Leopoldo Marechal, and Alejo Carpentier all belong to the "generation of '24," as distinguished by José Juan Arrom.[1] His generational scheme includes in this group the writers born between 1894 and 1924. Their period of predominance in literature should be the years 1924–1954. All four of these novelists were born early in the period assigned to their generation. In fact, the youngest of the four was twenty years old in 1924, the first year of the period of dominance. Therefore, it is reasonable to expect these writers to have published relatively definitive works in the late 1920s or early 1930s. They were, in fact, active writers during those years, but their definitive works of fiction were delayed. In the trajectory of each one, there is a hiatus in the writing of fiction, probably caused by external pressures related to the social problems of the day and to interest in the picturesque aspects of the New World experience.

Asturias published *Leyendas de Guatemala* in 1930 and did not publish another work of fiction until 1946. We know that he had written the new book earlier, that he was possibly working on it as early as 1922. It is true, of course, that political circumstances in Guatemala made publication unwise, but that is part of the problem that created the hiatus. Agustín Yáñez published an avant garde story, "Baralipton," in 1931. He wrote some highly personal prose narratives in the early 1940s, but the date of his first full-fledged novel is 1947. Marechal did not publish innovative prose in the early years. However, he did belong to the vanguardist group that published the magazine *Martín Fierro*; and we know he was writing *Adán Buenosayres* as early as 1931, although it was not published until seventeen years later. Carpentier published *Ecue-Yamba-O* in 1933; and although he, like Yáñez, published some short fiction in the early 1940s, he returned to the full-length novel form only in 1949.

The initial literary experience of these writers corresponds to the vanguardism promoted by literary magazines like *Contemporáneos, Revista de Avance, Martín Fierro, Proa,* and others not as well known. The collaborators on the reviews did not deny the objective reality of the world they lived in, but they were dedicated to the priority of art over social message. Major influences on them— though certainly not all these influences were operative in any one situation—were James Joyce, Franz Kafka, Marcel Proust, Benjamín

Jarnés, Sigmund Freud, Francis Jammes, and André Breton. Frequently, the writers who followed these leads were accused of hyperestheticism. Novels of protest seemed more relevant to the time. The internal problems of the Spanish American countries looked even darker against the background of world affairs—the economic depression, the rise of Hitler, the Spanish Civil War. It is entirely understandable that a novel using the narrative techniques of *El Señor Presidente* would appear to be creating unreality in a world that demanded attention to reality. Asturias's poetry written between 1930 and 1946 was one way of avoiding a difficult political issue, but it was also a way of perfecting the combination of vanguardist technique and American myth. All the novelists whose mature works were delayed during this period went through some corresponding process of discovery: Marechal in poetry, Carpentier in the problem of time and history, Yáñez in a mythic-autobiographical development toward awareness of self and of art. Eduardo Mallea, another member of this generation, differs from these four only in a way that confirms the nature of the hiatus. He first published fiction in 1926, in *Cuentos para una inglesa desesperada*. For some years after that, his principal writing was in the essay, in which he worked out his view of the Argentine circumstance within the framework of his cosmopolitan culture. His first major novel, *Fiesta en noviembre*, appeared in 1938; although this date is a decade earlier than the period of reaffirmation in the late 1940s, the difference in time probably is the result of Mallea's particular characteristics as a writer. His fiction frequently concerns itself with the same problems that appear in his essays. Therefore, the transition into long fiction was a very natural process.

The four major novels belonging to the years of the reaffirmation of fiction establish the author's right to create a world within the novel. The process of making this reality is consummately important, because what the novel says to its reader depends, to a considerable extent, on his appreciation of the growth of the novel itself. That is why fiction is different from history. The difference, however, is not as simple as it may sound. There are endless variations of narrative techniques that produce different experiences. Reading a novel does not necessarily require the reader to be consciously aware of these techniques; a listener does not have to read a score to enjoy a symphony. However, repeated readings (or listenings) of a really substantial work always reveal something new, and the experience of the creative process of a work is one kind of knowledge. These four landmark novels enjoy the support of quite a few others, published during the same years, in the establishment of a new period in Spanish American fiction. From this time on, we can refer to the "new novel" in Spanish America—a term that we use here to refer to the reaffirmation of fiction. This period is different from what is called the "boom," which dates from 1962 or 1963. The boom certainly is part of the new novel; but the boom itself produced an unprecedented international interest in the fiction of Spanish America.

El Señor Presidente is a novel inspired by the dictatorship of Estrada Cabrera in Guatemala. However, the narrator never mentions Guatemala, nor does he make a word portrait of Estrada Cabrera. It may be that the closest approach to portraiture is in the relative invisibility of the dictator himself. In an interview with Luis Harss, Asturias stated that no one ever saw the president. Everything was understood on the basis of rumors.[2] The strong man appears infrequently in the novel, and only in situations that emphasize the terror of his regime. The strong man's shadow is a persistent motif in Spanish American fiction, and Asturias would probably have seen his subject that way whether or not the historical record revealed Estrada Cabrera as a man who rarely appeared in public. The president's shadowy existence in *El Señor Presidente*—his intrusions that suddenly put matter into form—enhances the terrifying aspect of the regime, and of the novel. The sinister quality of this phenomenon contributes to the sense of distorted reality that is the novel's dynamic factor. Rather than melodramatic, or even satirical, the reality created by Asturias is a distortion of objective reality. In fact, one can regard the objective reality that supplies the novel's anecdotal base—that is, the dictatorship of Estrada Cabrera—as a distortion of the social function, and therefore the distortion within the novel actually makes the book more realistic.

The most apparent technical device in *El Señor Presidente* is language play. The novel is clearly a descendant of *Leyendas de Guatemala* and uses language for different effects that range from lyric beauty to animalization. The opening scene is on the steps of the cathedral in the capital city. The language play in the first paragraph is formed of words that suggest light and that approximate the sound of cathedral bells. The narration immediately following this paragraph is in third person, without any noteworthy characteristics except a tone that suggests oral storytelling. The city's beggars and thieves gather to spend the night. Their plight is not simply economic; they are grotesque distortions of humans, crippled physically and mentally. It is a scene all too familiar in Spanish American countries. Emerging from the scene, Pelele, who responds violently to the word *mother*, kills a man who utters the word, then flees. As we progress toward the end of the first chapter, some language play enters to help communicate Pelele's mental state and to indicate the teasing directed toward him.

However Spanish American this scene may be, it also achieves a further universality. Many of the words in the first paragraph begin with the syllable *al* and so suggest the mid-eastern cry to Allah. Certainly the paragraph is an invocation. It is also a distortion of a plea for light, one that asks for light but changes the nature of light. It is worth noting that the novel ends with a portion of the Litany and the Kyrie Eleison. These varied suggestions change the opening scene from a presentation of the city's flotsam and turn it into a broader possibility—that is, the degenerate state of human life under a terrorist dictatorship. In other words, the beggars and thieves extend into a kind of allegory that makes them not simply beggars and thieves within a society, but representatives of the society.

The understanding of *El Señor Presidente* depends to some extent on whether the distortion factor is read as satirical or as grotesque. Luis Harss points out that the novel's "rather crude satire" is one of several factors about the book that seem dated.[3] Possibly true; however, some characterization contributes more effectively to the tone set in the opening scene if it is taken as grotesque rather than as satirical. The difference is most apparent in the presentation of the president himself. It is satirical when, in praise of the leader, a public speaker calls for "a *viva* that echoes to the ends of the earth and never ends; *viva* His Excellency the Constitutional President of the Republic, Benefactor of the Fatherland, Chief of the Great Liberal party, Liberal to the core and Protector of Studious Youth."[4] This beginning is developed and repeated for the length of a page; and it is rather heavy-handed, relieved only by some language

161

humor—and even that probably would not be funny if it were not in a situation where it is part of the game. The orator, for example, confuses the phoenix with "tennis" bird (the Spanish words are phonetically similar), and this too is overly obvious, but works for Asturias because his reader expects it of him. Another view of the president, however, animalizes him; and this is grotesque, not satirical. During a scene in which the president is triumphantly drunk, his language degenerates into belching noises and idiotic laughter (the sound reproduced with a variety of vowels—series of *ja*, of *jó*, of *ji*, and of *jú*) as he chases a fly around the room, "shirttail out, fly unfastened, shoes untied, his mouth covered with spittle, and his eyes rimmed with excrescence the color of egg yolk" (pp. 232–233). In this scene, the distortion becomes grotesque. It is not a case of satire making a human being look ridiculous. The narrator actually dehumanizes the dictator, making him an object of loathing. The novel's treatment of the president in this way has an aspect of retribution—the narrator does to the strong man what the strong man has done to the people.

This grotesque quality is the very essence of the novel. A somewhat disconcerting factor is the love story of Cara de Angel (Angel Face), the president's favorite, and Camila. It is a straight love story and is related to the favorite's fall from grace. He suffers punishment that seems excessive; and we may discuss whether or not this fact is justified by the dictator's wariness regarding divided loyalty, or we may accept it as another grotesque factor. Cara de Angel himself may be taken, in part, as belonging to the system of distortion. His diabolical gentleness is not really convincing in terms of standard characterization. However, it is the love affair that does most to associate the novel with ordinary reality.

The association is fragile. The cultivation of the grotesque laces the novel with fear. Asturias employs free association, speaks from inside his characters, gives them independence or controls them at will, and provides a persistent line of reality. However, the language repeatedly destroys the reality, which we see always at a distance; it distorts what we would take to be the case, leaving us in a vulnerable position. The factor of time itself disintegrates. The first two parts of the novel refer to specific dates—a total of seven consecutive days; but the third part refers indefinitely to "weeks, months, years," leaving a sense of no release from fear. The epilogue

162

itself offers a crumb of hope that is immediately withdrawn. The prayers of the Litany intercede for many different kinds of people—for peace, justice, safety, and redemption. The last words of the novel, however, far from assuring us that the world will be kind to us, cry "Lord have mercy on us."

Al filo del agua, like many other novels published in these crucial years, existed in part long before it grew into a novel. Basically, it is an atmosphere study of a provincial Mexican town. The essence of this study operates as the "Acto Preparatorio" that begins the novel. In the narrative development, essence turns into a palpable town on the brink of the Mexican Revolution. The title of the novel is a rural expression that means to be on the edge of a storm or, by extension, to be on the brink of any happening. The town is unquestionably real in the sense that the author had known a prototype and also in the sense that the town created within the novel is as real as the prototype. The process of transformation is interesting because, in the "Acto Preparatorio," Yáñez has already essentialized the prototype; then, in the rest of the novel he progresses from this generalized reality to a more specific one in which people are not essence, but individuals with names and personalities.

The "Acto Preparatorio" uses several stylistic techniques to achieve the aggregate reality needed for communicating the atmosphere of the town. Omission of finite verbs, for example, avoids specific personal reference. In fact, omission of all verb forms is even more effective. A sense of movement or of duration can be created with words other than verbs, and it produces an unusual effect. In his opening paragraph, Yáñez writes: "Town of women in mourning clothes. Here, there, at night, in the dawn approaching, in the blessed river of morning, under the fiery brilliance of midday, in the afternoon light . . ."[5] In spite of the absence of verbs, there is movement in place and in time. However, the unusual syntax causes the sense of movement also to seem unusual. The reference to black-clothed women becomes a leitmotif, and its repetition evokes an increasingly complex set of responses. In addition, repetition not only of the leitmotif but also of other words and syntactical structures produces corollary effects. One is rhythm, which sets the "Acto Preparatorio" apart from ordinary prose; another is a resemblance to incantation, produced by the rhythm and by the fact that repeated phrases cease to inform, but communicate simply by being what they are.

Extended over approximately a dozen pages, this introductory chapter creates the feeling of a small town, isolated from big-city ways. The church is the reference point for everything that happens. Morals are puritanical and guilt feelings are both broad and deep. It is a hermetic town, collectively resistant to change, and most of its people are individually resistant to change. The crisis in the novel arises from the fact that some are not resistant. That crisis, however, belongs to the narrative. The "Acto Preparatorio" does not go beyond the closed-in character of the town. There are some elements in the description that evoke mental pictures of Mexico—the materials of which houses are built, for example. However, the general feeling is entirely universal, and the basic atmosphere could refer to any town in any part of the world where inhibitions have become the major cultural force.

The first chapter of the narrative consists of four episodes that deal with different happenings in the town on the same night. They are not related to each other except as all things in the town are connected in some way. Don Timoteo Limón, one of the pillars of the community, suffers guilt feelings caused by a complicated inner conflict. Leonardo Tovar, husband and father of a young child, sees the end of his wife's struggle with cancer. Merceditas Toledo is terrified because she has received a flirtatious note from a would-be suitor. Micaela Rodríguez returns with her parents from a visit to the city. She resents the necessity of having to come back to this humdrum town after enjoying the swirling activity of urban life. The narrator uses a third-person voice, but often places himself in the position of one of the characters, revealing the circumstances as they would appear to one or another of the people in the novel. The effect is very close to the effect of interior monologue. The intensity of this interiorization varies according to the needs of different sections of the novel.[6]

Following this chapter, the novelist reveals a number of personalities and customs of the town: the practice of penitence during Lent; the priest Don Dionisio and his nieces, who are named Marta and María and whose personalities suit their names; the ecstasy of a young religious fanatic; the arrival of Victoria, who brings all the disturbing qualities of a chic and sophisticated city lady; the phenomenal memory of old Lucas Macías, who is something of a prophet; and the intrusion of the young men who have been up north to work and who upset the town with their newfangled ways and ideas. These scenes are the material of seven chapters. They are followed by a chapter entitled "Canicas" (marbles), which makes a connection between the course of events in the town and the condition of the nation.

The stylistic techniques used by Yáñez in the "Acto Preparatorio" serve him well whenever he wishes to create atmosphere. Also, once he has materialized the town, in the narrative proper, he uses unidentified dialogue to communicate the town's attitude. These fragments of speech are a kind of chorus—voices from the crowd, or things a person in the town might be expected to say in a given situation—that contrasts with what is said by specifically identified people. No protagonist emerges, though the narrator provides an extremely adequate sense of the town as a whole. Often we know the results of an action before we know its cause. It is much like living in the town—later on we discover the cause of what we have seen. It is also apparent, by this point in the novel, that Yáñez makes characters stand out by giving them remarkable qualities. The civil-registry memory of Lucas Macías is the most spectacular example, but there are cases like the sophistication of Victoria and the fanaticism (or insanity) of Luis Gonzaga Pérez.

"Canicas," more than just a chapter, is an intermezzo. Its combination of themes recapitulates the characteristics of the town and prefigures the Revolution. The development of the second half of the novel proceeds on an expanded scale. In the second half, the implications of what happens in the town take account of a larger scene than in the first half. The workers returned from the north are the disruptive force in the first half; in the second half, the intruders are the revolutionaries. In many instances, the scale is enlarged this way. "Canicas" forecasts the change and introduces a new character, Gabriel, who is an embodiment of the enlarged concept. He is a nephew of Don Dionisio, the priest, and is the bell ringer whose music controls the pace of life. It is important that Gabriel be identified with the Revolution because his activity is creative. This role keeps change from being the result only of violence. It is also the result of creativity.

The following chapter, "Gabriel and Victoria," functions as an overture to the second part, much as the "Acto Preparatorio" serves for the first part. It is not exactly the same, because we are now within the story and cannot recover fully the aggregate reality of the "Acto." The "Gabriel and Victoria" chapter does become something of an abstraction, however. The narrator uses words that the characters might have said. They are elevated in style and in concept, highly improbable as real dialogue. The point is that they are not real dialogue. They are a fantasized representation of a wordless encounter. Gabriel, the artist, meets Victoria, the patron of art, the symbol of feminine beauty and sensitivity. Through her, the art of Gabriel extends itself toward a wider plane of activity.

The seven remaining chapters correspond to the seven chapters of the first part, creating a symmetrical structure that accords with the author's sense of rhythm. The chapters do not correspond to each other on a one-to-one basis, but the themes in general are exteriorized, given a more comprehensive importance. In the opening chapter of the narration, all four incidents indicate deep-seated rebelliousness, but no possibility of overt revolt. In part two, Micaela, instead of fuming about the drab old town, entices Damián Limón into a rendezvous. The individuality of Don Timoteo Limón's nightmare turns into the more comprehensive nightmare of Don Dionisio, who is concerned about saving his people. The religious crisis of Luis Gonzaga Pérez was dramatic, but had the effect of an interesting scandal rather than a disaster. The crisis provoked by Micaela's refusing to become one of the Daughters of Mary, in the second part, has repercussions that shake the very foundations of society. The small disobediences of María, in the first part, turn into outright alienation in the second.

The Revolution comes and sweeps part of reality away with it—María actually goes away with the troops. The hermeticism of the town has been broken. It may seal itself again, but the contents will be forever changed in some ways. As the hurricane passes on, Don Dionisio, in prayer and contemplation, wonders if the Revolution is, in some way, an agent of Providence that will bring about the results he has worked for (p. 386). We then realize that the novel has found a protagonist in the course of becoming a novel. It is Don Dionisio; a retrospective appreciation of *Al filo del agua* shows him as a unifying agent, and his concern as the motivating force of much of the action. Don Dionisio is not a symbol of the church, but a symbol of religion and numerous corollary social fuctors of moral significance. Yáñez's novel is not antichurch or even anticlerical, as some have wished to make it; it is very much anti the tyrannies men allow themselves to create and then suffer.

Adán Buenosayres is the story of an Argentine writer during the vanguardist years of the 1920s. Since the period of the reaffirmation of fiction, at the end of the decade of the forties, is the direct (if delayed) descendant of those years, Leopoldo Marechal's novel is a reaffirmation of itself. It is ironic that *Adán Buenosayres* received very little attention even in 1948. Orgambide comments that Marechal's *peronista* affiliation probably had something to do with the cool reception given the novel.[7] Its fate at that moment could hardly have had anything to do with the novel itself. It does for the *martinfierristas* what Gálvez's *El mal metafísico* does for an earlier generation of writers. It is, however, a much more complicated book, and a much longer one. In fact, it is one of those thick tomes with small print that are likely to be put on the shelf with a promise to read them next year.

A description of how the narrative is presented can be a source of encouragement to the potential reader who, unfortunately, may not even have the assistance of a table of contents.[8] The title itself provides the most basic key to the novel. "Adán" suggests universal man; the addition of "Buenosayres" specifies him by reference to a particular place. This combination turns out to be the conceptual framework of the book. Opening the volume, we find a section called "Indispensable Prologue" where the novelist explains the organization of his work and establishes the narrative point of view. This prologue, signed by Leopoldo Marechal, tells of the burial of Adán Buenosayres, whom we assume to be Marechal's alter ego. The date is an October morning in some year of the 1920s. Given the objects of the novel's satire, it is safe to place the year in the latter half of that decade. Marechal is one of six friends of the deceased who take part in the burial ceremony. Marechal then records how he read two manuscripts of Adán Buenosayres and decided to publish them. One is the *Cuaderno de Tapas Azules* ("The blue-covered notebook"), a series of autobiographical impressions and memories written by Adán Buenosayres and corresponding to the life of Leopoldo Marechal. The second work is the *Viaje a la Oscura*

167

Ciudad de Cacodelphia ("Journey to the dark city of Cacodelphia"), an account of a descent into hell where the author finds the objects of his displeasure in various stages of discomfort.

Having resolved to publish these works of his deceased alter ego, Marechal then decided he should present their author first, and in the form of a novel. For this narration, Marechal employs a third-person narrative voice. There are variations on this point of view within the development of the story, but third person is the basic narrative position. The *Cuaderno* and the *Viaje* are narrated in first person. There is nothing about this artifice that would cause a reader to think Marechal was not the real author; however, it does create a sense of separation with regard to the narrator. We feel that Marechal is writing about what he used to be, rather than about the present; and his attitude reveals a combination of satire and nostalgia. The volume entitled *Adán Buenosayres* purports to contain a novelized portrait of Adán Buenosayres and two works by him. The "Indispensable Prologue" is followed by seven numbered books, each divided into chapters or sections. The first five books are the third-person story of Adán, a poet and teacher. These five books make up substantially more than half the volume. The sixth book is the *Cuaderno*; it accounts for only about a twentieth part of the whole work. The seventh book is the *Viaje*, which is about one-third of the total *Adán Buenosayres*.

The third-person account is not supposed to cover a long period of time, but it covers in depth the world of Adán Buenosayres. That is the world of the vanguardist literati in Buenos Aires in the 1920s. More specifically, it is the reality of that city transformed by the young intellectuals and presented by one of them as he saw objective reality and transformation working together. The tone is gently satirical. There is something of the farce about the whole work, as if none of it ever had any serious intent. To a considerable extent, Marechal creates this effect by writing in an elevated style, then inserting a very earthy fragment to make a contrast. The earthiness of Marechal's style, incidentally, may be pornographic or obscene—his humor has a strong inclination toward the anal variety. It is genuinely humorous and is designed to deflate the pretentious.

The pretentiousness that provokes this disrespectful reaction on the part of the author is a reflection of the interests of the *martinfierrista* generation. Marechal communicates all this through the friends of Adán, each of whom is an interesting personality, though Adán himself is the only one who is characterized in depth. They include a man-about-town who is spectacularly nonintellectual, an unimaginative scientist, a philosopher, a folklorist, and an astrologer who has a theory about an Argentine superman. These people supply the intellectual-artistic milieu that inspires the novelist's satire and nostalgia. They represent the figures of an era, but are not portraits of individuals. (The fictional character who corresponds most directly to a real person is Luis Pereda, the folklorist-linguist, generally considered a caricature of Jorge Luis Borges.) Their usefulness in the novel, however, is not related to attacks on individuals. Rather, they make a composite portrait.

Taken together, these personalities create their own environment as they move about the city. This intellectually induced circumstance is the basis of Marechal's style. That is, he talks about philosophy and art, projects grandiose schemes that could change the world, discusses the *martinfierrista* brand of artistic nationalism, and comments on the superficialities of the period. It is all very cosmopolitan because he knows about myths and psychology. In fact, the story of Adán is a kind of Odyssey. Marechal penetrates deeply into the character of Adán by means of detailed reporting of the protagonist's reactions. The narrative voice is third person, but from the position of Adán. At times, the dialogue changes from speaker to speaker as in the theater, without the use of a narrative voice. The novelist also divides the personality of Adán so he addresses himself in the second person. His past self speaks to his present self and provides an appropriate foreshadowing of the *Cuaderno* (pp. 319–334).

Approaching the *Cuaderno* this way, we discover that it functions mainly as a characterizing device to penetrate more deeply into the psyche of Adán Buenosayres, in a form that is more confession than autobiography. It works as a complement to the third-person interiorizations of the first five chapters. Here the first-person narrator repeats some of what we learned about Adán in the first part, giving it greater intimacy in the first-person variation. A note by the author explains that the last pages of the *Cuaderno* were probably written at a time consistent with certain developments in the first five books. This note reinforces the idea of the *Cuaderno*'s autonomy.

The astrologer, Schultze, is possibly the most important of the friends in the first five books, because he serves as Adán's guide through the nether regions in the *Viaje*. Although the narration of this seventh book is first person, the tone is similar to the tone of the first five books. It takes place, presumably, the day after the time assigned to that first part. It shares also the humor created by using a commonplace to interrupt a mythic-epic narration. This effect is enhanced by the combination of the world of Marechal's time with a narrative that has characteristics of a literary classic. The result is amusing, but *Adán Buenosayres* contains many "in" jokes that are enjoyable in proportion to the reader's knowledge of Marechal's literary-intellectual circle. The dynamic factor in the novel is the effect of contrast; it points up the satire of a literary movement. By the end of the first five books, this dynamism has used itself up. The additional books do not detract from the work as a whole, but they add very little. The *Cuaderno* is dull except for the interest it takes on when we study it as part of the narrative device. The *Viaje* could stand as an independent work.

El reino de este mundo is a tale inspired by the circumstances surrounding Henri Christophe, black king of Haiti. The various scenes novelized have a unifying factor in the person of Ti Noel, a slave. He is not a protagonist, however—Carpentier's mythification of history prevents his being that, in any traditional sense. In fact, none of the characters are fully developed, but they are parts of a mosaic.

It is of considerable importance that the author refers to *El reino de este mundo* as a *relato* (an account) rather than as a novel. This term probably reflects Carpentier's special interest in the marvelous quality of reality in the New World—an interest that caused him to emphasize the historical accuracy of the work. It also explains the simple expository style of his narrative. He tells the story in the third person, and, by avoiding intimate detail, maintains a distance from the subject, giving the book a tone that suggests objective investigation of the subject. At the same time, this distance absolves the author of responsibility for supernatural happenings, such as the ability of two characters to transform themselves into nonhuman forms.

The story is divided into four parts which refer to (1) the rebellion headed by a mystic-leader named Mackandal, (2) the Bouckman massacre and the yellow fever epidemic, (3) the rule of

170

Henri Christophe, and (4) the coming of the mulattoes. Ti Noel's life, from youth to old age, parallels these four stages, and lapses in time in the narrative are always apparent in the age of Ti Noel. For example, twenty years pass between part one and part two; the information comes directly and is typical of the human but detached attitude of the narrator: "While all this was happening, twenty years had passed. Ti Noel had twelve children by one of the kitchen maids."[9]

The theme of the novel is the constant struggle against tyranny. The fact that Ti Noel is a unifying factor rather than a protagonist emphasizes the struggle in a general sense rather than the struggle of one man. At first, it seems to have a dominant racial ingredient—the oppressed black man against his white master. This opposition is particularly strong when General Leclerc, Napoleon's brother-in-law, comes to restore order to the rebellious country. The general is unable to control the hinterland and ultimately fails in his mission. The reign of Henri Christophe follows, and here the importance of racial difference diminishes, because the black ruler is as harsh as the white. It really comes down to the struggle between the powerful and the oppressed. After the fall of Henri Christophe, the mulattoes take over as the powerful factor. They constitute a mulatto oligarchy, and the poor are exploited as always.

The narrator underlines the alienation of the powerful—alienated from the people's reality, that is—by characterizing the voluptuous Paulina Bonaparte and revealing the life of Henri Christophe's widow and daughters in Rome. These episodes seem more "novel" than the rest of the book, but they are nonetheless stylized, or mythologized. In addition to the distance the narrator maintains between himself and his story, the sense of a special reality comes from the persistent presence of the supernatural. We are in the land of voodoo, of course. After the death of her husband, General Leclerc, Paulina turns to an unexpected and unexplained religiosity. It serves as a white man's counterpart to the ability of Mackandal and Ti Noel to transform themselves into nonhuman forms.

The people believe that Mackandal, when he was burned at the stake, changed himself into a mosquito and took flight. The narration of this event combines stylization and the illusion of matter-of-fact reporting. First we learn of the prophecy that Mackandal will save himself. The next step is a description of Mackandal at the stake. The narrator then describes a movement of Mackandal's body, which feeds the wishful thinking of the blacks, and the people speak with one voice, "Mackandal is saved" (p. 66). Immediately the narrator describes the events which few of the blacks saw but which deal with the death of Mackandal. The slaves return to their homes rejoicing; and in the last paragraph of the chapter, Ti Noel's owner tells his wife how insensitive the blacks were to the execution of one of their own, "drawing certain philosophical conclusions about the inequality of the races of humanity, which he proposed to develop in a speech decorated with Latin quotations" (p. 67).

This tendency to stylize or to make archetypes is one way of expressing Carpentier's notion of *lo real maravilloso* (marvelous or miraculous reality), which is an important part of his concept of the New World, and of its novelization.[10] Fundamentally, his idea is related to the French surrealists' idea of *le merveilleux*. Carpentier understands the sense of discovery inherent in this idea—the absoluteness of the creative moment when two apparently disparate elements are associated in such a way that the association itself is something new. The novelist, however, finds some of the natural juxtapositions in the New World as creatively stimulating as the unusual associations in a surrealist painting. The proximity of opera houses to half-civilized tribes is as extraordinary as a guitar hanging from the branch of a tree. The experience of seeing them should be more than appreciation of the contrast; it should embody the more positive reality of the association. Carpentier finds himself in the incredible reality of Haiti. It is not just a question of voodoo; the whole range of associations is stupendous: black slaves and French elegance, physical transformation, the nude Paulina Bonaparte being massaged by her black slave, the black baker-emperor, the failure of General Leclerc. Carpentier compares it to narrative romances like the stories of Amadís de Gaula and the Knights of the Round Table. The difference is that in Spanish America, it is real—therefore, *lo real maravilloso*. The objectivity of the narrator in *El reino de este mundo* emphasizes the reality. It is important, however, that the novelist recognizes its similarity to narrative romance, because this view of New World reality is entirely different from the cataloguing of objects and customs as in Gallegos's novels, for example. We may assume it is one of the bases of what critics, in

172

recent years, have called "magic realism." The importance of this term is not in an exact definition of it, but in a general attitude that embodies it—that is, the reaffirmation of the novelist's right to invent reality, to make up his story rather than copy what he has observed. Magic realism indicates a statement of acceptance of narrative romance.

Carpentier makes an ideological statement in *El reino de este mundo* that seems to disturb some readers. When Ti Noel is an old man, he discovers that, like Mackandal, he has the ability to transform himself. His life has been a struggle for freedom, and he has seen freedom denied him by one agent after another. Transformation is a possible exit from the dilemma, but experiments with this power prove unsatisfactory. The narrator sets forth Ti Noel's discovery that man can realize his true greatness in the Kingdom of This World (El Reino de este Mundo) where he is committed to other men, as contrasted with the Kingdom of Heaven where there are no battles to be fought (p. 197). Some readers take this discovery as a modification of the struggle for freedom. On the other hand, it seems to indicate dedication to a struggle that never ends. However one understands it, there certainly is every indication that the author's vision of *lo real maravilloso* does not blind him to the practical questions of how man comports himself. The same can be said for every one of these four basic new novels. The reaffirmation of the art of making fiction does not alienate the artist from society.

One of the major novels of the period is a second work by Asturias, *Hombres de maíz* (1949). Possibly the best description of this book is that it is the plenitude of *Leyendas de Guatemala*. Its inventive language is the dynamic factor of the novel. The author is as aware as any poet of the process of creating by naming; and Asturias's theory and practice in this regard make a contribution to the Spanish American novel comparable to Carpentier's reference to narrative romance. When interviewed, Asturias may comment expansively on the relationship of his novel to Maya reality; however, he also admits that he speaks no Indian language and that his appreciation of the Indian psyche is intuitive rather than scientific.[11] Maya culture is to *Hombres de maíz* what the history of Haiti is to *El reino de este mundo*. Asturias uses some language character-

173

istics that suggest or correspond to Indian speech habits: the repetitive-redundant phrasing characteristic of primitive speech, and the repetition of syllables within words. The language in general has an oral sound, is rhythmic, and seems exotic. These factors are what moves the novel. The stories are not sufficiently interrelated to provide a motivating force.

The basic proposition of *Hombres de maíz* is that the Indian culture is decaying—or, more accurately, it is gradually crumbling under the persistent assault of non-Indian progress. The "men of corn" who provide the book's title consider the plant a gift designated for their use. On the other side are those who commercialize corn, thus desecrating it. The novel is not a development of this contrast, however. Rather, Asturias composes six chapters, weakly interrelated, that reveal various aspects of Indian beliefs. The culmination of the experience is a descent into the underworld by a man who discovers the priority of instinct over reason. This ordering of values is appropriate because the experience of the novel is in that direction. The language play, always attractive and often amusing, enhances the nonrational communication; and so does the loose structure that makes us expect more unity than we get. The novel is not a somber experience. Readers are likely to have the feeling of being pleasantly tricked. An epilogue heightens this feeling because there is absolutely no need for an epilogue. It is quite useless and its very existence is absurd—and antirational.

There is an element of protest, of course, in Asturias's novel. It is not as apparent as in a proletarian novel, because the artistic act is the controlling factor in *Hombres de maíz*. In this respect it is very much a representative of the new wave. It should be clear, however, that during this same period there were novels of overt protest: the continued campaign of Jorge Icaza in *Huairapamushkas* (1948), an attack on the commercial oligarchs of the Bolivian tin industry in Augusto Céspedes's *Metal del diablo* (1946), and a kind of demythification of Asturias's Indian in *Entre la piedra y la cruz* (1948) by Mario Monteforte Toledo. Although Monteforte Toledo is one of the younger members of the generation of 1924, his novel seems older, probably because the richness of sentiment recalls an earlier manner of expression.

The study of society, whether concerned with *indigenista* problems or not, became more contemplative, often taking the form of analysis through highly detailed characterization. Eduardo Mallea's *El vínculo* (1946) is an example; another is Roger Plá's *Los Robinsones* (1946), though it is a very different kind of book. Using a group of four friends, Plá communicates the problems of the 1930s, in an Argentine setting, but with universal implications. The friends are from different backgrounds: one is rural, another is wealthy urban, one is middle-class Jewish, the fourth is also Jewish but poor. The basic story line extends from 5:00 P.M., July 18, 1936, to 8:00 P.M., March 4, 1937. Specific time references mark each narrative segment; and the procedure is meaningful because Plá uses flashbacks extensively. The four boys have been fellow students, and insights into their past are helpful; but the basic time span of the narrative marks a crucial point, and that is why the specific time references are important.

Plá controls narrative techniques that draw his reader into the scene of the novel. He opens the narration with a dialogue overheard by Ricardo, one of the four and really the novel's protagonist. Ricardo begins a conversation with Leonor, and the two dialogues are intermingled, with one of them fading gradually as they separate. The effect is cinematic. The date of the beginning of the novel corresponds to the outbreak of the Spanish Civil War; the newsboys, a man muttering about fascism, and an anti-Semitic placard greet Ricardo as he walks down the street. It is not an auspicious introduction. The first flashback recalls the year 1928 and introduces the four friends as schoolboys. The story circles to the present and to Ricardo, taking all four friends into account. They find nothing approaching a common direction, but the life of each one is set. Ricardo achieves an identification of himself with all humanity and convinces his father of his maturity. The other Jewish lad has terrible personal problems, but finds direction in an inner mysticism. The friend with the rural background is a failure in the university and is a political activist. The wealthy friend commits a murder in a tragic mistake and is saved only by being declared insane.

In rural settings, several novels reach toward epic dimensions. In *Lago argentino* (1946), Juan Goyanarte tells the story of Martín Arteche, a pioneer sheepherder in Patagonia. The narrator establishes the fundamental theme of the novel on the second page: Arteche's determination to bend natural forces to his will. After establishing the novel's present, the omniscient narrator goes back twenty-five years and returns to the present about halfway through the novel. We see the backgrounds of Arteche's workers, and that is an important part of the novel. The book is episodic, but Goyanarte has a good sense of what is interesting, and he expands or condenses the narrative accordingly. The third point of emphasis is that, when Arteche needs help, he gets none from the bureaucracy and has to depend entirely on himself. This rugged individualism is similar to the character in *Gran señor y rajadiablos* (1948) by Eduardo Barrios. The sense of dominion over a part of this earth (feudalism, if you will) is also the basis of Mauricio Magdaleno's *Tierra Grande* (1949). This novel deals with a family's response to the loss of their land during the Revolution. One of Magdaleno's favorite narrative techniques is to set up a present situation by giving the historical background in terms of his characters' ancestors. In *Tierra Grande*, the Suárez Medrano family controls not one hacienda, but a complex of haciendas. The background communicates the growth of identification between the owners and the land. It is almost a blood relationship, far deeper than economic considerations. The novelist combines the portrait of a family with the portrait of an epoch.

It is possible to see clearly, at this point in the development of the novel, a trend toward introspection that affects all kinds of thematic concerns, from social protest to character novels that have no tie whatsoever to Spanish America. At one end of this line, for example, is *Shunko* (1949), by Jorge W. Abalos. This work is a semidocumentary novel based on the author's experiences as a schoolteacher in a depressed rural area of Argentina. A few years earlier, a novel of this kind would have been characterized by vehement protest. In the present case, it turns out to be an unusually gentle book. The author reveals this impoverished world through his relationship with a schoolboy. In another book that might have become a standard novel of protest—*La dolida infancia de Perucho González* (1946), by José Fabbiani Ruiz—the emphasis is less on the child protagonist's economic situation than on the anguish he suffers because he lacks a sense of belonging. This emphasis is much more appropriate to the general trend of fiction at the time.

The other end of the spectrum—that is, where place is of little or no importance—is heavy with works by a wide variety of novelists: Rogelio Sinán, Clemente Airó, Ernesto Sábato, Rodolfo L. Fonseca,

Jorge Ibáñez, Andrés Mariño Palacios, Carlos Eduardo Zavaleta, and Yolanda Oreamuno. Among these novels, the relevance of place indicates the ability of the Spanish American novelist to deal with a locale entirely foreign to Spanish America, as in Fonseca's *Turris ebúrnea* (1948), or, on the other hand, to write with reference to a specific locale without restricting the experience of the novel, as in Airó's *Yugo de niebla* (1948). In narrative technique, the novels as a group seem much more sophisticated than a corresponding number of novels from a decade earlier. Interior monologue is frequent; simultaneity is useful in many cases. The Unamunesque—or Pirandellian—narrator in Sinán's *Plenilunio* (1947) uses not only the narrative techniques that are introspective, but also others that look outward, like newspaper headlines and radio.

Oreamuno's *La ruta de su evasión* (1949) is an enlightening and painful experience of human relationships. Aurora, the protagonist, comprehends the difference between life and death, through intimate ties to others and to her own self. The narrator uses interior monologue and also third-person exposition of very detailed reactions. Aurora's stability contrasts with the disintegration of her husband—a contrast very effectively communicated by their language. The anguish of the people in these books—resolved in this case by Aurora's attention to the simple details of living—is a common denominator among the introspective novels. Some of them are existentialist in a fairly strict Sartrean understanding of the term; others may not be so specifically defined, but are clearly the products of an age when anguish is the *mal du siècle*.

The anguished experience of alienation is particularly forceful in two novels published in 1948: *El túnel* by Ernesto Sábato and *Yugo de niebla* by Clemente Airó. Sábato's novel has become the standard example of existentialist fiction in Spanish American literature and enjoys the status of a modern classic. *Yugo de niebla* is not nearly as well known, but is another satisfactory example of the state of alienation, narrated in an entirely different way. Sábato creates the desperate situation of a single individual; Airó uses several characters in a single circumstance to create an overall sense of desperation, or at least of negativism.

The backbone of the structure of *El túnel* is a narrator-protagonist, Castel. This narrative voice gives a feeling of immediacy to his revelation of his anxieties—his need to belong to something, to establish a relationship. His problems extend through love, jealousy, and murder. Not even a sex relationship establishes communication. The basis of the structure of *Yugo de niebla* is a transient couple who rent a room in a pension-hotel. The assumption is that they will be there only a short while; but they do not appear when expected, and the narrator eventually reveals their suicide. This development is not a suspense-building device, however. The narration is third person, but always deals with reality as one or another of the characters sees it. The first is Patricio, husband of the woman who owns the house. His awareness of his own laziness and his dependence on his wife's property sets the tone for the down-at-the-heels situation. Then follow the thoughts and backgrounds of other people who live there—their frustrations, their need to feel fulfilled, their lack of anything that can be considered successful. The only person who has accomplished a degree of reconciliation with her fate is a maid, Alberta, who has had a child. Intercalated among these interiorizations are moments in the novel's present time that are mainly concerned with interest in the transient couple in room number seven.

These problems are of the kind we generally associate with a complicated urban society. Suicide is, of course, the perfect existential answer. It is important, however, to clarify the effect of *Yugo de niebla*. Our concern, in the experience of the novel, is not with an equation of the transient couple's problems and their suicide; rather, our concern develops an equation—or an association—of the other characters' problems with the transient couple's suicide. Airó creates this effect by means of the narrative structure. *El túnel*, on the other hand, is a psychophilosophical development of a single personality. The reader's experience is one of comprehending a set of ideas and attitudes, rather than of appreciating an association.

In general, these two novels do not concern themselves with location—that is, not with one place on the globe as distinguished from another. It might be possible to draw some conclusions regarding place. For example, if we associate the problems of *Yugo de niebla* with life in a modern urban setting, the novel suggests that life in Bogotá has reached that point by 1948. However, the main point addresses itself to human problems without regional significance.

Many novels, like the four that form the basis of this chapter, deal with New World situations in universal ways; others are primarily concerned with a universal human problem, and the New World experience is of secondary importance. In both cases, it is obvious that the Spanish American novel has by this time moved a long way from picturesque accounts of typically Spanish American situations. The change has affected themes, techniques, even the concept of what fiction does. Although some of the innovative steps are faltering, the general trend is healthy. The title of *Adán Buenosayres* says a great deal—it is symbolic of the new direction of fiction during the years of reaffirmation in its incorporation of universal man with regional man.

From *El reino de este mundo* to *Pedro Páramo* (1950–1954)

The maturity of Juan Carlos Onetti, in *La vida breve* (1950) and *Los adioses* (1954), sets a standard for the novel of alienation. The various shades of this condition—frustration, anguish, lack of communication, sense of inauthenticity, need for attachment—are evident with complete clarity in books by Eduardo Mallea, Clemente Airó, and Mario Benedetti. However, these writers are far from alone, because the same feelings are apparent in most other novels of this period, although their themes may be stated in different terms. For example, the effect of Colombia's politicoreligious strife, *la violencia*, is the basis of Eduardo Caballero Calderón's *El Cristo de espaldas* (1952); but the author deals with this external theme by means of interiorization that reveals typical twentieth-century anxiety. Other themes—some of them mythic in nature—reveal the same inner problems; even social protest becomes a factor in this complex. Whatever the circumstance, inhabitants of the world of fiction search for some ineffable moment or condition that persistently eludes them.

In *La vida breve*, the protagonist is tyrannized by his own conception of life as reality sandwiched between two walls of nothingness. In addition, this reality depends on one's having a sense of
fulfillment; and fulfillment is all but impossible in the world of
Onetti because his people need to recover something they have
lost or missed, rather than discover something they may look forward to or create. It is a somber world of disillusionment. Onetti
presents it in *La vida breve* by creating lives that extend outward
from other lives. Let us say that the protagonist is a man named
Brausen. The statement is a hypothesis rather than a fact because
we really don't know who the protagonist is. In fact, Brausen is also
two other men, Díaz Grey and Arce. We might say that they are
three aspects of a single person; however, the idea of three people
has merit since it enables us to think in terms of more than one short
life. Díaz Grey, moreover, is created by Brausen, supposedly for a
movie script.

Onetti sets up the novel in first person and in the mind of Brausen.
Interior monologue is of fundamental importance. Even when
Brausen is talking with someone else, the reader may be privy to his
thoughts, which appear in parentheses. What the reader may not be
privy to is information about who is talking—or thinking—that is,
whether it is Brausen, Díaz Grey, or Arce. Actually it is possible to
figure it out, but we do not always find out readily. The effect, of
course, is to make the protagonist neither three distinct people nor
a single person. This condition plays havoc with the reader's expression of empathy. To make matters more complicated, the author
is there too. Onetti often identifies with his protagonist; and that
fact is interesting in *La vida breve* because his association with
Brausen is reasonable enough and the creation of Díaz Grey fits in.
However, the other identity is not created, but is discovered by
chance.

Interpretation is probably no more dangerous anywhere than in
this novel. Returning to the experience of the book, knowing Brausen is like knowing a dead end. That is why the invention of Díaz
Grey is so important. He becomes the dominant facet of the protagonist entity and also appears in other novels by Onetti, so freeing
the author from participation. The invention of Díaz Grey is, therefore, a milestone in the author's career as a novelist. Although Díaz
Grey does not appear in *Los adioses*, the novel confirms the author's

independence. Here the narrator is a shopkeeper near a tuberculosis sanatorium. He remembers the case of a particular patient known to readers only as "the man." All the principal characters are referred to in similar general terms; the minor characters have proper names. We know only what the shopkeeper knows, and he knows only what he sees. After the man's suicide, some unclaimed mail provides a denouement, explaining—still through the shopkeeper—certain circumstances that had been misunderstood.

Los adioses is one of the author's lesser works, but it combines with *La vida breve* to mark a period of transition. The change, however, is in narrative technique rather than in theme or in tone. Onetti's novels continue to be despondent, full of a sense of futility. No matter how personal these qualities may be in the case of Onetti, surely they must be related to the social conditions in Uruguay and Argentina at the time. Government by committee in Uruguay's welfare state was indicative of an unproductive, passive society. In the late 1930s, Alfredo Baldomir returned the country to the commission-type government as a reaction to the increased executive power under Gabriel Terra. Various circumstances created by World War II shored up the nation's shaky economy temporarily. In fact, the awful truth was not generally apparent until the 1960s; meanwhile, the country was settling into a lethargic condition, satisfied and unproductive. The neighboring republic of Argentina, which Onetti knew as well as his own country, was hardly more inspiring. The Radical party, which offered hope at least for the lower-middle class, had lost its drive and its influence by the early 1930s, and Argentina reverted to the rule of the oligarchs and the military. The novels of Roberto Arlt are early reflections of popular disenchantment. The same feeling emanates from Onetti's *Tierra de nadie* in 1941. He resembles Arlt in both concept and carelessness of style. Two years later, Juan D. Perón was the real power in Argentina, and he controlled the nation until 1955. His regime awakened and supported the laboring class as had never been the case before; but it seriously damaged the intellectual and cultural life of the country and, in the long run, its economy. There was no cause for rejoicing by people like Onetti or the characters in his novels.

It is difficult to imagine characters less fulfilled than those in Mallea's *Los enemigos del alma* (1950). There are no tricks here about who created whom; Mallea controls his story and the people in it. The three protagonists are disoriented in their search for personal satisfaction. They are two sisters and a brother who live in the same house, loathing each other. They correspond to the soul's three enemies: the world, the flesh, and the devil—not in an allegorical way, but as people who multiply their own mistakes. One seeks satisfaction in being well thought of, another in promiscuous sex, the third in hating the first two. Completely removed from any creative possibility, they become ever more committed to their paths, which lead nowhere. Right at the end of the novel, in an epilogue, the author inserts a note of hope in the form of a look of pity, but he explains that this glance, which could change the world, has no place in the story, since the story is a closed case. The protagonist of *Chaves* (1953) is so disenchanted he hardly speaks a word. In order to make this short novel a reasonable experience, Mallea narrates in the third person, describing the emotions of Chaves and going back into the past to reveal situations in which he has spoken. The man has never used words for commonplace communication, but only when driven to use them in order to obtain what he needs. Even in this context, however, he has often found them ineffective. We experience the feeling that personal satisfaction will not be found through any available communication with others; the least amount of frustration comes from isolating oneself.

Different techniques provide a variety of experiences, but the anguish is always present. Even though reader involvement in *La vida breve* is puzzling when we think about it, the sense of participation is very real. In *Los enemigos del alma*, we feel involved all right, but involved with the author more than with the characters. In *Chaves*, we still tend to be with the author, but in a position closer to the subject. Mario Benedetti, in *Quién de nosotros* (1953), uses a very effective structure to develop the interplay of attitudes in the eternal triangle. Each of the three people involved tells the story as he sees it, and in a different form. The deserted husband writes a contemplative, diarylike narrative. The wife writes her farewell letter to the husband. The lover makes a fiction, using dialogue, changing names, and adding footnotes to explain why he uses certain techniques and how his story relates to reality. The result is to shift the reader from one position to another, thereby validating the last footnote's final words, which question whether anyone involved can blame anyone else. The message carries beyond the love triangle. Clemente Airó uses segmented narration in *Sombras al sol* (1951) not to produce parallel accounts, but to broaden the setting of his novel of alienation from the scene in the pension-hotel of *Yugo de niebla* to a scene that includes the whole city.

El sustituto (1954) by Carlos Mazzanti is an interesting combination of form and idea. The book's appearance is extremely forbidding. It consists of 136 pages filled margin to margin with words, except for two lines of suspension points thirteen pages from the end. Surprisingly, the narrative is fluent and interesting. It turns out that the typographical appearance has a meaning—Mazzanti believes men are tyrannized by a constant flow of thought that constitutes a barrier against their acting. The unbroken narrative represents the thoughts of the protagonist, revealed by a third-person narrator who witholds information at times in order to create suspense. Mazzanti keeps the experience entirely universal by leaving people and places unnamed. The protagonist, puzzled about the meaning of life and bereft of his family, decides to take the place of a young man accused of a crime. The process that leads to his decision covers about twelve hours. We experience his thought, beginning with a dream, passing into waking, and then continuing through the acts of one day. The narrative flow is broken for the only time when he admits guilt in order to save the other man. After this break, the narrator supplies some withheld information that makes the protagonist's decision more acceptable to the reader. The style resembles thought. Mazzanti's sentences are long and use lots of conjunctions. There are very few spoken words; and when they appear, they simply run into the flow of thought. The novel is somewhat marred by the fact that the narration of thoughts takes more time than the thoughts themselves require. In this respect, the novel violates reality, and the author uses no techniques to compensate for the distortion.

The identity aspect of the problem of alienation is particularly clear in novels that deal with the transition into adulthood—the story of initiation with different cultural connotations depending on the author's background. They usually contain some aspects of the picaresque, but the process of finding one's place is considerably more important than the social criticism normally expected in a picaresque novel. As for cultural contexts, they may be as diverse as *Huckleberry Finn* and *Don Segundo Sombra*; and the intensity of anguish varies, but the identity search is constant. It is in a novel of this kind, *Hijo de ladrón* (1951), that Manuel Rojas turned again to making fiction, after a silence of many years. He is still another member of the generation of 1924 who went through a quiet period. True, he was never a member of a vanguardist group; on the other hand, much of his early work, while not technically innovative, is more aware of the human psyche than is the case in *criollista* fiction with which Rojas's work is usually associated. As early as 1929, "El vaso de leche," one of the stories in *El delincuente*, penetrates deeply into the interior of a man to show a complex interweaving of shyness, pride, animal hunger, and disorientation. The association of human kindness with the idea of maternal love and with a glass of milk develops gently, with no dramatic fanfare.

This association is more impressive than the regionalist connotations and it is the characteristic that carries over to *Hijo de ladrón*. The present time of this novel is a period of about three days. The protagonist is Aniceto, a lad in his mid-teens, who has just been released from prison where he was sent for a burglary he did not commit. At the end of the period, he goes off with two friends he has met, all three dedicated to living as vagabonds. The greater part of the protagonist's story takes place in flashbacks, some of which are narrated in past tense and some in present. Since the protagonist is the narrator of all the episodes, this differentiation in the time of the flashbacks actually amounts to an evaluation by Aniceto of the aspects of his past. The product of this narrative system is considerable emphasis on Aniceto's wondering about his place and purpose in society.[1]

Two novels about young boys provide a freshness to the literature of this period that is very welcome in the midst of so much anguish: *Muchachos* (1950) by Juan José Morosoli and *El retoño* (1950) by Julián Huanay. Actually, because of their themes, they do deal with the process of individual identity, but they do not fit into any literary tradition. *Muchachos* is a series of sketches that show the protagonist's struggle to gain recognition as an adult. The milieu is a small town, and much of the book is gently humorous. In *El retoño*, the outstanding quality is a certain tenderness—of the narrator toward the boy, and between the boy and the people he meets. Juan Rumi is the boy, a twelve-year-old mountain lad who decides he just has to see Lima. His trip to the city is a journey of expanding experience. The goal is the realization of his dream. Juanito's fortune is not always good, but, for the most part, people help him. *El retoño* is a novel of poverty as well as of growing up, but it is not a novel of scrounging misery. Technically, the novel is simple. The narrative structure is lineal, the dialogue credible, and the narrative presentation of misfortune, of human concern, and even of human exploitation is matter-of-fact—which is the way Juan Rumi saw them.

The luminous simplicity of a novel like *El rotoño* raises some questions—not always fair questions—about the works of more literary authors. The reason the questions are not always fair is that, while Huanay's story may be like a breath of fresh air, a steady stream of books like it would be very dull, because technique is the most important cause of variety in fiction. Guillermo Meneses's *El falso cuaderno de Narciso Espejo* (1952) also deals with growing up, but in a much more complicated way. The first-person narrator invents an alter ego who then becomes the first-person narrator; but of course we must remember that one is an invention of the other. With this confusion of identities, which raises doubt as to who is the biographer and who is the subject, we confront the account of how a boy understands the circumstances in which he is growing up. Sometimes the novel comes very close to being an essay. However, it develops an archetypal quality because the incidents are standard ones in the process of maturing.

The role of myth becomes very important at this point in the Spanish American novel. There is awareness of universal archetypes, use of native myths as in the novels of Asturias, and the mythification of the New World experience (partly the case in the works of Asturias) as in Carpentier's *Los pasos perdidos* (1953). This novel undertakes a return into the American past, using a musicologist as a narrative instrument. Supposedly, he is making an anthropological investigation related to the origin of music. However, we know, even within the novel, that this trip is an excuse for him to get away from New York. His attitude places the research in second place. In fact, the protagonist himself is of secondary importance. The fullest appreciation of this novel evolves from its sense of history rather than from concentration on the importance of the protagonist and what he may symbolize. This book is another case of the author's awestruck response to the *real maravilloso* of the New World. The possibility at this time of moving back many centuries in civilization places history in an unusual perspective. Here is a key to the novel—it is not a matter of putting some situation in historical perspective, but of placing history in a perspective that is larger than history itself. To create this effect, Carpentier invents a thoroughly civilized protagonist with jaded tastes and blunted ambition (a specimen of inauthentic man) and allows him to tell his story. Gradually his adventure takes him back into time. He goes through stages that suggest the European conquest of the New World, the mythical Odyssey, the rediscovery of authentic human relationship, the redefinition of society, and the origin of art, arriving at the most elemental expression of feeling.

The suggested existence of multiple realities, in *Los pasos perdidos* and some other novels of this period, is highlighted by the absolute invention of a fictional world in Adolfo Bioy Casares's *El sueño de los héroes* (1954). In 1940, he had published *La invención de Morel*, a piece of science fiction often praised with the admonition that readers should take it more seriously than as a simple fantasy. The novel deals with a condemned man who invents a means of mechanically reproducing people he knows. The effect is to suggest a metaphysical consideration of reality and unreality. *El sueño de los héroes* also creates uncertainty as to the nature of reality, with particular reference to the perception of time. The protagonist, Emilio Gauna, tries to unravel the mystery of a part of his past that is a vacuum. He makes a circle; either an event is repeated exactly after a three-year lapse in time, or there is no lapse in time. Gauna's mentor and guide turns out to be an unworthy model; he kills Gauna. The question is whether what happens in 1930 is an enactment of what was supposed to happen in 1927, or a reenactment of what happened. Bioy Casares handles the balancing of possibilities carefully, but always from the outside. The narrative point of view is consistently third-person omniscient. In this and in other respects, the novel is typical of detective-story fiction. The story opens with some hints about the effects of the problem and then shows how the protagonist reached a particular point in the author's development of the plot. The style is direct, without metaphoric complications. Short chapters emphasize the progressive points in the development of the story. There is no attempt to draw the reader into the story, but it is attractive because obviously there

187

is a gimmick and one wants to discover it. In addition, the setting in Buenos Aires in the 1920s is interesting and sometimes funny.

It is entirely possible that the most interesting developments during the years 1950–1954—at least among established authors—are the maturity of Onetti and the new orientation of Miguel Angel Asturias. Although he does not completely give up the use of native myth, Asturias's novels immediately following *Hombres de maíz* are more specifically novels of social protest. *Viento fuerte* (1950) and *El Papa verde* (1954) denounce foreign exploitation—or better, commercial exploitation—of the author's compatriots. In *Viento fuerte*, he removes the stigma of national prejudice, at least partially, by having an idealistic couple from the United States attempt to form a cooperative among banana growers that will counteract the evil effects of "Tropbanana's" operation. By setting the conflict between two sides, both from the United States, he can avoid political considerations and emphasize the spiritual values that concern him. While the novel leaves no doubt about the company's economic power, Asturias's real complaint is that its methods are a denial of the joy that men ought to feel in planting and harvesting fruit. The folkloric element suggested in this attitude fits in with the reality of the workers, but not with their redeemers from the United States. The latter are not ugly Americans; they are just absurd. These improbable characterizations widen the credibility gap initiated by illogical plot development that seems strange in a novel of protest.

The opportunity for reform presented itself in Guatemala when the dictator, Jorge Ubico, was driven out of power by popular revolution in 1944. The United Fruit Company had been one of the beneficiaries of his regime. Under the administrations of Juan José Arévalo, 1945–1950, and Jacobo Arbenz, 1950–1954, Guatemala enjoyed a new freedom. A program of agrarian reform began in 1952 and, under its provisions, much of the land owned by United Fruit was expropriated. The action was taken, presumably, on the basis of economic considerations. *Viento fuerte* protests on a spiritual level as well as an economic one. It was a good idea, but not a very persuasive novel. In the world of economics and politics, the fruit company contended that it could not afford to lose the land, because in banana cultivation it is essential that some land lie fallow. Far

188

more effective than their contentions was the fear of communism on the part of the United States government. Its agents or representatives saw or thought they saw a dangerous infiltration from Moscow in the government of Arbenz, and they arranged a coup. In July of 1954, Carlos Castillo Armas took over the Guatemalan government by force, with the backing of the United States. That same year, the fruit company's lands were restored.

This political incident is, of course, a moment of crisis. *Viento fuerte* is concerned with a much longer time. An interesting companion novel to this one by Asturias is *Una manera de morir* (1954) by Mario Monteforte Toledo. With very little effort spent on artistic transformation, the author gives narrative form to the experience of a disillusioned Communist. The narrative is third person, and the story as well as the characters are completely controlled by the author. The ideological points are made in dialogue. They are categorical in tone and tend to dehumanize the speaker. This effect is the message of the novel, and it is also a partial definition of communism in Spanish America, where many have been attracted by the ideal but few by the dogma. In *Una manera de morir*, the conflict becomes a source of anguish through its relationship to the meaning and purpose of living.

Probably the most artistic treatment, during this period, of a specific social phenomenon is *El Cristo de espaldas* (1952) by Eduardo Caballero Calderón. The story is an intimate one of sacrifice and triumph, but its motivation is *la violencia* in Colombia. By extension, the novel addresses itself to the dangers of social polarization wherever and whenever it may occur. The situation in Colombia is not comprehensible unless we understand that the country has long found it impossible to differentiate between politics and religion. In 1946, the voters elected Mariano Ospina Pérez president. He was a conservative, and he won mainly because the liberals were divided into two principal groups, one headed by the radical Jorge Eliécer Gaitán. Violence burst out to such an extent that Ospina Pérez declared a state of siege in some parts of the nation. His administration was stymied by Laureano Gómez, an incredibly reactionary politician, as much as by Gaitán. A Conference of American States in April 1948 provided a showcase for threats and demonstrations. On April 9, Jorge Eliécer Gaitán was assassinated, and more than two thousand people were killed in the subsequent rioting in Bogotá. There was violence throughout the country—the most brutal kind of civil war. In 1950, Laureano Gómez was elected president because the liberals refused to put up a candidate. A thumbnail evaluation of Gómez's beliefs emerges from his condemnation of the United States for supporting the anti-Catholic government of Mexico. Needless to say, he did little to calm his country's troubles. He was deposed in 1953 by Gustavo López Pinilla; but there was no substantial move toward peace until 1957, when liberals and conservatives agreed to alternate control of the executive branch of the government for the next sixteen years. This act did not resolve the problems, but it reversed the trend toward national suicide.

The novelization by Caballero Calderón of this awful situation uses a provincial town as the setting. The plot grows out of an accusation of parricide. The accused man, a liberal, is suspected of having murdered his father, a conservative and a leader in the community. We learn the facts of this tragic situation through the role of the town's young priest. Outwardly, he fails in his attempt to save his people, but he gains an inner victory. The story does not depend on one crisis alone. Rather, there are moments of victory as well as defeat. A letter in which the bishop dismisses the priest is interrupted by insertions of the priest's knowledge of the facts. Since he may not make this information public, the counterpointing of fact with letter produces a feeling of hopelessness.

Gustavo Valcárcel's *La prisión* (1951), another contribution to Spanish America's ample prison literature, goes far beyond a denunciation of prison conditions and becomes a plea for human dignity. A novel of this kind is hardly a surprise in its time and place; and it is worth noting that the first edition was made in Mexico, rather than Peru.[2] After a brief flurry of liberalism in Peru, following World War II, dark conservatism returned. After the election of 1945, Raúl Haya de la Torre, the nation's very durable reform politician, was the real power behind President Bustamante. However, by 1948, both Bustamante and Haya de la Torre were out, and General Manuel Odría was in. Haya de la Torre sought refuge as an exile in the Colombian embassy in 1949 and had to stay there until Odría permitted him to leave the country in 1954. It was not a gentle regime.

Valcárcel's novel is basically a first-person narrative, so it is easy to assume the story is based on the author's personal experience. Actually, the elements of fiction are sufficiently important to make the biographical possibility relatively uninteresting. The story is a combination of the narrator's observations, memories, and dreams. Recall has two roles in the novel. One takes the story back to a time before the novel's present; the other recalls moments already experienced within the novel as parts of present time. When these moments are reexperienced in a new present, they are pertinent to the general situation in a different way. Therefore, they contribute notably to the feeling of change in the course of the book. The general nature of this change is the dehumanization of the narrator. The beginning is early and very gentle, a flow of associations that involve words (society—satiety) and remembered quotations. Ultimately, the novel reaches a point where the narrator is no longer himself, and then the point of view switches to third person. The sense of loss is shocking.

Argentina was in the midst of the epoch of Juan Domingo Perón. Without even suggesting an evaluation of this very complicated period, we can say with certainty that the significance of the class structure was radically altered. The laboring people acquired privileges—even dignity—that they had never enjoyed before. The oligarchy, while it certainly was not eliminated, witnessed what may be called the disappearance of a way of life. It was a time when those conventions that make up gracious living were given a rough working over. As a sample of the changing ambience, Martin S. Stabb, writing on literature during the time of Perón, says: ". . . formal attire was no longer required at the opera; and many of the public parks that previously had, by some unwritten law, been considered the semi-private preserve of the middle and upper classes, became crowded with picnicking workers and their families."[3]

People who might be inclined to resist change of this kind have made their peace with many of the particulars, or at least have declared a truce. Nevertheless, such processes always produce a complex sentiment composed of nostalgia, sorrow, resentment, and relief. The sense of an era of change is apparent in several novels of the place and time. We have seen that in the novels of protest the anguish of the individual joins forces with an expression of cultural anguish. In the Argentine novels which we may take to be some kind of response to a period of rapid change, anxiety emerges from the association of tradition with identity.

Beatriz Guido's *La casa del ángel* (1954), like many of her novels, deals with the reactions of adolescence. It is the setting within which these reactions operate that gives the novel a special atmosphere. Guido sets the stage by indicating the inhibitions that Ana Castro, at approximately sixteen years of age, feels toward Pablo Aguirre, a friend of her father. Ana herself is the first-person narrator, so her self-revelation is quite straightforward. We know that her feelings are particularly related to an event in the past, though we do not know what it is. In a flashback that recedes as much as five years, Ana re-creates the bourgeois world of Buenos Aires in the 1920s. The sketches of her childhood reveal a rather cold, withdrawn father and an extremely puritanical mother. The extreme nature of the latter characterization probably should be taken as an individual case rather than a generality. The crisis depends on a duel between Pablo Aguirre and a political antagonist. Ana fantasizes giving herself to Pablo before he dies in the duel, and, in fact, she does so. However, Pablo survives the duel.

The memoirs are somewhat excessive in quantity for the slender plot line. However, the gradual revelation of the cause of Ana's feelings moves the story nicely, and there is a consistent atmosphere of things past. Ana's romanticization of herself gives the whole situation an aura of fiction within fiction—a cultural pattern existing in a time when it is more imagination than reality.

A more clearly nostalgic novel is one by Manuel Mujica Lainez, called simply *La casa* (1954). It is the story of a house on Florida Street (a traditional symbol of elegance in Buenos Aires) from the time of its construction in 1885 to the time it is torn down in 1953. The story is told by the house itself, personified and functioning as a first-person narrator. This device causes some initial difficulty because there is no prose style particularly appropriate to a house. The original tone is what we might expect of a dignified lady well along in years. However, the narration really comes to have the effect of third-person omniscient, since the house knows everything that goes on inside it. The basic narration occurs during the days when the old dwelling is being torn down. Retrospective episodes take us back to earlier times. Several clever narrative inventions undergird the device of having the house tell its story: the *objets d'art* talk with each other, there are two ghosts seen (not heard) by the house and its appointments, and the place has an emotional reaction to other inanimate objects. Together, these factors create an attractive ambience.

The people who inhabit the house are a senator, his wife, and four sons. The family disintegrates. The property passes to one of the sons, who has an affair with an opportunistic servant. She and her sister get control of the house, and later their nephew sells it to a corporation. It is important to notice that not just the family and the house disappear—a way of life also disappears. By the end of the novel, Mujica Lainez has incorporated all these factors into the personalization of the house, and he effectively communicates their demise as the house notices its own disintegration, the disappearance of its ghosts, and finally degenerates into incoherent narration.

La casa de los Felipes (1951), by Luisa Mercedes Levinson, is the story of the disintegration of a hermetic family whose town house was torn down during the construction of Diagonal Sur (now a major street in central Buenos Aires).[4] The theme, or themes, have many Brontë-like aspects: incest, a mad half-sister, a mulatto mistress, some strange deaths, a few ghosts, an alcoholic and probably impotent young scion, and a lost young love. We should take the house to be real—one of those elaborate old buildings far enough removed from our own experience to excite the imagination. The gothic invention attached to the edifice is a comment on what the house really means. The story builds suspense—that is, we want to know how it turns out. It is constructed so that we know a good deal about the situation from the very beginning, but much remains unexplained. Then by focusing on a particular character, Levinson reveals or gives clues to part of the mystery. The process is not one of steady clarification, however; there are moments when the mystery deepens. This narrative structure, moving like an amoeba, is assisted by the narrator's keen sensitivity to the function of changing point of view—from third-person omniscient, to interior narrated in third person, to interior monologue.

The novel communicates beyond the action of its gothic story line. It is hardly possible to avoid the impression of a decadent, though persistent, aristocracy. However, this impression is likely to refer to the institution rather than to the individuals within the

193

novel. At the end of the story, as the house is being demolished, one workman asks another about the family that had lived there, and the second workman replies: "I don't know. People always talked more about the house than about them" (p. 151).

After the death of Perón's wife, Eva Duarte, there was considerable talk about his loss of influence. In April 1953 he called for a mass meeting of his supporters. The demonstration turned into an orgy of destruction. The rioting *peronistas* burned the headquarters of opposition political parties and—most worthy of symbols— the Jockey Club, including its library and art collection. The recording of this event should not be related, in a cause-and-effect way, to the novels discussed in the paragraphs immediately preceding. The coincidence, however, is noteworthy, because both fiction and current events appear to be marking the end of an era—or at the very least, a drastic change.

The dramatic popularization of a city is apparent at different times in more than one instance in Spanish America—the transformation of Mexico City after the Revolution or the first influx of *andinos* into Caracas in 1899, for example. In similar fashion, the problems delineated or suggested by the other novels in this chapter are more general than the national framework associated with individual cases. Common also to Spanish America as a whole is the deeper significance of social reality. It combines individual man with his surroundings in the search for identity—and in the expression of anguish. The only apparent road is toward deeper penetration of interior reality, individual and collective.

CHAPTER 14

The Year of *Pedro Páramo* (1955)

Juan Rulfo's *Pedro Páramo*—controversial in its early years, but never without impassioned advocates—has gradually come to be one of Spanish America's most prestigious novels. It is the story of a *cacique* and the people affected by his obsessions. This theme belongs to Spanish America, rather than to Mexico alone; and, taking one more step, we find emotions of ambition, self-preservation, greed, vengeance, and obsessive love that are entirely universal. However, rounding the other half of the circle, there are qualities that clearly identify the book with Spanish America and, even more specifically, with Mexico. It digs deeply into the reality of a culture—not so much by studying the complex characters of the people as by showing how they fit together in a cultural pattern. This pattern, in turn, has its own distinctive qualities, because it is not a picture of society in historical perspective or created by sociological analysis, but reality appreciated in terms of myths that take form during the actual experience of the novel (though their bases are sometimes folkloric). The effect is achieved by means of special narrative techniques, a process that is very different from what happens in a character novel.

Among the effects produced in *Pedro Páramo* are a negation of sequential time and the intercalation of cause and effect in such a way that neither takes precedence over the other. That is why Rulfo's novel is fundamentally different from a novel of character. The narrative procedures that create this product are point of view that changes unexpectedly, segmented and disordered story line, and the assumption that the moment of death does nothing to inhibit communication. This last characteristic is a novelization of the idea of *almas en pena* (souls in torment) that wander the earth even after death. Comprehension of such an unaccustomed reality requires a reading more like the experience of poetry than of prose fiction. Clues of all kinds are important—repeated images, references to people or to situations, stylistic changes—not to remake the novel into a rational experience, but to establish the proper relationships for a suprarational appreciation of the work.

A first-person narrator, Juan Preciado, begins the novel with deceptive simplicity: "I came to Comala because I was told that my father, a certain Pedro Páramo, was living there."[1] Juan Preciado then recalls his mother's admonition that he visit Páramo, and includes dialogue between mother and son. The narrator brings us back to the present by saying, "That's why I came to Comala" (p. 8). However, with no transition, explanation, or typographical change, the narrator asks, "What's the name of that village down there?" and the answer comes, "Comala, señor" (p. 8). Obviously, the narrator is not talking with his mother; but no other character has been introduced, mentioned, or even suggested. Over the next six pages, we discover that the new character is driving some burros, that he, like Juan Preciado, is a bastard son of Pedro Páramo, and finally that his name is Abundio. This sequence—or antisequence— is an early instance of one of the novel's characteristics.

During the conversation with Abundio, another basic characteristic presents itself. The man with the burros makes a gesture to indicate the extent of Pedro Páramo's holdings and says, "and all that land belongs to him" (p. 11). On the next page, the same man says, "Pedro Páramo died a long time ago" (p. 12). Let there be no mistake, the verb in the first statement is unmistakably present tense. Death is not incompatible with the ownership of land in this novel; and the reader will eventually become reconciled to the negation of the line between life and death, just as he becomes accustomed to the absence of a cause-and-effect sequence of happenings. These denials of what we ordinarily consider reality produce an element of uncertainty in the reader's experience; and this feeling is an appropriate effect since the people within the novel seem unable to hold on to anything. There is a persistent sense of being left alone. At the point in the conversation with Juan Preciado when Abundio says "Pedro Páramo is my father too," a paragraph of one sentence follows, standing by itself: "A flock of crows flew across the empty sky, crying *caw, caw, caw*" (p. 10). Immediately the narrative begins again, with no further exploitation of the image.

Pedro Páramo is not the only one who is dead. The whole village of Comala is dead, and as the novel develops we reach the point where Juan Preciado tells of his own death. Some conversations occur in the tomb, and whispers come from the resting places of the nearby deceased. In the story of Pedro Páramo that emerges, four lines of action take on importance. One is Páramo's ruthless accumulation of property without regard for principles of any kind; the second is corollary to the first: keeping his property throughout the period of revolutionary activity, with continued possession as the only motivating force. The third line of action is the accidental death of Pedro's hell-for-leather son, Miguel. The fourth is his obsessive love for Susana San Juan, the lyric memory of youth, unattainable by Pedro Páramo because her spirit belongs somewhere else.

The first fundamental narrator change takes place on the seventeenth page of the novel, where we look upon the childhood of Pedro Páramo from a third-person position. This narrative voice is not omniscient, however, and does not supply all the details we might wish. Interspersed throughout this third-person narration are passages in lyrical prose that are Pedro's memories of Susana. They are first person with Pedro speaking and are set off in a way that differentiates them from dialogue. We know that they are memories; but we also know that they must have come into being as memories at a time posterior to the account of Pedro's childhood. In other words, the novel takes us back to the protagonist's early years and, at the same time, projects us forward to a point in the future. In fact, the duality of these lyric memories makes them appropriate at any time, given the basic characteristics of the novel.

Possibly the most convenient way of appreciating Rulfo's novel is to think of it as a combination of Juan-passages and Pedro-passages.

The shifts from one to the other tend to combine the two men, though no statement is ever made to that effect. We must also note that when Juan Preciado is the narrator he sometimes turns the narrative voice over to someone else. There is also at least one passage narrated in first person that could not possibly be Juan's voice or even reported by him (pp. 93–96). These shifts in perspective provide a multiple source of information. Joseph Sommers points out that we learn of the death of Miguel Páramo in four separate episodes, and from the standpoint of three different people (two of the episodes focus on the priest, Padre Rentería—one is the event, the other is Padre Rentería's memory of it).[2] In order to understand the effect of this procedure, we must realize that it has nothing to do with the creation of a reliable witness. It is possible in fiction to create multiple, parallel accounts of an incident, showing how several people see the same thing, and presumably creating a more complete awareness of what really happened. These accounts of the death of Miguel, however, function in a different way. Since they are separated, and individually incomplete, they require the reader to hold his reaction in suspense. When a subsequent episode offers additional information, it recalls not only the earlier episode that is related to it, but also a lot of surrounding narration. Two of the episodes may be considered as existing in the realm of memory, but all four add up to the reality of Miguel's death. The disjointed way we learn of the incident adds to the elusive nature of fact in this novel.

This narrative structure does not produce detailed character studies. The various reactions to the death of Miguel, for example, contribute to the characterization of three people; but the incident itself seems more important. The effect is that we are not likely to feel we know the characters, but we are aware of the anguish of each one. Rulfo's prose style contributes substantially to this kind of characterization that is a combination of portrait and ambience. The language is the speech of country people, but sparse to the point of sometimes seeming cryptic. It has an earthy quality, and this characteristic stands out in contrast to the lyric passages about Susana. It is a style that seems to belong to no particular person, yet it seems to fit the situation admirably.

Near the end of the novel, the reappearance of a very minor character, Doña Inés Villalpando, provides a unifying factor in the story. Early in the novel, in one of the passages showing Pedro Páramo as a boy, his grandmother sends him to the store to buy something from Doña Inés Villalpando. Near the end of the story, we find the same woman sweeping the shop of her son, Gamaliel, when Abundio comes in and buys a drink. This setting is the initial step in the final episode. Abundio gets drunk to numb the sorrow of his wife's death. Then he encounters Pedro Páramo and Damiana Cisneros, who takes care of the old man. Events that take place from this point throughout the remaining few pages of the novel defy description. To say, as many have said, that Abundio kills Pedro Páramo, is about as adequate as describing the sea by saying it is wet—and considerably less accurate. In the first place, the narrator does not say that is what happens. In the second place, details of the narration deny a logical, step-by-step conclusion. We learn that Abundio has sold his burros, presumably before the death of Pedro Páramo (p. 149); on the other hand, we recall that he still owns them, presumably after Páramo's death (p. 12). This paradox reminds us that a cause-and-effect sequence is not a factor in Rulfo's novel. Given that condition, there is no rational basis for assuming that anybody killed anybody.

The experience of the last pages of *Pedro Páramo* is a synthesis of the experience of the novel as a whole. The range of emotions (the psychic states communicated) includes Abundio's blind grief, the complete lack of communication between him and the Pedro-Damiana combination, Pedro Páramo's stubbornness, his fear, his obsessive memory of Susana (there is a final lyric passage), and his awareness of his own death. All the stylistic factors operate here: the lyric memory, the rural speech, the brief dialogue. The imagery is very simple but has a strong visual impact. As the men are half dragging Abundio back to the village, "his feet scratched a long furrow in the dirt" (p. 151). The absence of cause and effect is important in the various steps of this final episode just as it is in the various episodes of the novel as a whole. Abundio appears to have killed Damiana Cisneros (p. 150), but she reappears to take care of Pedro Páramo (p. 152). The very last step communicates not the dramatic intensity of death by violence, but the protagonist's sense of his own disintegration. He watches the men and Abundio on their way to the village. Then he feels a hand go dead, notices leaves falling from a tree, returns to his train of thought (Susana), recognizes death, starts walking toward the house, and falls—"He struck a feeble blow against the ground and then crumbled to pieces as if he were a heap of stones" (p. 152).

A variable narrative point of view is the basic technique in two other important first novels of 1955. One is *El pentágono*, by Antonio Di Benedetto, a first-rate novelist who deserves much wider attention than he has received, and whose work shows many points of contact with the novels of Juan Filloy. The other is *La hojarasca*, by Gabriel García Márquez, an initial step toward his famous *Cien años de soledad*. Di Benedetto's novel takes its title from a love pentagon—that is, a love affair with five participants. To put it another way, it involves two love triangles that overlap at one point. Real love and ideal love are the characteristics of the two triangles. The narrative point of view skips capriciously from one position to another, and movement between the two realms (real and ideal) is equally active. Although the book has a contemplative aspect, its seriousness is colored by a slightly sardonic tone. Some stylistic techniques enhance this effect because Di Benedetto's alliterations and agglutinized words combine exactness with humor in the expression of the author's feeling.[3]

It is difficult to guess how one might react to *La hojarasca* as an introduction to the fiction of Gabriel García Márquez. It could well seem fairly heavy. Granted a kind of retrospective reading by someone already familiar with *Cien años de soledad*, however, it is fascinating for what it reveals of the author's mythical town, Macondo. The story concerns life there during the period 1903–1928. The basic scene is the home of a physician who has committed suicide. The first of three narrators is a nine-year-old boy. He uses the present tense to describe what happens around him as he sits stiffly in his dress-up clothes, his inertia nearly unbearable. Then the boy's mother becomes the narrative voice, and we learn from her that she and the boy are there because the grandfather wishes them to lend respectability to the occasion. The third narrator is the child's grandfather, who takes the story farther back into the past and tells most of what we know about the physician's life in Macondo. The effect of this narrative arrangement is different from the intercalation of small segments of narration. *La hojarasca* moves us back in time and more deeply into the underlying reality of a situation. It piques the reader's interest because effect is apparent before cause. That is one aspect of the novel's charm; the other is the wild inventions of the author, delivered straight and then left tantalizingly unexplained. The priest reads from the Bristol Almanac instead of from the Bible, and the word is as acceptable as the pronouncements of any other prophet. The newly arrived doctor requests some grass for dinner. Anyone who knows Macondo will feel at home with these people.

The first novel of David Viñas, *Cayó sobre su rostro*, is part of a cultural change in Argentina that is related to the political phenomenon of *peronismo*. Viñas belongs to a generation of writers called "angry" or "parricidal."[4] The attitudes of these writers (and, therefore, the tones of their novels) vary considerably among individuals. However, if we are to arrive at any kind of general understanding of their attitudes, it is necessary to remember that the Perón regime produced a sense of the failure or error of Argentine society, when it was examined retrospectively. This attitude was common among both *peronistas* and *antiperonistas* because the former regarded the new regime as compensation for past injustice while the latter considered it the onerous outgrowth of past mistakes.

These writers and critics are revisionist with regard to the understanding of what Argentina really is, and they intended to cut through the mist of unrealized dreams in order to discover that reality. The consequent reordering of literary stars brought Roberto Arlt to the forefront along with some writers of the realist tradition. At the same time, many prominent figures of Argentine letters were damned for their irrelevance. Jorge Luis Borges occasionally bore this opprobrium, but the object of the bitterest attacks was Eduardo Mallea. He was accused of bourgeois snobbery, unfeeling intellectuality, and unpatriotic cosmopolitanism. The virulence of the attack on Mallea is particularly significant because it reveals the backlash reaction of the new generation. Their criticism has very little to do with his creative process, but mainly with his definition of being Argentine. From their point of view, he had committed the unpardonable act—Mallea was as anguished over the Argentine dilemma as any of the new breed, but he did not save them from the moral crisis which was brought into focus by the Perón regime. The work of Mallea, of course, was not the only point of attack.

201

It was the *cas extrême* in the realm of literature. Historical figures and accepted traditions were attacked in the same way. The new insistence on seeing things as they really are included a new national awareness. It was not chauvinistic, but rather self-deprecatory. One aspect of it was clearly an identity search somewhat different from related tendencies—the revisionists intended to push aside hypocrisy, false patriotism, and hero worship so Argentines could face up to their true past.

One of David Viñas's targets is General (later President) Julio A. Roca, "the Conqueror of the Desert." The legend of Roca is based on his campaign against the Indians of Patagonia in 1879. This movement is, in some respects, like the opening of the West in the United States. When the cheering quiets, we become uncomfortably aware of inhuman violence and personal dishonesty. *Cayó sobre su rostro* has as its protagonist one of Roca's regional *caudillos*. The novel is an example of militant debunking. Not surprisingly, the author is more often recognized for that quality and for his central position among the revisionists than for his technical ability. The imbalance is not fair, because Viñas is a clever technician who knows how to put this ability at the service of his imagination.

The first chapter of *Cayó sobre su rostro* serves as an introduction to the novel (even as a prefiguration of it) in two ways: first, it defines the character and circumstance of the protagonist, Antonio Vera; second, the techniques employed in this chapter constitute an example of Viñas's narrative procedure in the novel as a whole. The action of the first chapter begins when Juan, a rancher, and his son see someone approaching on horseback. Juan tells his wife, Teresa, to stay in the house. She disobeys and stays outside with the dog. The person approaching is Antonio Vera, coming to collect the money Juan owes him. Juan does not have the money, but promises that his son will deliver it in a month. Vera insists that Teresa bring the money. This insistence angers the son and he steps toward the horse. At this point the dog starts running around the horse's hoofs. The horse rears; Vera falls and hurts his dignity.

The chapter opens in the middle of the incident. The third-person narrator offers no background explanation, but furnishes all necessary information in the course of the narrative. Viñas uses dry, sparse dialogue to build tension as Vera approaches. Although the narrative remains in the third person, the focus changes from the

Juan-son situation to the Vera situation. This shifting contributes to a *tempo lento* very reminiscent of the showdown scene in a western novel or film. The narrator intensifies the scene by beginning each of a series of consecutive phrases with the words *la plata* (silver, money), and then reinforces this repetition by having Vera's hand, shining in the sun, appear silver to Juan; still later, Vera's saliva appears to be silver.[5] All these factors, plus mental references to "it" (the money) and anticipation of what the other party will say, contribute to the slow ticking away of seconds as Vera approaches. When the horse rears, the narrative forsakes its measured pace and becomes a series of precipitous actions, changing rapidly but following one another in an unbroken sequence within the same sentence. It makes a paragraph that is like the breathless reporting of a crisis.

The narrative techniques employed in this chapter create two principal effects. One is the result of changing the focus of the narrative. Although the narrative voice does not change and there is no interior monologue, Viñas places us inside both parties to the tension. Therefore, the experience includes the whole situation rather than one side of it. The second effect, closely related to the first, is that the external, visible action functions as a symbol of what goes on inside the people. An external action triggers more analytical, internal narration.

The title of the first chapter is "El día del juicio" (Judgment Day). The bare facts we learn concerning the protagonist are that he is the local boss, that he keeps an eye open for the ladies, and that he is getting old. The title of the second chapter is "Los años" (the years), and it goes back in time to Roca's campaign against the Indians. Here we find Vera the soldier as very *macho* and as a strict disciplinarian, at least as far as others are concerned. These two chapter titles alternate throughout the novel. Those called "El día de juicio" deal with the novel's basic present—the early twentieth century, before the presidency of Hipólito Irigoyen. The chapters entitled "Los años" are flashbacks that always tell of Vera's career, his toughness, his success, his reputation as an old campaigner. There is also a past-time element in the "El día del juicio" chapters, however, because the present suggests the past. Just as external action triggers internal revelation in the novel's first chapter, conversation in the novel's basic present may trigger associated recall.

In some passages, the dialogue is minimal and is in italics while the evocation is in ordinary type. Here again, the external dialogue is a kind of symbol of internal reality. Gradually, these chapters reveal Antonio Vera as a man whose good days are over and who hates the signs of his advancing years. Nevertheless, his dignity diminishes in these chapters so that they counterbalance, and finally outweigh, the "Los años" chapters in which his dignity increases. His death in a brothel, face down on a woman, is a symbol of his feeling about growing old; it is also the realization of the condition foreshadowed by his loss of dignity in the first chapter.

The reader experiences a growing sense of the antiheroic that reaches the point of sarcasm by the end of the novel. The message deals with the treachery of false values—the past should admit its obsolescence. The inescapable residue of the experience of reading *Cayó sobre su rostro* is that Argentine history is, at best, farcical and, at worst, corrupt. There is a remarkable poignancy in the association of this bursting of the bubble of national pride with the frustrated dreams of the bourgeoisie in *Los viajeros*, by Manuel Mujica Lainez. In this book, as in *La casa*, the author novelizes a disappearing social order. The specific vehicle in *Los viajeros* is a family's evanescent dream of going back to Europe. The immigrant family has made it big, and they should have money enough for the triumphal return; but the diminishing value of the peso separates the dream from reality.

It is interesting that the revisionist attitude of the young Argentine writers even produced an *indigenista* concern—something of a novelty in a culture that tended to ignore its provinces, not to mention its isolated minorities. In *Donde haya Dios*, Alberto Rodríguez (h.) makes a novel around the progressive desolation of an area, in the name of progress.[6] The story has a basis in fact. Its scene is a lake region in the province of Mendoza where the Huarpe Indians live. A dam designed to irrigate the vineyards of another area has the effect of gradually drying up the lakes and leaving the Huarpes in a desert. Official indifference to their plight is absolute. As Angela Dellepiane points out, the novel implicitly questions the "civilizing" programs of Argentina's politicians from Alberdi and Sarmiento to Roca.[7] This attitude questions the very basis of the national image, which grew out of the nineteenth-century concept of progress. In many ways, this generational exposé of the national heritage resembles the reordering of priorities that began making headlines in the United States a decade later.

A comparison of *Donde haya Dios* with *Huasipungo* is tempting, but too simplistic. Alberto Rodríguez (h.) belongs to a later generation and deals with a different kind of problem. The presence of injustice, in *Huasipungo* and in many other novels of its era, represents a readily apparent and dominant characteristic of social reality. *Donde haya Dios* deals with a problem of injustice tucked away in a remote corner of a nation's conscience. The narrative techniques also show it is a product of a different generation. The use of interior monologue, for example, provides a dimension that is not common in novels on similar themes. The action is episodic and spotlights different characters. In very general terms, the story deals with the hope of divine intervention, always left unfulfilled. Its major unifying strands concern the persistent attempt of Cristino to maintain life in a blighted area, and the repeated attempts of the physician to leave. Basically the narration is third-person ominiscient and copious dialogue uses phonetic representation of regional speech. Interior monologue appears in italics. Sometimes the interior monologue is mainly a technique of characterization; on other occasions it moves the story. The narration is considerably more sophisticated than that of *El indio*, for example; however, the author sees the situation from outside and does not approach the deep perception of Rosario Castellanos in *Oficio de tinieblas* (1962).

It is possible to say that the social protest in *Donde haya Dios* is vigorous but subtle; and a similar statement would be fair with regard to *Casas muertas* by Miguel Otero Silva. The novel is set in the dying town of Ortiz — malaria infested, almost a ghost town, and ignored by political authority. Its sad condition may be taken as a protest against dictatorial government. However, the relationship of the town to the condition of the country develops very gradually. No obvious statement concerning the symbolism of the *casas muertas* (dead houses) appears until more than halfway through the book. Up to that time, a general sense of hopelessness grows, but on the basis of the town's poor economy and miserable health. Then a busload of student-age political prisoners stops in the town. On leaving, some of them speak of the dilapidated houses. One young prisoner says: "I didn't see the houses, or the ruins of the houses.

I just saw the sores on the bodies of the people." Another responds, "They are disintegrating like the houses, like the country we were born in."[8]

This episode is a natural development in a story that depends fundamentally on an extended flashback. The novel begins with the funeral of Sebastián, a young man who had been a spark of life in an ambience of death. The principal mourner is his sweetheart, Carmen Rosa, a second factor of vitality. Otero Silva emphasizes her role in two principal ways: she maintains a garden in a town where dying is more apparent than growing, and she seeks out people who remember the town as it was before it was damned by malaria and other ailments. By focusing on Carmen Rosa, the narrator takes us backward in time—to the immediate past (Sebastián's death), the past that corresponds to Carmen Rosa's childhood, and to a point in the life of the town before the girl was born. Then he brings the story forward to the point of beginning and slightly past that point. The time overlap with the first chapter occurs right at the beginning of the last chapter (p. 116), so the rest of the book has the effect of an epilogue.

The flashback structure of the novel establishes, from the beginning, the sense of death. When Carmen Rosa meets Sebastián, within the extended flashback, we already know that she represents the only possible hope of counteracting Sebastián's defeat. We witness his struggle in two ways. Initially, he is a strong personality, nothing more. When the political prisoners stop in Ortiz, he becomes a rebel. The plot to free the prisoners, in which he participates, fails, but he keeps his hope alive. We experience his struggle in another way when he is delirious with fever. He sees himself as a leader, but with no specific plan for government of the country. In the epilogue (the last chapter), Carmen Rosa persuades her mother and their employee to leave Ortiz and go to the province of Oriente where oil has been discovered. In terms of specific action, this is hardly a solution to the problem set forth in the novel. However, it is consistent with the characterization of Carmen Rosa, because she represents dynamism in a swamp of resignation.

Characterization is not particularly profound in *Casas muertas*, and there are no doubts about distinguishing between the heroes and the villains; however, the people are individually interesting. The narrative stucture establishes a relationship between the characters and the reader before social protest becomes apparent. That is why Otero Silva's novel is more convincing than the average socially committed novel is. We appreciate the circumstance by getting to know the people; then we become aware of the vigorous denunciation of injustice. The author's stylistic devices are also low keyed, but effective. Repetitions emphasize a personality characteristic—Celestino, for example, is always afraid to tell Carmen Rosa of his love for her because he dreads her probable rejection of him, and almost the same words describe his hesitation later on. Repetition also may end a chapter or a section of a chapter, emphasizing some aspect of the narrative; and on some occasions, repetitions combine with parallel syntactical structures to create special effects, like the passage of time (p. 62) or the deterioration of Sebastián's physical condition (p. 112). These techniques are never obtrusive; they serve their purpose without inviting attention to technique. Toward the end of the novel, the narrator goes more deeply into the inner awareness of Sebastián and Carmen Rosa. In the case of the former, it is a question of more detailed psychological insight; in the case of Carmen Rosa, the narrator selects those things that have influenced her most and uses them in a kind of stocktaking by her, but in third person. Gradually he has moved us to a fuller appreciation of the two main characters, and within this development is the subtle intensification of social protest. Both lines of change stem from two contrasts involving Carmen Rosa. One contrasts her victory with Sebastián's defeat; the other contrasts her persistence as opposed to Celestino's resignation.

The revisionist attitude of the young Argentine writers inspired a wide range of fiction, including the essayistic, philosophical novels of Héctor A. Murena. His *La fatalidad de los cuerpos* could be used as an example of a long list of things that should not happen in a novel; nevertheless, it is interesting because it is related to his essays and because it takes on meaning as a corollary to Viñas's novel published the same year. One of Murena's propositions, in his essays on the condition of being Argentine, is that the New World experience (specifically in Argentina, but more generally in all of America) may be characterized by a sense of being dispossessed.[9] This condition appears to be a specialized version of existentialist alienation. In the American context it involves a separation from history; and the resulting isolation leads to the fabrication of false fronts, of walls to hide behind. As examples, overemphasis on material well being is on a par with superficial intellectuality. It is in this sensitivity to the inauthenticity of Argentine (or American) culture that Murena's works complement those of Viñas.

La fatalidad de los cuerpos, the first volume of a trilogy, deals with the self-analysis of Alejandro Sertia, a wealthy industrialist. He suffers a heart attack and consequently comes to grips with a series of questions concerning the meaning of life—what he owes other people, what they owe him, what right he has to earthly happiness, how he tends to find a point between extremes. It is of some interest to note that his illness strikes after the material things he has enjoyed begin to lose their charm. Sertia's death occurs at the beginning of a trip, following his decision to retreat to a tropical isle.

In a prefatory chapter, the narrator—always third person—tells of the onset of the protagonist's illness and the circumstances surrounding it. Subsequent chapters use two lines of interest to illustrate Sertia's reactions. One has to do with his business affairs, seen mainly through his treacherous subordinate, Hussey; the other line is personal and develops mainly around Clotilde, the protagonist's daughter by an early marriage. The relationship with Clotilde involves a generation-gap problem, specifically the girl's lack of interest in marrying although she is pregnant. This line turns conventional at the end. The two interests of Sertia, business and personal, unite in Fernando, a trusted employee for whom the protagonist is a father figure. That relationship is tragically terminated.

Although Murena uses some flashbacks, the development of the story is basically lineal; there are no technical devices to make the novel transcend its expository nature. Some good imagery serves to create atmosphere and occasionally to define character. The characters, however, never quite separate themselves from the narrator, who prefers to tell about them rather than allow them to act. Dialogue is similar in function. It is rather stiff when it appears; but most often we find out about what people say, rather than hear them say it. The novel's dynamic factor, therefore, is an attitude toward living, which is set forth so it may be considered by the reader, rather than experienced by him. Even so, the concepts are elusive.

By the end of the novel—and particularly right at the end—we comprehend the protagonist's futility and the narrator's disgust. All through the book, Sertia's questioning of himself creates the image of a man who has always played the game in the middle, never really committing himself, in spite of his apparent success. This success has no real meaning, has nothing to do with his vital forces. When his story ends, it appears that his death is unrelated to the sequence of events in his life. It would have made more sense if he had died at a different time; but then his living did not make much sense either, at least as it is explicated by the narrator. There is, however, the suggestion of a kind of victory through defeat—if one really comes to terms with his loneliness, he achieves a realization of himself reintegrated. This transcendent expectation may make the reader wish to participate more actively in the development of the novel, but this experience is prohibited by the discursive and expository nature of Murena's work.

Two novels of 1955 require brief mention, though they are not closely related to any of the year's other novels. One is a highly sophisticated crime story, *Rosaura a las diez*, by Marco Denevi. The structure consists of four accounts of the same event, told by four different characters, plus a clarifying letter written by Rosaura. This narrative procedure is not unique with Denevi, of course, but he handles it as carefully and as effectively as anyone. It is quite likely that the novel has suffered some slight injustice on the part of the critics. The author belongs to the same generation as Viñas and Murena—a generation whose work we expect to have some profound significance. Denevi offers only a carefully wrought story— an experience of tension and release. Nevertheless, the narrative technique provides an appreciation of reality that may well be a deeper experience (though not a deeper intellectual exercise) than a novel like *La fatalidad de los cuerpos*.

The second novel is *Los Ingar*, by Carlos Eduardo Zavaleta, who published the highly contemplative *El cínico* several years before. Human relationships are important in *Los Ingar* just as in the earlier novel, but the circumstance is much more vital. The story is narrated in the first person by the fifteen-year-old member of a fighting, difficult, provincial family. The narrative point of view works extremely well as the young narrator anticipates a course of events that sometimes does not correspond to what actually happens. There is trouble with the law, unjust accusations and the like, but relationships within the family are just as important thematically. This balancing of factors supports the more general defense of the value of the individual over the social organization.

One of the most notable characteristics of the year of *Pedro Páramo* is the appearance of first novels by Rulfo, Gabriel García Márquez, David Viñas, Héctor A. Murena, Marco Denevi, and Antonio Di Benedetto. Five of these authors are now regarded as major Spanish American writers; the sixth, Di Benedetto, deserves much greater recognition than he has been accorded—probably as the result of limited cultural communication among the Americas, rather than of critical disfavor. The commitment of Argentina's "angry generation" is the most attractive literary phenomenon apparent during the year, especially because of the insight it provides into the Perón regime and the cultural patterns associated with it. However, the fascination of this literary-political combination should not be allowed to obscure the artistic importance of *Pedro Páramo* and *La hojarasca*. Regarding mastery of technique, the ten novels discussed in this chapter reveal writers who are confident of their craftsmanship, whatever failures may be apparent in specific cases. Multifaceted or segmented narrative structure involving changing point of view is commonplace and is handled with facility. The use of regional themes reaches a depth rarely even suggested in the novels of a quarter-century earlier. In short, this cross section shows mature, modern fiction.

CHAPTER 15

From *Pedro Páramo* to *Rayuela* (1956–1962)

Although the terms "new Latin American novel" and "the boom" sometimes appear synonymous, they really indicate two different aspects of a single phenomenon—the maturity of fiction in Latin America. Specifically with reference to the Spanish-speaking countries, it is convenient to think of the new novel as dating from the late 1940s, the years of the reaffirmation of fiction. The boom, on the other hand, best describes the unprecedented international interest enjoyed by Spanish American novelists in the 1960s, and the spectacular increase in the number of high-quality novels they produced. Although nobody thought of it as a boom until several years later, the change is readily apparent in the years following *Pedro Páramo*. The foundations had been laid: Spanish American novelists were technically sophisticated and sure that the novel was a valid artistic expression. The overwhelming number of good novels published in the period 1956–1962 could easily justify division into several chapters. Nevertheless, they belong in a single showcase of a remarkable period—one in which two generations are notably productive, in which there is wide variation in techniques and themes, and a period when Spanish American authors write with more confidence in their art than at any earlier time.

In order to provide an organization for the panorama, the present study will deal first with some of the younger novelists most closely associated with the boom. Then a review of the works published in 1956–1962 by established writers will show the relationship of the boom to the new novel. After that, some general thematic classifications of novels by other young writers will illustrate the diversity of fiction during these years. Some novels deal with specific, national scenes; within this classification are some works based on current politics while others are more concerned with the cultural heritage of the nation or region. Another large classification is a far more intimate kind of novel, more overtly concerned for people than for places or politics; within this group are some that are anguished to the point of nihilism while others are more objective studies of human relationships. Such classifications, of course, are oversimplifications of what the novels are. All classifications of this kind should be taken as organizational devices, never as critical opinions.

If someone were to make a survey, asking which Spanish American novelists are the best representatives of the boom, the chances are that the most frequently mentioned names would be Julio Cortázar, Carlos Fuentes, Gabriel García Márquez, and Mario Vargas Llosa (mentioned here in alphabetical order). In addition to their obvious excellence as writers, they share several other characteristics associated with the boom. They belong to an international literary set, travel extensively, spend much time in residence abroad (in some cases even most of the time), but find inspiration in their cultural heritage. To some extent they consider themselves handicapped by the unsympathetic cultural milieu of their native countries. There are practical reasons for this attitude; however, the reaction is occasionally similar to the *poète maudit* syndrome. Awareness of the creative act of making fiction causes the boom novelists to comment willingly (and sometimes eagerly) on the nature of fiction. Together they make an impressive declaration, in the forum of world literature, of the excellence of Spanish American letters; and it may be even more important that they have stimulated

212

communication among writers of the Spanish American countries— a condition that has never been as productive as during the 1960s. One undesirable effect of the boom is that a few writers in the spotlight tend to be lionized while many good writers are ignored. Such an effect is by no means the intention of the best-known writers, and, although their fame may shine brighter than the reputations of many worthy colleagues, it is equally true that they have attracted attention to a body of literature that badly needed publicity. The boom is not four novelists, or even six or seven. A large number of writers participate in the activities, attitudes, and rewards of the boom. Indeed, the rewards have benefited many novelists who probably would not even consider themselves part of the boom.

Three of the four big names appear as novelists during the 1956–1962 period. The fourth, Vargas Llosa, published an important volume of short stories, *Los jefes*, during this period, but his first novel, *La ciudad y los perros*, did not appear until 1963, the year of Cortázar's *Rayuela*. Cortázar himself published *Los premios* in 1960, a good novel that has been eclipsed by the fame of *Rayuela*. García Márquez published two works, *El coronel no tiene quien le escriba* (1961) and *La mala hora* (1962), that resemble his *La hojarasca* in two ways: they are generically somewhere between a short story and a novel, and are creations preliminary to the main event that turned into *Cien años de soledad* in 1967. The most active of the four was Carlos Fuentes, who established himself as a major writer through the excellence and variety of four works in a time span of five years: *La región más transparente* (1958), *Las buenas conciencias* (1960), *La muerte de Artemio Cruz* (1962), and *Aura* (1962).

Fuentes's first novel is complicated in structure, long, often discursive, but also highly entertaining. It is a panorama of life in modern Mexico City and, at the same time, an analysis of what it means to be Mexican, including what the Revolution has to do with that condition. There is hardly a reader who does not find the book exciting, yet almost everyone feels compelled to point out some imperfection. The objection may be to the author's unabashed and freely confessed adaptation of the styles of other novelists, most notably of John Dos Passos. Or some may object to the definition of Mexicanism, on the grounds that national cultural identity is out of style. Someone else may object to the melodramatic prose poems that open and close the novel. More than a few have felt the novel

213

attempts too many things. All these objections, and more, have some degree of validity. What it amounts to is that we may call Carlos Fuentes a pretentious novelist, without really speaking ill of his work. He is pretentious in the sense that he does not hesitate to undertake whatever strikes his creative fancy. It might be more accurate to say he is a flamboyant novelist. Whatever the word, in many respects his fiction comes close to being excessive, and it spills over at different places depending on where an individual reader's tolerance level is lowest.

In *La región más transparente*, Fuentes segments the narrative to achieve simultaneity in place-time relationships. By means of references that relate one segment to another, we know that two events separated in space are happening at the same time. The focal point at the beginning of the novel is a party attended by Mexico City's cocktail crowd. The basic scene is more than a view of life in a particular city; it is a revelation of some of the most superficial aspects of western culture. The overall picture, however, includes all social classes in the city, with economic and moral corollaries.

The central character in the novel's basic structure is an old revolutionary named Federico Robles. He is a financial tycoon, a self-made man whose power grew from the Revolution. As we know him in the novel, however, his position among the power elite has no real meaning since it serves only to feed itself. Robles has to find special relationships to maintain his hold on reality. His story is one of financial ruin and possible self-discovery. If this story were the central incident of the novel, it would be a far more compact work than it is in fact. The importance of Robles—and of the Robles story—is to provide a unifying factor that relates many lives and problems so that they form a mosaic of life in Mexico City; it is in this sense that Robles is the central character. Not through him, but in relation to him, we appreciate the reality of post-Revolutionary Mexico—a society changed in many ways from the years preceding, but one that is certainly not revolutionary in any common understanding of the term.

In spite of the very careful characterization of Federico Robles and the use of helpful narrative devices in the manner of Dos Passos, the basic narrative structure of *La región más transparente* apparently does not serve to create the complex of feelings and ideas desired by the author. Therefore, he adds two important characters,

214

Manuel Zamacona and Ixca Cienfuegos, who are laced into the narrative structure without being essential factors. They are interesting and important to what Fuentes apparently wishes to say, but the Robles story could stand without them. Zamacona is an intellectual poet who thrives on discussions of the meaning of being Mexican. His discourses—and the dialogues in which he participates—are more like essays than fiction. Cienfuegos is harder to define. He is a representation of the Indian influence in Mexican life. Part man and part myth, he suffers some human limitations, but goes beyond these limitations in his ability to be everywhere, inexplicably yet undeniably. We can never know exactly who he is, and this quality is an important element in his symbolic value; that is, the indigenous factor in Mexican culture is generally recognized but not well defined. Cienfuegos, even more than Zamacona, seems to exist in order to make a statement the author considered essential but could not express in any other way.

Fuentes pursues many of the same ideas and attitudes in *La muerte de Artemio Cruz*, his best novel. His technical virtuosity is as apparent as in *La región más transparente*, but is more controlled in a novel whose structure is essential to its meaning. The protagonist, Artemio Cruz, is similar in many ways to Federico Robles. The novel opens at a time shortly before his death and creates a multifaceted biography of the man, using narrative voices in first, second, and third persons. The first-person narrative is absolute present—Artemio Cruz taking account of his actual situation. The second-person voice (the familiar "you" in Spanish) moves back into the past and, from that point, looks toward the future. This future is, of course, already past in terms of the novel's basic present time. The use of a second-person narrative voice, though fairly common in very recent fiction, still tends to be a distracting technique that requires an act of generous acceptance by the reader. The effect it creates seems to depend not only on the author's intent, but also on the individual reader's reaction to the surprise. Some are put off, for example, by the imperative tone of the "you" sections of *La muerte de Artemio Cruz*. The fact is that several readings are possible. One reasonable and satisfying understanding of this narrative perspective is that Artemio Cruz is beside himself, observing his actions as a normally integrated personality. In addition to this placement of the narrator, the "you" passages exploit the time factor as a means of characterizing the protagonist. This narrative voice does not look back; the view is toward the future. This impulse is one of the major factors in the character of Artemio Cruz. It explains some of his actions, illuminates the tragedy of the moment of his death, and amounts to a moral commentary.

The third-person voice belongs to an omniscient narrator who recounts past incidents in the life of Cruz. Each episode is specifically placed in time. They are important moments rather than a full narration, and their placement is not in chronological order, but in a sequence that produces meaningful associations. Fuentes alternates the three narrative voices to create a fascinating character whose life represents modern Mexico—not as a symbol, but as a real person. The connotations of the characterization of Artemio Cruz are practically limitless. In very general terms, it is probably accurate to say that power is the protagonist's goal, the only thing he really values. He has very little sense of belonging—to another person, to a place, or to a culture. What little inclination he has in this direction falls victim to his will to be powerful. This attitude—still speaking in very general terms—is one way of describing Fuentes's sensitivity to the failure of the Revolution. These novels were published during a period that saw a strike of railroad workers summarily broken by the army in 1959 and the imprisonment of David Alfaro Siqueiros, the leftist painter, for "social dissolution," in 1960. It is not necessary to take sides on these specific issues to understand how they might symbolize the exercise of power at the expense of social justice that is part of the revolutionary ideal.

Fuentes is so skillful a technician that we can easily identify certain narrative procedures as the dynamic factors of his novels— the source of the change that takes place within the work, or the agent that transforms anecdote into art. These observations, however, can still leave much unsaid, because they do not necessarily indicate how interesting his novels are. It is a sad fact that, in recent fiction, some of the most spectacular narrative techniques grace some painfully dull novels. Not so in the works of Fuentes—at least not in those of the years 1956–1962. What analysis of technique cannot possibly communicate is the sheer joy of a mother-daughter dialogue on the correct pronunciation of Joan Crawford's last name, the insidious presence of old age in an episode about sugar-daddy Artemio in Acapulco with his luscious young dolly, or the combination of fun and cruelty among some lower-class fans at a bullfight. The author's sensitivity to reader interest makes him as competent a novelist on the small canvas as he is in the panoramic, murallike works.

A fine example of this small-canvas writing is Fuentes's second novel, *Las buenas conciencias* (1960). Rather than Mexico City, the scene is Guanajuato, a provincial town. Jaime Ceballos, a minor character in *La región más transparente*, is the protagonist. The book deals with well-meaning people who are inhibited by custom and tradition to the point of being unwittingly frustrated. *Las buenas conciencias* is in many ways the opposite of *La región más transparente*, almost as if Fuentes intended to show his critics how he could organize a novel economically and use traditional techniques effectively. *Las buenas conciencias* was originally intended to be the first of a series, later abandoned and, unfortunately, almost forgotten. It is an interesting link between the heroically proportioned novels and the more intimate works of writers like Sergio Galindo, Pedro Orgambide, and Haroldo Conti.

Aura (1962) is a novella that reveals another important aspect of Fuentes as a novelist—his love for the mysterious. In this respect, *Aura* recalls a number of his short stories and also the elusive Ixca Cienfuegos in *La región más transparente*. In the novella, a young scholar-narrator is employed by an elderly woman whose life reaches incredibly far back into history. However, she is also a young woman—the product of her own will. It is not likely to surprise many readers that the narrator falls in love with Aura (the young version) and finally discovers he has been duped. Here indeed is the novel's great fault: not many readers will be surprised by any of it. As a mystery story, it fails because the author gives away his secret. Attempts to find other meanings in the story include a social-protest reading which sees the old woman as a representation of the superannuated impediments to social progress in Mexico, the ash that covers the fire and refuses to move.[1] A more interesting aspect of the double personality is the question it raises concerning identity, and the second-person narrative tends to incorporate the reader into the identity problem, unless he rejects this narrative technique and removes himself from participation. Fuentes loves the identity game and plays it well, albeit too frequently, in his later work. This particular interest, however, shows Fuentes's relationship to still another group of recent novelists: those who play tricks with reality, almost always producing a problem of identity.

The two short novels of García Márquez continue the story of Macondo that begins in *La hojarasca* and culminates in *Cien años de soledad*. The epic quality of this body of fiction derives from a profound sense of history that mythologizes a culture, rather than from a panoramic vision like that of Fuentes. The retired colonel of *El coronel no tiene quien le escriba* is a combination of pathos and dignity. The story concentrates on him, but it suggests much more than it actually says. The man is a victim of dehumanized bureaucracy, for example; yet he continues to hope while trying to hide from others the fact that he is hopeful. This set of circumstances suggests—but only suggests—a detailed biography of the protagonist. *La mala hora* is a distillation of the fear and distrust that are essential parts of *la violencia* in Colombia. Someone puts up placards around the town undermining the security of the people who live there. What the placards actually say is not in itself of such devastating import. Much of it is equivalent to common gossip. However, two factors give them a special importance: the message is written, and no one knows who is posting them. The possibility of civil war turns to probability.

Except for a few devices like the multiple narrative voice in *La hojarasca*, García Márquez's narrative techniques tend to be rather conservative. His storyteller's imagination is the major creative tool. He has not the slightest doubt about his right to invent. Much of the unreality of his work, most of the feeling of myth, and a large portion of the humor come from this uninhibited invention. Often he deals with the extraordinary as if it were entirely commonplace. The colonel keeps his gamecock tied to the foot of his bed, and he does it as matter-of-factly as he pours a cup of coffee. Some of the inventions are preposterous. The newly arrived doctor in *La hojarasca* asks for grass for dinner, and we never find any explanation or exploitation of this unusual appetite. Wherever the inventions are used (and even where withheld information is itself a form of exaggeration), they create a special atmosphere—a new reality that springs from one that is more familiar.

Los premios (1960) is Julio Cortázar's major step toward *Rayuela* (1963), though he had written many short stories. This first novel is a playful yet serious consideration of a set of human destinies. The basic situation of the story is highly artificial—a diverse collection of *porteños* (people from Buenos Aires) are on a sea voyage because each has won the trip in a lottery. They are interesting as types recognizable in *porteño* society. Luis Harss points out that this fact is of secondary interest to the author.[2] Nevertheless, it would be foolish to overlook this factor of identity in a novel that deals with the problem of identity. In any work of this kind, there is a counterpointing of two qualities: one that emanates from the author's experience of belonging and another that comes from his experience of creating. They are not categorically separated, of course, but they certainly are recognizable as they function side by side. Carlos Fuentes, for example, might say he is only secondarily interested in the definition of the Mexican character, that he is really seeking the human reality beyond that definition. On the other hand, he might say exactly the opposite, and neither statement would change what he has written. So also with Cortázar. *Los premios* can be enjoyed as a gallery of types. Moving to an entirely different level, we experience the inconclusive self-identification of people who do not understand their destinies. As the novel develops, a sense of impenetrable mystery grows. The stern of the ship is forbidden to the passengers. Something strange—probably malevolent—is going on. We never find out what it is.

This withheld information is a major use of a technique that García Márquez uses in a minor way. In *Los premios*, it creates an atmosphere that should be enough of a message in itself. Cortázar, however, like Fuentes in *La región más transparente*, apparently thinks the basic structure of his novel does not say enough, so he inserts a character, Persio, who functions as an invented narrator. In expository passages that bear a limited resemblance to interior monologue (and printed in italics), Persio sees the group as a whole. The unifying effect is aesthetically desirable; but Persio is a presumptuous intruder, a nonentity who does not correspond to author, character, or reader, and his metaphysical wanderings are a bore. The diversity of the passengers is the interesting factor, whatever the level of appreciation. Among the several possibilities, one rather far-fetched one has a certain insistent appeal: that these *porteño* types, taken collectively, may represent the world view of a particular culture in their restricted understanding of their own reality, with a consequent accumulation of doubts and forebodings.

Whatever the shortcomings of particular works by these three writers who became big names in the boom, there is no doubt they are excellent novelists. It is important to notice, however (and it may be surprising to casual readers of Spanish American fiction), that they are not very notable for their technical innovation. In all fairness, the novelists themselves have never made that claim; critics and scholars have tended to emphasize their technical adventures because of a universal tendency to ignore their direct predecessors in Spanish America while eulogizing some of the least imaginative novels the region has produced. Carlos Fuentes freely admits his indebtedness to non-Hispanic novelists, and particularly to some in the United States. What he does not point out is that practically all the narrative techniques he learned reading North American novels had been used also in Spanish American fiction, by authors frequently not well known and, in many cases, not as gifted as Fuentes or the major writers who influenced him.

A number of the established writers who were productive during the period 1956–1962 belong to that delayed generation that tried its wings in the vanguardism of the late 1920s and early 1930s, and then went through a quiet period before participating in the reaffirmation of fiction in the late 1940s. Some established writers show little or no change from their earlier works; others are clearly different. Some participate in the boom, though not as intensely as the newer writers.

The works of Miguel Angel Asturias during this period belong to the negative side of his ledger. Protest dominates them—perfectly justifiable protest against the United States' imperialism, economic and political. Justifiable protest, however, does not necessarily make art; in some instances, Asturias's anxiety makes his work ridiculous. Agustín Yáñez continues to produce the portrait of Mexico begun in *Al filo del agua*. He never again achieves that excellence, but he comes very close in *Las tierras flacas* (1962). This is a novel of the high country—the land is poor and the people are persistently enduring. One of the major techniques used to portray these people is the proverb, the folk saying, not simply placed in dialogue, but used as the basis of stream-of-consciousness narration or as interior monologue. These sayings create a feeling of the sparseness of the land. The most basic representative of a technological age, a sewing machine, serves to illuminate the frustrations and faith of the people.

In a very carefully balanced narrative structure, the author sets this primitive technology against a more complicated one, and also the general concept of technological progress against the primitive endurance of the people.

Both Yáñez and Eduardo Mallea wrote novels on the creative act: Yáñez in *La creación* (1949) and Mallea in *Simbad* (1957). *La creación* is about a musician—a very difficult way to deal with creativity when the author is confined to words. The novel contains interesting suggestions about the process of making an artistic work, but there is no satisfactory communication of the feeling of the process itself. The novel is more interesting for its picture of the artistic world in post-Revolutionary Mexico. Mallea wisely creates a protagonist who is a writer. *Simbad* is an enormous book, a kind of stocktaking of the writer's relationship to the world. In this respect, it is reminiscent of *La bahía del silencio*—in principle, not in detail. Mallea's protagonist, Fernando Fe, imagines a work in which Simbad will end his quest, discovering his dream world. Fernando's imagined world overlaps with his real world, and this circumstance is the means of highlighting the nature of creativity. The author uses one of his favorite narrative devices: the double plot line. In this case the two are clearly related to each other, but create entirely different impressions of the duration of time. The five sections of the novel tell the life story of Fernando Fe; however, each of the sections has a prelude that deals with the protagonist's action during a short but crucial period of his life. Here, as in earlier novels, Mallea narrates defining. It is possible that the habits and customs of the characters (mostly intellectual bourgeoisie) may have some intrinsic interest, but the principal communication of the book is the never-ending quest of man as artist and as ordinary human.

Both Alejo Carpentier and Juan Carlos Onetti produced their best novels between 1956 and 1962. Carpentier's *El acoso* (1957) is a short novel generally recognized as a technical tour de force. The plot, basically a manhunt, develops in time and tension that accord with a performance of Beethoven's Third Symphony. The tension created by this structural requirement harmonizes with the emotional tension of the plot. The characters are recognizable Havana types, but that fact, as in Cortázar's *Los premios*, is secondary unless the reader is looking specifically for that characteristic.

El acoso is a virtuoso performance, but *El siglo de las luces* (1962) is the best of Carpentier's major works. He finds the basis of his magic in history, as in *El reino de este mundo*. The time is the French Revolution and the Napoleonic era. The protagonist is an obscure figure in French history, Victor Hugues. His exploits bring him into contact with an aristocratic family in colonial Havana. The story deals with the family and also with the partially separate line of Hugues's adventures. Cuba, the whole Caribbean area, France, and Spain are brought together in the story, so the concept of cultural heritage develops jointly with the idea of revolution. All this is another part of the New World experience. Carpentier's way of dealing with history, here as elsewhere, gives it a magical quality. Hugues is the man of action, ideas put in motion. The principle of revolution, along with its relationship to ambition and success, appears in a historical frame, but the transfer to contemporary implications is easy enough. Undoubtedly, Carpentier thinks of the Cuban Revolution as a restatement of a historical constant.

The lack of meaning that bedevils the characters of Juan Carlos Onetti becomes a kind of gamesmanship in *El astillero* (1961), one of the best novels—possibly the best—written by the dour Uruguayan. The title of the novel is the Spanish word for shipyard. This enterprise is located in Onetti's mythical town of Santa María. The protagonist, Larsen, returns to the town determined to make a name for himself. A position as general manager of the shipyard seems to be the perfect opportunity. Its owner, Petrus, is an aging businessman who pretends that the shipyard's affairs are about to take a turn for the better. The fact is that it is a collection of rusty machinery, a skeleton of what once existed. There is no business except the illicit activity of selling what remains of the machinery, without the owner's permission. General manager Larsen has two employees: a technical administrator and a business manager who pore over disintegrating blueprints and keep imaginary accounts of transactions that never happen. Everybody knows perfectly well that they're just playing a game, going through a set of motions. Larsen even courts the boss's daughter, a mentally retarded girl who lives in a musty old house about as lively as the shipyard.

The narrator tells the story of *El astillero* as if he himself witnessed part of it and learned the rest from other people. This point of view keeps the reader aware that the novel's characters do not see some facts that ought to be apparent to them. Therefore, we react to Larsen and the others not as we might toward people who are being deceived, but as we might toward those who deceive themselves. One reaction is to feel that they must hold on to this pretense because it is all they have. Another is that life amounts to playing a game that has no meaning beyond the game itself. It is impossible to dismiss *El astillero* without thinking about Uruguayan politics, which allow government by committee to promote civic inertia and the consequent corrosion, material and spiritual, of the nation. The exposé of life as a game demands more than a political answer, but the answer is not found in Onetti's novel.

Ernesto Sábato's *Sobre héroes y tumbas* (1962) tends to overwhelm readers. An initial experience with it creates an impression of a great mural depicting the present (last years of the Perón regime) and past of Argentina, with an extra dimension provided by the third of the novel's four parts, a penetrating interiorization of Fernando Vidal, possibly the novelist's protagonist.[3] Even after several readings, many questions remain unanswered, and two readers can easily become completely absorbed in asking each other what Sábato means by this or that character or act. Angela Dellepiane does the best job of relating his essays to his novels and it is through her analysis that we begin to see *Sobre héroes y tumbas* as an examination of values, an attempt to reindividualize human beings in the context of contemporary society.[4]

Sábato contrasts two characters, Alejandra and Martín, particularly in the first two parts of the novel. She is impure and belongs to a family that includes an unusually high percentage of the famous names of Argentine history. Martín, on the other hand, is innocent and is virtually without family ties and tradition. These two antithetical people seem irresistibly attracted to each other. Indeed, one of the less attractive features of the novel is the author's insistence on this deterministic relationship. It is a love affair more for a novel of the early nineteenth century than for one of the late twentieth. However, the telescoping of the emotion-time effect is one of the novel's narrative techniques. An account of the retreat of General Lavalle, a historical event of more than a century ago, functions as one element in the mural of contemporary Argentina and is particularly significant in its communication of a sense of honor and loyalty. There is a suggestion of the decadence of tradition, set forth in the character of Alejandra and the relationship within her family; but the Lavalle account is strongly affirmative. Martín, on the other hand, is devoid of tradition even to the point of being denied by his own mother; yet he is the character who carries the novel's spark of optimism. It is possible to suppose that Sábato wishes to set forth human values in such a way that they cannot possibly be confused with the process of passing time. Such an understanding would be far removed from an initial reading, because the story of the fatally attracted lovers plus a melodramatic development worthy of *King's Row* (incest, murder, suicide) overwhelm more subtle appreciations.

One critic provides a unified understanding of the novel through the archetypal explanation of Fernando as a hero.[5] He sees a pairing of General Lavalle and Fernando, the latter's interior descent into hell working as a contemporary parallel to Lavalle's heroic act. The nucleus of this reading is the third part of the novel, "Informe sobre ciegos," which may be taken as the journey through the underworld —an interior experience that recalls the journey of *Adán Buenosayres*. It is possible to find, in Fernando's experience, the seeds of Martín's salvation. This analysis, however, is a lot neater than the novel; it can illuminate the book, but should not be taken as an equivalent to the experience of the novel itself.

Manuel Mujica Lainez, already known for his aesthetic interests and his nostalgic novels based on the changing social structure of Buenos Aires, published *Bomarzo* in 1962. This book provided the story for Alberto Ginastera's opera. It is a historical novel that creates the flavor of the Renaissance. The author has been the art critic for the newspaper *La Nación* and for several years was connected with a museum. His sensitivity is not simply the enjoyment of artistic creations, but includes also a reaction of delight in the very act of evoking a past era. This evocation is one of the two important factors that make *Bomarzo* interesting. The other is the incorporation into the story of many well-known historical personages: Cervantes, Michelangelo, Lotto, Cellini, Charles V, and others. Mujica Lainez's work reveals his aristocratic attitude, and it is also a representative of the Argentine literary world's sophistication. The author is a latter day member of the Florida fellowship; his works contain many of the qualities that provoked the rebellion of the parricides, the revisionist writers of the Viñas group.

Another important writer, Ezequiel Martínez Estrada, may seem a strange addition to a group of established novelists, since he is more often thought of as an essayist. Actually he has made distinguished contributions to literature also as a poet and as a writer of fiction. While none of his works in the latter category have ever been considered major, they might well have enjoyed more attention if his essays had been less remarkable. The excellence of his stories and short novels is the result of several factors of great importance in the development of the genre: transformation of philosophical attitudes into fiction, association of narrative invention with the creative impulse, and use of stylistic variation to communicate the experience of the story.

His "Viudez" (1956) is the portrayal of a widow's confusion, indecisiveness, and eventual recognition of her state of being alone.[6] The dynamic factor in the novel is the progressively nightmarish quality of its three episodes. The scene is rural—the home and family of a small farmer. The first episode contains a labyrinth experience when the woman gets lost among the cattle (it is night) while going to seek aid from a neighbor. The second episode turns Carnival into a dead clown. The third tells of relatives who come and, instead of being helpful, make a fiesta that gets in the way of work the woman has to do. The reader identifies easily with the protagonist because the narrative, although in the third person, sees the situation as she would see it. It is also interesting that from this position the narrator is able to ask questions and answer them. They do not appear obtrusive because they seem to be the woman's natural questions. This advantage is a large contributing factor in the transformation of philosophical attitude into fictional experience.

Marta Riquelme is a Borgesian piece that cloaks subjectivity with a presumed objectivity. The story pretends to be a prologue written by Martínez Estrada for Marta Riquelme's memoirs. The book itself is presumed lost. It was supposedly given to Martínez Estrada for editing, by Arnaldo Orfila Reynal, who actually was director of Mexico's Fondo de Cultura Económica at one time. This setup gives the piece a desirable ring of authenticity. Beyond that, *Marta Riquelme* is a multiple satire: on the family-history type of novel, on literary scholarship of the "detective" kind, and on interpretive literary criticism. It is a stylistic tour de force because Martínez

Estrada says most of what he wishes to say simply by changing from one style to another. He uses at least four major style tones: scholarly exposition, the style used by the editor whose personal interest makes the prologue more intimate, Marta Riquelme's own style, and a style that may possibly not be Marta's.

The established novelists writing in the period 1956–1962 reveal few important changes in narrative technique. They did not need innovation. Their works of ten to fifteen years earlier established them as modern novelists. Even the best known of the younger writers used the same techniques. If it is possible—admittedly it is risky— to establish a difference between a large-screen, muralistic novel and a small-screen, salon-type book, it is correct to say that the large-screen type is more common among the established novelists. It is doubtful, however, that this preference indicates a generational choice. Among the younger novelists, the muralistic concept is very common. In any case, the established novelists of this period make up an unusual generation, because the fruition of their productive period was delayed so they often appear younger than they really are.

Separation of the new novelists of this period from the big names of the boom does not in any way mean that they are inferior writers. The well-known figures of the boom serve to define the phenomenon; they do not dominate it artistically. Another pitfall in discussing the boom is the temptation to separate writers who belong to it from those who do not; or, even worse, to make a complicated scale of relative "in-ness." If we allow consideration of the boom to go deeper than reaction to personalities, all the current novelists in Spanish America participate in the phenomenon in some way and to some extent.

Among the newer novelists of the period 1956–1962, a substantial number wrote novels that fall into our general classification of large screen or muralistic. Almost always these works are concerned with some understanding or explanation of a national (or regional or cultural) situation, developing it in terms and by means of techniques that make it a vital experience rather than a set of statistics or an objective account of an event already terminated. Making a subordinate classification within this large one, it appears that some

226

novels are primarily political, while others are more concerned with the heritage, history, or tradition of the place. The political concern seems to emphasize three countries: Colombia, Argentina, and Cuba.

One of the most vital political novels is *La calle 10* (1960) by Manuel Zapata Olivella. Its factual basis is the assassination of Jorge Eliécer Gaitán and the subsequent rioting in 1948. The novel was probably written at a time closer to the event than to the date of publication. It has a sense of immediacy; however, this particular vitality persists through repeated readings, probably because a compelling impression of mass insurrection operates in balance with portraits of individuals who are genuinely appealing. This way we feel the excitement of the mass movement while, at the same time, the attractive individuals create a natural sense of brotherliness. The association makes exhortations to brotherhood unnecessary, and the result is much more convincing.

The narrator opens with a morning scene: a cadaver, a family waking up, a man with a cart, a mule, and a dog. The prose is clear, direct, sparse. Yet it creates a feeling of great tenderness when the narrator speaks of emotions, always with simplicity that is convincing because it is unadorned. He brings the crowd to life by using unidentified dialogue. The narrative darts from one street scene to another. There is enough relationship between scenes to provide a sense of group unity, but the narrator does not develop a conventional plot line. That is, there are always people or situations that connect one scene with another, but these relationships may be of little importance in the total action that takes place in a given scene. There are moments that recall *Los de abajo*. The momentum of the novel develops in three stages: the circumstance seen in terms of an individual, then in the movement of mass insurrection, and finally back to an individual. Zapata Olivella portrays abject poverty without dramatic protest, but with tenderness. Class differences become apparent, but the novel's emphasis is on contrast rather than on indignation. The tone becomes disgust when politicians destroy the momentum of the rebellion by declaring, via radio, that they are the voice of the people and the people are triumphant. Finally, back once more to communication through an individual, one disillusioned rebel starts to break his rifle, but another stops him saying he will soon have use for it. This prediction—somewhat dramatic in the cold atmosphere of today's news report—is an entirely credible promise, even a consolation, in the context of the novel.

The feeling of frustration produced in *La calle 10* has a counterpart in another Colombian novel of the same period, Fernando Soto Aparicio's *La rebelión de las ratas*. It is a social protest novel, and, although it is not based on a specific political incident or problem, it deals with the dehumanizing effect of power. The circumstance is exploitation of the worker by a mining company. Soto Aparicio sets the tone, with no great subtlety, at the beginning of the novel: the advent of the mining company interrupts the bucolic quiet of the locale. Soto Aparicio moves from the general scene to the family of Rudecindo Cristancho and then shifts to the ideas of Rudecindo, his protagonist.

The time span of the novel is very specific, with narrative divisions indicated by days from February 10 to February 19. During this time, Cristancho's family suffers all the trials of poverty and exploitation by the company. Rudecindo is reduced to a number, sees his domestic happiness destroyed, and loses his life in a revolt against his exploiters. The narration is consistently third person, but from the standpoint of several different people. This procedure relates the social protest to the question of individual dignity. Therefore *La rebelión de las ratas* does not suffer from the doctrinaire effect that clutters the fictional experience of many proletarian novels.

The Argentine crisis of awareness is still acute during the years 1956–1962. David Viñas produced three novels that show he is as adept at the intimate study as he is in the muralistic books. *Los años despiadados* (1956) is the story, possibly autobiographical, of a schoolboy who feels imprisoned by the traditions of his family. It is important to note that they are not aristocratic but middle class. Even so, he feels restricted by a way of life that seems to him to belong to another age. Viñas states the message in one of his favorite ways—the development of an opposite. The protagonist's friend and opposite is the son of immigrants, and, so far as the protagonist can see, is not inhibited by any traditions. He has no apparent need to create any particular image or earn the approval of anyone. He is proletarian, *peronista*, even somewhat cruel; and his need for the protagonist's friendship is primitive. Although the novel deals only with this personal situation, we can hardly avoid the reference to change in Argentine society.

The narrative techniques Viñas uses are intended to emphasize a certain point he wishes to make. Sometimes the point is preconceived and the technique designed to bring it out. The author risks becoming didactic when he does so, but usually he is clever enough to make his characters so vital they mask his planning. That is the case in the development of the opposite. For the same reason, Viñas uses typographical effects, especially italics.[7] The first three parts (there are six in all) of *Los dueños de la tierra* (1959) are in italics, which properly set them apart because they are historical background. The novel, whose title means "the owners of the land," deals with the expansion into Patagonia, a frontier movement something like the United States' conquest of the West. In the three introductory parts of the novel, Viñas chooses three important moments in the history of the southward expansion: the Indian wars, development of the wool industry during World War I, and labor troubles between ranchers and peons in 1920.

The novel's present time—that is, the action that takes place in the last three parts—coincides with the third historical moment. President Irigoyen sends Vicente Vera to Patagonia as a conciliator. The change from italics signals the narrator's change from background to novel proper, and Vera becomes a symbol of what Viñas finds wrong with the official regime. The mood created by the story of Vera is surprisingly like the reaction to the protagonist of *Los años despiadados*. Vera, like the boy protagonist of the other novel, is so controlled by formulas there is little or no hope of his accomplishing anything. His approach is platitudinous. The difference between him and the boy is that Vera does not even know he is caught. In the next-to-last section Viñas sets up an opposite in the person of Yuda, a schoolteacher with progressive ideas. The love affair between Vera and Yuda softens the contrast, just as friendship shades the difference between the two boys in *Los años despiadados*. It is unproductive so far as Vera's mission is concerned. His government is too far removed from the nation's reality for him to be able to accomplish anything.

Beatriz Guido's *Fin de fiesta* (1958) is a successful though discouraging picture of the persistence of *caudillismo*. Guido, who likes to use young people as her protagonists, tells the story primarily through four cousins who grow up in the household of their *caudillo* grandfather. Multiple point of view contributes substantially to the effect of the novel, which alternates passages of first-person and third-person-omniscient narration. The presentation of the four cousins develops from their relationships during their early teens and continues into their political awareness. The death of the old *caudillo* fades into the rise of a new one (Perón, though he is not identified in the novel). The story suggests possible change in the quality of *caudillismo*, but it also suggests its indestructibility as an institution.

Concentration of power in one individual is the theme of *La alfombra roja* (1962), by Marta Lynch. It is a psychological study of what happens to several people during an election campaign which the protagonist, Doctor Aníbal Rey, wins. The focus is on his use of people and their reaction to him. The narrative point of view is the most important technical factor. It is consistently first person, but the identity of the first-person narrator varies from chapter to chapter. The chapter titles indicate who the narrator is in each case. The time perspective is also important—the narration is retrospective, but refers to the immediate past. The tone usually has an effect similar to a diary. The narration produces a more logical sequence of events than is characteristic of interior monologue, but the revelations made by the narrators are more intimate than we normally expect from a first-person narrator who functions in the novel on equal terms with the other characters.

Each chapter places emphasis on the person speaking, but we always learn something about the others. The candidate himself narrates chapter one (he also narrates several others) and reveals his growing taste for manipulating the crowd. In the same chapter, this euphoric demagogue introduces some of his supporters, so it is quite natural for one of them to act as the narrator of the second chapter. The technique of changing from one narrator to another produces a certain amount of simultaneity in the time covered by the various chapters. As the presidential campaign comes to a close, Lynch brings the novel to a climax. In one chapter (Beder), Rey's publicity man views the change that has taken place in the candidate. This episode is one of several where the first-person narration actually produces the effect of third-person omniscient. It is a description of the transformation of an intellectual into a power-myth:

". . . although the image of Rey that is current among the people has connection with reality, his myth is already in the making, created partly by himself, partly by history."[8]

The remaining chapters of *La alfombra roja* really constitute an epilogue. They all occur on election day; and the last, in which Rey is again the narrator, is called "El Señor Presidente," rather than "El Doctor." The basic facts of the campaign and election are commonplace, so the psychological insight into several characters is more interesting than the event itself. This fact, however, makes the mechanics of the campaign seem so cold and impersonal that its significance in the lives of human beings takes on a terrifying quality. Rey uses people more and more to gain his own ends, as he thinks of himself increasingly as a man of destiny. When Beder describes the transformation of the candidate, he describes him as unreal. By the end of the novel, the circumstance and the man are dehumanized—that is, they are not what we hope humanity is. The concluding chapters reveal the sacrifice of individuals to destiny, and at the end of the novel Aníbal Rey stands quite alone in his new residence.

The experience of political concern in these novels is preeminently one of objection to the concentration of power. There is also a strong revolutionary feeling—not in the specific threat or prediction of an uprising, but in the feeling that established political patterns must change. Nevertheless, hovering over the scene is the presence of the *caudillo*, the leader who will run the country. Marta Lynch's contribution to the literary life of this myth is portrayal of the change that takes place in the man as a corollary to the concentration of power. *La alfombra roja* deserves a place with *El Señor Presidente* and *La sombra del caudillo* in the literary picture of the phenomenon.

The novels that deal with the national heritage, rather than with a specific political situation, are even more like murals. Among the well-known novels of the boom, *La región más transparente* and *La muerte de Artemio Cruz* are good examples of this tendency. The narrative searches back into history and finds a way of illuminating a present-day reality. *Los dueños de la tierra* has something of the same effect, but the main experience of the novel turns out to be rather specifically centered on one proposition. The difference between it and *La muerte de Artemio Cruz* is interesting, because two obvious similarities attract our attention—both novels look back into the past, and both develop the plot around one man. The difference is that Artemio Cruz is the equivalent of the history in which he lives; Vicente Vera is an actor who plays his role against a historical backdrop. Viñas carefully sets the stage and clearly indicates the difference between the background and the story of Vera's mission. Fuentes, on the other hand, while he is careful to make Artemio Cruz a credible person, never separates him from history. The use of three narrative voices guarantees this result. The "I" passages make Cruz a completely individualized person; the "you" passages give him a past, and a special conscience; the "he" sections move him about in history, but never separate him from it. Therefore, the mural effect is stronger in Fuentes's novel than in Viñas's.

There is no specific set of procedures followed to gain the mural effect, but generally these novels find some way of bringing the past into the present, and they often use segments that are related to each other by associations more peripheral than the relationships required by traditional plot structure. Augusto Roa Bastos creates a sense of Paraguay's tragic history, in *Hijo de hombre* (1959), using nine chapters that are interrelated, but capable of standing independently (with possibly some minor editing in a few instances). However, the stories mean something different when they are associated with each other. There are some objective elements that link some or all of the stories: the invented narrator, the redemptive figure of Cristóbal Jara, references to place; but none of these factors is as important a unifying agent as the overall sense of oppression, of endurance, and of human dignity—always vulnerable, but always tough.

References in *Hijo de hombre* go back into the Colonial Period. One important factor in the total effect created by the novel is the feeling that the initial colonization of the area was as if by chance, when a Peruvian viceroy pointed to a spot on the map and told his subordinate to go there. However, the stories refer mainly to the twentieth century and include the Chaco War of the 1930s. Roa Bastos does not create clear-cut heroes. His profoundly humane attitude prohibits that. The values he espouses become apparent in a folkloric frame that depends on the feeling of provinciality arising from the relationships between characters, the use of repetitions to create special effects, and intelligent use of Guaraní Indian words. This last characteristic is important because it represents a fairly successful solution to an almost unsolvable problem. The Paraguayan writer must recognize the fact that he belongs to a bilingual culture, and that it is impossible to write in both Spanish and Guaraní. Roa Bastos uses many Guaraní words, but he places them with such care that an interested reader can usually tell what they mean. He never uses Guaraní in a pretentious way; rather, the strange expressions sound right. This extraordinary ability works well with his poetic attitude toward people and their problems. He is quite willing to invent, on the basis of historical incident, and his use of metaphor makes something special from something commonplace. *Don Goyo* often comes to mind, as well as some later work of Aguilera Malta and other novelists who probe ever deeper into the New World experience (Vargas Llosa and García Márquez, for example).

Antonio Di Benedetto deals with the past-present relationship in an entirely different way in *Zama* (1956). The spatial basis is much more restricted—in principle if not in objective measurement—because the scene of the novel is the Argentine province of Mendoza. The time is the last decade of the eighteenth century. Di Benedetto seems to take for granted the constancy of human behavior and the change of historical circumstances. His protagonist, Don Diego de Zama, is an existentialist antihero placed in an eighteenth-century provincial setting. In this way, the past is related to the present. The juxtaposition illuminates both of its components. The author uses unexplained phenomena (some might call them "magic realism") to intensify the mood of uncertainty created by the protagonist's vacillating character. The strange happenings contribute to a feeling of being detached from reality, and this reaction transfers to the twentieth-century alienation syndrome.

In Alvaro Cepeda Zamudio's *La casa grande* (1962), the depth of the experience comes from the communication of an event as it remains in memory, but always in the context of belonging to a family and to a town. The event is a strike of banana workers on the Colombian coast—the same strike occurs in García Márquez's *Cien años de soledad* (1967). It is put down by the army. Cepeda Zamudio's novel assumes the fact of a massacre, but does not actually present it. Two narrative techniques give the novel its special quality. One is that only generic names are used: The Soldiers, The Sister, The Father, The Town, The Decree, Thursday, and so on. These are the chapter titles, and they are the only identification. The other narrative technique is really a complex of techniques because the author changes his narrative manner from chapter to chapter, creating different effects.

Chapter one, "The Soldiers," is a description, in third-person narrative voice, of troop movement. The dialogue between two soldiers fits into the description. One of them says: "The country is not the government; the country is the flag. Stealing from the government isn't really stealing; everybody knows that."[9] And later, "The barracks and the churches are always together, always on the plazas" (p. 38). There is not much reason for the soldiers, as individuals, to oppose the strikers. However, they are individuals only to a limited extent. Since they are not given names, they tend to be identified ultimately with the collective body of soldiers, which is more receptive to the orders issued by the command.

The second chapter introduces the family of the *casa grande*. The narration is addressed to an unidentified "you," and the tone varies from accusatory to explanatory. Numerous allusions to family relationships suggest that the narrator is supplying partial information that will be supplemented later. The general effect is comfortably familiar to readers who enjoy William Faulkner or any of several family-in-history novelists. The following chapter is "The Father," and the narrative style changes completely to create first an illusion of objectivity, and later the tension of a building crisis. The opening sentences are like stage directions: "The Father is seated in a rustic chair made of wood and leather . . . The Father is sixty years old and is strong and hard" (p. 69). A section of drama-type dialogue follows this introduction; the speakers are The Father and The Girl. For several pages this type of dialogue alternates with passages of stage-direction description. Only The Father and The Girl (his daughter) participate, and the information set forth is that he is about to be killed and she is the inheritor of his strong will. The chapter concludes with ten segments of dialogue (no speakers identified), which build the feverish mood of the crisis. The tenth segment ends with a return to the stage-direction tone, but this last passage incorporates action with the description which verifies the death of The Father.

234

The narrative techniques continue to change throughout the ten chapters, always contributing to our appreciation of the situation. They vary from the legal terminology of the decree to put down the strike, as the ultimate in presumed objectivity, to a first-person reminiscence on the downfall of the family. The obvious constant is the unusual balancing of particularity and generality—or of individual identity and anonymity. Although one may dominate the other at one point or another in the novel, the balancing force becomes almost immediately apparent. The effect is to give the reader a sense of personal identification with the people—and even with the event; but the family and the event also take on a more generic significance. The major emotional concern involves the role of the family and its people in the showdown between the workers and the source of power.

The family history is of great importance in recent Colombian fiction—a possible reflection of a very conservative culture caught in the tide of change. Reading Héctor Rojas Herazo's *Respirando el verano* (1962), we think again of William Faulkner, and of Gabriel García Márquez. It is a novel of violent men and enduring women, and with a matter-of-fact acceptance of the extraordinary that particularly recalls *Cien años de soledad* and its sister novels. One of the women in *Respirando el verano*, Julia, is absent from home for a period of thirty-eight months, in the company of a peddler, *el libanés*. Then she comes back, with no explanation; she simply sits down and fans herself furiously.

The novel takes place mainly in the twentieth century, but looks back as far as 1871. An important part of the book deals with the civil war at the turn of the century—one of Colombia's eternal struggles between conservatives and progressives. An Iliad-reading grandfather is held prisoner during this conflict, and scavenging soldiers come to the house, which is really the center of the story. We experience this house as old, provincial, and with a glorious past—a once-great house. Its decay is the result of violence ranging from civil war to the internecine hate of two brothers, Horacio and Jorge. The means of looking back into the past is young Anselmo's way of understanding the reality he lives in. Past events do not appear in a logical sequence. We know Anselmo when he is nine years old, and the novel is to some extent an identity search of one person.

The problem of identity takes on a particular ethnic significance in José María Arguedas's *indigenista* novel, *Los ríos profundos* (1958). It is the story of a boy, Ernesto, who belongs to the white world by birth, but to the Indian world by cultural orientation. Ernesto is the fictional medium for the expression of the author's dual heritage, which is, by extension, characteristic of Peru.

The first part of the novel establishes the vitality of Indian culture in Ernesto's response to the world around him. Narration in the first person (Ernesto) provides the opportunity for him to point out aspects of his sensitivity that might not be apparent to an objective observer. His attitudes show a close relationship with living things and a regard for them that is similar to regard for another human. Beyond this identification, the boy finds a kind of life even in inanimate objects if they have a special meaning in his cultural heritage— the stone walls of Cuzco, for example. The boy and his father speak of things in the semireal world as if they were to be taken for granted. The author also reveals his taste for the surprising scene: when father and son enter Abancay, most of the population is kneeling in the streets, praying for the priest.

These elements all suggest a kind of mythmaking like that of Miguel Angel Asturias; however, Arguedas's novel changes course after the introductory section of thirty to forty pages. Ernesto's father leaves him in school in Abancay. From that point, the basic narrative is the traditional schoolboy story: the outsider who is uncomfortable with the other boys, the masturbation episode, growing awareness of girls, the big bully who is all brawn and no brains, the literary pupil who can write a letter worthy of a poet. What makes Ernesto special is that his feeling of being the outsider is allied with his tie to Indian culture; therefore, the problem of individual adjustment is also an ethnic contrast. The boy's Quechua heritage expresses itself in several ways: the use of Quechua words and the occasional explanation of Quechua terms, the insertion of *huaynas* (words to Quechua songs), verbal parallelisms, cultural shock arising from unfamiliar human relationships, and a more searching (or at least, very different) view of an object. An example of the last—by far the most effective manifestation of Ernesto's cultural difference—is a spinning top, a toy made by native craftsmen. In the reality of Ernesto, it becomes alive, a bird, a song, something that takes on life as we watch it. The feeling of creativity is strong. The personal relationships may hold some interest because they show that one culture does not meet the other squarely, as far as meanings are concerned. However, the impact is softened by our familiarity with the feeling of the outsider, which is real even within a single cultural context. The songs and expressions are folkloric addenda.

One of the characteristics of the new novel in Spanish America is that the authors who deal with the Indian come much closer to seeing the world from the Indian's point of view, thereby protecting the integrity of his culture and emphasizing the fundamentally human qualities of the Indians as individuals. Arguedas does so in *Los ríos profundos* because he actually feels himself to be a part of Quechua culture. Rosario Castellanos achieves similar effects in *Oficio de tinieblas* (1962), not by means of an ethnic narrator, but because she creates Indian characters who are genuinely individualized—not symbols, not components of an ethnic mass.

The geographical setting of Castellanos's novel is Chiapas, among the Tzotzil Indians. The time has two facets. What we may call the overt time of the novel is the 1930s, when revolutionary reform was at its height. The second facet of time is provided by an Indian rebellion that occurred more than a century ago. Some of the facts of this rebellion are part of the twentieth-century story—a melding that is entirely in order since the Indians have an atemporal world view. The story deals with relationships between the Tzotziles and their *ladino* (non-Indian) neighbors. It focuses on Catalina Díaz Puiljá, a Tzotzil woman whose sterility places her in an extraordinary position. In her characterizations of the Tzotziles, the author accepts the Indian culture as normal rather than exotic. Psychological development takes places within this cultural frame and with respect to each individual's role inside it. The Tzotzil culture itself is not a character trait. We see the people in three principal circumstances: the relationships involved in daily living, religious cultism, and the rebellion.

Castellanos's overall conception of the novel is more important than any specific narrative techniques, with regard to the effect achieved. The two facets of time are, of course, absolutely fundamental. The author uses a few stylistic devices that produce the effect of a different culture or circumstance: repetitions, syntactical rhythm, short sentences to create the illusion of simplicity. The narrative structure is essentially lineal with some flashbacks. These retrospective passages have nothing to do with the nineteenth-century episode that is one of the novel's facets of time, but serve only to clarify the background of some character in the story.

Oficio de tinieblas has three obvious stages: an introduction to the Tzotzil world, an introduction to the *ladino* world, and the conflict between the two. Much more subtle is the revelation of similarities and differences between them, because they are not diametrically opposed. In fact, there is a point where they neither parallel each other nor conflict absolutely—they dovetail. Holy Week is the time when this dovetailing turns into a crisis.

The mystical implications of this point in the Christian year combine with the priestesslike functions of Catalina and give a transcendent quality to the reality of the situation. The double-faceted time of the novel also differentiates it from a realistic work; and the narration of the legend of the *ilol* (Catalina) near the end of the novel creates the impression of something that happened long ago. There is an implicit criticism of the Mexican Revolution in *Oficio de tinieblas* because it shows the persistence of the Indian's problems, and placement of the story's overt time in the epoch of President Cárdenas, the most revolutionary of Mexico's presidents, eliminates the possibility of discussion centered on later conservative trends. Among the revelations effected by the dovetailing of the Tzotzil and *ladino* worlds, it is important to note that three social phenomena are experienced in parallel characters representing the two cultures: justice (Winiktón-Ulloa), fanaticism (Catalina-Mandujano), and decadence (Rosendo-Cifuentes).

The newer and deeper novelistic creation of the Indian reality seems more relevant, naturally, to the culture of the areas with high concentrations of indigenous population. Nevertheless, these novels do find wide acceptance throughout Spanish America, because the conflict between cultures is a vital part of the New World experience. Thinking of these wide-screen novels as an expression of Spanish-American reality, we need think only of how Castellanos's or Arguedas's novel complements and clarifies the role of Ixca Cienfuegos, in *La región más transparente*, in order to glimpse the fitting together of the common heritage.

In contrast to the novels dealing with the cultural heritage, writers during the years 1956–1962 published a substantial number of works that focus on human relationships. They do not avoid reference to their specific cultures, nor do they ignore its peculiarities. It is a fact, however, that a non-Hispanic reader would likely be primarily interested in the universal human problems experienced in these small-screen novels, in spite of the fact that regional and cultural differences are apparent in them. The same reader, on the other hand, would probably be most impressed by the different world he comprehends in the large-screen novels—this in spite of the fact that each and every one of them contains valid literary characterizations. José Donoso's *Coronación* (1957) has characteristics of both groups, but fits somewhat better with the salon novels because of his concentration on psychological development of characters. The protagonist is a Chilean *grande dame* who is nearing her hundredth year but refuses to die. It can be said with considerable justification that she never has really lived, but as she grows older she dies more and more. She and her frustrated son represent a famous old family. Their relationships with each other produce nothing but stubborn endurance; in their associations with people outside their social class, they appear ridiculous and futile, in spite of their persistence. Donoso uses some interior monologue to enhance characterization, and it is characterization, in fact, that provides the novel's dynamism. Except for one person (a friend of the son) who seems to tag along mainly to comment on the situation, the characters are interesting studies. Their obvious function as a commentary on the Chilean oligarchy, however, transfers the reader's attention to a specific political situation, in much the same way as in Viñas's *Los años despiadados*.

In many novels there is no such transfer. Their effect is to focus attention on how humans interact with each other, with the scope of the novel limited in some way (in space, in time, or in number of characters) so the study of a particular set of relationships is more penetrating. Often the characteristic anguish of twentieth-century man becomes an important part of the experience. There are many novels, however, that are more positive in tone but are still intensely intimist. Writers like Sergio Galindo, Pedro Orgambide, and Sara Gallardo have created novels in which the insistence is on reality—not in the sense of nineteenth-century realism, but with the intention of penetrating the reactions of people who are neither myths nor heroes. There is no division, of course, between the novels of anguish and the more affirmative ones. In the case of individual works, it is a matter of degree. However, it is possible to put aside temporarily some of the more negative views of the world while examining the affirmative.

Sergio Galindo published three novels in the period 1956–1962, including *El Bordo* (1960), a story limited in scope to the complexities of living within a single family—one that is economically secure, but not members of the idle rich. The major sources of income are a farm and the inherited fortune of a widowed aunt. The rural, provincial setting is not related to Mexico's agrarian problems. In fact, the principal characters are very sophisticated people, but the setting is important because the distance from standard patterns of urban life changes the perspective in which we see some universal problems.

Galindo begins episodes in the middle of the action and clarifies the situation as the action progresses. So the beginning of *El Bordo* opens on a preexisting scene which reveals basic traits of several characters and creates a sense of anticipation. This anticipated event is the arrival of one of the two brothers with his new wife, a stranger to the region. The result of establishing the base of the story is similar to the realist novels many people think of as traditional. The similarity, however, is only in the total result; the creative effect is entirely different. In Galindo's novel, the influence of the narrator is not apparent; his choice of detail is extremely perceptive and helpful in both characterization and plot movement; the use of retrospective dialogue (dialogue reproduced as it occurred in the past, but placed in the novel to reveal its present relevance) gives the novel depth in time without creating the sense of a flashback; the narrator is willing to settle for a brief introduction of a character if that will suffice. These techniques are more active than the procedures of traditional novels, and the resulting dynamism is attractive from the start, especially because it promises not just character study, but interaction.

In this first chapter, the narrator—either as third person or by surrendering the narrative voice to interior monologue—introduces the people, the place, and also the pattern of tensions on which the story is built. They include the strain between once-wealthy aristocracy and peasant materialism of the newly rich, between family warmth and parental rejection, between the need to love and the need to envy, between generosity and punitive stinginess, between the will to endure and the temptation to give up, between deliberation and passion, between pleasure and the wilful imposition of sadness. Early in the elaboration of the tensions, the narrator foreshadows an eventual tragedy, but does not destroy the suspense. In this elaboration, the novelist frequently moves into the poetic sphere, transcending the objective reality of a circumstance by evocation of the past, anticipation of the future, or an unusually deep and broad appreciation of a particular moment. Although three planes of time function in the novel, the narrator does not confuse them intentionally, but informs his reader by reference to material objects.

The story reaches a climax of secondary importance, which is related mainly to the aristocracy–newly rich line of tension. The denouement following this crisis leads into the major climax, which derives mainly from the love-envy tension. Two passages, both with characteristics of an epilogue, show two sets of reactions to the tragedy. One is superficial, the other enduring. It should be clear that there is never any doubt about where all this takes place. There are many references to Mexican places, customs, social institutions, and politics. However, they are not the point of the novel and they have nothing to do with its dynamism. What moves the story is the combination of characterizations-in-tensions and the consistent appropriateness in choice of detail, the latter having an effect similar to the choice of exactly the right word in a poem.

Pedro Orgambide's *El encuentro* (1957) is a deceptively simple novel that emanates from the author's particular set of values. In what Orgambide has written and said about prose fiction, he often appears aggressively anti-cosmopolitan.[10] Nevertheless, his novels rest on universal values. The apparent contradiction has an explanation that is important in the way Orgambide's generation understands reality and regional particularity. It seems that what he really objects to is the rootlessness of works like those of Borges. Literature, if it has a social role, is supposed to do more than make a neat imaginary structure—that is an approximation of the Orgambide position. The issue, however, involves more than a question of *engagement*; it rests upon a definition of what Argentine reality is. According to the criteria of Orgambide and many other Argentines about his age, some writers who are clearly *engagés* seem detached

241

from Argentine reality. The works of Mallea, for example, in spite of the author's concern for Argentina, seem unfamiliar at least part of the time. That is, the Argentina seen in them is not like the Argentina that seems real to the younger writers. Roberto Arlt, on the other hand, seems to be writing about a known Argentina. And Orgambide himself likes to go back to the costumbristic, satirical writers like Roberto Payró and Fray Mocho. He is a member of the revisionist generation, but he does not deal with the panorama of history. He talks about reality and social relevance; and it appears that another—and perhaps better—word for it might be familiarity.

El encuentro is about the members of a formerly wealthy family and their adjustment to life in a new house and to related new circumstances. The novelist develops the story through vignettes featuring each of the characters. He uses a combination of third-person-omniscient narration and interior monologue. One basic aspect of the adjustment is the decision of the husband, Aldo, that he will have to work. He is a good-time boy and this decision suggests a major social change. The most important character, however, is Ernesto, the wife's uncle. This cheerful type has long known that living is finding joy rather than conflict. He is a fifty-year-old flower child, and he falls in love with Cora, who works in her brother's bar.

It is Ernesto's joy in life that moves the novel, and his characterization is important in two ways. First, he is a maverick, a type that Orgambide likes very much (note the devotion to Fray Mocho) because the skeptical or dissident position provides a testing ground for generally accepted ideas. There is something of the *pícaro* in Ernesto, though he certainly does not have all the classic qualifications. The second importance of Ernesto is that he is really more than an optimist; he is an embodiment of the pleasure principle. While the novel as a whole has something to say about social change and the transition from an old society to new patterns, Ernesto's character points out an even more basic contrast: the difference between joy and humdrum existence. *El encuentro* may have a special significance in Argentina where quite a few people, including Orgambide, deplore the Argentine's solemnity. Nevertheless, the general value of the experience is not limited to any region. What stands out, in the long run, is the relationship between Ernesto's attitude and the way people interact.

Sara Gallardo's *Enero* (1958) is a perceptive and exceptionally neat, precise study of a pregnant teenager. The setting is rural Argentina. Sixteen-year-old Nefer is seduced more by the dramatic excitement of a situation than by specific sexual attraction. The novel recounts her thoughts and acts as her pregnancy progresses, showing her in different situations related to her dilemma: a visit to her godmother, a surreptitious visit to an abortionist cut short by a change of mind, a religious mission and Nefer's decision not to confess, her face-up with her mother, a visit to the physician, and arrangement of a marriage by the godmother. The problem is resolved by marriage to the man who is father of her child, not to the man Nefer would like to think is the father. Her fantasizing is the factor that makes the story itself interesting.

The narrative voices are third person and interior monologue. The latter contains very few surprising associations; the former is not omniscient, but sees only as Nefer sees. There is dialogue in which Nefer does not participate, but it is only what she hears. Both voices —or attitudes—are so clearly within Nefer that identification of reader with the protagonist is extremely easy—easier than with consistent interior monologue, because the third-person attitude requires less ego control on the part of the reader. The episodes of the plot tend to grow in dramatic intensity, with the abortionist incident providing a subclimax. The cultural ambience that surrounds these events retains its regional identity (particularly interesting is the maternalistic role of Nefer's godmother); but all this is of secondary interest, as in *El Bordo*. The trajectory of Nefer's exterior contacts has a parallel in her emotional attitude toward her pregnancy. First she rejects the "something" growing inside her; later she becomes reluctant to give it up; and then she is ambivalent in her acceptance and rejection. This inner trajectory is related to Nefer's fantasizing about the baby's father, and it amounts to the loss of an ideal. She would like to believe a dashing lover seduced her, but has to settle for the cloddish Nicolás. The arrangement of the marriage takes place just as she resigns herself to having the baby. The romance and drama of summer are gone. Gallardo frames the novel with two references to the harvest. The reference at the beginning of the novel (Nefer is pregnant when the novel begins) speaks of her desperate loneliness and the opprobrium she will suffer; the one at the end reveals the resignation of the almost wife.

These novels create an impression of dealing with essentials, probably because they are not about myths, heroes, and the drama of history, but also certainly because their reduced scope allows the author to focus on particular human problems. Sometimes the limited cast of characters reminds us of a play. Emilio Carballido, a playwright, is the author of *El norte* (1958), a novel that deals with only three people, though others exist as shadows in the background. They suffice to create the relationship between a middle-aged woman and her boy lover. Carballido's novel, however, is considerably less affirmative than the works of Galindo, Orgambide, or Gallardo. The anguish suffered by his characters—admittedly in their search for fulfillment—is closer to the psychic state of the people created by Mario Benedetti, or Salvador Garmendia.

Benedetti's *La tregua* (1960) is the story of an ephemeral moment of fulfillment. Its protagonist, Martín Santomé, tells the story in first-person diary form. He is an office worker, approaching fifty and retirement. He is also a widower; and although he lives with his three children, he really does not share their life. He is alone and he feels useless. Then he falls in love with a woman who works in the office (the title of the novel means "truce"), but this remission in his psychic malady is ended by tragedy. So his story begins and ends in loneliness and the passivity that accepts it. Benedetti adds depth to *La tregua* by showing that the period of happiness not only opens up the future, but also recalls Santomé's past potential. The protagonist's diary also adds to the depth dimension by revealing intimately the values of Santomé. The inconsequential matters that interest him are not in proportion to what his life might be if he chose to be less passive. This condition is a statement by the author not just about a single man, but about the Uruguayan people.

The office worker appears frequently as an embodiment of twentieth-century alienation, loneliness, or lack of self-identification. The routine character of his work—as it is generalized in fiction—provides an appropriate lack of distinctiveness. The technological society produces many jobs, of course, that are just as boring and removed from appreciable causes and results, but the point seems to be to place an individual in a situation where his identity is brought into question. Salvador Garmendia's *Los pequeños seres* (1959) is the story of Mateo Martán, whose problem is not simply one of knowing who he is and what his role is, but how he knows.

It has been said, with considerable justification, that this novel marks the beginning of urban problems in Venezuelan fiction, bringing the country's novel in from the plains and the forest to face the rapidly intensifying problems of the century.[11]

An external fact—let us say the death of Martán's boss—triggers the protagonist's slipping away from objective awareness. We must speak of the external fact with reservations, because in subsequent revelations of Martán's psyche, there are moments when his identity is equivalent to the identity of the deceased. Garmendia uses a third-person narrator when necessary, but depends heavily on interior monologue that occasionally surfaces to become audible. Martán's monologues reveal the intrusions of the past into present reality, and of a second past factor into the first. Some element in one situation causes the recall of another, so Martán finds himself in a situation of multiple time. This narration achieves a considerable degree of simultaneity, but it is not the complete overlapping cultivated by some other recent authors.

These steps back into interior monologue are the controlling factor in the narrative structure. Working within it, Garmendia uses a system of emphasis that enhances our awareness of Martán's preoccupations. The presence of a hand on his shoulder, during a discussion of company problems, takes on major proportions. The hand itself, for a while, becomes an independent entity. These emphasized details may function to develop characterization, to illuminate the problem that is the novel's basic theme, or to assure a particular orientation that will guide the reader's response. An example of this last phenomenon is the use of the word *slope* (*declive*) in the first paragraph of the novel to indicate the way a door appears in a mirror. Repeatedly throughout the novel, he uses this word and *inclined* (*inclinado*) to maintain awareness of the listing course of Martán's saga.

In another novel, *Los habitantes* (1961), Garmendia deals with an entirely different social class. The protagonist, Francisco, is a truck driver. It should be clear from the start that he finds satisfaction in his work. Truck drivers have identity; office workers, in *Los habitantes,* as elsewhere, do not. The problem is that Francisco is unemployed, and the novel develops around that situation rather than around an individual's alienation. The various episodes, involving mainly the different members of Francisco's family, are related to each other but do not follow a cause-and-effect development. The present time of each narrative segment belongs to the same day; therefore, they combine to create an appreciation of Francisco's situation.

Within any episode, the past may be recalled or the future antici-pated. Movement into a different time sphere is extremely smooth, but not deceptive. Narrating in the past tense, Garmendia signals a projection in time—a moment of fantasizing—by switching to the conditional (changing from what Raúl was doing to what he would do). Then, once within the projected moment, the tense switches back to past, and although we read what Raúl was doing, we know it is really what he would do. However, the feeling is different from that created by the conditional; the switch to the past, even though it is a projected past, seems more real.[12]

As in most other novels of this kind—that is, novels of twentieth-century anguish—the events in *Los habitantes* are antiheroic and the people are "little people." Without really deviating from this norm, Engracia, the wife of Francisco, takes on a special dimension. Her willingness to try to help her husband, even though she does not know what to do, confers on her the beauty of affirmation. Even in her failure, in her confusion, we understand it is the necessary act.

The urban environment is fundamental in the creation of the mood of anguish, and segmented narration is useful in relating the anguish of a circumstance to the anguish of a particular individual. Clemente Airó, in *La ciudad y el viento* (1961), creates a picture of transitional Bogotá. The principal factors that underlie the presenta-tion of the city are its change from an aristocratic stronghold to a modern metropolis, and the reflection of *la violencia* in the city's collective attitude. The particularized aspect of the situation de-pends on presentation of several different human conditions—the politician, the intellectual aristocrat, the alcoholic failure, the sexy working girl, the old beggar, and others—to exemplify the factors of the transition. Interior penetration of these people then enhances our appreciation of the basic factors operative in the city's transfor-mation.

A somewhat different manner of emphasizing society's complexi-ties is Enrique Lafourcade's *Para subir al cielo* (1958). The protago-nists (lovers) belong to different extremes of the social spectrum, and they try unsuccessfully to bridge the gap. The author's use of symbols—the book is almost an allegory—is excessive and tends to keep the reader outside. The castle and the brothel, for example, or the steps (the scene is Valparaíso) to climb up to the heights. In another novel, *La fiesta del rey Acab* (1959)—also supercharged with symbolism—Lafourcade relates a time of crisis in the life of a dictator, César Alejandro Carrillo. Naming a dictator Caesar Alexander is all right if the intent is simply to be funny, but it doesn't help a serious novel much. If we can somehow suspend our reaction to this type of painfully obvious suggestion, *La fiesta del rey Acab* provides a credible feeling of the strong man suffering. The time of the novel is confined to a twenty-four–hour period and Carrillo's sensitive awareness of time emphasizes his loneliness. In this respect, Lafourcade's novel makes an interesting complement to *La alfombra roja*.

Speaking in broad, general terms, the novels of 1956–1962 are a somber lot, although many of them are excellent. They initiate an intense bourgeois self-flagellation that still goes on in 1970. However, the years following 1962 saw several innovations or intensifications of tendencies already begun and related to the century's anguish. The most widely cultivated is the segmented narrative. This technique is valuable for creating new appreciations of reality. It also reflects the fragmented nature of contemporary society, and segmented narration turns out to be alternately centrifugal and centripetal.

No doubt in some instances readers may ask what became of the story. With this reaction in mind, it is important to point out that the raconteur's art has not disappeared. One important witness to this fact is Fernando Alegría's *Caballo de copas* (1957), a Damon Runyon–type story about a race horse imported into the United States from Chile. It is what Graham Greene calls an "entertainment"—smooth, professional writing, fun to read, no profound implications but quite a few matter-of-fact revelations of what life is like. Many novelists, particularly the innovative ones, would do well to learn from *Caballo de copas* or similar novels, and then innovate. The results could be rewarding, as in the case of *La muerte de Artemio Cruz*. Actually, the departure from an expected order of narration varies in nature. Many contemporary novelists tell the story fairly straight, but without explanations. Others do the unexpected, but take care that we follow them. Still others leave their readers to struggle.

The story is there; or, if it is not, there is a substitute. What has happened is that ways of presenting the story have changed, and, in addition, a circumstance may have taken the story's place. By 1962, the novelist is extremely aware of his creative function, though he talks about it more later on. Since he is so aware of creating, experience becomes more important than denouement. Of course, the experience of any novel is always the most important consideration, but it can become confused with or even hidden by the traditional plot-development sequence. The novelists after 1962 depend to a very great extent on the importance of experience.

CHAPTER 16

The Year of *Rayuela* (1963)

Although the Spanish American novel was obviously very sophisticated in matters of narrative technique well before 1963, the publication of Julio Cortázar's *Rayuela* emphasized technique as it never had been emphasized before. *Rayuela* is indeed something special because, in any probable description of the novel, some comment about how Cortázar composes it will precede any statement concerning what it is about. The novel invites general statements about what it is like—often impressionistic and almost always poorly related to each other. This critical reaction is eminently appropriate in at least one sense: the novel itself is a refutation of accepted concepts of order. Luis Harss has written that *Rayuela* is "at once a philosophical manifesto, a revolt against literary language, and the account of an extraordinary spiritual pilgrimage."[1] In all fairness, it is well to point out that Harss's statement is considerably more meaningful to someone who has read the novel than to someone who has not. However, the three characteristics he points out serve well as a general orientation. In addition, it is helpful to know that the rebellious aspect of the book affects more than literary language. *Rayuela* shows a general lack of respect for all kinds of accepted standards that are mindlessly followed. The attitude behind the book does not reject rationality, but reveals the absurdity of rationality taken to an extreme. This attitude produces many delightful incongruities within the novel.[2]

Rayuela means "hopscotch," the children's game. The title is important for several different reasons, but the first and basic importance, in the experience of a person reading the novel, is that it establishes the idea of play. Soon it becomes apparent that the title also refers to the structure of the novel. Later we appreciate its relevance to the search for fulfillment on the part of the protagonist. However, at the beginning, it is the suggestion of game that matters most.

Going past the title page but still before reaching chapter one, we find a page called "Instruction Chart" ("Tablero de Dirección"). Here the author informs us that *Rayuela* is many books, but principally two. The first of these two principal books, he tells us, consists of the first fifty-six chapters, read in the traditional manner. This news is heartening, for it is hard to keep from noticing that the book consists of 155 chapters printed on 635 pages. However, the promise of a fast and easy reading fades immediately when Cortázar announces sarcastically that "three sparkling little stars" appear at the end of chapter fifty-six and are equal to the word *end*. The condescending tone of this remark suggests that anyone who reads the book in the traditional manner is very unimaginative. The second principal book contained in *Rayuela* is a hopscotch reading of all the chapters, in an order indicated by Cortázar in the "Tablero de Dirección" (73-1-2-116-3-84-4, and so on). At the end of each chapter, there is a number indicating the next chapter to which the reader is supposed to hop.

The game gets to be fun. The reader is likely to find himself trying to comprehend *Rayuela* both ways at once, or at least trying to imagine it both ways at once. He is doomed to facing an impossibility, unless he has enough self-discipline to read the fifty-six–chapter version first and then start over again. Rayuela is set up in three parts. The first two parts constitute the fifty-six–chapter version. They tell the story of Horacio Oliveira and are entitled "About That Side" (Oliveira in Paris) and "About This Side" (Oliveira in Buenos Aires). The third part is called "About Other Sides" and carries the subtitle "Expendable Chapters." These chapters are not necessarily chapters at all. Some are narrative, but many are simply bits and pieces from the author's file, often quotations from other authors. Such a quotation may be no more than a single short sentence. In general, the effect of this third section is to enlarge on the story narrated in the first two sections and to cultivate an awareness of the act of creating. This characteristic—the awareness of the act of creating, within the act itself—is widely cultivated in recent fiction.

The plot of *Rayuela* deals with the attempts made by Horacio Oliveira to find himself, or, to put it somewhat more specifically, to understand what Horacio Oliveira is, without reference to anything but himself. His relationships in Paris with Maga and sundry jazz types, semibeats, and others fail to produce anything he can tie on to. On his return to Buenos Aires, he reencounters his childhood friend, Traveller, who has never been to Paris, but who certainly never worried about it. He has always been active in a variety of occupations and is in no way concerned about the meaning of his existence. Traveller is a kind of complement to Oliveira—the other side of the coin. In the course of the novel, Oliveira and Traveller tend to become one; or it may be more accurate to say that is what happens in the course of Oliveira's search. He also identifies Traveller's wife, Talita, with Maga, from the days in Paris. This process culminates in an episode often mentioned as one of the funnier parts of the book. Oliveira lives in a house directly across the street from Traveller. In the process of Oliveira's getting settled, he borrows some nails and some *mate* from Traveller, and the latter sends them by Talita, who crosses the street on a board extending from the window of one building to the window of the other. The crossing makes no sense (except that reason informs us it is the shortest route); and the incongruity of the situation—Talita midway, suspended several stories above the street, between two men who are vying for her favors—is funny, and revealing. The double-take reaction it produces is characteristic of much of Cortázar's humor. Similar effects come from the use of Latin and *porteño* slang in the same sentence, from the pretentious and redundant verbosities of Ceferino Piriz, from names like Talita Nightingale. They trigger a glimpse of reality revealed through the opening created by the contrast—an opening that occurs when an accepted pattern is broken.

The role of part three in *Rayuela* may be understood simply as several kinds of addenda, or it may be more fully appreciated for various functions in the novel. In other words, the "Expendable Chapters" are expendable only if they are allowed to be. Some of the chapters actually belong to the story of Oliveira; they fill it out. An important dimension is added when we read the "second" novel—that is, beginning with chapter seventy-three rather than chapter one. Reading this way, the awareness of the act of writing—the creative moment, the matter of invention and reality—is with us from the start. The traditional order of the "first" novel begins with Oliveira's search for Maga. The added dimension is enhanced by the invention of a writer, Morelli, who comments on creative writing. In addition, there are bits and pieces that often appear unrelated to the position in which they are placed.

Incongruity is certainly one of the novel's main characteristics, and surrealistic association is commonplace in it. It is important, however, to understand that the "second" novel—that is, the reading with the intercalation of the chapters in part three—does not simply produce a series of odd associations. The most important aspect of the experience is the actual participation of the reader in the structure of the book. It is not that the reader actually creates the structure—the "disorderly" sequence of chapters is really very strictly ordered. However, the unusual act of skipping around makes another fissure in commonplace behavior and enables us to see a bit farther (really, appreciate a bit farther) just as with all the incongruities in *Rayuela*.

The activation of the reader—the attempt to incorporate him into the process of making the novel—also depends on the use of the narrative voice. Ana María Sanhueza, in an analysis of how the narrative voice functions, points out that there are three obvious narrators: a third person who narrates most of part one, a first person who narrates some of that part, and a third narrator in part two.[3] This basic observation is only a start, however. Sanhueza shows the great number of changes in narrator identity and makes an essential observation: that in *Rayuela* the narrative is not a unifying factor, nor do the multiple narrative voices control the structure of the novel. She concludes that the reader is required to perform the narrator's traditional function. Again, the reader is activated, transformed into a participant.

This transformation is not simply a way of reading the novel, but a vital part of the experience of the work. When it brings the reader into the act of creating, it places him on the edge of becoming. Therefore, it reverses the process that creates appreciation of what has been experienced, and makes experience actual. This act is the essence of Cortázar's revolt. The incongruities in the novel constantly challenge the reader; the general sense of disrespect for reasonable behavior prohibits the expectation of events as they might reasonably happen; the author's experiments with the language itself indicate a willingness to start from nothing and build.

There are moments when Cortázar seems to have launched a search-and-destroy campaign against language itself. The fact is that he is disgusted with the treachery of language. It never really does what we need it to do. The experiments include many unusual techniques that are often amusing. In addition to the expected interior monologue and free association, Cortázar experiments in one passage with a tape recorder; in another he alternates lines of what a character is thinking with lines of a book the character is reading. The most extreme, and most amusing, is the invention of language in the famous passage that begins "As soon as he began to amalate the noeme, the clemise began to smother her and they fell into hydromuries, into savage ambonies, into exasperating sustales."[4] These language games also serve principally to challenge the orthodox.

It is easy to forget Horacio Oliveira, poor devil. He becomes the victim of the intensity of our own experience and our fascination with why we react as we do. His search never ends, though at one point it seems that he will be absorbed into Traveller, his double. That does not happen and, in fact, we do not find out what does happen to him. Maybe he commits suicide; maybe he is demented. Readers of the "second" novel do not even know where the book ends, because the next-to-last chapter, fifty-eight, sends the reader to the last chapter, 131; but the last chapter then sends the reader back to the next-to-last, and so on interminably.

La ciudad y los perros, by Mario Vargas Llosa, makes an interesting contrast with *Rayuela* because, although it is completely modern in narrative technique, plot development is the basis of the experience of this work. That is to say, Vargas Llosa creates a world, presents a problem, develops interesting characters, and works out a climax and denouement that hold his readers in suspense. A number of excellent narrative techniques guide reactions and color reality. One of the preeminent characteristics of *La ciudad y los perros* is that it is a moral novel, in much the same way and to the same extent that *Rayuela* is a philosophical novel. Many of its ardent admirers spend hours discussing its moral implications, and it can be a very rewarding novel in that regard, so long as the discussion does not obliterate the experience of the book's reality coming into being.

The title requires some explanation. Literally, it means "the city and the dogs." The city is Lima; the term "dogs" refers to the new boys in the Leoncio Prado Military School. It is a derogatory term like "rat" as used in similar institutions in the United States. In fact, the Leoncio Prado is hardly distinguishable, in a generic way, from a typical military preparatory school in this country. In Vargas Llosa's novel, the school is the principal setting. That is where most of the action takes place in the story's present time. Some concurrent incidents take place in the city, and retrospective narration takes us there to discover the backgrounds of some of the cadets.

An omniscient narrator opens the novel in the middle of an episode. Almost immediately we become aware of three things: we are observing an "in" group, a dangerous mission is being planned, and the leader of the group is a cadet named "El Jaguar." The earliest insight into characterization is the knowledge that El Jaguar is the strong-man type—tough, brutal, courageous.

The "in" group we have come upon is simply "The Circle," organized and controlled by El Jaguar since their days as *perros*. Now nearing graduation, the members no longer need the treaty of mutual defense that first united them, but find the organization convenient for breaking rules. The dangerous mission of which we are aware is the theft of a chemistry examination.

This adventure may seem to be small potatoes, schoolboy stuff. However, the actions of the cadets expand to involve them in the total society. The basic, restricted scene—handled so it provides a clear picture of a group of relationships—makes *La ciudad y los perros* similar to the works of some of the small-screen novelists, especially the novels that move out from the limited situation in challenging the values of a larger segment of society. Several of Galindo's novels, for example, enlarge in this kind of implication. In *La ciudad y los perros*, the movement is not immediately apparent. As soon as

254

the basic situation is presented, the author introduces several other threads of the story and, as a result, the first chapter is likely to be discouraging. After that, the novel starts to tie itself together.

Two principal characters, in addition to El Jaguar, take their place in the story. One is The Slave, the diffident victim of multiple psychic problems; the other is Alberto, the aspiring writer. The three cadets represent, to some extent, three classes of society.[5] Youths from different regions of the country also contribute to the notion of a cross section of Peruvian society. The moral problem, however, transcends national boundaries. Officers of the school discover the theft of the examination, but not the thief. They decree collective punishment in the form of denial of normal privileges. The Slave breaks under the strain and turns informer. When the cadets go into the field on military maneuvers, The Slave is killed by a shot in the head.

This action constitutes the first part of the novel. It is followed by a second part of approximately the same length, and then a brief epilogue. The first part, once all the lines of development become apparent, is very compact. Vargas Llosa likes to divide chapters into segments, and these segments are about equally divided between present-time action and background that directly concerns the present. Most of the narration is omniscient third person. However, there are two other narrative voices—one of them an unidentified first person. These two voices become more important in part two, and the effect is one factor in the novel's growing emphasis on individual differentiation, and the system as represented in the administration of the school appears more vulnerable—at least for a while. The loose handling of the narrative voice coincides with a sense of the weakness of the system. The whole second part deals with the accident, or possibly murder.

The administrators of the Leoncio Prado are very eager to write off the whole affair as an accident and forget it as soon as possible. Here is where the role of Alberto becomes important. He suspects El Jaguar of murdering The Slave, and reports his suspicion to Lieutenant Gamboa, the toughest but most trustworthy of the officers. Gamboa takes the matter to higher echelons, but they are not interested in searching out the truth. They wish only to avoid rocking the boat.

The general question of justice versus expedience takes on particular meanings arising from the role of the informer and the function of a subsystem, like The Circle, that exists within the power structure, living on it and undermining it at the same time. However, the same subsystem is a source of justice in some instances.[6] Certainly a very minimal observation is that Alberto's actions demonstrate the futility of telling the truth. However, the novelist colors this consideration by making Alberto less than a totally admirable person.

The dynamic factor in *La ciudad y los perros* is involvement of the reader in these moral questions through sustained interest in the plot. The author captures the reader by allowing the characters to react in ways that repeatedly complicate an issue. For the most part, this character development is the result of techniques that are entirely credible. One of the bothersome factors is the "I" narrator. The epilogue reveals that El Jaguar actually did murder The Slave and also that the tough guy is the anonymous narrator of the first-person sections. He confesses his crime in a note to Lieutenant Gamboa, shortly before the latter takes leave for a new and very undesirable assignment at an isolated post. Gamboa, understandably, has had enough, and he tears up the note. As for the identification of the "I" narrator, it is possible that a reader might be guessing in the right direction before he reaches the epilogue, but he could not possibly be certain. From the standpoint of narrative technique, it is interesting to wonder how the novel would have differed if the identity of the "I" narrator had been apparent from the beginning. In that case, the character of El Jaguar would have revealed some strong contrasts all through the book. Withholding the identity allows the reader to appreciate first El Jaguar's methods of accommodating himself to the system; then the revelation of the full character emphasizes the fact that he was out of place. The partial incorporation of him into the system is as frustrating as the futility of Alberto's telling the truth.

Right at the end of the novel, in the last of the epilogue's three scenes, we find El Jaguar in a mediocre job and, in some way, adjusted to society. He is no longer the strong man. The most notable quality of this last scene is that the author puts two time levels together, achieving not the simultaneity of the same time in several places, but the coincidence of different points in time. This technique appears in *La ciudad y los perros* only at the end, but is fundamental in Vargas Llosa's later novels.

Miguel Angel Asturias returns to the mythic implications of *Hombres de maíz* in a new novel, *Mulata de tal*. It is even less carefully structured than *Hombres de maíz*—a characteristic that makes the novel hard to describe—but still accomplishes a similar joining of mythical reality and material reality. The author says this novel is a version of the myth of the sun and the moon.[7] It is a nice idea; but if we deal with the novel rather than what the author thinks he has done, it is better to say that the novel is based on a man's pact with the devil. Guatemalan folklore has no particular claim on this story, but Asturias's imagination supplies all the individuality any book would need. His protagonist, Celestino Yumi, sells his wife to the devil and becomes enormously rich. One of his new treasures is a luscious mulatta whose presence is a mixed blessing. From this circumstance comes the title of the novel.

While this pact may provide a basis for a story, the real feeling of the novel comes through best in the opening scene where Celestino is presented as the Fly Wizard, so named because he has to attend mass with his fly open, thereby creating impure thoughts among the communicants.[8] All this is part of his agreement with Satan. It is this kind of humor that moves the book. The reader's experience is participation in Asturias's invention, particularly his playing with words. The story itself wanders around rather aimlessly. Some things happen as the result of others, but that does not really matter much. There are also times when it is not at all clear what is happening—partly because of the melding of myth and reality, and partly because Asturias does not worry about it.

The author's imagination controls the novel, and that is a little different from saying that the author controls it. There are no problems about narrative voice or segments or simultaneity. The narrative voice simply tells the story and with complete liberty. However, the characters and events do not make an impression of being controlled by an author unwilling to let his creations escape. On the contrary, the inventions in *Mulata de tal* spur the author's imagination on to other inventions.

Quite a number of episodes are worthy conversation pieces because they stimulate discussion by any two or more readers. When Celestino's pact with the devil turns into disaster, for example, the parallel event in material reality is a volcanic eruption. The result is the loss of property. It is Asturias's way of combining myth and materiality. The parallelism suggests the possibility of an interpretive reading of the novel. Another stimulating incident is Celestino's recovery of his wife, in the form of a dwarf. Symbolism and allegory seem useless in this case, however. The reduced size of the protagonist's mate appears to have its origins in the frequency of dwarfs in Guatemalan folklore, with no further significance. A third type of episode is one that contains social criticism, such as the struggle between Christian demons and Indian demons. However, none of these lines of development dominates the novel.

Bodily transformations are commonplace in *Mulata de tal,* and name changes accompany them. It is wise for the reader to submit to a corresponding phenomenon in his own role. That is, the novel is a better experience if the reader adjusts as he reads, allowing Asturias's exuberant humor to evoke a free-form response that accords with the shape of the novel. This process allows the book's myth factor to live in a way that might be impossible if it were restricted by a definable concept.

The mythmaking effect is the basis of another novel of this year, Elena Garro's absorbing but far less humorous *Los recuerdos del porvenir*. It is possible to read this novel as an account of the *cristero* rebellion (religious wars that followed the Mexican Revolution) and find it satisfactory. However, the violence of the novel becomes generalized, even abstracted; and when all is said and done, this violence is really the failure of love. The novel's major theme is love—the concept of love, particularized into cases of possessiveness, frustration, fulfillment, and violence.

Garro employs one narrative device that does not work very well. Her town, Ixtepec, tells its own story. The immediate problem is characterization of the town clearly enough to give the narrative voice an authentic tone. The author never really achieves this desirable goal. Fortunately, other aspects of the book are interesting enough to subordinate this deficiency. One positive effect of the personification of Ixtepec is the telescoping of time into only one of its three aspects, the present.

Given this condition of timelessness, it is not too surprising that some miraculous things happen. It is a world where people carry lighted oil lamps through storms as if there were neither wind nor rain; they smoke cigarettes without lighting them; they turn into stone. These incidents may belong to the category of magic realism;

258

however, they are significantly different from the history-based magic of Carpentier or Asturias's magic that has its roots in native myth. The magic factors in *Los recuerdos del porvenir* are pure inventions. Their corroboration exists in the form of an unexplainable character, Felipe Hurtado. He appears in the town without warning and is always "the stranger." He is the one to whom most of the magic things happen. Significantly, he teaches some natives of the town the meaning of theater—that is, how to put on a play. This act of inventing puts reality in an entirely different perspective for the people who are affected by it. When he leaves, he takes his love with him and evaporates before the eyes of his pursuers.

Hurtado, however, is the only character who achieves fulfillment. General Rosas is caught and destroyed in a trap between an unrequited love and one he does not return. Neither of the two principal women has a satisfactory love except as satisfaction for Julia may be inferred from her abduction by Hurtado. He is the one—Hurtado, the creative—who moves away from the sterility of frustration and violence.

Although the narrator-town is sometimes disconcerting, it does enhance the feeling of legend—one of the novel's best effects. Garro's ability to challenge the reader's imagination is the important factor. At the beginning of the book, the narrator looks backward in time, viewing the musty present and remembering the dynamic past: "Only silence and neglect. Yet memory holds a garden lighted by sun, radiant with birds, peopled with running and shouting."[9] The words *radiant* and *peopled* trigger the imagination. In another instance, near the end of the novel, Garro's imagery inspires a deeper contemplation; the town-narrator would have liked to give the participants in the story a more comprehensive view of reality: "Disoriented within themselves, they were unaware that a lifetime is not enough to discover the infinite flavors of mint, the lights of an evening, or the multitude of colors that colors are made of. One generation succeeds another, and each repeats the acts of the one before it. Only a moment before dying they discover it was possible to dream and to design the world in their own way . . ." (p. 249).

A second major factor in the creation of the sense of legend (or possibly myth) is the presence of extraordinary people. Felipe Hurtado, the messenger of illusion, is not the only rare character. Juan Cariño, the town loony, lives in a room in a brothel, wears a morning coat with ceremonial sash, and insists on being called "Mr. President." One of the officers in the military force that occupies the town has twin mistresses. There are things in this novel that are like the works of Gabriel García Márquez: the history and personality of the town, the fantastic happenings though they seem less normal than in García Márquez's novels, and the unusual people. Juan Cariño considers himself the guardian of words, and he keeps them in his room. Significantly, he is the only character in *Los recuerdos del porvenir* who has faith in reason.

In spite of the obviously attractive tendency to mythologize, the most regularly apparent characteristic of the novels of 1963 is the use of segmented narrative in different ways. After dealing with *Rayuela*'s "Instruction Chart," it is fascinating to discover the following announcement at the beginning of Enrique Lafourcade's *Invención a dos voces*: "This novel . . . can be read in the traditional manner—that is, following the progressive numbering of pages. Two lines of action can also be followed—the first on the odd-numbered pages (pp. 9–241) and the second on the even-numbered pages (pp. 10–242)—as two different plots, then continuing from page 243 in the normal manner. It is possible to read it from back to front. The system of skipping pages—used by some critics—is equally recommendable."[10]

Apparently the last two licenses granted by the author are made in jest. However, the basic announcement, concerning the intercalation of two plots, is an accurate description of how the reader may appreciate this novel. Its effect is to develop two lines of reaction to a materialistic world—one from the standpoint of pure science, the other from the standpoint of religion. Much of the author's satire is directed against life in the United States. It is weakened considerably by a very heavy-handed realization of the fundamental notion, especially in the form of overly obvious symbolism.

Segmentation is entirely different—and achieves a different effect —in Juan José Arreola's *La feria*. This novel is a portrait of Zapotlán, the author's hometown, and is a kind of autobiography because the book carries the stamp of Arreola's way of looking at reality— with affection, but with a quick sensitivity to the absurd. The novel opens with the town speaking collectively of itself—of its thirty thousand people and of its beginning. However, the novel consists of hundreds of fragments, and the narrative voice depends on the nature of each piece. The length of the segments ranges from a couple of lines to several pages.

Early in the reading of *La feria*, we understand that the author is combining Zapotlán's present and past. It is the act of the author—that is, an organizing force outside the novel—because there is no internal pattern of narrative voice. Soon we discover it is possible to join segments and so make story lines that deal with several different people. Once this discovery is made, there is a contrast between this game and the appreciation of Arreola's mosaic. If we read the novel as a mosaic, the town as a whole is more important than any of the individuals or situations.[11]

The portrait is of a small provincial city with quite a few interesting individuals. They constitute what the nineteenth-century writers called a "galería de tipos." Separated from Arreola's artistic treatment, they are just ordinary people; but in the realm of his magic, they seem very special. The same thing happens to the town as a whole—it is both ordinary and distinctive. The novel culminates in a celebration that marks the high point of the year—a blowout, an enormous explosion, with joy and fireworks and death. More than a celebration and a tragedy, it is a sign, an indication that the town exists and has reaffirmed itself.

The function of history in *La feria* is more as part of an atemporal sense of the present. In Lisandro Otero's *La situación*, the function of historical episodes is explanatory and they give the book some of the flavor of a historical novel. The effect of a past re-created emphasizes the segmented nature of the novel and suggests the possibility of reconstructing it in a more orthodox sequence. The reorganization would change the focus of the novel, of course, and so destroy its basic experience—a feeling of how life was in Cuba just before the second dictatorship of Fulgencio Batista.

Batista had surrendered the executive power in 1944 after ten years of dictatorship. He was followed by two civilian presidents whose administrations did not produce the expected reforms. Batista returned in March 1952 and once again established the dictatorship via a coup d'état. On July 26 of the following year, Fidel and Raúl Castro led students in an attack on the Moncada army barracks in Santiago. The present-time chapters in *La situación* refer to the half year immediately before the return of Batista.

Otero uses alternating chapters rather than small fragments like those of *La feria*. The basic chapters are identified by date or by reference to the season. Using a combination of third-person omniscient and interior monologue, they offer a picture of Cuba's dominant class at that time. The narrator depends mainly on dialogue—fast, lighthearted, and full of "contri clob" anglicisms—but there are some introspective passages. Intercalation of newspaper headlines, in the manner of Dos Passos, enhances the flavor of a particular time. The first chapter insinuates the tone of the novel by developing a panoramic scene of life at the beach on the last Sunday of vacation. The sense of being on the edge of change corresponds to the experience of the novel as a whole.

There are two sets of past-time chapters. Each has a title that always identifies the particular line, just as "Los años" and "El día de juicio" appear over and over as chapter titles in *Cayó sobre su rostro*. One of the lines in Otero's novel is "Oro Blanco"; the other is "Un padre de la patria." Both are printed in italics and are always clearly identified. They go back to the early part of the century and, in effect, supply the background for the present-time chapters. The "Oro blanco" chapters deal with the family of a wealthy planter; the "Un padre de la patria" chapters deal with the attainment of power through politics. These two lines constitute the power base of the bourgeoisie seen in the present-time chapters.

Two factors supply the dynamism of *La situación*. One is the attractiveness of the tell-it-like-it-is narration of what life was like for the "haves"; the other factor is the structure of alternating chapters, which accomplishes much of the effect of a historical novel without deemphasizing the present. It is important to recognize, however, that the two lines of historical chapters are chapters in fact—not reminiscences tied to the intimate experience of a particular character. Otero does create interesting characters and they seem very real; however, the historical chapters do not simply enhance this characterization. They explain the situation.

Carlos Martínez Moreno's *El paredón* is a case in which the retrospective factor is tied to one person. The novel deals with an Uruguayan newspaper man, Julio Calodoro, who goes to Cuba as a reporter, during the Castro revolution, then returns to his own country. The story actually develops in these three stages because the novel is not so much about Cuba as it is about Uruguay. *El paredón* communicates an Uruguayan reality that is static, or worse—a sense that will be far from strange to anyone who has read *El astillero*. The retrospective passages are related to Calodoro, and although they do concern themselves with history and politics, we appreciate it all through one man. This fact has nothing whatsoever to do with the validity of the novel. It illustrates a different effect achieved by a different method. Because the events in Cuba have the immediate importance of being newsworthy, they tend to impose themselves as the theme of the novel. Ideally, the time perspective in which Calodoro is characterized should provide a balancing factor. However, it is a double-take reaction that tells us the novel is really about the lethargic condition of Calodoro's own country.

Segments using different narrative voices may produce a generalized appreciation of a group. This is the case in Fanny Buitrago's *El hostigante verano de los dioses*. The controlling narrator (author) allows each of several characters to take turns telling about the others. The theme of the novel is boredom—how young people with nothing to do (no clear direction) burn themselves out spiritually. Buitrago sets up the story by having a newspaper reporter (female) go to a provincial city to meet and interview the anonymous author of a scandalous novel. Each chapter of *El hostigante verano de los dioses* carries, as a title, the name of the person who acts as narrator. A Stranger (the author-narrator) is the voice in alternate chapters, and in each of the others she concedes the narrative position to one of three women who are characters in the story. The technique is not as successful as it might have been, because the personalities of the women tend to meld into each other. The alternating point of view is capable of producing a sense of the circumstances in which the young people live, as a generation; and the intercalation of the "A Stranger" chapters provides an external balancing factor to the group's view of itself. It also relates Buitrago's novel-in-progress to the invented novel that inspires the visit.

The reader's experience with Buitrago's novel is likely to be one of ambivalent sympathy. The stranger-narrator, Marina, allows entrance into the situation; since she herself enters a strange group of people, the reader tends to be at her side. The people she discovers are, for the most part, an unlovely bunch, ranging from dull to depraved. They are accceptable only because of the narrator's "cool" —an insouciance that seems very carefully cultivated.

The picture of the novel in 1963 would be woefully incomplete without some reference to a less experimental kind of writing, one that is at the same time committed unquestionably to an obvious social crusade. This kind of fiction is much less apparent in 1963 than it was two decades earlier, but it still plays an important role. José A. Osorio Lizarazo's *Camino de la sombra* won the Esso Literary Prize in Colombia. It goes back into the nineteenth century to create the sense of eternal civil conflict, and to emphasize the plight of unfortunate individuals. Osorio Lizarazo uses an almost documentary technique. The facts of history are personified rather than transformed, and the experience of the novel is the author's concern for others.

Although it won no prizes, Manuel Peyrou's *Acto y ceniza* is noteworthy as an example of good narration and also as a protest against *peronismo*. The author is well known for his detective stories; and several stories, as well as two other novels, express his opposition to the former dictator. The anecdotal base of *Acto y ceniza* is the closing of Samuel Liberman's candy factory, by order of Eva Perón, and the effect on several different people. The primary focus is on Liberman.

The story opens on the occasion of the factory's closing. In a second stage, flashbacks tell the story of Liberman's youth, his growing success, and his family. In a third stage, the events leading directly to the closing of the factory bring the story up to the moment when the novel begins. The novel's most direct protest emerges in the campaign against Liberman. He is asked to contribute a large sum to Eva Perón's charitable enterprise. The question of whether to submit, refuse, or compromise makes his problem interestingly complicated. His decision displeases the powers and they launch a newspaper campaign that discredits his product.

The narrative then studies the effect on Liberman (he is a wreck of a man), his wife who has a love affair, and a former employee who dares face up to the regime. Peyrou uses dialogue to reveal a strong anti-Perón position and also a let's-wait-it-out attitude. The political question is complicated by Liberman's partial rejection of his Jewishness. In fact, the issue of anti-Semitism acts as a bridge between the political protest and the personal problem. It is this unification of elements that brings about the transformation that makes *Acto y ceniza* a good novel. Peyrou narrates in the third person and clearly controls the story. At times he describes the circumstances and characters, but he is also capable of letting them present themselves. This combination moves the story with a good balancing of dialogue and descriptive narration. A sense of frustration—the kind that comes from knowing that those who are powerful are also unjust— is inescapable.

In some ways, *Acto y ceniza* is like a historical novel: it creates the flavor of a time that is past—or that we usually think of as past. It is fairly apparent, however, that Peyrou sees *peronismo* as an ever-present danger. He published novels on the theme in 1960, 1963, and 1066, and current events have certainly not refuted his concern, though many would argue with his interpretation of Perón's politics.

CHAPTER 17

From *Rayuela* to *Cien años de soledad* (1964–1966)

The simple fact of proximity to recent fiction creates problems of organization and synthesis that are not present in the discussion of works set apart by the passage of time. These difficulties are compounded, in the case of Spanish American fiction, by the great productivity during recent years. The generally high quality of the novels makes selection a painful necessity. It is possible, of course, that casting *Rayuela* and *Cien años de soledad* in the role of landmark novels may be an error. However, the combination of current taste with dispassionate critical judgment makes them strong candidates. In the period of three years separating their dates of publication, it is not possible to define any major literary movements. The function of this period, in the story of the genre, is to point out a number of currents that identify recent fiction. Several characteristics of generic significance may be identified: (1) an invitation to the reader to participate in the composition of the novel, (2) an interest in having both reader and author himself observe the author in the act of creating fiction, (3) a special kind of realism in the fiction of disaffected youth, (4) an increase in the variety of techniques used to communicate the revisionist suggestions of small-screen novels, (5) the novelization of a concept, and (6) the transformation of regionalism. The six characteristics are observations only. It should be clearly understood that they are not movements, and they are not classifications of novels. Far from being mutually exclusive groups, several of these characteristics may be found in a single work.

Rayuela is a kind of standard of fiction that invites the reader's participation, most specifically because its structure is in process rather than predetermined, and because the novel has no definite end. In fact, it is endless in two different ways. One is that we never know for sure what happens to the protagonist; the other is that the novel really never comes to an end (that is, in the version that includes all the chapters) because the last two moves in the hopscotch pattern refer to each other endlessly. *La ciudad y los perros* invites the reader in entirely different ways, and less flamboyantly. The most obvious opening to the reader is in the two-level conversation at the end of the novel. Ideally, the reader goes beyond the figuring-out stage and actually comprehends the dialogue as an integrated reality. The other invitation to the reader is in the hidden identity of the "I" narrator. In this case, there is some doubt about the effect of the technique. If the reader reacts by guessing wildly or by feeling antagonistic toward the author, his experience of the novel suffers. On the other hand, if appreciation of the "I" narrator increases gradually—without reference to a specific character, but on its own terms—the eventual revelation makes the reader's appreciation of the "I" characterization a part of the novel's denouement.

There is always a valid question as to whether a given narrative technique actually does promote the reader's participation or simply constitutes a problem to be figured out. Undoubtedly, there are among recent novels some virtuoso performances that really do not offer anything beyond the technique itself. When that is the case, the experience of the technique needs to be satisfying in terms of the creative effort spent. The only reason for soliciting reader participation is to enhance appreciation of the work's artistic process.

Vargas Llosa increases the possibilities for reader participation in *La casa verde* (1965) by various means, including the intercalation of scenes as in *La ciudad y los perros*. He also achieves a melding of different points in time by using different tenses within the same sentence. The effect is similar to the repetition of motifs on different levels of time in Salvador Elizondo's *Farabeuf* (1965). In *La casa verde*, the points in time may be the moment of narration and the moment which is narrated. The technique involves a combination of dialogue and third-person narrative so they become one: "The Doctor said she was so tired she couldn't speak, sit down awhile, Doña Juana, tell us all about it, and she where is Antonia."[1] A passage like this can activate an attentive reader because it joins elements that normally appear separated from each other: (1) indirect quotation by the narrator of what the doctor said, (2) direct quotation of what the doctor says to Doña Juana, (3) narrator's elliptical reference to what Doña Juana says ("and she") but omitting tense, and (4) quotation of what Doña Juana says to the doctor. Vargas Llosa's reader may be puzzled at first, then may turn analytical, and ultimately may appreciate the effect of immediacy created by this kind of narration. The process itself removes us from the limitation of time.

In the case of Vargas Llosa, the novelist's persistent respect for the development of a plot operates as a modifying factor in the openness of his work. *La casa verde* consists of at least five identifiable story lines. Their interrelationship is not a reader option, but active appreciation of the process of bringing them together is necessary for the fullest experience of the novel. Participation by the reader in this way is a different matter from the usefulness of Vargas Llosa's narrative techniques in the creation of Peruvian reality. Whatever the degree of participation in the process itself, Vargas Llosa's narrative techniques produce a feeling of the enormous contrasts in Peruvian society. These are contrasts of conditions that ought to be separate in time but actually exist concurrently (feudalism and technological progress, for example); and the author's handling of time makes the fact more comprehensible than it might be in an objective presentation.

Special uses of narrative point of view can be extremely effective in activating the reader. Fernando del Paso's *José Trigo* (1966) uses a first-person narrator (an outsider, but with a special commitment to the situation in the novel) and a character, José Trigo, who actually never functions as an orthodox protagonist. He is more of an abstraction; and, indeed, a stimulating uncertainty grows from the beginning of the novel because the title of the first chapter is "¿José Trigo?" The relationship of this mysterious character to the specific (and relatively simple) plot line, depends on the reader's cooperation with the author's narrative techniques, and, even then, much is left to the individual reader's imagination. The reader must coordinate the sources of the narrative voice in Gustavo Sainz's *Gazapo* (1965). In fact, reference to a narrative voice in this novel is of questionable value. The novel uses narrative aids: telephone conversations, a tape recorder, diaries, dreams, and letters. To a considerable extent, the narrator is removed from the novel, and the reader takes over. This phenomenon is not as complete in *Gazapo* as in some other novels (Manuel Puig's *La traición de Rita Hayworth*, 1968, for example), but it is enough to involve the reader in the process that is the normal responsibility of a controlling narrator. The resolution of *Gazapo*'s plot—the love story of a boy and girl in the process of becoming adults—depends entirely on the experience of coordinating the narrative sources. There is no outcome in the traditional sense, but an affirmation that is meaningless or trite except in terms of the multiple associations that make up the novel.

The segmented structure of Vicente Leñero's *Los albañiles* (1964) involves the reader and then ends on a question, just as *Rayuela* does. Leñero's novel opens with the knowledge of a murder, then examines the motivations of several possible killers. We never find out which it was; but that fact is essential to the experience of the book, which is not a detective novel, but a consideration of the meaning of justice. The process of suspicion and defense involves the interweaving of facts and personalities, and one aspect of the moral question is the conflict between truth and expediency, which is raised also in *La ciudad y los perros*. A major difference in the reader's experience is that in *Los albañiles* we put the pieces together with the hope of clarifying the issue, but the culprit is never identified.

One of the problems related to novels that require the reader's active participation is that the experience must be worth the time it requires. Not many people can read a book like *La casa verde*, for example, with full appreciation unless they have been provided some good orientation to the novel or are willing to read it twice. A second reading is a lot to ask for a book of several hundred pages. Generally speaking, a novelist must make the human beings he

269

writes about interesting enough and visible enough for his readers
to care about them. Failure to do so is not likely to win a large
public. *Gazapo, La casa verde,* and *Los albañiles* all manage to
make the characters interesting in the early stages of the novel,
though the amount of concrete knowledge about them is different in
each case. *Gazapo* accomplishes the necessary attraction more rapidly than the other two. *La casa verde* establishes the interest, then
nearly loses it in the complicated narrative technique. Not all novels
are this successful, and frequently they show little respect for the
reader.

Closely related to reader participation in the composition of the
novel—or activation of the reader—is the authors' fascination with
the act of novelizing. Novels comment on literary life and ambitions,
use the act of writing as the basis of narrative structure, contain
criticisms of literary modes, set forth a theory of the novel in the
composition of the work itself, and ultimately even observe the
creation of the work within its own creation. This fascination on the
part of the novelists emphasizes the factor of creation in progress,
and it is the most apparent link with other techniques that activate
the reader.

Los geniecillos dominicales (1965), by Julio Ramón Ribeyro, includes literary ambition in a general frame of a search for something meaningful. Ribeyro's novel deals with a young man who rejects a routine job; then it develops the problem of whether this
renunciation will eventually have more meaning than the job had.
The narration is in third person, but really sees things as the protagonist, Ludo, sees them. His search for meaning involves much
literary activity, including the founding of a magazine. The high
point of literary activity in the novel is a public reading of short
stories by some of the young literary lights. The incident is a satire
of exaggerated narrative techniques, but more important is Ludo's
awareness of doing something he does not want to do, for people
who are not interested.

Satire is also an important factor in the picture of the aspiring
writer in Eduardo Caballero Calderón's *El buen salvaje* (1966).
The experience of this novel, however, goes beyond the characterization of the protagonist, because it is actually the protagonist's
story of his literary ambitions. For the sake of clarity, it should be

understood that the general tone of the novel is satirical, and that much of the satire is directed against Spanish Americans abroad. The protagonist is a young Colombian novelist who resides in Paris and intends to write a great novel. What he actually writes is his autobiography, filling the "notebooks" that are the chapters of *El buen salvaje*. He writes about what happens to him and about the plans for his novel. The proposed great work changes according to the circumstances in which the aspiring author finds himself. At one time it is a historical novel about his country; then it turns into a masterwork on the Cain and Abel theme, later into a novel based on political ideology, and then a hard-hitting slice of life. Descriptions of these projects are always pretentious and always come to nothing. The plans for the proposed novel are, however, the controlling factor in the narrative structure of the "notebooks."

It is also important to note that use of any substitute for a normal narrative voice places the act of novelizing in a different perspective. The tape recorder in *Gazapo*, for example, does more than simply enhance the characterization of its owner, Menelao; it actually places him in the position of putting the story together. There is nothing satirical about this phenomenon although there are satirical elements in the novel. The activation of the reader by this and other means brings him into the process of invention, and that is the nucleus of most of the novelists' fascination with observing their own function. In *Rayuela*, Cortázar actually sets forth ideas on the theory of the novel through his invented author, Morelli. These observations appear in the Expendable Chapters; therefore, they become functional when the reader is in the act of putting together the novel according to the author's directions. Morelli's ideas point toward a negation of accepted, rational procedures, emphasizing the novelist's right to make the experience of fiction a matter of absolute invention.[2] Acceptance of the nonrational finds support, in *Rayuela*, in the contrast made by Ceferino Piriz and his plan for universal peace—an example of the absurdity created by taking logic to an extreme.

Many of the techniques used to invite the reader into the composition of a novel appear at times to express a profound lack of respect for conventionality. This effect is the basic characteristic of young novelists who write about disaffected youth, often in a seriocomic way. Precise definition is impossible. The establishment of a set of characteristics simply invites an enumeration of exceptions as seen in one novel or another. Probably the most fundamental characteristic is the use of language that belongs to youth, in a way that distinguishes one generation from its predecessor. This honesty in language is one aspect of a tell-it-like-it-is attitude that becomes both confessional and critical.

There is no doubt that the influence of J. D. Salinger has been considerable in this kind of writing. The shadow of Holden Caulfield, the protagonist in *The Catcher in the Rye*, is apparent in the characterization of the protagonist-narrator of José Agustín's *De perfil* (1966)—much more apparent than the influence of Joyce's *Ulysses*, which has been mentioned often in this connection, presumably because the novel deals with the narrator in the process of becoming a man. The basic difference between Salinger's novel and *De perfil* is that Holden Caulfield is the creation of an artist who understands an age group different from his own, while the author of *De perfil* actually belongs to the generation whose reality he creates. One of the questions raised by the particularity of this kind of novel is whether it has lasting value; or, more specifically, whether a book like *De perfil* has continued validity, since both the author and his subject have passed beyond the moment of youth.

The question cannot be answered very well in terms that would satisfy a traditionalist in matters of art, and this is certainly no place for a treatise on aesthetics. It may be helpful, however, to think of the posters that have adorned the walls decorated by young people for a decade or more. They are not intended to be lasting; however, they transcend the humdrum of daily experience. Their ephemeral quality is the very essence of their universality. They belong to an age of rapid change, of dynamic experience. The same kind of dynamism promotes narrative techniques that activate the reader.

The immediately attractive aspect of *De perfil* is its humor—an infrequent characteristic in Spanish American fiction, but a growing tendency in the 1960s. The conversational, incredibly realistic style is the principal source of humor in *De perfil* and several other novels of youthful disaffection. José Agustín has a good ear for dialogue, and his language is so right—and so uninhibited—it is funny. In addition to this fundamental homage to reality, he also agglutinizes words, making adjectives of what might ordinarily be clauses; he

272

refers to people by names that describe the narrator's reaction to them (Hacedor de Plática—Conversation Maker). The air of frankness created by these techniques is intensified by the narrator's habit of offering alternative words in parentheses, or by inserting a parenthetical modifier. Sometimes these additions have the effect of a theatrical aside; always they suggest the possibility of ingenuous honesty. There is a certain objectivity, possibly an illusion, in the results of these techniques. The narrator sees below the surface and discovers the absurd truth—in himself as well as in others.

Both *De perfil* and *Gazapo* deal with the search for what is genuine. People committed to this search frequently find conventionality unacceptable. Their reaction may be bitter, or they may laugh. Indeed the two reactions may be mixed. The comportment of the protagonist in each of these novels is designed to be "cool"—that is, with a casual air. Actually, the experience of both novels is an appreciation of the difficulties both protagonists have trying to live up to this ideal. The narrative tone, however, retains the "cool" that either protagonist might lose in a given incident. This tone makes it quite reasonable that both novels should end on a low key—actually, a nonending.

The basic plot of *Los geniecillos dominicales* is a break with routine, and there is an honesty about the novel that also reveals how things are in the world of youth. The author is older than his protagonist, possibly looking back on his own life. However, we do see the world as his protagonist does. In the opening scene of the novel, Ludo leaves his office job after three humdrum years. He invites his friends to a New Year's orgy at his uncle's house, which Ludo is caring for. The party turns out to be resoundingly dull, and the description of it is detailed and frank to the point of being funny. There is a mildly patronizing factor in the tone of the narrator, possibly because the author is at a greater distance in time from this work than Agustín and Sainz are from theirs.

A similar disgust with the established order is amply apparent in Oswaldo Reynoso's *En octubre no hay milagros* (1965). Probably its best expression is in a passage of interior monologue when Manuel describes how he intentionally failed the oral examination for admission to the University of San Marcos.[3] He is offended by the feeling of distance established between the examiners and himself, by their asking questions that he considers personal, and by academic questions that are, in his opinion, either too obvious or too difficult. The passage is funny because it is satirical and partly true of all such situations. It is also disquieting because it reveals Manuel's enormous ego—not in the sense of his being a braggart, but in his dedication to his own plight and interests.

Reynoso, although only thirty-two years old when his novel was published, is also at some distance from the young people he describes. There is an additional factor that makes *En octubre no hay milagros* different from many other novels of youth: it is committed to political action. The novel's message emerges from the parallel development of two plot lines, as well as through the nonconformism of Manuel. The family of Manuel is modest middle class in every way. The crisis in the story deals with the father's search for housing to replace the home that was torn down and replaced by a modern building. The parallel story line focuses on the wealthy entrepreneur who is the power that precipitates the crisis. The author creates a good deal of warmth toward the characters in the first story line through various interiorizing techniques; the second story line seems removed, untouchable, because third-person narration keeps it at a distance. The title refers to the fact that the last day Manuel's father has to find a house coincides with the day of the procession of Nuestro Señor de los Milagros (Our Lord of Miracles).

The obvious social commitment of *En octubre no hay milagros* does not mean that novels like *De perfil* are entirely uncommitted. Quite the contrary, they are deeply committed to anticonventionality; however, their protest is less specific—and probably more fundamental—than the suggestion in Reynoso's novel that the system should be reformed. Both *De perfil* and *Gazapo* suggest a more radical revision of values. It may be of some significance that two other Peruvian novels (that is, in addition to *En octubre no hay milagros*) evaluate the system rather than make fun of it, even though they contain elements of humor: *Los geniecillos dominicales* and Luis Loayza's *Una piel de serpiente* (1964). Loayza's novel associates youth with radicalism—or, perhaps better said, revolutionary idealism. The author organizes the narrative in two parts, the first one establishing the revolutionary impulse (principally through publication of a periodical), the second revealing the inevitable victory of the bourgeois establishment whose numerous self-defense mechanisms subvert the revolutionary impulse quite handily.

It is an interesting speculation, and quite possibly un endless one, that the nature of social commitment in these Peruvian novels may be some indication of special conditions in the country. Fernando Belaúnde Terry became president in 1963 and instituted many greatly needed social reforms. He was opposed by the oligarchs, by the right-wing political forces of ex-dictator Manuel Odría, and by the left-wing *apristas*. The latter were in substantial agreement with many of Belaúnde's reform programs, but apparently were unwilling to support reforms instituted by anyone but themselves. In 1968, before the end of Belaúnde's term in office, the executive power was seized by a military junta, which proceeded with substantial social reforms. The idea of a reformist military government is surprising; however, it can be explained partially by the fact that Peruvian military men have for some time been put through a social awareness program—instituted, surprisingly, by Manuel Odría.

The possible relationship of this situation to the novels discussed here does not mean that these books favor this kind of reform. Indeed, *Una piel de serpiente* and *En octubre no hay milagros* very obviously do not show much faith in the possibility of reform within the system. They do assume, however, that there is a debatable issue. Some other novels communicate a kind of disaffection that does not even recognize the debate. In this connection, it is important to remember that this same period saw not only the development of the Castro regime in Cuba, but also the growth of the legends of Fidel and of Che Guevara. The legends are different from discussions of political ideology; rather, they are legends of freedom from convention, of the denial of paternal or paternalistic authority. They are related to the revolutionary impulse that deals with radical change, not with the reform of systems. Its most easily triggered weapon is an attitude of disrespect.

The social concern of the authors of small-screen novels is apparent in their treatment of the middle class, whatever the economic shading of the particular group. If youthful writers are disrespectful, their elders reflect a feeling of guilt. Sergio Galindo's *La comparsa* (1964) captures a particular moment in the lives of the people of Jalapa, the capital and cultural center of the Mexican state of Veracruz. The controlled study of human relationships in this case operates in a different way from *El Bordo* where the focus is on a single family. *La comparsa* deals with the whole town, but concentrates on the celebration of Carnival—a period of two days which allows us to see the people masked and unmasked. The cross section affords several contrasts: generational differences, variation in social status (e.g., traditional family versus social climbers), university people, and townspeople. The particular time setting of the novel combines with these contrasting factors to reveal what the people are really like. Galindo makes good use of his special sensitivity for significant detail.

The reader's experience in this novel begins in the home of Alicia Esteva, daughter of obviously bourgeois parents. We hear her side of a telephone conversation with her parents who are vacationing in New York. It is their wedding anniversary. Alicia is of college age, and the conversation reveals a generational difference which, on Alicia's side, is reflected in a mixture of love and impatience. She is disturbed by the hypocrisies that exist within the framework of her living. This condition is basic to her characterization and, as the novel develops, we appreciate her situation as a prisoner of convention, but at the same time she finds security within its confines.

This case is only one of many that make up the world of *La comparsa*. It is a sample of the novel's searching view of middle-class values. Often the presentation is humorous, the product of a gentle but perceptive satire that unmasks the characters. Since Galindo's narrative deals with so many people, but is so confined in time, he has to make very careful use of segmented narration. The pieces vary from a single line to several pages, and although many appear to have the qualities of good anthology selections, very few can stand alone. The author relates them intricately to each other, and quick changes of scene are made more plausible by Galindo's three-step transition from third-person omniscient narration to interior monologue, in which a kind of third-person interiorization operates between the two narrative voices.

The relationship of time to space is of great importance in *La comparsa*—time is confined and space is practically endless. Of course, the actual geographical size of the novel's setting is relatively small since it deals only with Jalapa and one place outside the city. However, the space is actually the same as the variety of characters, and while the basic reference is to the people in a single town, their variety expands their reality into infinitely increasing waves of human identification. Time, on the other hand, is strictly confined—not simply to two days, but to the two days when human beings can be revealed in the two states of being masked and unmasked.

The time-space relationship is also important to the intimate experience of *Cuerpo creciente* (1966) by Hernán Valdés. In this case, space is strictly confined, but time develops outward. It is the story of the growth of a boy's awareness of the people about him, mainly in terms of his grandfather. By the end of the novel, he is old enough to have a life larger than that of his family, and time (that is, his life) stretches out to no foreseeable end. Although the time-space factor is almost the reverse of the way it is in *La comparsa*, it serves in both cases to illuminate a particular set of human relationships, revealing qualities that might be hidden if the novel took in the full scope of both time and space. Another effective variation is the use of two specific points in space, plus the expansion of time in memories and dreams. This combination is the basis of Jorge Edwards's *El peso de la noche* (1965). Actually, the element of time functions as one basic point: the last illness and death of a matriarch, "La señora Cristina" (the Chilean oligarchy again). The two points in space are her grandson, Francisco, and her wastrel son, Joaquín, Francisco's uncle.

In Edwards's novel, each of the two male protagonists is, in a sense, a projection of the matriarch. Each is rebellious in his own way, and each is tied to tradition. The spatial development of the story alternates between the focus on Joaquín and the focus on Francisco. Time expands, through the memories and dreams of both men, into past and future, always intercalated with the present.

The first-person narrator is extremely important in novels of this kind; however, there are many variations in the way this narrative voice functions. In *Cuerpo creciente*, it is the basis of the characterization of the child protagonist. The narrator tells what life looked like when he was a preschool boy. One of the fine qualities of Valdés's novel is the effectiveness of this view. Rather than nostalgic memory by an adult narrator, the novel is unusually consistent in presenting reality as the child might see it. A first-person diarist in *Mientras llueve* (1964), by Fernando Soto Aparicio, uses a good deal of immediate present (e.g., "The men go away and I stand quiet, dumbstruck.")—that is, action as if it were happening while

277

being recorded. The technique communicates satisfactorily the sense of duration of time while the narrator is in prison. The novel deals with a woman sentenced to a prison term for poisoning her elderly husband. The narrative is addressed to a poet who was the love of her youth. The experience of this novel is not a matter of guilt or innocence, but of the struggle to protect one's integrity against the destructive forces of prison.

In Pedro Orgambide's *Memorias de un hombre de bien* (1964), the first-person narrator is close to the picaresque tradition. The protagonist belongs to a once-wealthy Argentine family, and his life corresponds generally to the course of change in Argentine society during the twentieth century. He is similar to Ernesto in *El encuentro*. However, *Memorias de un hombre de bien* is closer to the old *costumbrista* tradition, recalling particularly the stories of Fray Mocho, to whom the novel is dedicated. Two layers of irony work together—one in the characterization of the narrator-protagonist, the other within the observations made by him. The result is a funny book, but not a happy one. The many facets of Argentine society all seem false. It is a criticism of the conventions of the middle class.

A very neatly confined picture of a disappearing segment of society (the landed gentry) emerges from the first-person narration of *Los burgueses* (1964), by Silvina Bullrich. The situation is a family reunion at the patriarch's *estancia*. The narrative voice is never identified—it is not even clear whether the speaker is a man or a woman—but he (she) is closely related to the people there. This semi-identity gives the reader a sense of partial objectivity, but still with a feeling of involvement. Nostalgia combines with a sense of relief. The changing society is evident in the different situations of various members of the family; however, meanness of spirit seems constant.

The isolation of problems of human relationships continues as an important factor; however, the novelists find more sophisticated narrative devices to create the effect of interiorization.[4] The revelation of the weaknesses of the bourgeoisie becomes increasingly functional in the novels of intimate searching. José Donoso's *Este domingo* (1966) is the story of a crisis in the life of a well-to-do family, but the crisis reveals a double disrespect for the humble: one in the form of unadorned class discrimination, the other in the guise of charitable attention. The structure of the novel allows us to see a set of grandparents as they know themselves and also as their grandchildren see them. To the young, one grandparent appears more modern than the other; but the intimate revelation shows them as simply employing two different ways of exploiting the poor.

The revisionist aspect of the small-screen novels—that is, with regard to conventional middle-class values—sometimes calls into question our concept of reality. What happens is that conventionality is associated with a certain perception of reality. If a given pattern of behavior persists even though it is not in accord with that perception, the result is hypocrisy. If a given appreciation of reality persists, it may instigate change in conventionality or at least cast doubt on the validity of convention. In the give-and-take correspondence of the two possibilities, there are situations that provoke doubts about what reality is. This complex of experiences is expressed in a considerable number of novels that are fictionalizations of concepts rather than developments of characterization or plot in the ordinary sense.

In order to appreciate these works, it is helpful to understand that some develop from the standpoint of conventionality, and others are based on the perception of reality. Examples of these respective cases are Carlos Droguett's *Patas de perro* (1965) and Salvador Elizondo's *Farabeuf* (1965). The point of Droguett's novel is that everyone is a misfit, but society forces the individual to conceal his nonconforming characteristics. To make the point, the author invents a boy with dog's paws, a nonconformity he obviously cannot hide.[5] Of course, the condition is in itself a distortion of reality; however, the effect of Droguett's invention is to illuminate human behavior rather than define our basic perceptions. In *Farabeuf*, on the other hand, Elizondo subtitles his work "the chronicle of an instant" and proceeds to develop the novel outside ordinary concepts of space and time. It might be said that he fuses all aspects of both phenomena, or simply that he "suppresses all logical concepts of time and space."[6] The novel challenges perceptions, but does not concern itself primarily with apparent human behavior. Nevertheless, both novels fictionalize concepts; and the reader's experience in both cases is much more likely to be an appreciation of these concepts than an identification with particular characters or with a familiar situation.

Patas de perro appears to have more pragmatic value. That is, it contains an idea that can be interpreted into a presumably useful lesson. In this regard there is a certain similarity between it and the novels of the naturalist school, though Droguett's novel uses narrative techniques that are not part of the nineteenth-century manner of storytelling. The major device, however, is similar to the naturalist's *cas extrême*. José Donoso employs a procedure that is similar, in a general sense, in *El lugar sin límites* (1966). The weird nature of the people and their story makes more apparent their inability to say anything important to each other, so creating a kind of hell on earth. The scene is a brothel where the fading young madame lives with her transvestite father. A bizarre situation, certainly. To fill out the picture, it is necessary to know that the father, known as "La Manuela," is biologically a father, but psychologically a mother. There is a kind of irony in the daughter's reference to him as her father. To make matters worse, the poor man is bedeviled by the passionate advances of a truck driver. The paradox contained within the personality of La Manuela (one might even call it a relationship within a single person) contains the germ of the experience of frustrated relationships throughout the novel. Several people are dependent on each other, yet mutual help is impossible. This dilemma emerges from a narrative procedure that makes frequent use of flashbacks and interior monologue. However, the technique that best communicates the human condition of the novel is indirect quotation in which the narrator tells (or paraphrases) what someone says. It may be that interior monologue reveals the characters' moments of deepest anguish, but the indirect quotation creates the reality of frustration.

Although it is possible to accept the people in *El lugar sin límites* as real, the dilemma probably stands out more strongly than the people, except insofar as they are freaks—and that is part of the dilemma. The feeling of frustrated relationships is similar to the sense of elusive truth or justice in *Los albañiles* and *La ciudad y los perros*. The people are even less important in *Farabeuf* because the experience of the novel is not convertible into a moral or ethical lesson. Rather, it is the creation of a sense of reality. This effect is different from what we normally think of as the novelist creating his own fictional world. Elizondo's novelization is not so related to questions of invention or of transformation of visible reality; rather it has to do with the restructuring of the concept of reality. The concept he creates is, in fact, the experience of the work. It is not a predetermined concept explained through fiction, but the expansion of a rudimentary notion, in which the act of expansion constitutes a new perception.

Most critics of literature would agree that the novel in recent years has been taking on characteristics usually associated with poetry. That is clearly the case with *Farabeuf*. The intricate interweaving and repetition of incidents create an effect which cannot be defined in words other than those used by the writer. The fact that the novel deals with an incident in history really has nothing to do with the total effect, since its historical significance is demolished in the process of making the novel. It is possible to say that the incident took place during the Boxer Rebellion and involves the dismemberment of a human. It is also possible, though less satisfying to the literal minded, to say that Dr. Farabeuf is related to this incident and also to a woman who plays more than one role. Taking the development a step farther, we know that dismemberment is associated with coitus, and orgasm with death. However, all this says very little, because it is the experience itself that contains the novel's only truth.

Although other novels that are strictly the experience of concept have appeared since *Farabeuf*, there is no other novel quite like it in the period covered by this chapter. However, it is probably fair to mention, in this connection, a very important novel by José Lezama Lima, *Paradiso* (1966). Readers who know the novel may well find it in a strange context here, especially because it is autobiographical and the characters seem more firmly attached to this world than do the actors in *Farabeuf*. However, it is a highly poetic book in which the narrator's sensory perception makes its whole reality seem special—something different from the ordinary world. The book is a story of a boy's coming of age, an appreciation of his finding a reconciliation with the idea of death, and an awareness of the act of writing. This last characteristic involves the meaning of creativity and counterpoints the concern with death. The experience of the reader is a sense of the combination of creative need, awareness of life, and the identity search. The combination produces a kind of wholeness in *Paradiso* that is not present in many novels. Its dynamism comes mainly from Lezama Lima's imagery, which humanizes the feeling of wholeness.

Paradiso does have a locale. It is Cuba; and in a way, the country corresponds to the protagonist in this novel of initiation. However, it really is not regional in any accepted sense of the term. Quaintness is not one of its characteristics. Indeed, it is generally true of contemporary fiction that regionalism, far from being of the "delightfully different" school, searches deeply into the reality of its setting and transforms it into an illuminating experience. This practice, of course, is not an invention of the 1960s. It has been characteristic of the mainstream of Spanish American fiction since the late 1940s, the period that marks the beginning of the new novel. The interesting development in this kind of novel is not an abrupt change but the persistent increase in the use of complicated narrative techniques.

The range of technical virtuosity varies from the rather straightforward structure and style of Manuel Zapata Olivella's *En Chimá nace un santo* (1964) to the interweaving of several story lines and the telescoping of time in *La casa verde*. All these novels develop a principal idea; however, this idea is less abstract than in novels like *Farabeuf*, and they depend on careful characterization. Awareness of these "real" people attaches the novel to the familiar world; then various narrative techniques serve to produce an epic or mythic quality. The combination produces a work that is regionalistic and transcendent at the same time.

Pointing out *En Chimá nace un santo* as an example of uncomplicated narration really shows how much novels have changed over the course of the century. Zapata Olivella uses segmented narration, shifting from one place to another and also cutting into the trajectory of time. Nevertheless, since he does not change the logical order of events, but simply fences in particular moments, we react to his novel as being fairly traditional. Actually, its transcendent quality is the product of a contrast seen mainly in the cinematic movement between the isolated village of Chimá and the town of Lorica. The people of Chimá form a heretical cult around a crippled youth who has a reputation for working miracles. The consequent struggle with orthodoxy (its seat is in Lorica) shows one side as fanatical as the other. Corollary to this experience is the awareness of a great need felt by the people of Chimá. Similar techniques produce a panorama of the reality of Peru, in José María Arguedas's *Todas las sangres* (1964). The most notable characteristic of this novel, from the standpoint of its position among the author's other works, is that the persistent "I" disappears. The author's hypersensibility to Indian culture, so apparent in *Los ríos profundos*, ceases to be a participating factor in the story. However, there is no reason to think his attitude has changed, and he is certainly behind the third-person narrator of *Todas las sangres*. Considering this novel without reference to other works by the same author, its most interesting feature is the treatment of characters, of types, and of institutions as if they were all endowed with qualities that enabled them to act within the same framework of capability. That is, a civic institution tends to be anthropomorphized, and types are accepted on the same terms as particularized characterizations. This equalization casts a special light on the novel's cultural contrasts.

The narrative procedure of *La casa verde* is much more complicated, and its quality of transcendent regionalism depends on more than an anthropological contrast, though that factor is amply apparent. The effect of simultaneity in this novel is about as complete as a narrator is likely to make it. Not only does it create an appreciation of what happens in different places at the same time, it also brings together different points in time. Vargas Llosa's use of tense works effectively to this end. There is a telescoping of time which is related to the interweaving of several story lines. These lines of narration deal with various matters which, when brought together, create a series of contrasts: feudalism and progress, pleasure and puritanism, civilization and barbarism. One story is the rise and fall of an adventurer who rules his backwoods domain in a manner appropriate to the Middle Ages. Another line is the Green House itself, a brothel built on the edge of town. Since the town is on the margin of civilization, the moral threat of this pleasure palace is intense and, in the experience of the novel, the house takes on the phoenixlike quality of self-regeneration. Another line deals with an Indian leader who forms a rubber-marketing cooperative. Probably the most astonishing line has to do with missionary nuns who actually capture Indian girls and intern them in the mission school.

All these lines are interrelated, and they work together to make a Peruvian epic. However, the time effect created by Vargas Llosa keeps the novel from having the aura of history that normally characterizes an epic. Yet it does not seem confined to the present either. Rather, it is a reality without time. In this respect, the novel goes far beyond traditional regionalism. Its transcendent character is enhanced by a view of the New World that is somewhat like Carpentier's—there is something marvelous, something nearly incredible, about the hemisphere.

The transformation of regionalism is a different matter if the focus is a particular event or situation. Colombia's *la violencia* is the thematic base of Manuel Mejía Vallejo's *El día señalado* (1964). The feeling developed in the course of the novel is that there is no apparent solution and that acts of violence will continue indefinitely. The basis for this impression is a prologue which could stand quite well as a short story. Its effect is to create awareness of a man's being drawn into violence against his will. After this introduction, the author alternates two story lines: one built around a frightened town and the presence of unwelcome government troops, the other around a matter of personal vengeance. The narration in one story is third person and in the other is first person, thereby reinforcing the difference between the general situation and the individual concern. The contrast is resolved as the two lines of action meet, but that does not mean that the problem is resolved. The conclusion of the novel may be taken as a temporary resolution, but the circularity of the situation suggests interminable repetition of the same. As this realization takes form in the reader's experience, the human problem becomes generalized without losing, of course, its fundamental Colombian reference.

The particular circumstance in Fernando del Paso's *José Trigo* is that of the provincial who comes to the city and needs to integrate himself into the working class. The scene is Mexico City; however, the theme itself takes the novel beyond the boundaries of a single place. In addition, José Trigo himself is more myth than man, more concept than tangible reality, made so by the fact that he never becomes a living reality in the novel's present. What we know about him we know through what others say. The time of the novel is basically retrospective. The "I" narrator is searching for José Trigo, and we find out about things that have already happened. The structure of the narration inverts itself, the second set of chapters carrying numbers in reverse order, ending in "One" and leaving us at the point of origin. There is a plot concerning a strike of railroad workers which serves as a foundation of reality for the mythologizing of José Trigo.

The theme of political exile is transformed into a universal experience in two novels by Gabriel Casaccia, *La llaga* (1964) and *Los exiliados* (1966). The author's nationality, Paraguayan, makes him a natural authority on long-term repression and rejection. The country has not enjoyed a happy political history and, since 1954, has lived under the repressive government of Alfredo Stroessner. This tyrant, who has never paid more than lip service to civil rights, rules as if the country were threatened by immediate invasion. Plots form, rebellions are put down, and exiles nourish diminishing hope. The circumstance is not exclusively Paraguayan, and that is one reason Gabriel Casaccia's novels transcend their regionalistic base.

The two novels constitute a more satisfactory artistic transformation of the theme than either book offers by itself. *La llaga* involves a revolutionary plot in the capital city, Asunción. The structure of the novel, however, also depends on the complications of a relationship involving a mother, her son, and her lover. Much of the characterization is revealed in interior monologue, and this intimacy keeps the novel from being strictly political. *Los exiliados* moves across the border to a colony of Paraguayan exiles. There is a continuation of the story from *La llaga*, but the narrator interweaves this line of action with several others, all concerning the exiles. Individuals refer to themselves—a kind of identity—by mentioning the year of the rebellion that caused the exile of the person speaking. One of the principal story lines concerns Doctor Gamarra, an intellectual who has been in exile for twenty years. He dreams of the triumphant return, but really knows it will never take place. In different circumstances, he might have been a leader, but, in reality, he is an example of disintegration both physical and spiritual. What happens to him personally is indicative of the general tendency in the community of exiles. Their situation does not improve, they lose their sense of purpose, and character disintegration sets in. This process is the dynamic factor of the novel, and its success is largely the result of relating the lives of other exiles to the story of Doctor Gamarra.

The realistic base of the novels of transformed regionalism shows their affinity with the small-screen, more intimate novels of human relationships. In the development of the realistic base, we find a continuation of the difference, already observed, between the epic-type, panoramic novel and the intensely searching, finely focused novels that show how individuals get along together. By this time, there is little difference in the variety of narrative techniques employed by the novelists. The youth novels and the concept novels are the most innovative tendencies thematically. However, they too show the same wide range of techniques. Regarding the technical virtuosity of Spanish American novelists during these years, it is fair to say—in a very general statement—that the most interesting effect of their artistry is the activation of the reader.

CHAPTER 18

The Year of *Cien años de soledad* (1967)

It would be difficult to find a better indicator of the boom in Spanish American fiction than the fact that at least a dozen novels published in 1967 deserve detailed analysis. It is equally indicative of the period that half of them, or more, are so innovative they should have much longer analyses than are practicable in a study of this kind. Some of them depend to such an extent on the inventive power of language—that is, creativity by language and within language itself—they boggle the resources of standard criticism. In some cases it is difficult to say more than that experience of the novel is in the vitality of the language itself. These characteristics intensify the tendencies noted particularly in the years 1964–1966.

Three novels furnish a suitable basis for this chapter: *Cien años de soledad* by Gabriel García Márquez, *Tres tristes tigres* by Guillermo Cabrera Infante, and *Cambio de piel* by Carlos Fuentes. Several other books of this year certainly belong in the same value category with these three; however, they will be dealt with more briefly and with reference to the basic works. Of the three, *Cien años de soledad* is by far the best known and most widely discussed. Three general characteristics form the basis for its wide appeal. First, the author insists on the artist's right to invent his own reality. In the case of *Cien años de soledad*, it is a very strange reality, but it is entirely accessible to the reader since there are no barriers created by difficult narrative techniques. Second, the book has several interest-provoking characteristics, not just one: unusual people, fantasy, and plot suspense. Third, it is a very funny novel—a fact which does not make it a frivolous book, but a profound and humane one.

The novel opens with this sentence: "Many years later, as he faced the firing squad, Colonel Aureliano Buendía was to remember that distant afternoon when his father took him to discover ice."[1] It is a remarkable introduction. Immediately, the narrator involves us in the three aspects of time; we look forward to "many years later" than the presumed present and, at the same time, backward to "that distant afternoon." As the novel develops, the whole matter of time takes on a certain magical quality that obscures its pragmatic significance and leaves the reader in a situation of uncertainty—and probably unconcern—about the relationship of past to present to future. In addition, the sentence establishes plot suspense by informing us that Colonel Buendía is going to face a firing squad for some reason or other—a situation that arouses interest even though we do not know who the colonel is. Still another highly suggestive factor in the sentence insinuates what is probably the novel's outstanding characteristic: "his father took him to discover ice." This act of identifying basic things is in effect the act of bringing-into-being by naming. With only one sentence intervening, the narrator reaffirms this idea on the same page: "The world was so recent that many things lacked names, and in order to indicate them it was necessary to point." So informed, we are ready for the creation of a reality within the experience of the novel.

The sentence that intervenes between the first suggestion of discovery and its affirmation refers to the town of Macondo, a village of twenty houses when Aureliano's father took him to discover ice. Macondo is the town invented by García Márquez. It is his standard locale, just as Yoknapatawpha County is a standard locale in the works of William Faulkner. *Cien años de soledad* is a culminating point in his fiction, bringing together various facets of earlier works. Right at the beginning of the novel, already forgetting sequential time, we are aware of the first days of Macondo. The story covers the town's history, from its beginning to its end when the wind sweeps it away. The story of the Buendía family parallels that of Macondo. The patriarch founded it; the last of the line is destroyed with the town.

Still in the first paragraph of the novel, we learn that every March a family of Gypsies would come and put on a display of new inventions. The narrator recalls the advent of the magnet, dragged through town by a Gypsy named Melquíades, pulling all the pots, pans, and other metal objects from the houses, and even making their frames squeak as the nails became restive under the magnet's influence. This part of the opening paragraph sets forth two more fundamental aspects of the novel. First, the kind of exaggeration— or fantasy—seen in the magnet incident is characteristic of many presentations of things, people, and actions: they have a larger-than-life quality. Second, the extraordinary feat is performed by Melquíades, who persistently adds a miraculous touch to the story.

The life of Macondo reflects much of the history of Colombia; however, its implications make widening circles that include Spanish American and even universal experience. It is preeminently the sense of origins, of creating—almost biblical at times—that is basically responsible for the level of universal experience. The town is in the Colombian jungle, where a band of pioneers settled. It grows, suffers epidemic and flood, prosperity and misery. Macondo enjoys its greatest prosperity when a company from the United States establishes a banana plantation in the area. Later, the planters leave and misery takes their place. The specific source of ephemeral prosperity has a clearly Spanish American connotation; however, the cycle of prosperity and depression, created by similar commercial or industrial events, is a common experience in the world. Macondo reflects the influence of revolution and of technological progress. Both phenomena seem to be intrusions; they come from the outside world, just like the touches of cosmopolitanism that enliven the place.

Macondo has its own life that is a separated, isolated existence. Nevertheless, that life is forever affected by attack or intrusion from the outside. For this reason, the reality of García Márquez's town is somewhat like that of a laboratory specimen, and this condition enhances the feeling that everything about the place is special in some way. Even its epidemic is different—its inhabitants suffer from insomniac amnesia. It is an extraordinary place, and the people who live there are as strange as the town.

The Year of *Cien años de soledad* (1967)

The narrative structure of *Cien años de soledad* might be said to depend on the history of Macondo or on the generations of the Buendía family. Such a statement, however, would be meaningless without explaining that the generations of the family are as elusive as the historical time of the setting. Illegitimacy is commonplace, fertility is astonishing, and generational lines are consequently skewed in such a way that an aunt or uncle may very well be younger than the niece or nephew. Regarding the basic organization of the story, García Márquez plays it down. The novel is divided into sections, but they do not carry numbers or chapter titles. Once the important elements in the novel are insinuated into the reader's experience (all within the long initial paragraph), the narrator tends to immerse us in a flowing of his invention, allowing us to lose track of time and even of objective reality.

Within this flow is a subtle structure based on the extraordinary qualities of the characters. Early in the novel, we learn of the first José Arcadio Buendía's obsession with technology. He wants to use Melquíades's magnet to extract gold from the earth. With an early camera he darts around trying to take a picture of God, on the theory that, if God is everywhere, the camera should record his likeness. All this is fun to read. It starts out with the extraordinary and mildly amusing discovery of ice. Soon it turns into rich merriment. What happens is that the nearly incredible people amuse us—or fascinate us—into acceptance of the author's invention; and the real joy of *Cien años de soledad* depends on reading it as a rollicking, made-up story. The nature of the book invites readers to explore it for hidden meanings, but this activity can easily kill the joy of the book's experience.

The story deals with five generations of Buendías—or it might be safer to say approximately five generations.[2] Throughout the story there is much that might be called "magic realism." Colonel Aureliano Buendía has seventeen illegitimate sons by seventeen different women, and each son carries the mark of penitential ashes indelibly fixed on his forehead. All seventeen are named Aureliano. Remedios la bella, the most beautiful woman in the world, lives in the purity of innocence and ascends into the heavens, carried away by a sheet while hanging out the laundry. José Arcadio Buendía (one of them—there are three), the labor leader, sees a massacre of workers that nobody else sees. Melquíades, whose age is not clear but is beyond rational belief, is present even when he is away; and his room stays in immaculate condition even when he does not visibly live in it and no one takes care of it. These strange things are not exactly fantasy; García Márquez prohibits their being fantastic by dealing with them as if they were commonplace. This special state is the condition of the family history, from settling the town, through all the trials and tribulations of life, to the last Aureliano, a bastard son who is a recluse separated from the world. He is drawn out by the vivacious Amaranta Ursula after her return from Europe. They have a child, not knowing that she is Aureliano's aunt. The child is born with a pig's tail, fulfilling a family prophecy that was the obsession of the first Ursula, wife of the Buendía who founded Macondo. All three die, Aureliano just as he is deciphering Melquíades's mysterious books, which inform him that the Gypsy (the bringer of inventions) wrote the family history a hundred years in anticipation of the events.

This revelation is the final reaffirmation of the role of fictional invention in *Cien años de soledad.* Although much of the novel seems strange, it is never difficult. The unreality has a flavor of legend. Everything is prodigious: the size of the José Arcadios, the beauty of Remedios, Rebeca's passion for eating dirt, the sexual activity of various characters, the size of someone's private parts, the gentility of Fernanda. In some cases it is possible to imagine prosaic bases for the fabulous elements in the novel. The attempt to photograph God could be the novelization of a family joke or a spiritual crisis. Remedios's ascent is the destiny of someone who is too beautiful for this earth. Colonel Buendía, who fought in thirty-two civil wars and lost them all, is a novelization of the constant revolutionary. The dirt-eating Rebeca may be an interpretation of a childhood reprimand. It is probable, indeed, that the reality of *Cien años de soledad* has its basis in childhood. That is, it may be that the novel uses the way a child sees reality, then places that view in the larger context of an adult world. The narrator then maintains this childhood view within the unfamiliar context, without making allowances for different levels of sophistication.

Obviously García Márquez is not interested in being clear about all the effects created in his novel. He seems to write from inspiration, using what he remembers combined with what he thinks of during the process of writing. His novel has a high level of spontaneity; it does not have a carefully worked out pattern of meaning. His style is direct, accurate. The sense of unreality in the novel has nothing to do with language invention; it is created by events, by what the author says happens. We may have doubts about the probability of what happens, but there is never any doubt about what the narrator says.

With regard to the use of language for direct and clear communication, Guillermo Cabrera Infante's *Tres tristes tigres* is almost at the opposite pole from *Cien años de soledad*. The experience of Cabrera Infante's book is not entirely a matter of inventive language play, but it comes very close to being so. This fact invites comparison with James Joyce, and it is true that Cabrera Infante, like many other recent novelists who have discovered the nature of language, is indebted to Joyce. On the other hand, only a very superficial critic would dismiss the author of *Tres tristes tigres* as "a Cuban Joyce." The locale, Havana, is important; Cabrera Infante is inventive in his own right; his tone is one of skeptical nostalgia, hardly an imitation of Joyce.

Tres tristes tigres is a novel in movement. It communicates a sense of its own development, somewhat the way *Rayuela* does. Such a feeling—that the novel is always in progress—is very likely the product of the author's concept of creating fiction. He makes changes in the various editions—an attitude that made translation possible. Complicated language play forces the translator to make parallel versions of many passages, sometimes adding, sometimes eliminating; therefore, the possibility of variation is extremely important.[3]

The present time of the novel is 1958, some months before the victory of the Castro revolution. It is the end of an era, and the sense of this kind of finality permeates the novel. In addition to the feeling of being on the brink of change (or of disappearance), Cabrera Infante employs a dimension of moderate depth in time, though it never exceeds the lifetime of people who participate in the novel. Placing the era in international terms, it is the period of the rumba, Latin lovers, and the paradise of palms. The action of *Tres tristes tigres* catches this crepe paper world at its moment of crisis— probably more accurately, its moment of agony.

292

The novel opens on a Havana night club scene. We hear the master-of-ceremonies' stream of patter. *Hear* is a good word in this connection because Cabrera Infante has an excellent ear for oral language. The emcee introduces personalities among the clientele, makes dumb jokes, laughs at his own remarks, mixes Spanish and English to please the international crowd. This prologue establishes a mood of meaningless fun searching. It concludes with his announcement that the show is about to begin.

The show we see, however, is not what follows our jolly emcee on the stage of the Tropicana night club, but the doings of some of the people who frequent the place. These actions take place in the novel's present time. However, between the prologue and the chapters dedicated to Havana night life, runs a series of scenes that remove us from the night club world. These scenes ought to reveal a more authentic appreciation of life since they seem to deal with ordinary people, but their lives are just as vapid as the emcee's line. As far as effect is concerned, it doesn't matter who narrates these passages. They are more important for the feeling they create than for specific identity. Cabrera Infante often changes narrative voice with no warning and uses devices like telephone conversations and letters to eliminate the traditional narrator role. These techniques open the novel to the reader, inviting him to active participation.

The principal lines of narration—those that deal with night life in Havana—are narrated by three active participants: a photographer named Códac, a television actor named Arsenio Cué, and Silvestre, a writer. The inane life of the let's-have-some-fun world looks pretty stupid. However, Cabrera Infante does not make us feel we are in some way superior to these silly people. Here is where the nostalgia comes in, and it is the nostalgia itself that gives poignancy to the sense of cataclysm.

In sections of the novel (not consistently throughout it), Cabrera Infante alternates two series of episodes, one made up of a woman's sessions with a psychiatrist, the other telling the story of a singer, La Estrella. These two series have opposing relationships to the night-life story. The psychiatric episodes are identified simply as "First Session," "Second Session," and so on. They are monologues consisting entirely of what the patient says to the doctor. Their length varies from several pages to a single sentence in which the patient asks whether *psychiatrist* is spelled with or without a *p*. This particular session functions as a *reductio ad absurdum* in the series. In the experience of the novel, we have every reason to expect psychotherapy to add a dimension of depth. Quite the contrary, it turns out to be as meaningless as the night life.

The episodes of the series alternating with the psychiatric sessions are always entitled "I Heard Her Sing." La Estrella's career as a singer places her directly within the spinning superficiality of cabaret life. We can reasonably expect from her a corresponding superficiality, but we actually experience more depth. In this connection it is important that she insists on being called "La Estrella," rather than simply "Estrella." The name means "Star" and is a reasonable Spanish name for a woman. However, "La Estrella" means "The Star" and is a declaration of status. The uniqueness implied by the article is appropriate to the archetypal value of La Estrella as compared with other entertainers who are characters in the novel. She is an enormous black woman whose exaggerated mannerisms set her apart from ordinary humans. She insists on singing without instrumental accompaniment, and her artistic personality evolves into the essence of sound.

Undoubtedly, La Estrella's dedication to pure vocal sound has the effect of emphasizing the author's insistence on the authentic sound of Cuban Spanish and, in a larger sense, his interest in the creative power of language. While this more general dedication refers to the novel as a whole, it also has a specific representation in a character named Bustrófedon. He is the incarnation of language, and that role is the best way to describe his function in the novel. He participates in the action with some of the other people in the story, but he is never quite the same as they. We do not really know who he is or where he came from. His characterization may be well described as the spirit of inventing reality. Under his influence, the novel produces mandalas, backward writing, mirrored typography, puns, spoonerisms, and neologisms. This inventive language is fun; however, beyond that description, it has two effects which may become either paradoxical or complementary, depending on an individual reader's response. In one direction, the language play adds to the chaotic character of the novel and to the fragmented personalities of the people who live within the story. In another direction, the creative nature of the language continues to produce a sense of invention—of making—that has a redemptive significance. It is possible that the maximum experience of the novel is to reduce reality to nothing and then start over again. This process, however, is not a message within the novel. If it takes place, it must do so through the action of the reader in the role of narrator, or controlling organizer.

It is possible that a reader may not be aware of his potential activity in *Tres tristes tigres* until he gets to a series of literary parodies. All of them deal with the death of Leon Trotsky, and each one imitates a Cuban writer. They are a delightful tour de force. They are also a devastating satire on linguistic conventionalities. In the experience of the novel, they contribute to our awareness of how vital language is; however, they are not really necessary to the success of the book. Anyone who has read *Rayuela* may well recall its Expendable Chapters and wonder if these parodies are of the same kind. At that point, if not before, the reader is sufficiently activated to wonder if other parts of Cabrera Infante's novel may have the same characteristic.

The probability is that not much of *Tres tristes tigres* could or should be left out without spoiling its effect. However, it is important to remember that *Rayuela* is really two different novels—not one novel with optional chapters. In other words, the Expendable Chapters are not expendable at all in terms of experiencing the whole work. They can be excluded only if we are willing to accept a different experience. So in *Tres tristes tigres*, the activated reader has numerous options. He may omit or he may change order. Unlike Cortázar, Cabrera Infante does not offer a patterned alternative. His book is more open than *Rayuela*, and the reader is on his own. There is no doubt that any variation may alter the experience, particularly by changing emphasis. However, there is one constant that will appear whatever the arrangement—the absurdity of life, the ridiculous nature of momentous events, the insignificant cause of catastrophic effect. It would be possible, for example, to extract the story of La Estrella from the novel and let it stand independently. Because of her archetypal qualities, that is the factor in *Tres tristes tigres* that promises the deepest insight. Yet she dies from overeating. This apparent irony—that the woman who is the essence of sound should die from such a prosaic cause—is faithful to the total experience of the novel. It may be expanded or enriched in many different ways, but the nature of the ultimate experience must depend largely on the activated reader's effecting a reconciliation of disparate elements.

Readers who define Carlos Fuentes (rather than simply recognize him) as the author of *La región más transparente* and *La muerte de Artemio Cruz* are likely to be disconcerted by *Cambio de piel*. The novelist appears to be teasing his reader when, more accurately observed, he is playing games with the relationship of narrator to story. The novel also produces the effect of shared identity of characters, and even more apparent is the folding of time and of place so that multiple times or multiple places may appear as a single time or a single place. While one or another of these factors—or techniques— may be analyzed and explained in a way that makes the novel more accessible to the reader, their combined function in the novel tends to be disorienting rather than communicative. By 1967, of course, novels tend to be vague, confused or confusing, and generally difficult. Often the effects achieved, once the difficulties are overcome, amount to a dazzling experience, and readers tend to forget the desire for clarity and logic. However, the thematic material and even some of the narrative techniques of *Cambio de piel* promise a clearer resolution than Fuentes ever produces.

To a considerable extent, the deficiencies of *Cambio de piel* can be traced to the same creative impulses that inspired *Aura*. Some of its successes come from the same source. The double identity situation in *Aura* is one aspect of the novelist's preoccupation with the nature of individual identity, particularly as it relates to continuation of life beyond the normal span. However, it is not simply a question of immortality or of reincarnation; rather, it is part of a larger consideration—one that deals with a reality different from what we usually consider real. This idea, in turn, refers to the act of creating fiction as well as to the content of a specific work. In other words, the question of what is reality has to do with the techniques used in making a novel and also with the concepts that inspire the work and grow with it. In order to remove the barriers that ordinarily limit a reader's experience, Fuentes experiments with inventions that appear to be distortions, particularly in dealing with time and space. He also experiments with the position of the narrative voice, often with the effect of adding a dimension to the invented reality of his novel.

At the beginning of *Cambio de piel*, Fuentes deals with the questions of narrator and time in the novel.[4] In a quotation that serves as an epigraph, he sets the circumstance by saying it is as if we were on the eve of an improbable catastrophe or the morrow of an impossible fiesta. The short initial passage also points out that the book begins after the Narrator finishes his tale, and that the Narrator, like the character in a ballad, asks permission to begin. This first part of the novel is called "An Impossible Fiesta." The reader, therefore, may know vaguely what his situation is. However, in the actual experience of the novel, the prefacelike page does not make much of an impression at the beginning. It is more likely to take on meaning when and if it is remembered later on in the novel.

Immediately following the preface is a section describing the Mexican city of Cholula, at the time of Cortés and during the present time of the novel, 1965, creating a kaleidoscopic union of past and present. The effect is mainly the creation of ambience. Some characters are mentioned, but the section leaves no clear idea of them. The narrator addresses himself to one of them, Elizabeth, and then to another, Isabel (p. 17). *Isabel* is the Spanish form of *Elizabeth*. At the end of the section, an aged Lincoln convertible rolls into Cholula, and from it emerge the hippie-type members of a rock ensemble which is soon identified as "The Monks." Finally, the narrator drops a clue that is picked up in the last episode of the novel. This repetition is significant, but only if we remember the first clue after reading 419 intervening pages.

Cambio de piel builds a mood of desolation through persistent reference to decaying reality: the pre-Hispanic ruins in Cholula, the ancient ruins of Greece, burned out haciendas, New York slums, a down-at-the-heels hotel in Cholula, and a Nazi concentration camp. The principal characters suggest a corresponding state of decay. Javier, a Mexican poet who has been unproductive since a youthful moment of glory, toys with ideas in a futile attempt to convince himself that he is both man and poet. He finds it convenient to believe that his wife's sexual demands have stifled his poetic voice.

His *yanqui* wife, Elizabeth, needs love as a means of confirming her individual identity. She knows well that Javier, even in his moments of passion, makes love to Woman rather than to Elizabeth.

Franz, Elizabeth's lover, is a German immigrant who was once a Nazi. He seeks and finds expiation for not having saved a girl from murder. The fourth member of the quartet is one of Javier's students, Isabel. Javier, fascinated by the girl's carefree youthfulness, has changed his relationship from teacher to lover. Isabel is the only one of the four who is not in a state of decay. However, there is little to be found in her personality beyond her obvious sensuousness. In fact, she is better understood as an extension—or possibly an aspect—of Elizabeth.

The characterizations and the mood of desolation develop in the second part of the novel. The first part serves as a prologue and as the bait in the narrator's trap. In the second part, we find Javier and his three playmates in a hotel in Cholula, forced to stop over because of automobile trouble on their way to Veracruz. The third-rate hotel is indicative of the way Cholula looks to them. It is a sad place indeed, but they really have as much to interest them there as anywhere else—sex.

While they are in Cholula, we learn about their backgrounds: Elizabeth's childhood in the slums of New York, Franz's Nazi experience, Javier's pitifully anxious mother, Elizabeth and Javier in Greece. The narration uses many points in time, some reaching up to the recent past—for example, Isabel and Javier in a motel room while the taxi waits outside. To appreciate how *Cambio de piel* develops, it is helpful to think of the protagonists' past lives as a vertical dimension. The development also employs a horizontal dimension, created by reference to events occurring at one point in time, but in widely separated places and with no apparent relationship to each other. In our experience of the novel, the two dimensions cross and make a kind of cube of reality. There is no individual in the novel who appears to be affected by all the criss-crossing circumstances; however, each one is a part of the development, both vertical and horizontal, and seems to exist within both dimensions. The vertical dimension, therefore, is not a movement backward in time, but a recognition of one aspect of present-time reality.

The most striking factor in this past-present combination is the guilt of Franz. Although the novel is rich in moral implications,

Franz's situation stands out most sharply because it deals with man's persistent self-brutalization. Or to put a different light on the matter —man's apparent need for the sacrificial act. It is primarily in connection with this need that the third part of the novel turns into a trial put on by The Monks at the expense of the four protagonists. This procedure takes place in the setting of Cholula's pre-Hispanic ruins. At this point, the novel becomes so full of possible symbolism, many readers grow weary. The reaction has a last-straw quality, because the novel is complicated enough from the beginning. It is full of clues that should be remembered, and many suggestions of possible significance.

The trial scene itself has an air of madness, of nonrationality, of condemnation not only of deeds but also of conventional values. In this respect, *Cambio de piel* is clearly a novel of the value revolution. However, it does not make a cut-and-dried proposition. The nonrationality of the last part seems personified in youth that judges, condemns, and at the same time continues its antecedents. Many readers would prefer a clearer, specific resolution. There is a catastrophe at the end of the novel, and the truth about who survives depends on the way the book is read. The difference may also change the general experience of the novel to some extent; but it would be difficult, whatever the experience, to make a case defending man's respect for man. On the contrary, hate and evil seem destined to live on. Nevertheless, Fuentes adds one last flourish. His narrator reveals his identity at the end; and we are faced with two levels of invention at that point—in case we did not catch on while reading the first page. The problem is whether or not all this is invented by the narrator, who is invented by Fuentes. Like so many of his contemporaries, Fuentes is fascinated by the awareness of the narrator in the act of creating.

All three novels, *Cien años de soledad, Tres tristes tigres,* and *Cambio de piel*—almost certainly the best known of the many fine works published in 1967—are good examples of the transformation of regionalism. *Cien años de soledad* may be appreciated as Colombian, as Spanish American, or as completely universal. *Tres tristes tigres* has its roots in a very specific period of Cuban history, and one of its characteristics is a persistent nostalgia with respect to that time. However, the total experience of the novel transforms that immediate concern into a sense of crisis and possible disaster—and maybe even redemption. *Cambio de piel* makes use of Mexico's pre-Hispanic mythology, as well as contemporary cultural particularities, in developing a complicated notion of evil-sacrifice-justice.

In addition to this transformation of regionalism—one of the several characteristics of current Spanish American fiction—all three novels reveal in other ways that they are typical of a new epoch. The three authors obviously insist on the novelist's right to invent reality, and all three books are in some way creation within creation. To put it another way, all the authors seem to enjoy observing the act of making fiction. They are all adventurous in technique and tend toward the communication of concepts rather than the lives of characters. In one way or another, language takes on special values in all these novels, even though *Tres tristes tigres* plays the most intricate game in this respect. Given their general cosmopolitan nature, it is important that the regional base is vital to all three novels. This combination of cosmopolitanism and regionalism is also present in *De donde son los cantantes,* by Severo Sarduy, and *Los hombres de a caballo,* by David Viñas.

Sarduy's book consists of three parts ("fables," according to the author) that deal with three aspects of Cuban culture: Chinese, African, and Spanish. Three characters take part in all three fables. The principal character changes identity from fable to fable, ultimately taking on a redemptive connotation. The two girls who appear in all three stories change identity frequently, even within a single fable.

Describing the narrative technique used in *De donde son los cantantes,* Sarduy calls it "un *collage* hacia adentro" (a collage that moves inward).[5] The collage is made up of different narrative manners and the changing identities of the protagonists. One part of the book, for example, is based on a poem written as an epitaph. Following the poem are ten scenes (one for each line of the poem) written in dramatic form. As for the changing identities, they relate to the three aspects of Cuban culture. As the novel develops, the three aspects become interrelated. The collage, in effect, moves inward, and the activation of the reader by the variation in narrative manner also deepens the significance of the work.

One of the more interesting—and puzzling—features of the novel is the author's explanatory note at the end. He analyzes the novel almost as if someone else had written it. True enough, the reader can use a little help, and it could be argued that Sarduy might put his note at the beginning. However, in that position it could make some readers think they need not experience the novel itself. As it stands, it clarifies the experience of the work, but takes away some of the magic. The novel does, in fact, move inward—to a Havana completely alienated from itself, and then the author pulls us away so we can admire his tour de force.

Viñas's *Los hombres de a caballo* is similar, in many ways, to his first novel, *Cayó sobre su rostro*, and also the better known *Los dueños de la tierra*. The author adopts a skeptical attitude toward Argentine history, and the novelization of the material produces a revisionist effect. The relevance of past to present becomes apparent through alternating narrative lines in the novel's structure. *Los hombres de a caballo* is based on the Argentine military tradition. One critic says it is a novel of the decadence of the South American military.[6] It is significant, with respect to the transformation of regionalism, that he sees the phenomenon as South American rather than as Argentine. The facts of history actually do induce this effect, as novelized by Viñas. However, the most important aspect of the transformation is the development of the concept of decadence.

El espejo y la ventana, by Adalberto Ortiz, transforms regionalism in a different way—it makes an intimate experience of history. The novel, taken in its broadest sense, deals with the history of Ecuador during approximately a quarter of a century before the Second World War. However, it is not a mosaic of the nation. The experience of the novel tends to concentrate on the story of a family and even on one member of the family. The title means "the mirror and the window," and it suggests the combination of inward searching and outward concern that forms the base of the novel. In fact, the diminishing focus creates, in *El espejo y la ventana*, a strong similarity to the small-screen novels of human relationships.

Concern for the quality of human relationship seems to lessen in many novels that activate the reader to participate in the composition of the work. They are deeply concerned about humaneness, but the people who live in the novels tend to lose their individual wholeness and become symbols or myths or absurdities or fragments of personalities. We often identify with a circumstance rather than with a person. To a considerable extent this effect is produced by a

301

sense of fragmented reality—a condition that may well be related to recent cultural phenomena that evoke expressions like "getting it all together." However, there is a complementary trend that achieves unity in the midst of fragmentation. A kind of intuited unity develops from the association of seemingly disparate pieces— a program develops. The process is amply apparent in José Agustín's *Inventando que sueño* (1968) and Humberto Costantini's *Háblen- me de Funes* (1970). The reason for anticipating these two books at this point is the nature of a novel published in 1967 by Eduardo Mallea, *La barca de hielo*. It is a series of nine pieces which are both independent and related.

A narrative structure of related stories is not an innovation by any means. Thematic or character relationships among stories are numerous. Mallea himself published a more innovative book during the vanguardist years of the 1920s, *Cuentos para una inglesa deses- perada*, composed of different pieces that are united by stylistic de- vices and by a gradually emerging sense of overall development. This book is very different from a collection of related stories or an episodic novel. It is much closer to *La barca de hielo*, and the latter bears a clear similarity to the works of some youthful writers. Ma- llea's nine pieces in *La barca de hielo* are related to each other by their characters. However, a more important unifying factor is the growing loneliness of the narrator's father. We also appreciate this condition in a larger sense, which may be described as a deepening human concern that enlarges as the book develops.

The basic narrator is first person, though he shifts to third person when relating events in which he has not participated. This proce- dure tends to produce a warm relationship between narrator and reader, especially since the first-person chapters are primarily re- sponsible for the intensification of the father's loneliness. What hap- pens in the experience of the novel is that the collage of nine chap- ters moves inward, making the experience deeper and more intimate as the novel develops. In spite of the great difference in subject matter, the narrative technique makes the experience similar to what happens in *De donde son los cantantes*. (It should be clearly stated, in this connection, that readers who look only for theme and plot—for what the story is—will find absolutely no similarity between *La barca de hielo* and Sarduy's novel.)

It is apparent that both *El espejo y la ventana* and *La barca de hielo* have some of the characteristics of small-screen novels; however, there are other books of 1967 that belong more clearly to the tradition of limiting the scope of the story so that human relationships may be developed in an intricate pattern. Among them is Carlos Martínez Moreno's *Con las primeras luces.* It is a story of growing up that uses scenes from both childhood and adulthood. Much of what is said in the childhood scenes is communicated in terms of the theater—the acting—performed by two boys and a girl. This narrative procedure, of course, brings up the question of the nature of reality, and the role of the mask.

Haroldo Conti's *Alrededor de la jaula* is also a story of self-identification with emphasis on a childhood experience. Its protagonist, Milo, is a waif who is deeply attached to his adopted "Pa." When the latter's illness deprives the boy of the affection he needs, the characterization of Milo develops a transfer of relationship from Silvestre, the foster father, to an animal in the zoo—specifically a mongoose. The change is seen mainly through a single characterization, that of Milo. A third-person narrator describes what the boy feels and also indicates his feelings by means of his actions. Conti uses some interior monologue, but the use is limited, and not very apparent since it reinforces the third-person narration instead of contrasting with it. The narrative follows a straight, chronological line except for some brief retrospective passages. Movement in time is indicated by reference to the seasons and to the weather. When there is a lapse in the course of events reported, the narrator states briefly all that is needed to keep the story and the characterization moving. There are no chapters, only scene changes. The experience of *Alrededor de la jaula* takes on a particular subtlety as the novel develops: as Milo transfers his relationship from his protector to the animal, he also changes his position by assuming responsibility for the animal rather than receiving protection from Silvestre. We feel the persistent need for a relationship, in spite of the changed position.

Several novels of 1967 invite attention because of their particular uses of the narrative voice, even though certain idiosyncrasies in each case discourage general association of the work with other novels of the same year.

Filisberto Hernández's *Tierras de la memoria* is a humorous memoir that is reminiscent of some of Juan José Arreola's sketches. The book uses dialogue at the beginning, but turns into simple first-person narration. This narrative point of view is very appropriate because Hernández is more *raconteur* than novelist. His tone may be described as fond exaggeration. The narrator, at twenty-three, recalls episodes from his childhood and youth. The predominant first-person voice sometimes speaks of his own body in third person. This separation reaches its most interesting stage when the narrator's fingers refuse to obey as he plays the piano.

El testimonio, by Alsino Ramírez Estrada, deals with the transition of the protagonist, Anselmo, from the restricted circle of family experience into the larger world of social responsibility. Anselmo's experiences as a young man are counterpointed by letters from his mother, whose experience remains within the confines of family life. The story develops a sense of New Testament redemption. Then in the final chapter, the narrator destroys his allegorical pattern and confesses that the neat outcome of his novel represents what he would like, rather than what reality is. This revelation places the act of making fiction in an entirely different perspective and, therefore, alters the reader's experience.

Siberia Blues, by Néstor Sánchez, is a novel that comes close to denying the possibility of understandable critical comment.[7] The narrator-protagonist uses interior monologue as an essential part of the creative process. However, the relationship of one sentence to another is more like variations on a theme than a sequential development of ideas. The experience of the novel, therefore, resembles making a design more than organizing a series of events. The event, in *Siberia Blues,* is the making of the sentence. This process creates a feeling of groping, of yearning. It is likely that Sánchez's novel will interest only a small group of readers attuned to radical innovation, unless it is a forerunner of a great change in literary taste.[8] It is clearly the most radical novel, with respect to technique, published in 1967.

CHAPTER 19

After *Cien años de soledad* (1968–1970)

Following the year of *Cien años de soledad*, the novel in Spanish America appears increasingly self-assured. It creates an impression of professional and artistic adequacy. Narrative techniques that activate the reader have become more frequent and more daring. Equally important is the frequency of humor—not simply because it provides a brief period of pleasure, but rather because it reflects a new attitude toward literary creativity. Carried a step farther, of course, it suggests a new attitude toward the reality in which we live.

One of the most discussed novels of recent years is *La traición de Rita Hayworth* (1968), by Manuel Puig, and it is interesting both as an example of the activated reader and as a showcase of rollicking humor. It also has several of the other characteristics of recent fiction, described in the chapter on novels between *Rayuela* and *Cien años de soledad*. The anecdotal base of the novel is the growth of Toto (closely related to the novelist's autobiography) from infancy in 1933 to adolescence in 1948. Some might even think of it as the miseducation of Toto, since many of the influential factors around him appear to limit his potential as a human being. The scene is a provincial Argentine town and the principal cultural activity is the movies. In the case of Toto, the cinema becomes a way of life, the idiom through which he expresses himself, interiorly as well as overtly. To some extent, this cinema metaphor functions with respect to the total experience of the novel, but Toto is always its focus.

The most interesting characteristic of *La traición de Rita Hayworth* is how the cinema metaphor functions within the narrative structure of the novel.[1] The chapters are varying situations with different narrators, and even written documents, that provide insight into the character of Toto and his friends and family. There is a minimal amount of direction by the author. The first chapter is called "Mita's Parents' House, 1933." With no further introduction we find ourselves in the middle of a conversation. Not only are we not told who Mita is, we don't even know who is speaking, because Puig's novel uses no stage directions to indicate who says what. Nevertheless, we know immediately, by what is said, that the conversation is among women, that one of them is making a crib coverlet for Mita's new baby, and gradually we gather most of the information needed as a basis for the story. The second chapter is identified as "Berto's House, Vallejos, 1933," and completes the basic information. Berto is the father of Toto, and the conversation of two maids in this second chapter communicates a feeling of the life and problems of this young family, and emphasizes the provincial nature of Vallejos.

The third chapter moves forward six years in time and is entitled "Toto, 1939." In this and the next eight chapters, titles refer to the narrative voice rather than to the place. This change has the effect of focusing attention on individual characterization, once the basic situation has been established. The year is stated in each case. Toto is six years old in chapter three, and time moves forward in orderly fashion throughout the succeeding chapters. It is important to note that Puig does not direct his reader beyond what the chapter title says. Looking back on the experience of reading *La traición de Rita Hayworth*, it appears that the novel sets the scene and then introduces the characters, including a protagonist. The procedure seems close to the realist tradition. The big difference is that the author-narrator is almost entirely absent from the work, and the reader puts the pieces of the novel together. Therefore, the reader is more active in the actual experience of the book than he is in his memory of the

306

experience. It is equally important to note, however, that Puig does not abdicate completely the role of guiding narrator. His chapter titles identify what is going on and, therefore, the novel is much more satisfying than many contemporary works that leave readers groping for clues.

Following the series of chapters that are essentially monologues, the oral voices disappear and the novel is completed in five written forms: two diaries; an essay, "My Favorite Movie"; an anonymous note; and a letter from Berto to his brother, dated 1933. This last chapter reveals some information withheld in the first two and tends to transport us back to the beginning of the novel to reconsider and, to some extent, relive the experience. The written items emphasize the absence of communication in the novel, which consists mainly of monologue even before the "written" chapters. It is this lack of communication that emphasizes the importance of the cinema metaphor, since references to the movies are the most convenient framework the characters find for expressing their own feelings. The fact constitutes a kind of paradox because extremely clever use of language is the book's best quality. People speak the way they should—with a rightness that is actually amusing because it is so appropriate.

The nature of language, in *La traición de Rita Hayworth*, is a product of the cinema metaphor, and it is a key to understanding how the novel creates its unique atmosphere. The rightness of what the characters say (and write) depends on Puig's sensitivity to the effect of movies in their lives. That is, their speech is different from what it would be if they were not dependent on films as a means of expression. Our awareness of this condition suggests that the inhabitants of Toto's world are in some way separated from their authentic selves. The movies they see are a make-believe world, and they betray their genuine selves when they accept films as a frame of reference. Therefore, our reaction to them may shift to an awareness of meager life, or, as Emir Rodríguez Monegal puts it, a life of mediocrity.[2]

With keen perception, Rodríguez Monegal also points out that the characters in Puig's novel, although they are funny, are not caricatures. Other Argentine writers, dealing with the same kind of people, set them apart from an acceptable standard associated with the author. Puig, like Cabrera Infante, avoids looking down on his

307

characters. This effect is enhanced, of course, by the near absence of a narrator. The activated reader is in direct communication with the characters, and there is no need for the author to interpret them.

There are several interesting points of contact between *La traición de Rita Hayworth* and Alfonso Calderón's *Toca esa rumba, Don Azpiazu* (1970). Calderón's book is a series of sketches, technically speaking, that are related to each other mainly by reference to a particular period and by the hypnotic effect of alterations in the narrative point of view. Thematically, the sketches deal with aspects of reality in a provincial Chilean city during the years when the author was growing up, in that epoch dominated by the Second World War. In *Toca esa rumba, Don Azpiazu,* the screen goddess is Ann Sheridan. Along with many other celebrities of the time, she enters the life of the community via movies and radio.

The narrative voice occasionally sacrifices its personality to the flood of associations. It continues to be heard, however, in various guises, and adjusts itself to the kinds of experience that form the basis of the sketches. Some of the references are local, others are international, but they are equally significant. The material may vary from a description of the attitudes of students to a newspaper human-interest story or to an anxious father addressing his son. The narrative may be third person, or it may be in the form of second-person address. The latter style communicates a sense of the author speaking to himself (the narrator partially immersed in the multiple associations of the narrative), but at the same time invites the reader to assume the narrative position.

The joining of narrator and reader becomes a strong unifying factor in the experience of the book. Since most of the sketches are thematic collages, the invited reader easily becomes enmeshed in the story. This phenomenon avoids caricature or satire, and produces a seriocomic effect. The preoccupation with a certain period of time, in this book and in Puig's and Cabrera Infante's novels, suggests that there is more to the message than the portrayal of mediocrity. The nostalgia present in all three works suggests the possibility that the reality they create is a highly desirable condition.

Activation of the reader takes place in many different ways, and with varying success. In *La traición de Rita Hayworth* and *Toca*

esa rumba, Don Azpiazu, the self-willed (or self-conceded) dis-
placement of the narrator allows the reader to step in. On the other
hand, in Cortázar's *62. Modelo para armar* (1968), the reader's participation is required by the novel's structure, which, in turn, is
produced by the concept underlying the work. The number in the
title refers to chapter 62 of *Rayuela,* in which the invented author,
Morelli, speaks of the possibility of a novel based on random notes
and observations. People would act and things would happen, but
these phenomena could not possibly be evaluated by psychological
means. Psychological validity is not a possible criterion for judging
62. Modelo para armar, or for reacting to it. Logical sequence is
equally irrelevant.

The action takes place in London, Paris, Vienna, and the City.
Space amounts to several specifics that are absorbed into a generality. It might even be reasonable (if reason mattered) to say that the
specific places are real, and the City is invented. There is a similar
treatment of characters in which real people are counterpointed by
abstractions. The story contains enough associations to create tantalizing possibilities of logical order. However, any attempt to make a
plot novel must end in frustration.[3]

A reader, in making something of this Cortázar novel, may experience the fragmented quality of contemporary society. Whether
or not he needs this experience is another matter. At least this kind
of communication may justify the factors that make the novel seem
difficult and obscure. It is often hard to say whether a recent novelist
requires participation by the reader as part of the book's message, or
is simply careless. One example among many that provoke this question is *En caso de duda* (1968), by Orlando Ortiz. The novel can
withstand criticism on this point, because it is basically a sound
work—one that produces an excellent appreciation of youthful dropouts from Mexican society. A reasonable objection to the novel is
that it changes scenes, characters, and narrative points of view so
frequently it cannot be comprehended in a single reading. Unlike
62. Modelo para armar, En caso de duda deals with a sequence of
events that can be placed in a logical pattern, though the author
does not do so. Whether Ortiz's reader resigns himself to the technique of withholding details that would be enlightening, or struggles
to reorder what Ortiz has written, the result is likely to be a sense

of fragmentation. This sense, however, is quite different from that of *62. Modelo para armar*, since logical sequence is a possibility in Ortiz's novel and is not a possibility in Cortázar's.

José Balza's *Largo* (1968) involves the reader not in making the structure of the novel, but by creating an unusually intimate identification of reader with narrator. The human relationships in *Largo* are extremely complicated, but there are no problems of logical sequence, and we always know what is happening. The narrator-protagonist anticipates suicide. His name never appears in the novel, so specific identity does not discourage the reader from sharing his role. The narrative is in first person and in actual time. That is, the account corresponds exactly to the moment of action. Therefore, the reader may become the narrator and tell the story. This procedure is much gentler than the techniques that force readers to create the structure or in some other way act in place of the narrator. In *Largo*, he is simply assimilated into the narrative position.

Jorge Guzmán requires his reader's participation by forcing a choice upon him in *Job-Boj* (1968). The novel is based on two contrasting characterizations. One is anxiety-ridden, hounded by misfortune, and miserable; the other extroverted, happy, and sure that time and luck are on his side. Both are entirely credible characterizations. They are involved in two story lines, which are developed in two sets of alternating chapters. One set is identified by arabic numerals, the other by roman numerals. The major difference in the two lines is greater use of interior monologue in the introspective characterization. Within these passages, Guzmán's language indicates clearly the confused and deteriorating psychic state of the protagonist. Language is equally effective in the counterpointing story line, where its lighthearted quality coincides with the personality of the main character and creates humor mainly through exaggerated frankness.

There are points in the process of counterpointing when the *joie de vivre* of one characterization makes the other's anguish seem absurd—and humorous, in a bitter way. It is probably at these points that we are most intensely bedeviled by the relationship of the two. The question is whether they are two different men, two facets of a single personality, or two periods in the life of one man. Each story line ends at a point where the other might begin, and there are associations between them that suggest either sequence

310

or simultaneity, depending on the reader's participation in the novel.[4] The experience of the novel is likely to have several facets or levels. The characterizations are individualized enough so we may comprehend them as individuals and react accordingly. However, there are obvious implications beyond that point which deal with the cultural process of western man. The free spirit of Boj may be an earlier state which we have left in order to take part in a kind of progress that produces Job's anxiety. On the other hand, if the two conditions of man are reversed, *Job-Boj* becomes a prophetic novel. This understanding is very attractive to someone reading contemporary Spanish American fiction, because it coincides with the humor and anticonventionality (sometimes, but not always, a factor in the humor) that seem to propose a new attitude toward fiction and toward life.

Obviously, the alternation of chapters in *Job-Boj* is the technique that activates the reader. If one story followed the other, our response would be much more passive. The narrative structure (the sequence of narrative material, that is) in recent fiction is a primary factor in the experience of a book, and, in the end, it exercises major control over what a book says. The range of this effect extends from segmentation that accomplishes simultaneity to involvement of the reader in the composition of the novel, as in works that are called "open." The influence of Julio Cortázar in this respect has been tremendous—not only as an innovator in the open novel, but also, in a larger sense, as a challenge to conventionality. Many younger writers find the attitude as important as the techniques, because it provides an atmosphere of freedom for creation. *Mateo el flautista* (1968) by Alberto Duque López, declares itself the offspring of *Rayuela* and extolls its own freedom.[5] The overt structure of the novel is in two parts—two versions of Mateo. Two people remember him. However, in each part, the person remembering is less a narrative voice than an organizer of the narration. The source of the narration changes according to the requirements of memory. The two accounts complement each other, the second illuminating the first. Illuminating, that is, insofar as illumination is possible in a novel of this kind. It is a matter not of ultimate revelation, but of further suggestion. No logical order appears. In fact, it is entirely possible that Mateo is an illusion.

In novels like this, much of the communication depends on how

311

narrative point of view is used. Indeed, the term "point of view" may not be sufficiently inclusive to describe all the possibilities. Something like "source of narrative information" may be more useful. In *La traición de Rita Hayworth*, the narrative is delivered by several different characters, by documents, and by dialogue in which no single character occupies the position of narrator and in which there is no indication of an objective narrator. In novels where the authors view the creation of fiction while it is in progress, the narrative source becomes the most important technique.

Although there is no way to prove such a hypothesis, it seems likely that the novelist's interest in seeing himself writing bears some relationship to the attack on conventionality and to the importance of humor. This apparently self-centered interest is, at its best, an acute awareness of the creative process, in a world where creativity is repressed rather than encouraged. The techniques employed in the novelization of this awareness vary somewhat among the many novels in which it appears; however, the general principle may be described by reference to Pirandello or Unamuno, whose creations bring the author into contact with the characters born of his creative effort. It is also helpful to recall the moment of truth in Jorge Luis Borges's story, *Las ruinas circulares*, where the protagonist ideates a man, creating him by thinking him into being, only to realize that the protagonist himself has been created by the same process. To put it another way, there are many novels that raise the question of who creates whom, or of who creates what. If we include the sense of fiction making that characterizes novels in which the reader is forced into active participation in the composition, the interrelationship of *being* with *creating* involves novelist, character, and reader. The result is always surprising and often amusing. The extent to which the effect may be enlightening depends on how many novels of this type one happens to read. The fact is that recent fascination with the phenomenon has produced a very large number of examples, and it is not certain that the cases are sufficiently different from each other to maintain interest in more than one or two.

There are some books in which the identity of the true narrator is a vital part of the experience even though it is not apparent throughout the novel—*Cambio de piel* and *Cien años de soledad*, for example. In *Los contados días* (1968), Fernando Alegría gives the novel a documentary slant by identifying the narrator at the end of the story. The book deals with unpretentious people in a way somewhat reminiscent of William Saroyan's stories. Ordinary people, pictured in the frame of their commonplace activities, turn into memorable characters because of the narrator's ability to view, with equal compassion, both the humorous and the sad aspects of their lives. The tone of the novel suggests that it is dealing with these people as they really are. Alegría uses interior monologue very successfully; however, the basic narrative voice is third person. Then at the end of the novel, one of the characters, Anita, assumes the narrative role and addresses the basic narrator as "Alegría." In response, Alegría speaks directly to Anita. This exchange—a revelation of narrator identity right at the end—greatly increases the credibility of the fiction.

The role of the narrator is considerably more complicated in novels where the act of invention is the fundamental experience of the fiction. A novel by Vicente Leñero, *El garabato*—one of the good novels half-submerged in the riches of that formidable year, 1967—is built on a series of writers of novels, one leading to another. Leñero invents a friend who sends him the manuscript of a novel by a man named Moreno. Within Moreno's novel, Moreno himself reads the manuscript of a novel by still another writer. This last novel never ends, unless we choose to make the end.

This kind of telescoping creativity is even more tantalizing in the third part of Humberto Costantini's *Háblenme de Funes* (1970)—the part entitled "Fichas." Costantini invents a novelist, and the first frame of narration is the story of this nameless writer's construction of a novel. Novelist Costantini comments on the process from the standpoint of a critical observer. The nameless, invented novelist invents a protagonist named Corti—a druggist who inherits a card file of case histories from a friend. These histories contain information about a strange illness. Corti is supposed to continue the study. With the information on the cards, Corti also invents characters. The development is far too intricate for brief exposition. However, it is fair to say that the experience of the story is an infinite series of authors creating characters.

In a clearly Pirandellian fashion, Corti deals with and even comes into conflict with the characters he creates. In *Piedra de mar* (1968),

313

by Francisco Massiani, the narrator writes the novel within the novel itself. He addresses his friends in the process of creating them as characters and even telephones them to ask what they are doing. They are never doing anything, and Corcho, the narrator-protagonist, has to invent something. Implicit in this situation is a sense of boredom with the world of objective reality. The novel is about teen-agers, and it seems they have nothing to do; or it may be more accurate to say they think that what they have to do is nothing. Theirs is the bleak side of human potential and it corresponds to the Job side of *Job-Boj*. Its counterpoint, in Massiani's novel, is creative imagination.[6]

Jorge Onetti, in *Contramutis* (1969), develops the notion of who invents whom; however, the proposition is enclosed in a paradox rather than open ended. There are two possibilities that face and reflect each other like two mirrors. Onetti invents two young people, Hilda and Pelo, who observe a suicide. They decide to invent the life of the dead man, Roberto Lupo. An important part of their game is their right to absolute freedom of imagination. The major part of the novel consists of alternating inventions by Hilda and Pelo. However, we then find ourselves within the flow of awareness of Lupo and discover that he is not dead, but is, in fact, the creator of Hilda and Pelo. It is at this point that the absolute freedom of invention, practiced by the two young people, takes on special significance. Throughout the chapters in which they are inventing the life of Roberto Lupo, the fictional reality is full of extraordinary events that are obviously unreal in terms of ordinary experience. Since we know that Hilda and Pelo are inventing these things, we assume Hilda and Pelo are real. Therefore, when we discover that they are themselves invented, our certainty about the nature of reality is knocked awry. Having been lulled into peaceful acceptance of the combination of extraordinary circumstances with invention, we are hard hit by the revelation that commonplace circumstances are also invented.

There are some novels in which these experiences regarding the nature of reality resemble the novelization of a concept, as we find it in Salvador Elizondo's *Farabeuf*. Indeed, Elizondo uses the author-meets-the-character principle in *El hipogeo secreto* (1968). In novels of this kind, the quality of the reader's experience frequently depends on the extent to which individual characterization is sacrificed in order to use devices that novelize the concept or leave a general mood, a vague notion. The most accessible meaning of Rodolfo Izaguirre's *Alacranes* (1968), for example, is a sense of disintegration. Or as another example, Luis Britto García's *Rajatabla* (1970) communicates an impulse to destruction. There is enough appreciable characterization in *Alacranes* to suggest a contrast between decay and a resolution to survive; however, the contrast is more prominent than the people themselves.[7] *Rajatabla* is more like a series of sketches than a novel, except that an element of unity operates via a growing sense of undermining the foundations of society. Even this unifying factor is modified by narrative fragmentation that is in accord with social disruption. As for characterization, the book contains no memorable achievements. It is the mood that lingers in memory, just as it functions in the experience of reading the book.

Even in a much more complicated work like Gustavo Sainz's *Obsesivos días circulares* (1969), the final impression (and the most lasting aspect of the reader's experience) is a feeling of self-defense in the face of imminent disaster. The novel's structure is extremely complicated; one reference device is the narrator's reading of Joyce's *Ulysses*, and another is a trip on a commercial airline. The notion of the narrator as an island develops throughout the novel, sharpening the book's satire on what we may refer to, oversimplifying, as the consumer society. At the end of the novel, language disintegrates. The final phrase appears typographically larger and larger. It is a kind of refuge for the narrator, used by him to counteract his uncertainty while the plane is landing. The letters of the phrase become abnormally large, only partial words are visible, and finally a single letter appears on the last page, and even that letter is disintegrating.

At times, readers may wonder if novels like *Obsesivos días circulares* are replacing small-screen novels that illuminate problems of human relationships. The concepts that become the principal communication of some novels may be a substitute for the anguished protagonist of the existentialist tradition. There are many novels in which problems of human relationships are fundamental to the story and more apparent than in Sainz's novel, for example. However, there is often some other aspect of the book that is more spectacular and more likely to invite comment. The narrative source of *La trai-ción de Rita Hayworth* is much discussed; little is said about the penetrating view of Toto's family which the author presents in a very restricted frame to emphasize the protagonist's special person-ality and the way it is produced by his parents. The narrative tech-niques used are likely to invite attention to themselves or to the general sense of cultural mediocrity rather than to Toto as an individual.

Sergio Galindo, in *Nudo* (1970), maintains the focus on the prob-lems of individual humans as steadily as any novelist in several years. Nevertheless, his readers seem to agree that *Nudo* is the most complicated, technically, of his works. The cause of this observation is the narrative structure, which depends on some fairly complicated time sequences to present the information needed for support of the central problem. The anecdotal base of the story is the relationship between a middle-aged couple and a younger man about a half-generation removed from them. As always, Galindo chooses details and creates perspectives that question commonplace responses, and *Nudo* is his most radical book in this respect. For the sake of credi-bility, he has had to weave supporting circumstances very care-fully. The scope of the novel is limited by careful and explicit ref-erence to the basic relationship novelized.

Human relationships constitute the theme of the second section of *Háblenme de Funes*. In this case, the scope of the observation is controlled by a single incident which transforms—perhaps only for a moment—the life of a neighborhood. However, the compelling and extraordinary unity achieved in the experience of this book is more remarkable even than what happens to the neighborhood. *Las suicidas* (1969), by Antonio Di Benedetto, is an extremely intimate study of emotional growth; nevertheless, the stark sim-plicity of its prose style is likely to evoke the first comments.

Salvador Garmendia's *La mala vida* (1968) is more similar to the fiction of existentialist anguish. As is often the case in Garmendia's novels, his protagonists are trapped. They are losers, and it is only through memory that the central character of *La mala vida* escapes the limitations set by his office and his club. The narrative voice is the protagonist, who speaks from a present position, recalling the past. The sequence of the incidents recalled appears chaotic; how-ever, this apparent chaos turns out to be the best characterization of the protagonist. That is, the way he remembers things is important to the characterization. A sarcastic, disillusioned ending reveals the narrator's utter disrespect for life, and this extreme reaction tends to overshadow the rest of the novel.

It is entirely possible that some of the best comment on the behavior of human beings with respect to each other may be found in the novels of youthful writers who deal with youth. These novels are also among the funniest. However, it is important to note that, while the new emphasis on humor may well have had its first great promotion in what may be called "youthful fiction," laughter has long since passed beyond those boundaries. Very often, but not always, the source of the humor is a skeptical view of human behavior.

The dropouts in *En caso de duda,* although they face problems and even tragedy, are humorous in two ways: the perspective in which the author sometimes places them, and the humor they create as one of the characteristics of their culture. Their language is colorful and amusing. The tell-it-like-it-is tone of the novel is a companion of laughter. The rightness of language is often a major factor in humor—*La traición de Rita Hayworth* is a good example, as is *De perfil.* Names are funny. Pelo in *Contramutis* is Peloquieto (Calmhair), because he applies a substance to hold it in place. In José Agustín's *Inventando que sueño* (1968), a boy and girl seeking a secluded rendezvous go to the Hotel Joutel (a phonetic version in Spanish of the way "hotel" is pronounced in English). Word play of this kind is frequent and often intricate. The important consideration is that it is not simply funny. It also communicates a flagrant lack of respect for conventionality.

In Héctor Libertella's *El camino de los hiperbóreos* (1968) is a page, in the form of a single-sheet advertising handout, that announces the burning of the book. The attitude suggested by this episode is reinforced by an interview with the author—after he has won a literary prize—in which he answers questions with belches. It is hilarious, within a limited frame of acceptance—just what the trite questions deserve. This reaction, however, is modified, in the total experience of the novel, by the desperation that becomes apparent in this rejection of predictable behavior. *El camino de los hiperbóreos* is a search for some kind of ideal, centered around a protagonist named Héctor Cudema. It is difficult to say more about

317

him, because he appears to be more than one person. This is no traditional novel, and description comes hard.

Like Néstor Sánchez, Libertella depends on language and the actual moment of using it to establish the sense of seeking that is the vital part of the book. Cudema seems to live somewhere between a dream of man fulfilling the best of his human potential, and a discouragingly dull reality from which the only escape is exaggeration of animal instinct. All this comes to the reader in a very chaotic form that uses many different sources of narration, including all three voices and a variety of documents. The negative world of Cudema is similar to the mediocrity of life in *La traición de Rita Hayworth,* only worse. In fact, it is so intense it casts doubt on the proposition of mediocrity and raises questions concerning the creative initiative of people who see the world this way. Therefore, the reader's experience may have one, two, or three stages—from hilarity to sympathy with the desperate search, and then to disgust with the paucity of inner resources.

It is worth while, in connection with this kind of fiction, to point out that these complex attitudes are not the exclusive property of young authors. In 1969, Héctor A. Murena, known for his rather heavy novels of ideas, published the first volume of a new trilogy, *Epitalámica.* It marks a radical change from his earlier novels. *Epitalámica* is first of all a caricature of courtship and marriage; however, it is by implication a caricature of social conventions in general. Taking one more step (and it is a dangerous step because there is no way of knowing how many readers will take it), the novel may be read as a satire on novels that make caricatures of conventionality. It is funny—unreasonably so—exaggerated in its treatment of subjects that were once taboo, to the point of causing some readers to react against the humor.

Murena's novel offers no problems concerning structure. The narrator's presence is apparent from the beginning and the organization is a straight chronological line. The bases of humor are contrast and exaggeration. Spanish of the Golden Age appears alongside *porteño* slang and constitutes one example of joining the sublime with the commonplace.[8] The language play in the novel uses neologisms, agglutination, phonetic equivalents, and double meanings. In addition to language play, Murena uses frequent wisecracks with satirical intent. Many of these features resemble the novels of

318

much younger writers. What is missing is the combination of creation-in-progress with the sardonic world view. The anguish is there, but it is static.

It is also important to see that youthful disaffection continues to acquire more specific political overtones in some novels. Once more a Peruvian is the convenient example. Edmundo de los Ríos, in *Los juegos verdaderos* (1968), writes the novel of a captured guerrilla fighter. The frustration of youth changes its mode of expression from scorn of conventionality to protest against oppression. The narrator illuminates three stages in the life of a man we may presume to be the same person in all three stages. However, the novel's structure allows us to experience these stages in a disjointed fashion and put them together. They refer to imprisonment, to separation from family, and to childhood. By presenting the story in this way, De los Ríos develops a protagonist who is more specific than the mass protagonist of an old-fashioned novel of social protest, but still more general than a protagonist developed in the manner of the realist novel. Humor disappears, of course; there is no laughter here. The bitterness is, in a sense, a practical application of the discontent communicated by novels like *El camino de los hiperbóreos*.

Reference to a feeling of bitterness may be too strong a way to describe the youth novel in general. In many books that look very skeptically at the habits and customs of an older generation, there is a good deal of tenderness. Massiani's *Piedra de mar*, Sainz's *Gazapo*, and Agustín's *De perfil* are all examples of this combination. In 1968, José Agustín published *Inventando que sueño*, a book that is best described as a "program novel." It is characterized by the same combination of satire and tenderness and, in this respect, resembles *La traición de Rita Hayworth* and *Tres tristes tigres*, because the narrator does not place himself in a position superior to the subjects of his satire. It is a program novel because it consists of several parts that differ greatly from each other, but still combine to make a literary experience that is different from the experience of any one of the parts. In this respect, *Inventando que sueño* is similar to some recordings of rock music, in which the pieces are not related in any formal way, but still make a program whose effect is much more satisfying than any one of the pieces heard separately.

José Agustín shows clearly, in *Inventando que sueño*, that his writing need not be restricted to a particular kind of character, or to

319

a single theme. The themes—at least the most apparent themes—vary widely; however, the unifying factor that exists throughout the book is the feeling that the world is very silly, but nonetheless very dear. This feeling is not really a theme. It amounts to an intensification that takes place because of the persistence of the tone in a variety of fictional situations developed by many different narrative techniques.

Some unity of a kind as unusual as this is a source of satisfaction in a number of works that appear to be collections of stories or short novels. The phenomenon works contrary to an apparent fragmentation; however, there are no particular techniques that are always used, and the nature of the unifier is not always the same. Miguel Briante's *Hombre en la orilla* (1968) consists of four stories that are related to each other by setting and by some characters. Each story can be read independently, but one of them may increase the reader's understanding of another. It is particularly apparent in the function of the fourth story as the background of the first three. As the reader becomes aware of this function, he reconstructs the experience of reading the preceding stories—now in the light of the new information. The effect is not exactly like finding withheld information, because we accept the information we have in any one of the stories—we accept the fact without knowing the cause. Therefore, when the explanation comes, it enriches, but is not essential.

The tone is important in *Hombre en la orilla* just as it is in *Inventando que sueño*. It creates a sense of change. Specifically, it comes from the fact that a place is becoming less rural as the metropolis encroaches upon the locale. This sociological reality comes to the reader in a feeling that a known situation is slipping away. The effect of evaporation is enhanced by an intricate procedure of shading and changing the narrative voice in the fourth story.

Humberto Costantini's *Háblenme de Funes* offers an especially satisfying program because the questions raised about reality and invention in the third part, "Fichas," are a climax to the frustration of joyful living in the first two parts. At the same time, the narrative techniques used by Costantini (they are different in each of the three parts) are a showcase of the art of novelizing. The title story is an account of the life and death of the musician-protagonist, Funes. Each musician who worked with him tells what he knows, characterizing himself in the process. These changes in point of view, assisted by a chorus effect, gradually fill out the story. The secret revealed in the course of the narrative is Funes's September-April love affair with a young girl. This idyll is the source of his joy in living; it is also the cause of his death when it sets off the jealous rage of the ardent fans who come to hear him play.

The second part is called "Amarillo sol, amarillo pétalo, amarillo flamante, amarillo poema." It captures a moment in the life of a neighborhood when loneliness might turn to fellowship, but the normal condition prevails. This story uses a single narrative point of view, but sees all the people in the neighborhood at the same moment. Costantini's style creates the effect of a cosmogonic myth by using periodic sentences and repeated first words. Then he modifies the portentous effect by repeatedly using the same noun-adjective combination so it becomes funny, and then makes an adverb of the adjective to describe the action of the character who is identified by the adjective. These effects are in themselves joyful, and they add to the possibility of vitality in the neighborhood. In this case, frustration comes to a group rather than to an individual, and, instead of death, it is in the form of spiritual lethargy.

"Fichas," the third part, is important as an example of the novelist viewing literary invention. The effect of this commentary on creativity is necessarily impressive in the wake of two experiences that communicate the meanness of the human spirit.

Persistent attention to spectacular innovations and intricate subtleties in recent fiction, though certainly well deserved, may create the impression that novels are less and less related to a locale. It might seem that regionalism has disappeared and that fiction no longer has anything to do with the reality of daily living. The fact is quite different. Novels often reflect the reality of both place and problem, even when their main interest has little or nothing to do with locale or with the problems of society. What happens to the phenomenon of regionalism in contemporary fiction is that the writers are less and less defensive about it. In a sense, they care less about it; they feel less compelled to define themselves in terms of place.

In practice, place and the real world are eminently functional in novels where they are not really expected. The guise in which they appear may vary from the typical language of *Piedra de mar* and dozens of other novels to the reflection of *peronista* Argentina in *La traición de Rita Hayworth* to the use of an adjective like "ofeliaguilmainesca" in *En caso de duda*. (Ofelia Guilmain is a Mexican actress.) In two recent novels, Sebastián Salazar Bondy and Reynaldo Arenas mythologize, respectively, a cultural type and a historical personage, and both novels provide keen insight into a culture.

Salazar Bondy's *Alférez Arce, Teniente Arce, Capitán Arce . . .* (1969) is an unfinished novel, published after the author's death. Its theme is the intricate maneuvering of a military coup d'etat, seen in one man as his ambition is reduced to fear. The most important narrative technique is the change of point of view from chapter to chapter. The novel's editor and prologuist, Tomás G. Escajadillo, describes the novel's structure very clearly in an introductory essay.[9] Chapter one is the interior monologue of Nicanor Arce moments before his execution. In it we first sense the replacement of ambition by fear, though some aspects remain obscure—naturally, since this chapter is reminiscence by Arce. In the second chapter, the narrative voice is third person and portrays Arce as seen by a man in the adjoining cell. By removing the reader a short distance from the protagonist, the narrator emphasizes the indignity of fear. Chapter three is a third-person-omniscient account of preparations for the coup. It detaches the reader from Arce and shows the revolutionary movement as entirely opportunistic, without ideology or patriotism. The fourth chapter is a first-person reminiscence by Arce's brother, Pedro, a Marxist. Pedro talks with a political colleague at the time of the coup. Here we appreciate two opposing facets of middle-class values: Nicanor Arce's support of law and order (so long as it suits his purposes), on the one hand, and Pedro Arce's dreamy, ineffective Marxism, on the other. Chapter five is a third-person-omniscient account of Nicanor's decision to support the coup. This episode corresponds to the third chapter in narrative point of view and describes an individual just as opportunistic as the movement revealed in chapter three. The man and the movement become one, and personality joins with social phenomenon. The result is especially effective because Nicanor Arce does not become the stereotyped strong man. Quite the contrary, he is a miserable loser. This fact also colors our appreciation of the coup. In addition to creating a specific reaction to the protagonist, it heightens the sense of futility created by the movement itself.

Reynaldo Arenas's *El mundo alucinante* (1969) deals with one of Spanish America's most interesting personalities, Fray Servando Teresa de Mier, a Mexican cleric of the late eighteenth and early nineteenth centuries.[10] He lived during the years of the fight for independence from Spain. His nonconformism is a reflection of the time. The legend of Fray Servando portrays a man likely to say what he thought, argumentative and pugnacious. He was imprisoned more than a dozen times and escaped with a frequency that must have shaken the confidence of authorities. He sometimes had an income, but sometimes eked out a living on the edge of starvation. He lived in a Jewish community for some time and is said to have converted two rabbis through his formidable powers of persuasion. All these things took place in Mexico, Cuba, Spain, France, and Portugal.

Arenas takes this legendary image and actualizes Fray Servando, making him vitally present in our own time. The man's career has many picaresque qualities, and the novelist cultivates this aspect. At the same time, he uses supernatural or magic circumstances that transport the characterization into the realm of myth, creating an effect similar to characterization in *Cien años de soledad*. Arenas's principal technique is the use of three narrative voices. The narrator addresses Fray Servando in the second person, placing himself and the protagonist on the same time plane. Fray Servando speaks in the first person, and there is also a third-person voice that completes the description of the man and his world. All three voices may deal with the same episode. The essence of the experience of *El mundo alucinante* is the sense of struggle against conventional restraint.

There is no doubt at all about the cultural identity of these novels. It is more common, however, to find an epic effect—an attempt to reach the soul of a country or region. Adriano González León, in *País portátil* (1968), situates his protagonist, Andrés Barazarte, within a specific moment in Caracas, but expands the narrative, through Andrés's inner awareness, to a larger appreciation of the city, and also to the provincial heritage of the Barazarte family. The basic time span of the novel corresponds to Andrés's running a political errand—a question of hours. His family tradition takes us into the feudal social organization of the provinces, and the life of metropolitan Caracas has its feudal aspect, too. González León interweaves the three aspects (or levels) of the novel's development, but maintains the identity of each by changing the narrative voice and the general characteristics of the prose style in each case.

Lizandro Chávez Alfaro's *Trágame tierra* (1969) also deals with more than one generation, showing a change of attitude among Nicaraguans. The older one is reconciled to the spiritual oppression created by the country's abject relationship with the United States. The younger people consider that their elders have sold out for an economic stability worth far less than they have paid. The author's ability to move inside a character right in the middle of a statement tied to external actuality produces characterizations that combine great depth with qualities typical of a region. In *En noviembre llega el arzobispo* (1968), Héctor Rojas Herazo penetrates the character of a region, coastal Colombia, by segmented narration that makes a cross section of a town's reality. He captures the essence of the town within a time span that makes reality appear to stand still— the final episode is at the same time as the opening episode.

A very different, much less Faulknerian, relationship to place becomes apparent in *Los niños se despiden* (1968), by Pablo Armando Fernández. It is an allegory of the author's concept of Cuban reality, which is different from saying that it is an allegory of Cuba. The action focuses on the founding of a Utopian community, Sabanas. This story telescopes all of Cuban history, juxtaposing people from different epochs. It involves examples of civic loyalty, those who accept the new society, and those who reject it. The allegory is not absolute—it is not possible to fit all the suggestions into a pattern. This characteristic makes the novel confusing. Fernández does not help much, because he moves around in tenses and changes narrative tone without being clear about the meaning of the change.

Among the long-established novelists, Demetrio Aguilera Malta and Miguel Otero Silva have published novels recently that are regional in the best sense of the word and that show clearly the liberating effects of narrative techniques generally used in recent fiction. Aguilera Malta's *Siete lunas y siete serpientes* (1970) creates the mythic town of Santorontón where indigenous American, African, and European Christian cultural factors join. Segmented narrative structure in antichronological sequence, miraculous happenings, and the author's sharp sensitivity to phonetic rhythm combine to create a sense of magic. Folklore of the Asturias variety mingles with everyday problems; wild fantasy frolics by the side of Aguilera Malta's persistent concern for social justice. Readers who know *Don Goyo* are likely to feel that *Siete lunas y siete serpientes* is a kind of intensification of the earlier novel—a case of the creative imagination given full rein.

Language play is a basic ingredient in the experience of the book. It is rhythmic and humorous, serves to color the narrative tone in a number of instances ranging from a feeling of primitivism to the suggestion of sexual prowess in one of the characters. Aguilera Malta, like Agustín Yáñez, is fond of the unforgettable, extraordinary character: the good priest and his talking crucifix, the indomitable hell raiser, the black witch doctor. Folklore, real people, animals, and pure invention operate on the same level. There are many contrasts between good and evil, the good being represented by those who feel good will and unselfishness toward their fellows. It is important that the novel is by no means a crusade for some social program, but is an affirmative statement of brotherhood. The central conflict between good and evil involves the redoubtable Candelario Mariscal, son of Satan and godson of Padre Cándido, the simple and good priest. Candelario is supreme in matters sexual and military. He is the incarnation of *machismo* and of *caciquismo* and is, therefore, a representation of two important characteristics of Spanish American culture. A major theme of the novel deals with the way Candelario runs into trouble and then seeks a solution for his problem.

The extraordinary characteristic of Miguel Otero Silva's *Cuando quiero llorar no lloro* (1970) is attractive and effective use of innovative narrative techniques by an author who insists on social relevance and has been openly propagandistic at one time or another. The structure of this novel carries its message. Three youths, all named for Saint Victorino, are born at the same time and also die simultaneously. The first part of the book identifies Saint Victorino in historical perspective and moves into mid-twentieth-century Caracas. Headline effects and a collage of history operate as a frame for Saint Victorino's Day, 1948. A young Venezuelan critic, R. J. Lovera de Sola, points out that this part of the novel establishes the idea of youth as a victim of established order.[11] The three youths whose stories are the content of the novel are Victorino Pérez, son of a humble family; Victorino Peralta, who belongs to a wealthy, upper-class family; and Victorino Perdomo, who is modest middle class.

With reference to the three births (and it must be remembered that all three men are, in some sense, a single man), Otero Silva establishes the principle of similarity-difference by speaking of the three mothers as Mamá, Mami, and Madre. Following the introductory chapter is a brief reference to Victorino's eighteenth birthday. After that, alternate chapters refer to each of the three Victorinos—four chapters for each. Part of each chapter deals with the situation of each man on his eighteenth birthday; another part is a flashback to an earlier time in his life. Pérez is a criminal; Peralta is a playboy-prankster; Perdomo is a member of FALN (Armed Forces for National Liberation). Perdomo's father is an oldtime Communist who cannot understand his son's concept of revolution without the proletariat. This conflict is the factor in the novel that contains the greatest amount of ideological explication. It is possible that the author's creative flow may be inhibited by some anxiety in the presentation of these opposing views.

Otero Silva injects humorous notes—almost always based on incongruities—into the process of mounting tension. His narration often has the quality of dialogue because the narrative voice speaks in a way appropriate to the person who is being spoken about. There are other shadings in the point of view that give the novel variety and move it rapidly. The alternating presentation of the triple protagonists creates a feeling that all men have the same destiny, but clearly not that all men are the same. Throughout the book, there is a steady intensification of the idea of wasted lives. The view of life is humanistic, and one might reasonably guess that the author was trained in the classics. The final chapter bears the title of the novel and is a kind of epilogue referring to the three funerals.[12]

Cuando quiero llorar no lloro is, to a considerable extent, the voice of an older generation commenting on youth and the revolutionary impulse in Spanish America. The author was born in 1908. The voice of an entirely different generation deals with similar themes when Mario Vargas Llosa (born in 1936) weaves the complex narrative tapestry of *Conversación en La Catedral* (1969). Association of these two novels with each other can enhance an appreciation of contemporary Spanish America, but only if the generational sequence is clearly understood. Vargas Llosa was born one generation later than Otero Silva, but he does not belong to the same generation as the Victorinos, who came into this world in 1948. Vargas Llosa's protagonist, Santiago Zavala, belongs to the author's own generation and is, therefore, a half-generation older than the Victorinos.

Conversación en La Catedral is basically a political novel, but only basically, because it encompasses many aspects of human behavior in Peru during the regime of Manuel Odría, 1948–1956. The novel focuses principally on these years, but actually moves forward to 1963, through the second administration of Manuel Prado and the beginning of the presidency of Fernando Belaúnde.[13] Vargas Llosa's novel, like many political novels in Spanish America, deals with the influence of the *caudillo*—his effective power is always present though the man himself is hardly ever seen. Santiago Zavala grows up under the shadow of the power. His characterization is a commentary on the situation.

To appreciate fully the dilemma of Santiago Zavala, it is helpful to know something of Peruvian politics. Manuel Odría represents a backlash against the power held by Raúl Haya de la Torre and the *apristas* in the government of José Luis Bustamante, a moderate liberal who was elected in 1945 over an oligarchy-supported opponent. The progressive programs set forth by the *apristas* alarmed the oligarchy and ultimately led to the assumption of power by a junta which General Manuel Odría headed. His eight-year regime was more corrupt than brutal, more stultifying than oppressive. In effect, he restored the Peruvian way of life—the order favored by the nation's famous families even though they know it will not work.

In 1956, Odría—to the surprise of most people—permitted free elections. Former President Manuel Prado was elected with the support of his old enemies, the *apristas*. One of the defeated candidates was Fernando Belaúnde, who had alienated the *apristas*. Prado's second administration was an economic disaster and accomplished nothing in the area of social reform. Near the end of Prado's term, in 1962, elections were held. There were three candidates: Odría, Haya de la Torre, and Belaúnde. Haya de la Torre won the largest number of votes, but not enough to be elected. There followed a period of political and military maneuvering, a brief reign by a military junta, and the eventual election of Belaúnde in 1963. It is noteworthy that Belaúnde received 39 percent of the vote, Haya de la Torre 34 percent, and Odría 26.

It is approximately at this point in history that the conversation takes place in La Catedral, a bar where the two basic characters spend four hours talking. The dialoguists are Santiago Zavala and Ambrosio Pardo. Waves of dialogue spread out from this conversation and recede in time to 1948. They refer to many different places in Lima and to several in the provinces, and incorporate sixty to seventy characters.[14] The experience created by this montage of dialogues is very complicated and subtle; however, it leans heavily on the characters and novelistic functions of Santiago and Ambrosio.

Santiago is a complex of frustrations. He is the son of a prominent family, and he rejects their values and the role of the oligarchy in Peruvian society. Nevertheless, he finds it impossible to take an affirmative position. He marries a provincial girl whose prosaic tastes and aspirations recall the cultural ambience of *La traición de Rita Hayworth*. Santiago becomes a dissatisfied nonentity, in his personal life and in his career. He functions in the novel as an example of a generation—the same one presented in Luis Loayza's *Una piel de serpiente*. It is a dissident generation frustrated by political circumstances. Its members have not passed beyond the point of being committed to ideologies, as have some more recent dissidents; rather, they seem ideologically passive or frustrated. There are similarities between these Spanish Americans and the quiet generation of the 1950s in the United States.

Ambrosio Pardo is from the provinces and from the lower class. He has long been in contact with powerful people, in the role of employee. He is a stable and honorable man. However, it becomes apparent that these qualities are in part the result of his surrender to a system he does not have the courage to try to change. Ambrosio serves as an important unifying factor in the novel, through his contact with various people. He knows Santiago because he once was chauffeur for Santiago's father. They meet by chance when the younger Zavala has to reclaim his dog from the pound. The ex-chauffeur works there.

In the waves of dialogue that emanate from their four-hour conversation in La Catedral, two characters stand out as contrasting factors to Santiago and Ambrosio. The elder Zavala, Fermín, is the standard oligarch and contrasts with his son's dissidence. Cayo Bermúdez comes from a background as humble as Ambrosio's, but has risen to power through opportunism. Neither Cayo nor Ambrosio takes a position against the oligarchy, but their responses to it are entirely different. Ambrosio, in fact, has worked as chauffeur for both Cayo and Fermín. This fact hints at Ambrosio's role as a unifying factor and also suggests how the waves of dialogue interweave many facets of the narrative.

Vargas Llosa makes use of the same narrative position, somewhere between dialogue and third-person narration (or a combination of the two), that is so effective in *La casa verde*. He also signals the relationship of a piece of dialogue to the general montage, by using key words that advise the reader. With respect to the phenomenon of time, *Conversación en La Catedral* eschews chronological progression and concentrates the essence of an epoch within a limited time span. The reality, therefore, is not the historical sequence, but all that we experience through knowing Santiago and Ambrosio during their conversation. In addition to the telescoping of time, Vargas Llosa also telescopes space by cutting rapidly from one scene to another. The effect—even though it may be only partially accomplished—is not a panorama, but a melding of several scenes.

There is little doubt that Vargas Llosa is one of the most interesting innovators in the Spanish American novel. It is also a fact that his techniques produce results that communicate beyond the experience of the technique itself. The most justifiable complaint about his work is that his techniques have to be learned so the reader can relax and stop trying to make the novel over into a commonplace experience. Once this step is taken, the novel can be appreciated on its own terms, but that may require a second or third reading. That is a lot to ask when a novel is published in two volumes totalling 675 pages. This complaint does not mean, of course, that *Conversación en La Catedral* is not worth reading. Far from it. It does mean that the reading is not to be undertaken lightly.

The author could respond, in turn, that he does not undertake the writing lightly. In fact, serious composition of fictional work is increasingly apparent in Spanish American fiction. Surely it is this artistic dedication that produces the sense of novelists who feel secure in their art. The attitude of certainty also pervades the expression of regionalism. The ability to make regionalism transcendent removes the creation from the possibility of censure on that point. It is a state of maturity with regard to technique and with regard to material—which is equal to saying that the Spanish American novel, by 1970, is a mature artistic medium.

CHAPTER 20

Conclusions

The function and value of conclusions are necessarily uncertain at the end of a study which is not the proof of a hypothesis. Nevertheless, the process of exposition in this book suggests the desirability of some concluding comments on two questions: (1) the practicability of dealing with the Spanish American novel as a whole, without resorting to subdivisions by country or region, and (2) the extent to which the disappearance of regionalism, in the traditional sense, affects the role of the novel as the expression of a region's culture.

Judgment of the first proposition rests, to a considerable extent, with the readers who make use of this book. They alone can say whether this organization of the material makes a convenient and reasonable presentation. The author can speak not of the usefulness of the study, but of his own experience in making it. Inevitably, the question presented itself from the very beginning. Some differences are immediately apparent in the novelistic traditions of the several nations, and an investigator must wonder if he can satisfy himself by subordinating divergencies to the general picture, or whether exceptions will be so frequent he will be uncomfortable in making generalities. At the conclusion of the study, it seems to me that the Spanish American novel can be usefully considered as a whole. It follows a course of development in which the straight line is altered by some minor outcroppings and by at least two major ones. The two major outcroppings (this word is preferable to "deviations") are caused by extraliterary phenomena: the Mexican Revolution and the Perón regime.

The distinctive factors added to the novel by the Mexican Revolution belong to the works published in the late 1920s and early 1930s, rather than to the immediate time of *Los de abajo*, which was during the Revolution itself. Obviously, there are many points of contact between Azuela's novel and the later novels of the Revolution, but the latter are less accommodating to the general trajectory of Spanish American fiction. *Los de abajo* is a highly experimental novel, in spite of all the derogatory statements its author may have made regarding vanguardist literature. The author invented a narrative process—quite different from his earlier work—to accommodate the new circumstance that is the basis of the book. It anticipates the vanguardist movement of the 1920s, but it uses the observed reality surrounding the author as its material. In this latter respect, it is very similar to other regionalist novels.

It is fundamentally important that Azuela novelized his anecdotal material. In the later novels of the Revolution, there is much reminiscence, and many of the books could be described as tales rather than as novels. They tend to be individualized accounts of how it all happened—a catharsis, in terms of exact or nearly exact recall. These books appeared at a time when the flurry of vanguardist fiction was waning, temporarily overshadowed by social protest. On the general trajectory of Spanish American fiction, the novels of the Revolution find their most likely companions among the novels of social protest. However, they do not quite fit, because the Mexican works are more highly personalized.

The extraordinary effect caused by the Perón regime is found in the novels of the "generation of parricides," beginning in the middle of the 1950s. The revisionist attitude of these writers is different from anything else going on at the time. In David Viñas's work, conventional concepts of Argentine history are called into question, and the attack spreads to include the whole "Argentine way of life" —the stereotypes that provided the standard of *argentinidad*. The novels emerging from this attitude reveal a kind of neorealism—an attempt to see the country as it really is. The reaction promoted interest in the neglected works of Roberto Arlt and rejected Mallea's optimistic view of the "invisible Argentina." Such a view of reality is not the same as the tell-it-like-it-is attitude of some young writers of the 1960s. The latter reveal far more of themselves. The *parricidas* were less self-centered, more concerned with the society. The directness of their expression creates a certain similarity to the small-screen novels of the time—novels that also tend to be revisionist with regard to social mores. The specifically national—sometimes even nationalistic—orientation of the Argentines sets them apart.

With these two exceptions, the line of development is fairly regular in Spanish America as a whole. At the beginning of the century, fiction is characterized by a combination of hyperaestheticism with realism-naturalism. The two tendencies, as opposed as they may seem, sometimes operate together. The first tends to disappear, and the second becomes stronger, making itself particularly useful in the expression of unique features of Spanish America, as opposed to Europe. In the 1920s and early 1930s, the cultivation of vanguardist fiction makes some headway. To a certain extent, this movement may be confused with the hyperaestheticism of an earlier generation. However, its narrative techniques are more radical. It stands out from other literature of its time because of these techniques and because of the authors' belief in their right to invent rather than reflect reality.

In the 1930's, this vanguardism is almost eclipsed, in the view of historians and critics, by the realistic tradition which turns toward social protest. It is important to notice the persistence of the vanguardist position, and particularly that some novels of protest—or involving protest—also adopt the vanguardist attitude toward invention of reality and technical innovation. During the same period, there is an evolution toward a novel of anxiety based on the question of personal identity. Gradually this kind of novel becomes dominant over the novel of social protest and, at the same time, tends to reaffirm the artist's right to invent his world.

It is important to understand that this process is not a matter of one phenomenon starting where another stops, but of a constantly shifting pattern of emphases. By the late 1940s, the role of the novelist as creator of his fictional world is amply clear. The 1950s saw a general increase in the quality of fiction—quality based on the writers' awareness of their role as creative artists, and on the cultivation of narrative techniques that transform the anecdotal material into aesthetic experience. The material of the novel, therefore, becomes subordinate to the artist. He is no longer dominated by the material; he controls it, uses it for what it is—material.

The boom in the 1960s is not related to a change in the nature of Spanish American fiction; it marks international recognition of its quality. The novel continues along the lines apparent in the 1950s, with a gradual selection process reinforcing its sounder characteristics. The major innovation of the 1960s is related to man's dissatisfaction with the signs, symbols, and forms of the culture he has created. This mood has produced the fiction of dissident youth, and an apparent anarchy in the making of fiction. On the more positive side, the same phenomena offer a possibly salutary new view of reality, a shifting of values, and an invitation to creative activity.

Such is the general development of the genre. In addition to the two major outcroppings already described, several interesting characteristics in various places invite attention, but do not seriously alter the general course. Among them are the variation in the intensity of vanguardism in various countries during the 1920s and 1930s, the Peruvian preoccupation with short fiction, the longevity of realism-naturalism in Chile, the overwhelming influence of Proust and Faulkner in Colombia, the recent *costeño* development in the same country, the possibility of the Cuban Revolution creating a third major outcropping, and the importance of a small group of writers in Ecuador. We must also remember that an imbalance appears when the general development is particularized into countries, because more fiction has come from some than from others. The possible explanations are many. However, if we study the Spanish American novel, rather than the countries, no problem arises.

Regarding the role of the novel as the expression of a culture, my experience in the course of this study has been that the role does not bear a direct relationship to the kind of literature we normally call regional. It is true that, within a specific frame of expectation, the regional novels of the first third of the century are typical of satisfactory fiction. This frame of expectation is the one that prefers to have the novel describe reality so that the reader, having experienced either the novel or the reality, may see the other and exclaim joyfully, "That is exactly right."

It is an interesting commentary on reader response that some people who greatly admire this reflection of reality in traditional regionalism reject a similar one-to-one correspondence in some recent novels where dialogue is an absolutely accurate reflection of reality. They are less disturbed, but not entirely comfortable, with the accurate portrayal of human relationships in the small-screen novels. It seems likely that the degree of comfort may correspond to the reader's lack of intimate involvement with the subject.

The transcendent regionalism present in many novels of the past quarter-century probes deeply into the character of a region. It is not photographic; it is not even a painting. It is a collage, or a happening, or both. It produces the experience of knowing a region intimately. In order to produce such an experience, the author is increasingly conscious of making his work itself an experience— this is the reason for using narrative techniques that are sometimes difficult. Given this attitude on the part of the author, it is apparent that his real concern is for the creation of the experience, rather than for the fact of having portrayed a region. The activity required by the experience makes the new, transcendent regionalism a more intimate experience than is possible in traditional regionalism of the oh-yes-I've-seen-that variety.

There remains a question about those novels that contain absolutely no suggestion of a definite place on this earth and also about those that deal with place only incidentally. The fact that the culture of a region produces this kind of fiction generally says something about the culture itself. The condition may indicate a degree of cultural maturity. However, there are nuances in any novel that are related to the particular reality in which it is born. In some specific cases, the relationship becomes so tenuous it is hardly worth considering, but there can be no doubt that, in general, the Spanish American novel in 1970 is still the voice of Spanish America—the voice, not the portrait—and more profoundly so than ever before.

A LIST OF NOVELS BY YEAR AND COUNTRY

[This list is not a bibliography. It contains the novels on which this study is based. Some volumes of short stories are also included because they have particular significance in the development of the novel.]

1900

ARGENTINA   *Montaraz* by Martiniano A. Leguizamón
CHILE   *Un idilio nuovo* by Luis Orrego Luco
URUGUAY   *Raza de Caín* by Carlos Reyles

1901

VENEZUELA   *Idolos rotos* by Manuel Díaz Rodríguez

1902

CHILE   *Juana Lucero* by Augusto D'Halmar
VENEZUELA   *Sangre patricia* by Manuel Díaz Rodríguez

1903

MEXICO   *Santa* by Federico Gamboa

1904

CHILE   *Los trasplantados* by Alberto Blest Gana
ECUADOR   *A la costa* by Luis A. Martínez

1905

CHILE   *Memorias de un voluntario de la patria vieja* by Luis Orrego Luco

1906

ARGENTINA   *El casamiento de Laucha* by Roberto J. Payró
Redención by Angel de Estrada
Cuentos de Fray Mocho by José S. Alvarez
COLOMBIA   *Polvo y ceniza* by Clímaco Soto Borda
MEXICO   *La chiquilla* by Carlos González Peña

List of Novels by Year and Country

1907

COLOMBIA *Pax* by Lorenzo Marroquín
MEXICO *María Luisa* by Mariano Azuela
VENEZUELA *El desarraigado* by Pablo J. Guerrero
El hombre de hierro by Rufino Blanco Fombona

1908

ARGENTINA *Pago chico* by Roberto J. Payró
La gloria de don Ramiro by Enrique Larreta
CHILE *Casa grande* by Luis Orrego Luco
MEXICO *Los fracasados* by Mariano Azuela

1909

ARGENTINA *Plata dorada* by Benito Lynch
MEXICO *Mala yerba* by Mariano Azuela
VENEZUELA *El Cabito* by Pío Gil

1910

ARGENTINA *Aventuras del nieto de Juan Moreira* by Roberto J. Payró
CHILE *El inútil* by Joaquín Edwards Bello
COLOMBIA *Grandeza* by Tomás Carrasquilla
VENEZUELA *Los oprimidos* by Carlos Elías Villanueva

1911

MEXICO *Andrés Pérez, maderista* by Mariano Azuela

1912

CHILE *En familia* by Luis Orrego Luco
El monstruo by Joaquín Edwards Bello
MEXICO *Sin amor* by Mariano Azuela

1913

VENEZUELA *Política feminista* [later *El Doctor Bebé*] by José Rafael Pocaterra

1914

ARGENTINA *La maestra normal* by Manuel Gálvez
CHILE *La lámpara en el molino* by Augusto D'Halmar
A través de la tempestad by Luis Orrego Luco
La reina de Rapa Nui by Pedro Prado
VENEZUELA *Villa Sana* by Carlos Elías Villanueva

1915

CHILE *El niño que enloqueció de amor* by Eduardo Barrios
COLOMBIA *Diana cazadora* by Clímaco Soto Borda
VENEZUELA *El hombre de oro* by Rufino Blanco Fombona

1916

ARGENTINA *El mal metafísico* by Manuel Gálvez
Los caranchos de La Florida by Benito Lynch
GUATEMALA *El hombre que parecía un caballo* by Rafael Arévalo Martínez
MEXICO *Los de abajo* by Mariano Azuela
URUGUAY *El terruño* by Carlos Reyles

1917

ARGENTINA *La sombra del convento* by Manuel Gálvez
Raucho by Ricardo Güiraldes
CHILE *Un perdido* by Eduardo Barrios

1918

ARGENTINA *Raquela* by Benito Lynch
Nacha Regules by Manuel Gálvez
CHILE *La cuna de Esmeraldo* by Joaquín Edwards Bello
MEXICO *Las tribulaciones de una familia decente* by Mariano Azuela

1919

BOLIVIA *Raza de bronce* by Alcides Arguedas
CUBA *Los inmorales* by Carlos Loveira
MEXICO *Fuertes y débiles* by José López Portillo y Rojas
La fuga de la quimera by Carlos González Peña
Ejemplo by Artemio de Valle Arizpe

1920

CHILE *El roto* by Joaquín Edwards Bello
Zurzulita by Mariano Latorre
Alsino by Pedro Prado
CUBA *Generales y doctores* by Carlos Loveira
VENEZUELA *El último Solar* by Rómulo Gallegos
¡En este país! by Luis Manuel Urbaneja Achelpohl

1922

ARGENTINA *La evasión* by Benito Lynch
CHILE *El Hermano Asno* by Eduardo Barrios
CUBA *Los ciegos* by Carlos Loveira

339

List of Novels by Year and Country

MEXICO *Doña Leonor de Cáceres* by Artemio de Valle Arizpe
PERU *Escalas melografiadas* by César Vallejo
URUGUAY *El embrujo de Sevilla* by Carlos Reyles

1923

ARGENTINA *Xaimaca* by Ricardo Güiraldes
Tinieblas by Elías Castelnuovo
Las mal calladas by Benito Lynch
CHILE *Montaña adentro* by Marta Brunet
MEXICO *La Malhora* by Mariano Azuela
PERU *Fabla salvaje* by César Vallejo

1924

ARGENTINA *Pata de zorra* by Gustavo Martínez Zuviría
El inglés de los güesos by Benito Lynch
CHILE *La sombra de humo en el espejo* by Augusto D'Halmar
Un juez rural by Pedro Prado
COLOMBIA *La vorágine* by José Eustasio Rivera
CUBA *La última lección* by Carlos Loveira
VENEZUELA *La trepadora* by Rómulo Gallegos
Ifigenia by Teresa de la Parra

1925

ARGENTINA *Palo verde* by Benito Lynch
El Capitán Vergara by Roberto J. Payró
CHILE *Bestia dañina* by Marta Brunet
MEXICO *El desquite* by Mariano Azuela

1926

ARGENTINA *El juguete rabioso* by Roberto Arlt
Don Segundo Sombra by Ricardo Güiraldes
Zogoibi by Enrique Larreta
Cuentos para una inglesa desesperada by Eduardo Mallea
El empresario del genio by Carlos A. Leumann
CHILE *El habitante y su esperanza* by Pablo Neruda
MEXICO *Pero Galín* by Genaro Estrada
El Café de Nadie by Arqueles Vela

1927

ARGENTINA *Royal Circo* by Leónidas Barletta
CUBA *Juan Criollo* by Carlos Loveira
MEXICO *Margarita de Niebla* by Jaime Torres Bodet

340

1928

ARGENTINA   *Escenas de la guerra del Paraguay* by Manuel Gálvez
CHILE   *Un chileno en Madrid* by Joaquín Edwards Bello
COLOMBIA   *La novena sinfonía* by José María Vargas Vila
  La marquesa de Yolombó by Tomás Carrasquilla
MEXICO   *El águila y la serpiente* by Martín Luis Guzmán
  Novela como nube by Gilberto Owen
  El joven by Salvador Novo
PERU   *El pueblo sin Dios* by César Falcón
  La casa de cartón by Martín Adán
  Matalaché by Enrique López Albújar

1929

ARGENTINA   *Los siete locos* by Roberto Arlt
  Papeles de Recienvenido by Macedonio Fernández
CHILE   *María Rosa, flor de Quillén* by Marta Brunet
  Cap Polonio by Joaquín Edwards Bello
  Tronco herido by Luis Orrego Luco
  El delincuente by Manuel Rojas
MEXICO   *La sombra del caudillo* by Martín Luis Guzmán
  La educación sentimental by Jaime Torres Bodet
VENEZUELA   *Doña Bárbara* by Rómulo Gallegos

1930

ARGENTINA   *Miércoles santo* by Manuel Gálvez
COLOMBIA   *La casa de vecindad* by José A. Osorio Lizarazo
ECUADOR   *Los que se van* by Demetrio Aguilera Malta, Enrique Gil Gilbert, and Joaquín Gallegos Lara
GUATEMALA   *Leyendas de Guatemala* by Miguel Angel Asturias

1931

ARGENTINA   *Los lanzallamas* by Roberto Arlt
  Larvas by Elías Castelnuovo
CHILE   *Valparaíso, ciudad del viento* by Joaquín Edwards Bello
ECUADOR   *Río arriba* by Alfredo Pareja Díez-Canseco
MEXICO   *La asonada* by José Mancisidor
  Campamento by Gregorio López y Fuentes
PERU   *El tungsteno* by César Vallejo
  Hollywood by Xavier Abril
VENEZUELA   *Las lanzas coloradas* by Arturo Uslar Pietri
  Cubagua by Enrique Bernardo Núñez

List of Novels by Year and Country

1932

ARGENTINA   *El amor brujo* by Roberto Arlt
GUATEMALA   *El tigre* by Flavio Herrera
MEXICO   *Tierra* by Gregorio López y Fuentes
La luciérnaga by Mariano Azuela
La ciudad roja by José Mancisidor

1933

ARGENTINA   *¡Quiero trabajo!* by María Luisa Carnelli
45 días y 30 marineros by Norah Lange
COLOMBIA   *Toá* by César Uribe Piedrahita
CUBA   *Laberinto de si mismo* by Enrique Labrador Ruiz
Ecue-Yamba-O by Alejo Carpentier
ECUADOR   *El muelle* by Alfredo Pareja Díez-Canseco
Don Goyo by Demetrio Aguilera Malta

1934

ARGENTINA   *Op Oloop* by Juan Filloy
CHILE   *Cagliostro* by Vicente Huidobro
Papá, o el diario de Alicia Mir by Vicente Huidobro
Capitanes sin barco by Augusto D'Halmar
COLOMBIA   *Cuatro años a bordo de mi mismo* by Eduardo Zalamea Borda
ECUADOR   *Huasipungo* by Jorge Icaza
MEXICO   *Desbandada* by José Rubén Romero
Mi general by Gregorio López y Fuentes
Primero de enero by Jaime Torres Bodet
PERU   *Duque* by José Díez Canseco
URUGUAY   *El paisano Aguilar* by Enrique Amorim
VENEZUELA   *Cantaclaro* by Rómulo Gallegos

1935

ARGENTINA   *Madre América* by Max Dickman
Historia universal de la infamia by Jorge Luis Borges
CHILE   *La chica del Crillón* by Joaquín Edwards Bello
La última niebla by María Luisa Bombal
COLOMBIA   *Mancha de aceite* by César Uribe Piedrahita
La cosecha by José A. Osorio Lizarazo
Risaralda by Bernardo Arias Trujillo
El criminal by José A. Osorio Lizarazo
ECUADOR   *Canal Zone* by Demetrio Aguilera Malta
La Beldaca by Alfredo Pareja Díez-Canseco
MEXICO   *El indio* by Gregorio López y Fuentes

PERU   *Agua* by José María Arguedas
      La serpiente de oro by Ciro Alegría

1936

ARGENTINA   *La ciudad junto al río inmóvil* by Eduardo Mallea
           Hasta aquí no más by Pablo Rojas Paz
CHILE   *La ciudad de los Césares* by Manuel Rojas
CUBA   *Cresival* by Enrique Labrador Ruiz
ECUADOR   *En las calles* by Jorge Icaza
MEXICO   *Mi caballo, mi perro, y my rifle* by José Rubén Romero
URUGUAY   *Cielo en los charcos* by Juan Mario Magallanes
VENEZUELA   *Mene* by Ramón Díaz Sánchez

1937

MEXICO   *El resplandor* by Mauricio Magdaleno
        Sombras by Jaime Torres Bodet
VENEZUELA   *Pobre negro* by Rómulo Gallegos

1938

ARGENTINA   *Fiesta en noviembre* by Eduardo Mallea
CHILE   *La amortajada* by María Luisa Bombal
       Los hombres oscuros by Nicomedes Guzmán
COLOMBIA   *Hombres sin presente* by José A. Osorio Lizarazo
ECUADOR   *Cholos* by Jorge Icaza
         Baldomera by Alfredo Pareja Díez-Canseco
MEXICO   *San Gabriel de Valdivias* by Mariano Azuela
        La vida inútil de Pito Pérez by José Rubén Romero
PERU   *Los perros hambrientos* by Ciro Alegría
VENEZUELA   *Puros hombres* by Antonio Arráiz

1939

COLOMBIA   *Garabato* by José A. Osorio Lizarazo
MEXICO   *Huasteca* by Gregorio López y Fuentes
URUGUAY   *El pozo* by Juan Carlos Onetti

1940

ARGENTINA   *La bahía del silencio* by Eduardo Mallea
           La invención de Morel by Adolfo Bioy Casares
CUBA   *Anteo* by Enrique Labrador Ruiz
GUATEMALA   *Anaité* by Mario Monteforte Toledo
MEXICO   *Avanzada* by Mariano Azuela
        Espejismo de Juchitán by Agustín Yáñez
PERU   *Yawar fiesta* by José María Arguedas

List of Novels by Year and Country

1941

ARGENTINA *Una novela que comienza* by Macedonio Fernández
Todo verdor perecerá by Eduardo Mallea
El jardín de senderos que se bifurcan by Jorge Luis Borges
COSTA RICA *Mamita Yunai* by Carlos Luis Fallas
ECUADOR *Hombres sin tiempo* by Alfredo Pareja Díez-Canseco
Nuestro pan by Enrique Gil Gilbert
MEXICO *Nueva burguesía* by Mariano Azuela
Sonata by Mauricio Magdaleno
Los muros de agua by José Revueltas
Flor de juegos antiguos by Agustín Yáñez
PERU *El mundo es ancho y ajeno* by Ciro Alegría
URUGUAY *El caballo y su sombra* by Enrique Amorim
Tierra de nadie by Juan Carlos Onetti

1942

ARGENTINA *Alamos talados* by Abelardo Arias
ECUADOR *La isla virgen* by Demetrio Aguilera Malta
Media vida deslumbrados by Jorge Icaza

1943

ARGENTINA *Las águilas* by Eduardo Mallea
El balcón hacia la muerte by Ulyses Petit de Murat
CHILE *La sangre y la esperanza* by Nicomedes Guzmán
COLOMBIA *Babel* by Jaime Ardila Casamitjana
ECUADOR *Juyungo* by Adalberto Ortiz
MEXICO *El luto humano* by José Revueltas
Archipiélago de mujeres by Agustín Yáñez
URUGUAY *Para esta noche* by Juan Carlos Onetti
VENEZUELA *Sobre la misma tierra* by Rómulo Gallegos

1944

ARGENTINA *Ficciones* by Jorge Luis Borges
CHILE *Tamarugal* by Eduardo Barrios
COLOMBIA *Cada voz lleva angustia* by Jorge Ibáñez
El hombre bajo la tierra by José A. Osorio Lizarazo
ECUADOR *Las tres ratas* by Alfredo Pareja Díez-Canseco
MEXICO *Los peregrinos inmóviles* by Gregorio López y Fuentes
VENEZUELA *Dámaso Velásquez* by Antonio Arráiz

1945

ARGENTINA *Plan de evasión* by Adolfo Bioy Casares
URUGUAY *El asesino desvelado* by Enrique Amorim

1946

ARGENTINA *El retorno* by Eduardo Mallea
El vínculo by Eduardo Mallea
Lago argentino by Juan Goyanarte
Los Robinsones by Roger Plá
BOLIVIA *Metal del diablo* by Augusto Céspedes
CHILE *Humo hacia el mar* by Marta Brunet
En el viejo almendral by Joaquín Edwards Bello
GUATEMALA *El Señor Presidente* by Miguel Angel Asturias
MEXICO *La mujer domada* by Mariano Azuela
VENEZUELA *La dolida infancia de Perucho González* by José Fabbiani
Ruiz

1947

CHILE *Playa negra* by Luis Orrego Luco
COLOMBIA *Tierra mojada* by Manuel Zapata Olivella
Donde moran los sueños by Jaime Ibáñez
MEXICO *Al filo del agua* by Agustín Yáñez
PANAMA *Plenilunio* by Rogelio Sinán
PERU *El cínico* by Carlos Eduardo Zavaleta
VENEZUELA *El camino de El Dorado* by Arturo Uslar Pietri

1948

ARGENTINA *Adán Buenosayres* by Leopoldo Marechal
El túnel by Ernesto Sábato
CHILE *Gran señor y rajadiablos* by Eduardo Barrios
COLOMBIA *Yugo de niebla* by Clemente Airó
ECUADOR *Huairapamushkas* by Jorge Icaza
GUATEMALA *Entre la piedra y la cruz* by Mario Monteforte Toledo
URUGUAY *Turris ebúrnea* by Rodolfo L. Fonseca
VENEZUELA *Los alegres desahuciados* by Andrés Mariño-Palacios

1949

ARGENTINA *Shunko* by Jorge W. Abalos
El aleph by Jorge Luis Borges
CHILE *Raíz del sueño* by Marta Brunet
COSTA RICA *La ruta de su evasión* by Yolanda Oreamuno
CUBA *El reino de este mundo* by Alejo Carpentier
Trailer de sueños by Enrique Labrador Ruiz
GUATEMALA *Hombres de maíz* by Miguel Angel Asturias
MEXICO *Tierra Grande* by Mauricio Magdaleno

List of Novels by Year and Country

1950

ARGENTINA *Los enemigos del alma* by Eduardo Mallea
CUBA *La sangre hambrienta* by Enrique Labrador Ruiz
GUATEMALA *Viento fuerte* by Miguel Angel Asturias
PERU *El retoño* by Julián Huanay
URUGUAY *La vida breve* by Juan Carlos Onetti
    Muchachos by Juan José Morosoli
VENEZUELA *Cumboto* by Ramón Díaz Sánchez

1951

ARGENTINA *La casa de los Felipes* by Luisa Mercedes Levinson
    La torre by Eduardo Mallea
CHILE *Hijo de ladrón* by Manuel Rojas
COLOMBIA *Sombras al sol* by Clemente Airó
PERU *La prisión* by Gustavo Valcárcel

· 1952

CHILE *Coirón* by Daniel Belmar
COLOMBIA *El pantano* by José A. Osorio Lizarazo
    El Cristo de espaldas by Eduardo Caballero Calderón
VENEZUELA *El falso cuaderno de Narciso Espejo* by Guillermo Meneses

1953

ARGENTINA *Chaves* by Eduardo Mallea
CUBA *Los pasos perdidos* by Alejo Carpentier
    El gallo en el espejo by Enrique Labrador Ruiz
GUATEMALA *Donde acaban los caminos* by Mario Monteforte Toledo
URUGUAY *Quién de nosotros* by Mario Benedetti

1954

ARGENTINA *La casa* by Manuel Mujica Lainez
    El sustituto by Carlos Mazzanti
    El sueño de los héroes by Adolfo Bioy Casares
    La casa del ángel by Beatriz Guido
GUATEMALA *Una manera de morir* by Mario Monteforte Toledo
    El Papa verde by Miguel Angel Asturias
URUGUAY *Los adioses* by Juan Carlos Onetti

1955

ARGENTINA *El pentágono* by Antonio Di Benedetto
    Donde haya Dios by Alberto Rodríguez (h.)
    Rosaura a las diez by Marco Denevi

Cayó sobre su rostro by David Viñas
Los viajeros by Manuel Mujica Lainez
La fatalidad de los cuerpos by Héctor A. Murena
COLOMBIA   *La hojarasca* by Gabriel García Márquez
MEXICO   *Pedro Páramo* by Juan Rulfo
PERU   *Los Ingar* by Carlos Eduardo Zavaleta
VENEZUELA   *Casas muertas* by Miguel Otero Silva

1956

ARGENTINA   *Tres cuentos sin amor* by Ezequiel Martínez Estrada
Marta Riquelme by Ezequiel Martínez Estrada
Los amigos lejanos by Julio Ardiles Gray
Los años despiadados by David Viñas
Las tierras blancas by Juan José Manauta
Zama by Antonio Di Benedetto
ECUADOR   *La advertencia* by Alfredo Pareja Díez-Canseco
GUATEMALA   *Weekend en Guatemala* by Miguel Angel Asturias

1957

ARGENTINA   *Hombres en soledad* by Manuel Gálvez
Simbad by Eduardo Mallea
Un Dios cotidiano by David Viñas
El encuentro by Pedro Orgambide
CHILE   *Coronación* by José Donoso
María Nadie by Marta Brunet
Caballo de copas by Fernando Alegría
CUBA   *El acoso* by Alejo Carpentier
MEXICO   *Los motivos de Caín* by José Revueltas
Balúm Canán by Rosario Castellanos

1958

ARGENTINA   *Fin de fiesta* by Beatriz Guido
Perdido en la noche by Manuel Gálvez
Enero by Sara Gallardo
CHILE   *Para subir al cielo* by Enrique Lafourcade
MEXICO   *El norte* by Emilio Carballido
La región más transparente by Carlos Fuentes
Polvos de arroz by Sergio Galindo
PERU   *Los ríos profundos* by José María Arguedas

1959

ARGENTINA   *Las hermanas* by Pedro Orgambide
Los dueños de la tierra by David Viñas

347

List of Novels by Year and Country

CHILE   *La fiesta del rey Acab* by Enrique Lafourcade
        Puerto Engaño by Leonardo Espinoza
MEXICO *La justicia de enero* by Sergio Galindo
        La creación by Agustín Yáñez
PARAGUAY   *Hijo de hombre* by Augusto Roa Bastos
URUGUAY   *Una tumba sin nombre* by Juan Carlos Onetti
VENEZUELA   *Los pequeños seres* by Salvador Garmendia
        A orillas del sueño by José Fabbiani Ruiz

1960

ARGENTINA   *Las leyes del juego* by Manuel Peyrou
        Los premios by Julio Cortázar
COLOMBIA   *La calle 10* by Manuel Zapata Olivella
GUATEMALA   *Los ojos de los enterrados* by Miguel Angel Asturias
MEXICO   *El Bordo* by Sergio Galindo
        Las buenas conciencias by Carlos Fuentes
        La tierra pródiga by Agustín Yáñez
PERU   *Crónica de San Gabriel* by Julio Ramón Ribeyro
URUGUAY   *La tregua* by Mario Benedetti
        Los días por vivir by Carlos Martínez Moreno
        La casa de la desgracia by Juan Carlos Onetti

1961

COLOMBIA   *La ciudad y el viento* by Clemente Airó
        El coronel no tiene quien le escriba by Gabriel García Márquez
URUGUAY   *Cordelia* by Carlos Martínez Moreno
        El astillero by Juan Carlos Onetti
VENEZUELA   *Los habitantes* by Salvador Garmendia

1962

ARGENTINA   *Dar la cara* by David Viñas
        Bomarzo by Manuel Mujica Lainez
        Sobre héroes y tumbas by Ernesto Sábato
        La alfombra roja by Marta Lynch
CHILE   *Según el órden del tiempo* by Juan Agustín Palazuelos
COLOMBIA   *La casa grande* by Alvaro Cepeda Zamudio
        La mala hora by Gabriel García Márquez
        La rebelión de las ratas by Fernando Soto Aparicio
        Manuel Pacha by Eduardo Caballero Calderón
        Respirando el verano by Héctor Rojas Herazo
CUBA   *Maestra voluntaria* by Daura Olema García
        El siglo de las luces by Alejo Carpentier

348

MEXICO   *Oficio de tinieblas* by Rosario Castellanos
           La muerte de Artemio Cruz by Carlos Fuentes
           Aura by Carlos Fuentes
           Las tierras flacas by Agustín Yáñez
VENEZUELA   *La misa de Arlequín* by Guillermo Meneses

1963

ARGENTINA   *Acto y ceniza* by Manuel Peyrou
           Rayuela by Julio Cortázar
CHILE   *Invención a dos voces* by Enrique Lafourcade
COLOMBIA   *Camino en la sombra* by José A. Osorio Lizarazo
           El hostigante verano de los dioses by Fanny Buitrago
CUBA   *La situación* by Lisandro Otero
           Gestos by Severo Sarduy
GUATEMALA   *Mulata de tal* by Miguel Angel Asturias
MEXICO   *La feria* by Juan José Arreola
           Los recuerdos del porvenir by Elena Garro
PERU   *La ciudad y los perros* by Mario Vargas Llosa
URUGUAY   *El paredón* by Carlos Martínez Moreno

1964

ARGENTINA   *Límite de clase* by Abelardo Arias
           Los burgueses by Silvina Bullrich
           Memorias de un hombre de bien by Pedro Orgambide
           Asfalto by Renato Pellegrini
CHILE   *Toda la luz del mediodía* by Mauricio Wácquez
COLOMBIA   *Mientras llueve* by Fernando Soto Aparicio
           En Chimá nace un santo by Manuel Zapata Olivella
           El día señalado by Manuel Mejía Vallejo
MEXICO   *La comparsa* by Sergio Galindo
           Los errores by José Revueltas
           Los albañiles by Vicente Leñero
PARAGUAY   *La llaga* by Gabriel Casaccia
PERU   *Todas las sangres* by José María Arguedas
           Una piel de serpiente by Luis Loayza
URUGUAY   *Juntacadáveres* by Juan Carlos Onetti
VENEZUELA   *Día de ceniza* by Salvador Garmendia

1965

CHILE   *Patas de perro* by Carlos Droguett
           El peso de la noche by Jorge Edwards
MEXICO   *Gazapo* by Gustavo Sainz
           Farabeuf by Salvador Elizondo

List of Novels by Year and Country

PERU   *La casa verde* by Mario Vargas Llosa
        En octubre no hay milagros by Oswaldo Reynoso
        Los geniecillos dominicales by Julio Ramón Ribeyro

1966

ARGENTINA   *Minotauroamor* by Abelardo Arias
             Se vuelven contra nosotros by Manuel Peyrou
             En la semana trágica by David Viñas
             La cordillera del viento by Carlos Mazzanti
CHILE   *Cuerpo creciente* by Hernán Valdés
         Este domingo by José Donoso
         El lugar sin límites by José Donoso
COLOMBIA   *El buen salvaje* by Eduardo Caballero Calderón
            Los días más felices del año by Humberto Navarro
CUBA   *Paradiso* by José Lezama Lima
MEXICO   *De perfil* by José Agustín
          José Trigo by Fernando del Paso
PARAGUAY   *Los exiliados* by Gabriel Casaccia

1967

ARGENTINA   *Siberia Blues* by Néstor Sánchez
             Los hombres de a caballo by David Viñas
             La barca de hielo by Eduardo Mallea
             Alrededor de la jaula by Haroldo Conti
CHILE   *El compadre* by Carlos Droguett
COLOMBIA   *Cien años de soledad* by Gabriel García Márquez
CUBA   *Tres tristes tigres* by Guillermo Cabrera Infante
        De donde son los cantantes by Severo Sarduy
ECUADOR   *El testimonio* by Alsino Ramírez Estrada
           Los prisioneros de la noche by Rafael Díaz Ycaza
           El espejo y la ventana by Adalberto Ortiz
MEXICO   *Cambio de piel* by Carlos Fuentes
          Zona sagrada by Carlos Fuentes
          Morirás lejos by José Emilio Pacheco
          El garabato by Vicente Leñero
URUGUAY   *Tierras de la memoria* by Filisberto Hernández
           Con las primeras luces by Carlos Martínez Moreno

1968

ARGENTINA   *62. Modelo para armar* by Julio Cortázar
             El camino de los hiperbóreos by Héctor Libertella
             Nanina by Germán Leopoldo García

350

La traición de Rita Hayworth by Manuel Puig
Hombre en la orilla by Miguel Briante
CHILE   *Los días contados* by Fernando Alegría
Frecuencia modulada by Enrique Lafourcade
Job-Boj by Jorge Guzmán
COLOMBIA   *Mateo el flautista* by Alberto Duque López
En noviembre llega el arzobispo by Héctor Rojas Herazo
CUBA   *Los niños se despiden* by Pablo Armando Fernández
MEXICO   *En caso de duda* by Orlando Ortiz
Inventando que sueño by José Agustín
Pasto verde by Parménides García Saldaña
El hipogeo secreto by Salvador Elizondo
PERU   *Los juegos verdaderos* by Edmundo de los Ríos
VENEZUELA   *Alacranes* by Rodolfo Izaguirre
Piedra de mar by Francisco Massiani
Largo by José Balza
La mala vida by Salvador Garmendia
País portátil by Adriano González León

1969

ARGENTINA   *Boquitas pintadas* by Manuel Puig
Contramutis by Jorge Onetti
Epitalámica by Héctor A. Murena
Los suicidas by Antonio Di Benedetto
COLOMBIA   *Las maniobras* by Héctor Sánchez
CUBA   *El mundo alucinante* by Reynaldo Arenas
ECUADOR   *Henry Black* by Miguel Donoso Pareja
MEXICO   *Obsesivos días circulares* by Gustavo Sainz
Cumpleaños by Carlos Fuentes
NICARAGUA   *Trágame tierra* by Lizandro Chávez Alfaro
PERU   *Conversación en La Catedral* by Mario Vargas Llosa
Alférez Arce, Teniente Arce, Capitán Arce . . . by Sebastian Salazar
Bondy
PUERTO RICO   *El francotirador* by Pedro Juan Soto

1970

ARGENTINA   *Háblenme de Funes* by Humberto Costantini
Cancha rayada by Germán Leopoldo García
CHILE   *Toca esa rumba, Don Aspiazu* by Alfonso Calderón
COLOMBIA   *Cola de zorro* by Fanny Buitrago
CUBA   *En ciudad semejante* by Lisandro Otero
ECUADOR   *Siete lunas y siete serpientes* by Demetrio Aguilera Malta
Las pequeñas estatuas by Alfredo Pareja Díez-Canseco

351

List of Novels by Year and Country

MEXICO *La muchacha en el balcón* by Juan Tovar
Nudo by Sergio Galindo
Yo soy David by Alfredo Leal Cortés
Acto propiciatorio by Héctor Manjarrez
VENEZUELA *Cuando quiero llorar no lloro* by Miguel Otero Silva
Rajatabla by Luis Britto García

NOTES

1. The Heritage (1900–1915)

1. Hernán Vidal, "*Sangre Patricia* y la conjunción Naturalista-Simbolista," *Hispania* 52, no. 2 (May 1969): 183–192.

2. Andrew P. Debicki, "Díaz Rodríguez's *Sangre patricia*: A 'point of view' novel," *Hispania* 53, no. 1 (March 1970): 59–66. Debicki points out, in a note, that Luis Monguió has discussed the theme of the ideal versus the practical in the work of Díaz Rodríguez, in his *Estudios sobre literatura hispanoamericana y española* (Mexico City: Ed. de Andrea, 1958), pp. 71–77.

3. Debicki, "Díaz Rodríguez's *Sangre patricia*," p. 59.

4. *Diana cazadora*, by Clímaco Soto Borda, is a good example of the satire. It was written in 1900, but first published in 1915. Another work by the same author, *Polvo y ceniza* (1906), is a fine example of the desire to shock readers. It is a volume of stories, printed in blue ink, with roman numerals, and with type running the long dimension of the page.

5. In Pedro Orgambide and Roberto Yahni, *Enciclopedia de la literatura argentina* (Buenos Aires: Ed. Sudamericana, 1970).

6. Seymour Menton, "Federico Gamboa: Un análisis estilístico," *Humanitas*, no. 4 (1963), pp. 311–342.

7. Gerardo Sáenz, *Ideología de la fuerza* (Mexico City: Herrerías y Alvarez S., 1971).

8. Fernando Alegría, *Historia de la novela hispanoamericana* (Mexico City: Ed. de Andrea, 1965), p. 108.

9. Orgambide and Yahni, *Enciclopedia de la literatura argentina*, pp. 128–129.

10. Ibid., p. 166.

11. In the second edition (1918?), the title is changed to *El Doctor Bebé*.

12. Guillermo Meneses, "Notas sobre *El Cabito*," *Letras Nuevas*, no. 5 (August–September 1970), pp. 6–8.

13. Enrique Gil Gilbert, "Homenaje a Luis Martínez," *Cuadernos del Guayas*, July 20, 1969, pp. 38–40.

14. Personal letter from Iván Droguett Czishke, June 14, 1970.

15. Luis Leal, *Mariano Azuela: Vida y obra* (Mexico City: Ed. de Andrea, 1961); pp. 44–45 list the innovations in this novel and also show how it is related to Azuela's cycle of the Revolution.

16. Ibid., p. 44. The Azuela quotation is from his *Obras completas*, III, 1072.

2. The Year of *Los de abajo* (1916)

1. Luis Leal, *Mariano Azuela*, p. 20. This book is a good general summary. It is the source of most of what is said here about Azuela's life, and of some of the analysis of his work.

2. Arturo Torres Rioseco, *Novelistas contemporáneos de América*, p. 16; Fernando Alegría, *Historia de la novela hispanoamericana*, p. 146; Leal, *Mariano Azuela*, p. 125; Seymour Menton, "La estructura épica de *Los de abajo*," in *La novela Iberoamericana contemporánea* (Caracas: Universidad Central de Venezuela, 1968), pp. 215–222.

3. Leal, *Mariano Azuela*, p. 104.

4. Carlos Reyles, *El terruño* (Santiago: Ed. Ercilla, 1936), e.g., pp. 34, 143.

5. Benito Lynch, *Los caranchos de La Florida* (Buenos Aires: Troquel, 1958), pp. 28–29.

6. Torres Rioseco, *Novelistas contemporáneos de América*, pp. 162–163.

7. Ibid., pp. 158–159.

8. Pedro Orgambide and Roberto Yahni, *Enciclopedia de la literatura argentina*, pp. 212–213.

9. Manuel Gálvez, *El mal metafísico* (Buenos Aires: Ed. Tor, n.d.), p. 5.

10. Daniel R. Reedy, "La dualidad del 'yo' en *El hombre que parecía un caballo*," in *El ensayo y la crítica literaria en Iberoamérica* (Toronto: University of Toronto Press, 1971), pp. 167–174.

3. From *Los de abajo* to *Don Segundo Sombra* (1917–1925)

1. Arturo Torres Rioseco, *Novelistas contemporáneos de América*, pp. 93–94.

2. Juan Carlos Ghiano, *Ricardo Güiraldes* (Buenos Aires: Pleamar, 1966), p. 36.

3. Ibid., p. 74.

4. "New Worldism" is a translation of *novomundismo* or *mundonovismo*, a term used by Spanish American critics with reference to novels that emphasize things, persons, customs, or experience that characterize the New World as different from Europe.

5. Joaquín Edwards Bello, *El roto* (Santiago: Ed. Universitaria, 1968). The review by Omer Emeth was published originally in *El Mercurio*, August 2, 1920. It is on pp. 160–165 of this edition of the novel.

6. Torres Rioseco, *Novelistas contemporáneos de América*, p. 285.

7. Edwards Bello, *El roto*, "Nota preliminar" by Alfonso Calderón, p. x. *Alessandrismo* refers to Arturo Alessandri who was elected president of Chile in 1920.

8. Ibid., p. 8.

4. The Year of *Don Segundo Sombra* (1926)

1. Fernando Alegría, *Historia de la novela hispanoamericana*, p. 182.

2. Juan Carlos Ghiano, *Ricardo Güiraldes*, p. 104. A slightly different division, still into three parts, would consider part three as consisting only of the last chapter. This division takes into account the major time lapses.

3. Ricardo Güiraldes, *Don Segundo Sombra* (Mexico City: Ed. Porrúa, 1971), p. 125.

4. Alegría, *Historia de la novela hispanoamericana*, p. 187.

5. Ghiano (in *Ricardo Güiraldes*, pp. 108–109) makes substantially the same evaluation. He also refers to an interesting statement by Amado Alonso to the effect that, in his narrative voice, Güiraldes does not distort literary language, but works in the other direction, adding artistic dignity to the normal speech of an *estanciero*.

6. Ibid., p. 113.

7. Iván Droguett Cz., "Antecedentes para la comprensión de *Don Segundo Sombra*," *Signos de Valparaíso* 1, no. 1 (Second Semester 1967): 28.

8. Roberto Arlt, *El juguete rabioso* (Buenos Aires: Ed. Losada, 1958), p. 88.

9. Pedro Orgambide and Roberto Yahni, *Enciclopedia de la literatura argentina*, pp. 51–52.

10. Ibid., p. 48.

11. Ibid., p. 50.

12. Arqueles Vela, *El Café de Nadie* (Jalapa: Ed. Horizonte, 1926), p. 13.

13. The use of the word *vanguardist* here refers to new techniques used by writers in the 1920s. I mean to use the word, however, in the general sense of "avant garde," not in the sense of vanguardism as a specific literary school or group.

14. An example is an article by the philologist Pablo González Casanova, "Las metáforas de A.V.," *La Vida Literaria* 1, nos. 10–11 (November–December 1970): 8–10. The article was originally published in *El Universal Ilustrado*, in 1927.

15. Eduardo Mallea, *Cuentos para una inglesa desesperada* (Buenos Aires: Gleizer, 1926), pp. 13–14.

16. Genaro Estrada, *Pero Galín* (Mexico City: INBA, 1967), p. 4.

5. From *Don Segundo Sombra* to *Doña Bárbara* (1927–1928)

1. See Boyd G. Carter, *Historia de la literatura hispanoamericana a través de sus revistas* (Mexico City: Ed. de Andrea, 1968)

2. "Novela como nube," in Gilberto Owen, *Poesía y prosa* (Mexico City: Impr. Universitaria, 1953), pp. 155–209. This reference is to p. 156.

3. Martín Adán, *La casa de cartón* (Lima: Juan Mejía Baca, 1971), p. 15.

4. Firpo was an Argentine heavyweight prizefighter.

5. Tomás Carrasquilla, *La marquesa de Yolombó* (Medellín: Ed. Bedout, 1968), p. 31.

6. John Englekirk, "Doña Bárbara, Legend of the Llano," *Hispania*, no. 31 (August 1948), pp. 259–270. This study identifies most of the prototypes of the novel's characters. In an entirely different kind of article, a prominent sociologist praises the accuracy of Gallegos's picture of Venezuela (see Raymond E. Crist, "Some Aspects of Human Geography in Latin American Literature," *American Journal of Economics and Sociology* 24, no. 4 [October 1962]: 407–412).

6. The Year of *Doña Bárbara* (1929)

1. Rómulo Gallegos, *Doña Bárbara* (Buenos Aires: Espasa-Calpe Argentina, 1959), p. 37.

2. Sturgis E. Leavitt, "Sex vs. Symbolism in *Doña Bárbara*," *Revista de Estudios Hispánicos*, no. 1 (May 1967), pp. 117–120.

3. André S. Michalski, "*Doña Bárbara*, un cuento de hadas," *PMLA* 85, no. 5 (October 1970), 1015–1022. J. Riis Owre (in "The Fauna of the Works of Rómulo Gallegos," *Hispania* 45, no. 7 [March 1962]: 52–56) deals with animals mainly as a means of foreshadowing. Michalski emphasizes the myth of transformation because he is interested in revealing Doña Bárbara's witchlike qualities.

4. Martín Luis Guzmán, *La sombra del caudillo* (Mexico City: Compañía General de Ediciones, 1970), pp. 9–10.

5. Roberto Arlt, *Novelas completas y cuentos* (Buenos Aires: Compañía General Fabril Editora, 1963), I, 177.

6. Pedro Orgambide and Roberto Yahni, *Enciclopedia de la literatura argentina*, p. 230.

7. A good example, which I do not care to translate, is "Tan es así que si tan es así no fuera todo lo que de él se sabe no se ignoraría todavía" (Macedonio Fernández, *Papeles de Recienvenido. Poemas. Relatos, cuentos, miscelánea* [Buenos Aires: Centro Editor de América Latina, 1966], p. 23).

7. From *Doña Bárbara* to *Don Goyo* (1930–1932)

1. Arturo Torres Rioseco, *Novelistas contemporáneos de América*, pp. 273–274.

2. Roberto Arlt, *Los lanzallamas* (Buenos Aires: Claridad, 1931), p. 2.

3. Thomas E. Kooreman, "Urban Emphasis in the Contemporary Colombian Novel" (Ph.D. dissertation, University of Missouri, 1970), pp. 55–56.

4. Osvaldo Larrazábal Henríquez, *Enrique Bernardo Núñez* (Caracas: Universidad Central de Venezuela, 1969), see especially pp. 34–36.

5. Fernando Alegría, *Historia de la novela hispanoamericana*, p. 287.

6. Miguel Angel Asturias, *Leyendas de Guatemala* (Buenos Aires: Losada, 1967), p. 31.

7. Richard Callan, *Miguel Angel Asturias* (New York: Twayne Publishers, 1970), pp. 123–124.

8. Demetrio Aguilera Malta, Enrique Gil Gilbert, and Joaquín Gallegos Lara, *Los que se van* (Quito: Casa de la Cultura Ecuatoriana, 1955).

9. The general understanding of *cholo* is a mixture of Indian and white, or an Indian assimilated into white culture. However, in the coastal region of Ecuador the word has a different significance. It refers to the indigenous inhabitant of the seacoast and the nearby islands. He is, therefore, differentiated from the indigenous inhabitant of the river area, who is called *montuvio* or *montubio*.

8. The Year of *Don Goyo* (1933)

1. Demetrio Aguilera Malta, *Don Goyo* (Buenos Aires: Editorial Platina, 1958), pp. 44–45.

2. Pedro Orgambide and Roberto Yahni, *Enciclopedia de la literatura argentina*, p. 368.

9. From *Don Goyo* to *Todo verdor perecerá* (1934–1940)

1. Alberto Escobar, *Patio de letras* (Lima: Ediciones Caballo de Troya, 1965), pp. 180–257.

2. José María Arguedas, *Yawar fiesta* (Lima: Populibros Peruanos, n.d.), p. 14.

3. "Película de negridumbre y de vaquería, filmada en dos rollos y en lengua castellana," on title page of Bernardo Arias Trujillo's *Risaralda* (Manizales: Casa Editorial y Talleres Gráficas Arturo Zapata, 1935).

4. Nicomedes Guzmán, *Los hombres oscuros* (Santiago: Ediciones Yunque, 1939), p. 25.

5. María Luisa Bombal, *La última niebla* (Santiago: Nascimento, 1941), pp. 15–17.

6. It is certainly not my intention to make a great thing of early unpublished works. It is well known, however, that Onetti had written a novel, *Tiempo de abrazar*, as early as 1933, and that *El pozo* was written some time before it was published (see Luis Harss and Barbara Dohmann, *Into the Mainstream* [New York: Harper and Row, 1966], p. 179).

7. Bernardo Verbitsky deals with this phenomenon in his introduction to the modern edition (see Juan Filloy, *Op Oloop* [Buenos Aires: Paidos, 1967], pp. 7–17).

8. Vicente Huidobro, *Cagliostro* (Santiago: Zig-Zag, 1934). The composition of *Cagliostro* may date back as far as the early 1920s. Details of the Huidobro bibliography are too complicated for exposition here. The edition cited contains a note that may be of interest to specialists.

9. Attilio Dabini on Mallea in Pedro Orgambide and Roberto Yahni, *Enciclopedia de la literatura argentina*, pp. 410–411.

10. The quotation is from Alis de Sola's translation of *Fiesta en noviembre*, in a Mallea anthology edited by John B. Hughes, *All Green Shall Perish, and Other Novellas and Stories* (New York: Alfred A. Knopf, 1966), pp. 4–5. This translation of *Fiesta en noviembre* is the best English version I have seen of any of Mallea's novels.

10. The Year of *Todo verdor perecerá* (1941)

1. The quotation is from Isaiah, 15:6. The second epigraph is Ecclesiastes, 9:12.

2. Eduardo Mallea, *Todo verdor perecerá* (Buenos Aires–Mexico City: Espasa-Calpe Argentina, 1945), p. 14.

3. Translation by John B. Hughes, in *All Green Shall Perish, and Other Novellas and Stories*, p. 137.

4. All quotations in this paragraph from Mallea's *Todo verdor perecerá*, p. 106.

5. Quoted in Luis Harss and Barbara Dohmann, *Into the Mainstream*, pp. 176–177.

6. Juan Carlos Onetti, *Tierra de nadie* (Montevideo: Ediciones de la Banda Oriental, 1965), p. 129.

7. Alfonso González, "Las técnicas narrativas en dos etapas del novomundismo hispanoamericano" (Ph.D. dissertation, University of Kansas, 1971), pp. 71–72.

8. Mauricio Magdaleno, *Sonata* (Mexico City: Botas, 1941), p. 226.

357

Notes to Pages 140–185

9. See Rodrigo Solera, "Carlos Luis Fallas: El novelista de su propia vida," *Hispania* 53, no. 3 (September 1970): 403–410.
10. Alfredo Pareja Díez-Canseco, *Hombres sin tiempo* (Buenos Aires: Sudamericana, 1941), pp. 7–8.
11. F. Scott Helwig, "Narrative Techniques in the Rural Novels of Enrique Amorim" (Ph.D. dissertation, University of Kansas, 1972), pp. 121–122. I am also indebted to this study for many other comments on the novels of Amorim.

11. From *Todo verdor perecerá* to *El Señor Presidente* (1942–1945)

1. This *guerrilla* was settled at the Río conference in January 1942. Ecuador was pressured to settle and lost a substantial amount of territory. The settlement has continued to be a source of dissatisfaction.
2. Hugo Wast is the pen name of Gustavo Martínez Zuviría.

12. The Years of the Reaffirmation of Fiction

1. José Juan Arrom, *Esquema generacional de las letras hispanoamericanas* (Bogotá: Instituto Caro y Cuervo, 1963).
2. Luis Harss and Barbara Dohmann, *Into the Mainstream*, p. 72.
3. Ibid., p. 78.
4. Miguel Angel Asturias, *El Señor Presidente* (Buenos Aires: Losada, 1959), p. 102.
5. Agustín Yáñez, *Al filo del agua* (Mexico City: Porrúa, 1955), p. 3.
6. A detailed study of this technique is Samuel J. O'Neill's "Interior Monologue in *Al filo del agua*," *Hispania* 51, no. 3 (September 1968): 447–456.
7. Pedro Orgambide and Roberto Yahni, *Enciclopedia de la literatura argentina*, p. 16. Julio Cortázar was one of the few to comment on the novel (*Realidad*, no. 14 [March–April 1949]). The essay is also published with Marechal's *Las claves de Adán Buenosayres* (Mendoza: Azor, 1966), pp. 23–30.
8. The edition used here is Buenos Aires: Sudamericana, 1967. Some disoriented reader may find the following helpful: Prólogo indispensable, p. 7; Libro I, p. 11; II, p. 63; III, p. 157; IV, p. 249; V, p. 317; VI, p. 369; VII, p. 405. The last page is 644.
9. Alejo Carpentier, *El reino de este mundo* (Mexico City: E.D.I.A.P.S.A., 1949), p. 74.
10. The prologue of *El reino* (pp. 7–17) contains Carpentier's explanation of the term.
11. Harss and Dohmann, *Into the Mainstream*, pp. 80–90.

13. From *El reino de este mundo* to *Pedro Páramo* (1950–1954)

1. See Fernando Alegría's *Historia de la novela hispanoamericana*, pp. 214–215, for a description of this generalized type in Chilean fiction. The distinguishing characteristic of the type as portrayed in *Hijo de ladrón* is the element of anguish communicated through narrative techniques usually considered innovative in Chilean fiction. Jaime Valdivieso, in his "Realidad y ficción en Latinoamérica" (unpublished at this writing), explains that Carlos Sepúlveda Leyton, in his *Hijuna* (1934), used techniques that were innovative within the Chilean tradition as a means of conveying the popular sense (feeling for the

358

common people) also evident in the work of Rojas. Valdivieso points out this popular sense in a line of Chilean writers, including Sepúlveda Leyton, J. S. González Vera, Manuel Rojas, and Fernando Alegría. It is also interesting in the history of the genre to note the proximity of *Hijuna* to Bombal's *Niebla*. The latter was in no way related to the popular sense, of course, but the characteristic of narrative invention relates them to each other.

2. The first edition was published by *Cuadernos Americanos*. The present edition is Lima: Editora Paracas, 1967.

3. Martin S. Stabb, "Argentine Letters and the Peronato: An Overview," *Journal of Inter-American Studies and World Affairs* 13, nos. 3–4 (July–October 1971): 435.

4. The second edition, with revisions, is Buenos Aires: Santiago Rueda, 1969. The second edition is the one used here.

14. The Year of *Pedro Páramo* (1955)

1. Juan Rulfo, *Pedro Páramo* (Mexico City: Fondo de Cultura Económica, 1963), p. 7. The English translation is by Lysander Kemp (New York: Grove Press, 1959), p. 1. Further page references are to the Spanish edition. The translations are Kemp's.

2. Joseph Sommers, *After the Storm* (Albuquerque: University of New Mexico Press, 1968), p. 75.

3. Angela B. Dellepiane, "La novela argentina desde 1950 a 1965," *Revista Iberoamericana* 34, no. 66 (July–December 1968): 275–276.

4. See ibid.; Emir Rodríguez Monegal, *El juicio de los parricidas* (Buenos Aires: Deucalión, 1956); Martin S. Stabb, "Argentine Letters and the Peronato: An Overview," *Journal of Inter-American Studies and World Affairs* 13, nos. 3–4 (July–October 1971): 434–455.

5. David Viñas, *Cayó sobre su rostro* (Buenos Aires: Jorge Alvarez, 1955), pp. 11, 12, 14.

6. The author's name may be puzzling to non-Latin readers. The "(h.)" means "hijo" (son)—a way of saying "junior."

7. Dellepiane, "La novela argentina," p. 266.

8. Miguel Otero Silva, *Casas muertas* (Santiago: Editorial Universitaria, 1968), p. 76.

9. The idea is contained in Héctor A. Murena's *El pecado original de América*. For a discussion of this work, including its relationship to similar lines of thought, see Martin S. Stabb, *In Quest of Identity* (Chapel Hill: University of North Carolina Press, 1967), especially pp. 178–181.

15. From *Pedro Páramo* to *Rayuela* (1956–1962)

1. Salvador Reyes Nevares, "Una obra maestra," *La Cultura en México*, July 22, 1964, p. 19.

2. Luis Harss and Barbara Dohmann, *Into the Mainstream*, pp. 225–226.

3. For an analysis of his role in the novel, see Raymond D. Souza, "Fernando as Hero in Sábato's *Sobre héroes y tumbas*," *Hispania* 55, no. 2 (May 1972): 241–246.

4. Angela B. Dellepiane, *Ernesto Sábato, el hombre y su obra* (New York: Las Américas, 1968).

5. Souza, "Fernando as Hero."

6. This work is one of three pieces of prose fiction in Martínez Estrada's *Tres cuentos sin amor* (Buenos Aires: Goyanarte, 1956). The title indicates that "Viudez" is a short story; however, its three stages of development produce a complicated trajectory of emotional change that makes the story seem anything but short. In terms of typographical length, it is fifty-seven pages in this edition.

7. Angela B. Dellepiane, "La novela argentina desde 1950 a 1965," *Revista Iberoamericana* 34, no. 66 (July–December 1968): 255–256.

8. Marta Lynch, *La alfombra roja* (Buenos Aires: Losada, 1966), p. 204.

9. Alvaro Cepeda Zamudio, *La casa grande* (Bogotá: Ediciones Mito, 1962), p. 33.

10. Dellepiane, "La novela argentina," p. 266. Orgambide also commented on this matter in an interview on April 17, 1971.

11. This point is made in many places. A good statement of it is an introduction by Francisco Pérez Perdomo to Salvador Garmendia's *Los pequeños seres* (Montevideo: Arca, 1967).

12. The scene referred to, too long to quote as an example, is on pp. 72–75 of Salvador Garmendia's *Los habitantes* (Caracas: Monte Avila, 1968).

16. The Year of *Rayuela* (1963)

1. Luis Harss and Barbara Dohmann, *Into the Mainstream*, p. 212.

2. For an expansion of this subject, see Hana Muzica, "El humor en Cortázar," *Letras nuevas*, no. 4 (June 1970), pp. 4–5.

3. Ana María Sanhueza, "Caracterizaciones de los narradores de *Rayuela*," *Revista chilena de literatura*, no. 1 (Autumn 1970), pp. 43–57.

4. Julio Cortázar, *Hopscotch*, translated by Gregory Rabassa (New York: Signet Books, 1967), p. 311.

5. Frank Dauster places this representation in proper perspective in "Vargas Llosa and the End of Chivalry," *Books Abroad* 44, no. 1 (Winter 1970): 41–42.

6. One of the more interesting discussions of these matters is Jorge Lafforgue's "*La ciudad y los perros*, novela moral," in *Nueva novela latinoamericana*, ed. Jorge Lafforgue (Buenos Aires: Paidós, 1969), I, 209–240. See also George R. McMurray, "The Novels of Mario Vargas Llosa," *Modern Language Quarterly* 29, no. 3 (September 1968): 329–340. José Miguel Oviedo makes very good use of the McMurray article, and of many other discussions of this novel, in the best overall analysis of the work (*Mario Vargas Llosa: La invención de una realidad* [Barcelona: Barral, 1970], especially pp. 80–121).

7. See Harss and Dohmann, *Into the Mainstream*, p. 97.

8. The English version of Celestino's nickname is from Gregory Rabassa's translation of the novel: *Mulata* (New York: Delacorte, 1967).

9. Elena Garro, *Los recuerdos del porvenir* (Mexico City: Joaquín Mortiz, 1963), p. 11.

10. Enrique Lafourcade, *Invención a dos voces* (Santiago: Zig-Zag, 1963), p. 7.

11. Emmanuel Carballo says he is tempted to write that Arreola conceived the novel in a traditional structure, then cut it up to create the mosaic effect ("Cada quien habla de *La feria* según lo que leyó en ella," *La cultura en México*, March 11, 1964, p. xix).

17. From *Rayuela* to *Cien años de soledad* (1964–1966)

1. Mario Vargas Llosa, *The Green House*, translated by Gregory Rabassa (New York: Harper and Row, 1968), p. 144.

2. Luis Harss and Barbara Dohmann, *Into the Mainstream*, pp. 236–237.

3. Oswaldo Reynoso, *En octubre no hay milagros* (Lima: Wuaman Puma, 1966), pp. 25–26.

4. It is helpful to note, in connection with changing techniques in small-screen novels, that a writer may follow an entirely different road leading to deeper perception and to a revisionist attitude. Abelardo Arias is a good example. He changes the kind of novel, rather than his techniques of narration. As early as 1942, he published a novel about a youth's transition into manhood, *Alamos talados*. Passing over other novels that reveal his deepening perception, we find that his *Límite de clase* (1964) is a spatially restricted study of a group of people with many individual differences. In *Minotauroamor* (1966), the experience of the novel depends on contrast. Fundamentally, the novel is a retelling of Greek myth. The counterpoint is the sale at auction of a prime-quality Argentine bull. The effect of this juxtaposition is to illuminate, via the contrast, the quality of being human.

5. For further discussion of the relationship of this novel to other Chilean fiction, see Ariel Dorfman, "La actual narrativa chilena: Entre ángeles y animales," *Los Libros*, nos. 15–16 (January–February 1971), pp. 15–17, 20–21.

6. This is the way George R. McMurray puts it in "Salvador Elizondo's *Farabeuf*," *Hispania* 50, no. 3 (September 1967): 596–600. The critic shows how Elizondo creates the effect by the manipulation of three fundamental incidents.

18. The Year of *Cien años de soledad* (1967)

1. Gabriel García Márquez, *One Hundred Years of Solitude*, translated by Gregory Rabassa (New York: Harper and Row, 1970), p. 1. The Spanish version is *Cien años de soledad* (Buenos Aires: Editorial Sudamericana, 1967), p. 9.

2. The English edition has a genealogical chart opposite p. 1.

3. The English edition is *Three Trapped Tigers*, translated by Donald Gardner and Suzanne Jill Levine (New York: Harper and Row, 1971). The Spanish title of the novel is part of a tongue twister. Literally it means "three sad tigers." The English title is a very apt translation and is indicative of a generally excellent English version.

4. Carlos Fuentes, *Cambio de piel* (Mexico City: Joaquín Mortiz, 1967), p. 9.

5. The statement is made by Severo Sarduy in "Las estructuras de la narración," *Mundo Nuevo*, no. 2 (August 1966), p. 20. For a discussion of the technique, see Donald Ray Johndrow, " 'Total' Reality in Severo Sarduy's Search for *lo cubano*," *Romance Notes* 13, no. 3 (Spring 1972): 445–452.

6. Antonio Acosta, review in *Revista mexicana de la cultura*, November 26, 1967.

7. The best essay on this novel is by Julio Ortega, in *La contemplación y la fiesta* (Caracas: Monte Avila), 1969, pp. 189–204. It is a difficult essay because it recognizes that traditional critical approaches will not suffice; it deals with the novel on its own terms.

8. One cannot guess what changes may take place in canons of taste and means of expression. *Siberia Blues*, at this moment, seems to dismay readers and intrigue them at the same time. As a complement to my own reading, I requested a careful reading by a graduate student, Michael Nelson, who is a competent and imaginative critic and whose view of literature is certainly that of a still-youthful generation. His reading suggests the need for the reader to give form to the novel. However, he finds the clues so indefinite that participation by the reader is unlikely beyond the point of saying or feeling "perhaps . . ."

19. After *Cien años de soledad* (1968–1970)

1. The best explanation of this structure is by Emir Rodríguez Monegal, "A Literary Myth Exploded," *Review* 72, Winter 1971/Spring 1972, pp. 56–64.

2. Ibid., pp. 62–63. Rodríguez Monegal makes an interesting comparison between this mediocrity and the quality of Argentine life revealed by the Perón phenomenon.

3. See a review of the novel, by José María Carranza, in *Revista Iberoamericana*, no. 69 (September–December 1969), pp. 557–559.

4. On this point, see Ariel Dorfman, "La actual narrativa chilena: Entre ángeles y animales," *Los Libros*, nos. 15–16 (January–February 1971), pp. 15–17, 20–21. The particular reference to *Job-Boj* is on p. 20.

5. For characteristics in *Mateo el flautista* that resemble other famous modern novels, see a review by Germán D. Carrillo in *Revista Iberoamericana*, no. 73 (October–December 1970), pp. 663–666.

6. One section of the novel is particularly interesting for its comments on the creation of fiction (see Francisco Massiani, *Piedra de mar* [Caracas: Monte Avila, 1968], pp. 49–57).

7. See "Alacranes" in Osvaldo Larrazábal Henríquez, *10 novelas venezolanas* (Caracas: Monte Avila, 1972), pp. 77–86.

8. On the language of this novel, see Julio Crespo, "Informe sobre la literatura argentina en 1969: Narrativa," *Nueva Crítica*, no. 1 (1971), pp. 3–19. The specific reference to *Epitalámica* is on pp. 11–14.

9. Sebastián Salazar Bondy, *Alférez Arce, Teniente Arce, Capitán Arce . . .* (Lima: Casa de la Cultura del Perú, 1969), pp. 7–17.

10. The fact that Reynaldo Arenas is Cuban gives his story larger significance than identification of Fray Servando as Mexican.

11. R. J. Lovera de Sola, "*Cuando quiero llorar no lloro*: Tres vidas paralelas de jóvenes venezolanos vistas por un novelista pesimista," *Letras Nuevas*, no. 5 (August–September 1970), pp. 32–33. Lovera de Sola sees only one of the three (Perdomo) as a victim of the establishment. He also believes that Otero Silva does not understand Perdomo. This judgment has to be accepted with

caution. It may well be correct; however, it is necessary to remember that the critic himself could be less than omniscient.

12. The title is from a well-known poem by Rubén Darío in which the poet mourns the disappearance of his youth, and then says "Cuando quiero llorar, no lloro / y a veces lloro sin querer" (When I wish to weep, I weep not / and sometimes I weep without wishing).

13. Regarding the time span of the novel, see Raymond L. Williams, "Los quince años de *Conversación en La Catedral*," *La Nueva Crónica*, March 30, 1972, p. 7.

14. The reference to "waves of dialogue" comes from José Miguel Oviedo, whose book on Mario Vargas Llosa contains an excellent analysis of *Conversación en La Catedral* (*Mario Vargas Llosa: La invención de una realidad* [Barcelona: Barral, 1970]).

A SELECTED BIBLIOGRAPHY

[The following titles are selected with two purposes in mind: (1) to suggest a group of studies that provide a general knowledge of the subject in more detail than is possible in a single book, and (2) to indicate the different kinds of studies available. The list specifically omits books not limited to prose fiction (except in one case) and books on the works of single authors. Studies mentioned in notes are not necessarily listed in this selected bibliography. The most complete single bibliography on the subject is contained in the Schwartz history, listed below.]

Alegría, Fernando. *Historia de la novela hispanoamericana.* Mexico City: Ediciones de Andrea, 1965.
> History of genre in outline form. Entries by author vary from several pages to brief, single-statement comment. Divided by periods and countries.

Bibliografía de la novela venezolana. Caracas: Centro de Estudios Literarios, Universidad Central de Venezuela, 1963.
> Two listings: alphabetical and by year. Title index.

Bollo, Sarah. *Literatura uruguaya, 1807–1965.* Vol. 1. Montevideo: Orfeo, 1965.
> Organization by period and genre. Useful mainly as source of biobibliographical data.

Castillo, Homero, and Silva Castro, Raúl. *Historia bibliográfica de la novela chilena.* Mexico City: Ediciones de Andrea, 1961.
> Listing alphabetical by author only. Title misleading—this is not a history.

Castro Arenas, Mario. *La novela peruana y la evolución social.* Lima: Ediciones Cultura y Libertad, 1965.
> Rather superficial treatment of subject, but occasional good insights (e.g., the vanguardism of Martín Adán).

Curcio Altamar, Antonio. *Evolución de la novela en Colombia.* Bogota: Instituto Caro y Cuervo, 1957.
> Colonial Period followed by organization according to major literary movements. Bibliography to 1956, listing by author.

A Selected Bibliography

Dellepiane, Angela B. "La novela argentina desde 1950 a 1965." *Revista Iberoamericana* 34, no. 66 (July–December 1968): 237–282.

Exposition of general characteristics of period; emphasis on *peronismo* and *los parricidas*; sections specifically on Viñas, Guido, A. Rivera, Manauta, Rodríguez (h.), Orgambide, Murena, Mazzanti, Di Benedetto, Ardiles Gray, Denevi, and Adolfo Jasca. Attitudes, themes, descriptions of techniques.

Dorfman, Ariel. "La actual narrativa chilena: Entre ángeles y animales." *Los Libros*, nos. 15–16 (January–February 1971), pp. 15–17, 20–21.

Interpretation showing how recent Chilean fiction communicates essence of the culture, by younger generation critic. Comments on Donoso, Droguett, Jorge Edwards, J. Guzmán, and others.

Englekirk, John E., and Ramos, Margaret M. *La narrativa uruguaya*. Publications in Modern Philology. Berkeley: University of California Press, 1967.

Bibliography with alphabetical listing by author. Introductory essay giving general idea of development of genre in Uruguay.

————, and Wade, Gerald E. *Bibliografía de la novela colombiana*. Mexico City, 1950.

Listing alphabetical by author. Dates and places of birth.

Escobar, Alberto. *La narración en el Perú*. Lima: Juan Mejía Baca, 1960.

Anthology with introduction and notes. Sound critical comment, but not a full history.

Fell, Claude. "Destrucción y poesía en la novela latinoamericana contemporánea." In *III Congreso Latinoamericano de Escritores*, pp. 207–213. Caracas: Ediciones del Congreso de la República, 1971.

Points out special predilections of very recent Latin American fiction.

Franco, Jean. *An Introduction to Spanish-American Literature*. New York: Cambridge University Press, 1969.

Several unusual perspectives shed light on the subject—e.g., Franco concentrates on the Ecuadorean novel as example of socialist realism in Spanish American fiction.

Fuentes, Carlos. *La nueva novela hispanoamericana*. Mexico City: Joaquín Mortiz, 1969.

One of several statements by the boom novelists about what the genre is. Good analytical view, but brief, very condensed presentation.

Ghiano, Juan Carlos. *La novela argentina contemporánea*. Buenos Aires: Dirección General de Relaciones Culturales, n.d.

Long essay primarily dealing with period 1940–1960 but referring to books as far back as early years of century. Dispassionate, brief descriptions and evaluations.

Goić, Cedomil. *Historia de la novela hispanoamericana.* Valparaiso: Ediciones Universitarias, 1972.
> Basic organization by generations. Within each generational division, a selection of authors and emphasis on a major novel by each author. Critical analyses not as exhaustive as in *La novela chilena.*

———. *La novela chilena.* Santiago: Imprenta Universitaria, 1968.
> Excruciatingly detailed analyses of eight Chilean novels: three from nineteenth century, plus *Casa grande, Zurzulita, Hijo de ladrón, La última niebla,* and *Coronación.* Eight corresponding sections of bibliography and notes.

Gómez Tejera, Carmen. *La novela en Puerto Rico.* San Juan: Universidad de Puerto Rico, 1947.
> Classification by theme, with brief description of each novel. Covers to 1929.

Guibert, Rita. *Seven Voices.* New York: Knopf, 1973.
> In-depth personality interviews with Asturias, Borges, Cabrera Infante, Cortázar, García Márquez, Neruda, and Octavio Paz.

Guzmán, Augusto. *La novela en Bolivia 1847–1954.* La Paz: Juventud, 1955.
> General comments on periods followed by brief descriptions of novels in each period. Covers well to 1938.

Harss, Luis, and Dohmann, Barbara. *Into the Mainstream.* New York: Harper and Row, 1966.
> Essays based on interviews and readings. Includes Asturias, Borges, Cortázar, Carpentier, Fuentes, García Márquez, Onetti, Rulfo, and Vargas Llosa. Background generalities misleading.

Lafforgue, Jorge. *Nueva novela latinoamericana.* Vol. 1. Buenos Aires: Paidós, 1969.
> Anthology of analytical essays on Arguedas, Yáñez, Rulfo, Martínez Moreno, Lezama Lima, García Márquez, García Ponce, Leñero, Vargas Llosa, Cabrera Infante, and Fernando del Paso. Critics range from world renowned to very perceptive newcomers.

Larrazábal Henríquez, Osvaldo. *10 novelas venezolanas.* Caracas: Monte Avila, 1972.
> Critical essays on the novels of one year, 1968. Author's name appears erroneously as Oswaldo Larrazábal.

Madrid-Malo, Néstor. "Estado actual de la novela en Colombia." *Inter-American Review of Bibliography* 17, no. 1 (January–March 1967): 68–82.
> An up-dating of Curcio Altamar's history. Basic bibliographical information with observations on the novels.

A Selected Bibliography

Menton, Seymour. "En torno a la novela de la revolución cubana." In *III Congreso Latinoamericano de Escritores*, pp. 214–222. Caracas: Ediciones del Congreso de la República, 1971.
>Divides the Cuban novel of the decade 1959–1969 into three stages. General characteristics of the three stages and brief analytical comments on some novels.

———. *Historia crítica de la novela guatemalteca*. Guatemala: Editorial Universitaria, 1960.
>Some chapters based on movements, others on particular writers. History and criticism. Also bibliography, listing by author.

———. *Prose Fiction of the Cuban Revolution*. Austin: University of Texas Press, 1975.
>An extensive study of the material dealt with in his article "En torno a la novela de la revolución cubana." Not yet in print when this bibliography was made.

Ocampo de Gómez, Aurora M., and Prado Velázquez, Ernesto. *Diccionario de Escritores Mexicanos*. Mexico City: UNAM/Centro de Estudios, 1967.
>Biobibliographical information with some critical comment. Entries alphabetical by author. Introductory essay by María del Carmen Millán.

Orgambide, Pedro, and Yahni, Roberto. *Enciclopedia de la literatura argentina*. Buenos Aires: Editorial Sudamericana, 1970.
>Entries written by Orgambide, Yahni, and eighteen collaborators. Listed alphabetically by author. Also some topical entries (e.g., "literatura social," "ultraísmo").

Ratcliff, Dillwyn F. *Venezuelan Prose Fiction*. New York: Instituto de Las Españas, 1933.
>Covers subject from beginning to early work of Gallegos. Mainly description of themes and synopses of plots. Critical comments of a general kind.

Rodríguez Monegal, Emir. *El juicio de los parricidas*. Buenos Aires: Deucalión, 1956.
>Title refers to the revisionist generation of writers produced by *peronismo*. Combines critical analysis with social relevance.

———. *Narradores de esta América*. Montevideo: Alfa, 1962.
>Essays that include criticism, biography, and bibliographical comments. Emphases vary from essay to essay. Azuela, Gallegos, M. Rojas, Marechal, Borges, Amorim, Brunet, Carpentier, and Onetti.

Rojas, Angel F. *La novela ecuatoriana*. Mexico City: Fondo de Cultura Económica, 1948.
>Subject divided into three epochs. Works discussed novel by novel, with regionalistic characteristics emphasized. Also bibliography, listing by year.

Schwartz, Kessel. *A New History of Spanish American Fiction.* 2 vols. Miami: University of Miami Press, 1972.

History from beginnings to late 1960s. Divisions by period and by country, not always indicated clearly. Indications of what novels are about, plot synopses, some critical comment. Best bibliography available on subject; divided into general works on Spanish American fiction, general works on fiction in different countries, works about particular authors.

Sommers, Joseph. *After the Storm: Landmarks of the Modern Mexican Novel.* Albuquerque: University of New Mexico Press, 1968.

Extensive analytical essays on *Al filo del agua, Pedro Páramo, La región más transparente,* and *La muerte de Artemio Cruz.* Introductory and concluding chapters place these four works in Mexican fiction.

Spell, Jefferson Rea. *Contemporary Spanish American Fiction.* Chapel Hill: University of North Carolina Press, 1944.

Life-and-works style essays on Gálvez, Azuela, Loveira, Barrios, Horacio Quiroga, J. E. Rivera, Güiraldes, Gallegos, J. Icaza, and C. Alegría.

Stabb, Martin S. "Argentine Letters and the Peronato: An Overview." *Journal of Inter-American Studies and World Affairs* 13, nos. 3–4 (July–October 1971): 434–455.

Essay on the general cultural ambience of the period, with the focus on literature.

Torres Rioseco, Arturo. *Novelistas contemporáneos de América.* Santiago: Nascimento, 1939.

Life-and-works style essays, based on interviews and readings: Azuela, J. E. Rivera, Gallegos, Güiraldes, B. Lynch, Barrios, Gálvez, J. Edwards Bello, Reyles, Díaz Rodríguez, Prado, and Arévalo Martínez.

Villanueva de Puccinelli, Elsa. *Bibliografía de la novela peruana.* Lima: Ediciones de la Biblioteca Universitaria, 1969.

Two listings: alphabetical by author, and by year. Also years of birth and death.

Zum Felde, Alberto. *Indice crítico de la literatura hispanoamericana: La narrativa.* Mexico City: Editorial Guaranía, 1959.

History from beginnings to mid-1950s. Strongest in Río Plata area. Emphasis on ideas and attitudes in fiction. Hard to use because it is poorly indexed.

INDEX

Abalos, Jorge W. (Argentina, 1915–), work by: *Shunko*, 176

Acción Democrática (Venezuela), 155

Acose, El (Carpentier): narrative structure of, 221–222

Acto y ceniza (Peyrou): narration of, 264–265; as a protest against *peronismo*, 264–265

Adán, Martín (pseud. Rafael de la Fuente Benavides; Peru, 1908–), 60. Work: *La casa de cartón*, 62–64

Adán Buenosayres (Marechal), 158, 179; importance of, 157; narrative structure of, 167–170; satire in, 168–169, 170; treatment of vanguardist literati in, 167, 168–169, 170

Adioses, Los (J. C. Onetti), 180; narrative technique of, 181–182

Aguila y la serpiente, El (M. L. Guzmán): narrative technique of, 66

Aguilera Malta, Demetrio (Ecuador, 1909–), 69, 106, 112, 146. Works: *Don Goyo*, 96, 97, 98–101, 102, 104–105, 150, 233, 325; *La isla virgen*, 150; *Los que se van*, 93–95; *Siete lunas y siete serpientes*, 94, 324–325

Aguirre, Lope de, 88

Agustín, José (Mexico, 1944–), works by: *De perfil*, 272–273, 274, 317, 319; *Inventando que sueño*, 302, 317, 319–320

Airó, Clemente (Colombia, 1918–), 176, 180. Works: *La ciudad y el viento*, 246; *Sombras al sol*, 184; *Yugo de niebla*, 177, 178, 184

A la costa (Martínez): portrayal of social disruption in, 14–15

Alacranes (Izaguirre), 315

Alamos talados (Arias), 361 n. 4 (chap. 17)

Albañiles, Los (Leñero), 269, 270, 280

Alberdi, Juan Bautista, 204

Alegría, Ciro (Peru, 1909–1967): political involvement of, 138. Works: *El mundo es ancho y ajeno*, 130, 136–138, 140, 142, 145, 148; *La serpiente de oro*, 113

Alegría, Fernando (Chile, 1918–): on *costumbrismo*, 11–12; on *Don Segundo Sombra*, 46, 47; on *Los de abajo*, 20. Works: *Caballo de copas*, 247; *Los contados días*, 313

Alem, Leandro N., 7

Alessandri, Arturo, 33

Alfaro, Eloy, 8

Alférez Arce, Teniente Arce, Capitán Arce . . . (Salazar Bondy): depicts military coup, 322; narrative technique of, 322

Al filo del agua (Yáñez), 220; characterization in, 164–166; importance of, 157; narrative structure of, 163–167; portrait of small town in, 163–165; protagonist of, 166–167

Alfombra roja, La (M. Lynch), 247; narrative technique of, 230–231; portrait of despotism in, 230–231

Alienation: emergence of, as theme in fiction, 180; and search for identity, 184–185; sources of, 31–32

Alonso, Amado: on Chilean literary

Index

Index

Index

Index

Index